Endorsements

Bryan Elliott's new book, *As in Heaven,* is a glorious documentation of his journey into a life that, despite hard beginnings and unimaginable heartbreak, is a demonstration of a son who's in constant connection with the Father's heart for him, his family, his workplace and the precious lives all around him. Bryan lovingly illuminates for us in principles and stirring examples how the healing power of Heaven will manifest now, on Earth, in our daily lives, when we operate as God intended - in Divine power as his Ekklesia wherever we go, 24/7/365. Read Bryan's story and let your faith arise for Heaven to visit your own part of Earth in ways that will astound you.

— **Ed Silvoso**, *Founder of Transform Our World Network*

Bryan Elliott has written a "Kingdom masterpiece." No matter how much theory one can put into a book, it always comes down to practical application for the reader's life... and Bryan has given us the application! He has proven the words on these pages with testimony and results, revealing how the Kingdom can transcend every area of our lives, demonstrating the reality of Jesus Christ to the world. "As in Heaven" is a Handbook for Kingdom manifestation in all areas of our lives.

— **Derek Schneider**, *History Makers Society and History Makers Academy*

It can be said we never stop growing in our spiritual journey. Regular renewals, vulnerability, and an environment of transparency are a must. Bryan Elliott challenges us in his book to walk toward spiritual maturity by using his own story and biblical principles for wholeness. You will learn and flourish as you walk through this material as a tool for growth.

— **Glenn Shaffer**, *Director of Apostolic Teams International and Overseer at DestinyLife Church*

Bryan is a man who now seeks first the kingdom of God. The evidence is in his writing on these pages and was also evident when I met him in person. His hunger for Jesus and His kingdom was palpable. It's very encouraging to read of a marketplace leader discovering and expressing wonderful kingdom truths in business life. A testimony of God's kingdom advancing in this sphere of influence. An inspiring and provoking read!

— **Tony and Marilyn Fitzgerald**, *Church of the Nations*

Bryan Elliot has done it again! *As in Heaven* is a powerful study that will cause you to grow in your knowledge of the kingdom of God. Bryan writes with great transparency and humility, but also with great wisdom and insight regarding so many different kingdom concepts and truths. This book will educate you, it will encourage you, and it will challenge you to believe for 'on earth as in heaven.'

— Brendan Witton, *Lead Pastor of Toronto City Church*

St. Augustine is recorded as saying, *"God wants to give us something, but cannot, because our hands are full – there is nowhere for Him to put it."* Bryan's life has been one of *"letting go"* so that he can receive from God. Bryan has let go of pain, condemnation, loss, and unforgiveness, as well as success, financial independence, and self-reliance, so that God may fill him with His love, His compassion, His grace and a dependence on Him. This book, therefore, is more than Bryan's personal story, and more than a "how to" book on kingdom living. It is a chronicle of one man's journey in the kingdom and the insights and lessons learned and applied in daily life and in business. *As in Heaven* is a relevant addition to the library of anyone who desires to establish His kingdom *"on earth as it is in heaven."* I encourage you to read it thoroughly, meditate on its questions and prayerfully apply its principles.

— Kevin Dowling, *Lead Pastor of Desert Stream and Director of Reaching Kids International*

This is a book to study, not just read. The book is filled with insight, understanding, and application. The weaving of Bryan's story brings down-to-earth reality that we can all understand and live out in our lives. The selection of questions at the end of each chapter helps to bring home key thoughts and ideas. I would recommend every small group, business owner and ministry school use this as a textbook on the kingdom.

— Randy Cox, *Lead Pastor of Legacy Life Centre*

As we read through Bryan's latest book, *As in Heaven*, we found we really liked having in one place so many of the major principles of the kingdom of God. What a treasure chest of revelation. However, we found ourselves especially drawn to "The Kingdom Principles of Business." As we read through these, we found ourselves wishing we had known these many years ago. We could have been much better stewards of the revelations Father gave to us, as we led ministries and brought healing transformation to individuals and businesses. But it is never too late in God's kingdom, not for us and not for you. It is also exciting to see how Bryan and team have benefited from the "Transforming Your Business" revelation, deliberately renewing the foundation of their company, and then continuing to implement TYB principles and other kingdom principles to become the kingdom business God intended. They are truly demonstrating creative stewardship.

— Chester and Betsy Kylstra, *Founders of Restoring The Foundations International, RTF Healing House Network and Transforming Your Business*

Are you longing for more of God's promised life? *As in Heaven* reveals liberating kingdom life nuggets! Bryan Elliott provokes us to be awakened in the spirit to receive the fullness of the kingdom. If only the natural mind is touched, the transforming reality of the kingdom will elude us. Bryan grasps the essence of kingdom life on earth with clarity. He doesn't sidestep the present demise of culture; rather he offers testimonies of redemptive life moments and declares that the ideals of kingdom life are our present inheritance. These pages underscore the promises of kingdom life. Embark on the journey, no longer only hoping for a better tomorrow in a heaven yet to be attained, but rather walk in the fullness of the kingdom now!

— **Michael Pierce**, *Co-founder of Christ For Your City*

Bryan Elliott's *As in Heaven* isn't just a book; it's a transformative roadmap that illuminates how the principles of the kingdom can revolutionize our lives and our world. With profound experiential wisdom, Elliott guides readers on an empowering journey, showcasing the tangible impact of embracing Jesus's teachings. Through vivid narratives and insightful guidance, he navigates the path of personal transformation and unveils the profound potential within each of us to become kingdom agents. *As in Heaven* equips us to embody the essence of salt and light, enabling us to transcend boundaries and influence every facet of society. This book isn't just about theory—it's a practical, empowering guide that empowers us to deploy our faith in action, making a meaningful impact in every sphere of influence.

— **Bruce Friesen**, *Co-Founder of Kingdomize Global*

*All emphasis in Scripture added by the author.

*Bolded scriptures highlight the words of Jesus.

Cover and images by Chelcea Cummings

Edited by Jessica Glasner and Allison Ulloa

Printed in the USA

First Edition

www.m46ministries.com

@M46Ministries

Index

Dedication

To my spiritual father and dear friend, Kenn Gill,

I will be forever grateful for your unwavering friendship and the revelation of the nature of our Heavenly Father that I have received, having you as my spiritual father. Your guidance has been instrumental in accelerating my journey as a son, contributing significantly to my growth in the kingdom. Over the years, you've imparted invaluable lessons, particularly in understanding the relational nature of the kingdom. Through our shared experiences, my love and reverence for the Word of God have deepened. This book stands as a tribute to you, your teachings, your community, your family, your resourcing, your wisdom, and the impact you've made on my life.

Acknowledging the Holy Spirit's vital role, and despite the detailed footnotes, it's challenging to individually credit everyone who has influenced this book through their friendship, teachings, sermons, writings, and discipleship. Many have also contributed by meticulously proofreading and assessing the concepts and principles for their adherence to biblical truth. I deeply honour all pioneers and educators whose insights have enriched the world and profoundly influenced this book. Special honour and thanks go to Jessica and Allison, my ministry partners, who have skillfully refined my engineering-based raw writing style and significantly shaped the final manuscript.

With much love and honour,

Bryan

Foreword

As we crossed into the third decade of the 21ˢᵗ century, in the midst of great global turmoil, Bryan Elliott, a university graduate and corporate business owner of many years, was, I believe, enrolled by the Heavenly Father in the University of the Spirit. It is like he's working on his "master's in Discipleship" with "the Master Himself" leading, guiding, and equipping him in this kingdom journey.

One of the fantastic aspects of true discipleship is the process of unlearning. This is necessary because of the vast number of things we've learned, experienced, or been taught in life, up to the point of our inner transformation, that have no biblical roots or kingdom of God worldview. The great need is to have our "minds renewed" by the Holy Spirit and the Holy Scriptures while engaging with Christ in a complete unlearning and relearning process. This transpires as we are guided through the Word by the Holy Spirit, teachers, coaches, mentors, and fathers and mothers in the faith. Most discipleship concentrates on "learning more," not "unlearning," which I believe reflects only one side of the coin. Bryan summons the courage in this book to address both "sides of the same coin" through openness, surrender, honesty, humility, and overt vulnerability.

While meditating on Romans 12 many years ago, I engaged the Holy Spirit in conversation with a question. I asked, "What are the evidences of a transformed mind?" Verse 2 speaks of being "transformed by the renewing of our minds." My query was, "How would I know if my mind was being renewed, transformed?" As a brilliant teacher, He responded gently, saying, "Keep reading, son!" I reached verse 9, and my spirit "lit up" with fresh revelation and brand new insight. My question was being answered. As I combed through verses 9–21, I discovered 25 in-plain-sight injunctions delineated by the Holy Spirit for my understanding, pursuit, and alignment, which would lead to a lifelong metamorphosis in my thinking, acting, and behaviour.

It is evident to me that the author, Bryan Elliott, has been and is being transformed over the past seven years. The pages before us are the shreds of evidence of the work of the Spirit, the study of the scriptures, connection to the body of Christ, seasoned believers, and the role of intentional investors in his personal life, family, and business enterprise. His desire to replicate what Father has done for him in the lives of others is amazing. As I read his insights and connect to his thought processes, I am simply overwhelmed by what God has done and what Bryan has given Him space to do. Truly, a metamorphosis is at work.

Bryan postures himself as a son in His kingdom, and from that place of submission and surrender, the Holy Spirit is illuminating his journey with insights that can assist everyone in navigating our way as kingdom people in whatever sphere of life we find ourselves.

Enjoy the sojourn through the pages of this book, manual, and guidebook that is filled with insight, counsel, story, opportunity for life assessment, reflection, introspection, and clear direction coming from the scriptures. The questions posed at the end of each chapter give us an opportunity to "go deeper and further" in our kingdom journey and, when answered honestly, trigger the master disciple, Jesus, the King, His opportunity to unfold the expanse of His kingdom to us.

Fellow Kingdom Sojourner
Kenneth Gill
Ripple Effect Ministries
Calgary

Preface

"As you passionately seek his kingdom, above all else, he will supply your needs. So don't ever be afraid, dearest friends! Your loving Father joyously gives you his kingdom with all its promises!"

Luke 12:31-32, TPT

For those of you who have not read my first book, *More Than Gold: Reflections on Living in Glorious Freedom*, you do not yet know that my life story is one of both great tragedy and great redemption.

My life totally changed when I finally embraced the Gospel after 45 years of living life my way and on my terms. As a lukewarm "believer," I considered myself a Christian but didn't experience any of the actual transformation that comes from knowing and following Jesus. Before knowing Jesus, I grasped for things of the world to fill the emptiness in my soul. My peace was circumstantial. Happiness was my aim. I lived life my way, which was full of compromise. By the world's standards, I had a good life, and my wealth affirmed it.

In 2016, when I declared Jesus the Lord of my life, my motivations and priorities all began to shift. I finally decided to remove myself from the little throne of my life. When I submitted or yielded to the Lord, I made the choice to place my life and desires beneath the desires and will of Jesus, daily dying to self. This is what it means to make Jesus Lord. This decision changed everything. However, I didn't yet know about the kingdom and was soon to know the King more deeply. I knew that He was now my King or better put, I began a beautiful process of making Him King in every area of my life. As promised in Scripture, my loving Father joyously gave me His kingdom!

The more I understood the realm of the kingdom of God and His purposes for me, the more I saw how dim the world's trappings were. As King Solomon confirmed at the end of his life, the things this world offers us are meaningless.[1] Where I had once looked to money and success to find security and fulfillment, God began to reveal to me that true peace and fulfillment solely come from Him. Had I not taken the step to trust in and follow after Jesus, I would not be here to share with you the glorious freedom He offers to all. It is the freedom to live above our circumstances and thrive in the midst of suffering, enjoying the goodness of God no matter what we face. Right here, right now.

Modern Christianity Is Falling Short

Embracing God's truth including the full gospel of the kingdom of God and abiding in His presence are the most transformative experiences you will ever have. Doing so will impact every aspect of your life and your spheres of influence for the kingdom. Yet, why do the most "Christianized" families, communities, and nations still struggle with the same issues as their non-Christian counterparts? The root of the problem lies in the adoption of a narrow focus on the gospel of salvation, neglecting the comprehensive, redemptive, and transformative power of the gospel of the kingdom of God. The result is a version of Christianity that provides personal redemption but fails to achieve societal transformation that reflects heaven on earth. We are called to follow Jesus's example and become Isaiah 61 kingdom ambassadors.

As I came to the close of writing this book, I came across this powerful statement in *The Old Testament Template* by Landa Cope which sums up the state of our world (and the church) today:

> If the gospel does influence all of society, how could America, with 78 percent of people identifying as Christian, be slipping from biblical values in so many arenas? Slipping in justice, health care, and literacy? Slipping into crime, immorality, poverty, corruption, drug addiction, homelessness, and more? How was it that I, and the myriad of committed Christians I knew, had never realized this?[2]

Or as senior leader of Bethel Church Bill Johnson puts it, "We have repented enough to be saved, but not enough to see the kingdom."[3] Despite the overwhelming nature of our declining cities, nations, and the world, the answer to our biggest and smallest issues is the kingdom of God.

The Kingdom of God: The Ultimate Solution to Everything

> The early church transformed Israel, revolutionized the Roman Empire, laid foundations for Western European nations to become the most prosperous in the world. What a different impact we see in modern mission history.
> — Landa Cope[4]

Repentance means changing the way we think. *NOW* is the time for a divine reset for the body of Christ to align with heaven. The proclamation of the kingdom of God, as clearly understood by the early church, is essential for humanity and is unparalleled in significance and impact. Since all things were created by Christ and for Christ, everything in heaven and on earth will be brought back to Himself, back to original intent. There is no sacred/secular divide; everything belongs to Him and is important to Him.

Transcending geographical and national confines, God's kingdom stands sovereign over everything, uniting all 195 nations, 40,000 denominations, various social classes, and diverse groups. Creation eagerly awaits the manifestation of the kingdom through God's sons and daughters, as it holds the key to global and cosmic restoration and transformation. This core message of Jesus's teachings offers the ultimate solution, reshaping our earthly lives to mirror heaven by the grace of God.

As in Heaven

In Matthew 5-7, we read Jesus's Sermon on the Mount, which He delivered to a crowd of people. Midway through, He paused to teach the people how to pray in what is known as "the Lord's Prayer."

"Pray, then, in this way:
'Our Father, who is in heaven,
Hallowed be Your name
Your kingdom come.
Your will be done,
On earth as it is in heaven.
Give us this day our daily bread.
And forgive us our debts, as we also have forgiven our debtors.
And do not lead us into temptation, but deliver us from evil.
For Yours is the Kingdom, the power and the glory forever and ever. Amen.'"
Matthew 6:9-13, NASB

This prayer goes beyond praising God, asking for forgiveness, and requesting our daily needs from Him. "Your kingdom come. Your will be done, On earth as it is in heaven" is a divine directive, a grace mandate from the King of heaven to spread and establish His kingdom on earth. It declares that His will would be done *on earth as it is in heaven.* Though we will not experience the fullness of His kingdom until we are united with Him in heaven or until Jesus comes back to restore fully what was lost in the fall, we have the opportunity, every day, to enter His courts, bringing heaven to earth as we model our lives after the King. The kingdom is available to us *NOW* if we are willing to walk in God's presence and receive His goodness, grace, and mercy.

"Yet through it all, the good news of heaven's kingdom will be proclaimed all over the world, providing every nation with a demonstration of the reality of God."
–Matthew 24:14, TPT

THIS is the crux of *As in Heaven: Life in God's Kingdom NOW.* It is a collection of reflections based on deep study in God's Word, time spent with Jesus, influence of the Holy Spirit, and wisdom gleaned from spiritual mentors on what it means to live in the kingdom of God, which I discovered in the wake of my beloved daughter Abbe's murder. Kingdom living describes what life as a son or daughter of God is meant to look like while we journey through life. His kingdom is expanding *NOW* in and through us.

What delight comes to the one who follows God's ways! He won't walk in step with the wicked, nor share the sinner's way, nor be found sitting in the scorner's seat. His passion is to remain true to the Word of "I AM," meditating day and night on the true revelation of light. He will be standing firm like a flourishing tree planted by God's design, deeply rooted by the brooks of bliss, bearing fruit in every season of life. He is never dry, never fainting, ever blessed, ever prosperous.

–Psalm 1:1-3, TPT

The kingdom of God is rooted in Psalm 1. It is a heavenly reality that we can experience in our lives on earth. As we delight in God's ways, His presence empowers us to live *on earth as it is in heaven*, producing fruit in every season.

I have written this book intending to guide the body of Christ towards the glorious kingdom of God, knowing the great awakening or revival unto the great harvest of souls is imminent. Revival must look like something. Transformation starts in the heart, extends to the family, and expands outward. This means we must go out into the world and outside of the walls of the church. This means embracing a lifestyle of sacrificial or selfless love and putting others ahead of ourselves.

Faith must be accompanied by action, His love moving in and through us as the hands and feet of Jesus on the earth. It must lead to reformation as His kingdom comes across the earth. There must be a practical application of kingdom principles and real-world solutions to the problems we experience every day as an expression of an inward transformation and the coming of His kingdom. The outward expression is the manifestation of the kingdom on earth, not by might nor by power, but by His Spirit. This is why I have focused on both the spiritual and the practical aspects of the kingdom of God in this book.

I have wrestled to articulate what I've learned about living as a citizen of the kingdom of heaven over the last few years, and I ask for your grace as this book represents where I am now, with much growth ahead. I hope that my story will serve as a catalyst to jumpstart your life in the kingdom through specific truths and practices that I've picked up on my journey so far. Every "practice" is a key, unlocking doorways that accelerate your journey into this exciting realm, experiencing life as God intended. With the Holy Spirit, we can bring heaven to earth in every area we apply kingdom keys. Using them daily will help us overcome and live above the storms of life.

I invite you to come alongside me and adventure into His glorious kingdom.

May God bless you every step of the way and give you with the grace to receive the revelation of His kingdom realm. Afterall, living for eternity NOW is the best life on earth!

Shalom!

Bryan Elliott

1. Ecclesiastes 1.
2. Linda Cope, *The Old Testament Template*, (YWAM Publishing, 2011).
3. Bill Johnson, *When Heaven Invades Earth*, (Destiny Image: 2009).
4. Linda Cope, *The Old Testament Template*, (YWAM Publishing, 2011).

"YOUR KINGDOM COME.

YOUR WILL BE DONE,

ON EARTH AS IT IS IN HEAVEN."

MATTHEW 6:10, NASB

Introduction

The teachings of the godly ones are like pure silver, bringing words of redemption to others, but the heart of the wicked is corrupt.
—Proverbs 10:20, TPT

In early 2023, I had just released my first book, *More Than Gold*, a discipleship book about the foundations of faith, and I was planning to continue with this theme in my next book called *Greater Than Silver*. However, as I wrote the introduction, fresh inspiration from the Holy Spirit struck. I kept writing, and soon, that introduction became a whole new book—the one you are reading now. From start to finish, it has been a labour of love.

Life on earth is meant to be lived in the kingdom, *as it is in heaven*. This revelation came from a season that started in 2017 when the Lord began to highlight His kingdom to me, specifically regarding my business.

During this time, the Lord gave me a vision for a Christian company with God having majority ownership, which in my mind meant 51 percent. Then, in 2020, it became increasingly clear that everything I had was already His (100 percent ownership), and I was only a steward of what He had entrusted to me. I had more revelations about this in the coming years, which I will share later. This began my shift from a religious mindset to a kingdom mindset. I began to see that my external reality was a manifestation of my inward reality. As I took responsibility for my life, filled myself with the truth of Jesus, the living Word, and sought inner-heart healing, my world began to change, and my perspective became increasingly aligned with heavenly realities.

In 2022, with the Holy Spirit, I put together something titled the *Kingdom Manifesto*, where I outlined different elements of the kingdom and how they applied to life, family, relationships, business, wealth, etc. My theology, my view of God, my view of the world, and my priorities were all changing. My mind was being transformed by the Word of God and the Holy Spirit's presence in my life. I had read the Bible and all the scriptures about the kingdom of God before, but they started to look different. I was thinking differently. I was seeing differently. I understood differently.

WHAT IS LIFE IN GOD'S KINGDOM?

Jesus is *the way* into His kingdom.

His primary message is: the kingdom of God has come to earth for the restoration of all things.

His one new command is: to love others as He loves us.

His top priority and focus is: to seek first His kingdom and His righteousness.

His resulting promise is: to live above our circumstances knowing God is with us, ahead of us, and adding all things unto us, knowing that everything is by grace alone.

Our new identity is: as sons and daughters, kings, priests, kingdom ambassadors, and citizens of heaven.

Our purpose and mandate: We are chosen and born again from heaven to establish His kingdom on earth. We are conduits between heaven and earth, tasked with making the invisible kingdom visible. We are alive to experience the love of God and to share that love with others. To know God and make Him known. To serve and bless others. To be discipled and to disciple others. To grow God's family by making sons and daughters who become fathers and mothers who make sons and daughters. To be fruitful and multiply. To rule and reign in life by taking responsibility, each playing our part by tending our gardens, aligning our life, family, giftings, community, and business with heaven. To glorify Him with our lives, bringing heaven to earth from our life union with Jesus and in unity with the body of Christ to fulfill our destiny.

The centrepiece of the good news gospel, salvation by grace through faith is: that the just shall live by faith. Everything is by the extravagant grace of God. Grace is the power of God - God's unmerited, completely underserved and freely given favour. It cannot be earned. Grace is divine enablement. Grace is God's empowering presence that leads to His divine influence in our lives. Grace is the manifestation of God's unconditional love and mercy towards humanity. Grace is a sin conquering power. We live in grace-consciousness, not sin-consciousness as we yield to the dynamic life and power of the Holy Spirit.

They conquered him completely through the blood of the Lamb and the powerful word of his testimony. They triumphed because they did not love and cling to their own lives, even when faced with death.
—*Revelation 12:11, TPT*

Loving our lives even unto death means that we know our lives are not our own. It means knowing that we are each given a certain number of days on earth to steward what God has placed in our hands. Ultimately, not loving our own lives is a "stewardship" model of living.

How we steward what we've been given becomes our testimony. There is a difference between a biography and a testimony. A biography is about me. A testimony is about Jesus, the story of what God has done in me, with me, and through me. A testimony proclaims the greatness of God.

Every believer has a testimony of how Jesus became real to them personally. Our stories are different but equally powerful. Our testimonies help us and others overcome trials and tests. The word "testimony" comes from the Hebrew root word *odot* (עֵדוּת), which essentially means "do it again." Every time we share our testimony of God's faithfulness in our lives, we welcome the power of God to *do it again* in the lives of others. The Gospel is the testimony of Jesus, the power to destroy evil and give eternal life. Our testimonies are about how our stories fit into God's greater story of the Gospel of Jesus Christ. As we share our testimonies, we release the power of God for transformation to be released into the lives of others.

The spirit of prophecy is the testimony of Jesus. As we share what God has done in our lives, we become prophetic messengers and multiply the grace we have received to be activated in the lives of others. Every believer is meant to share their testimony, glorify God, and create the faith for others to receive breakthrough. Our lives serve as a living testimony of the kingdom of God, embodying the words of Jesus in Matthew 5:16: "**Let your light shine before men, that they may see your good works and glorify your father in heaven.**" Our Heavenly Father is no respecter of persons.[1] He shows no favouritism. What Jesus did for me, my daughter Bryn, or any other person, including all the people in Scripture, He can do for you!

Though our personal stories include tragedy and extreme loss, Bryn and I have been redeemed by Jesus and transformed into testimonies of Jesus. We tried life our way, then we did it Jesus's way, the better way. His way is so different from anything the world has to offer. As we remember with gratitude what God has done for us, it builds our faith and honours God. It allows others to see God's goodness. As we share our testimonies, God is glorified, and faith is ignited.

…For the testimony of Jesus is the spirit of prophecy [His life and teaching are the heart of prophecy].
—*Revelation 19:10, AMP*

To understand how I came to write this book, I need to back up a few years to 2018. This was during the aftermath of my daughter Abbe's murder. To summarize the events that occurred on the day Abbe died, I've included an excerpt from my first book, *More Than Gold*.

> *Over the next hour in the hospital waiting room, I experienced a host of conflicting feelings. Heaviness, sadness, disbelief, hope… emotions overlapped, started, and stopped at strange intervals. I didn't know what to think or feel. No one would tell our family or me what was going on. There was no follow-up explanation. The only direct information we had was from that first call telling us Abbe had been stabbed. Family members arrived, one after another, gathering in silence as we waited for someone to tell us what was happening. When that moment finally came, the news was nearly impossible to believe. The doctors pronounced Abbe dead on arrival. The cause? She experienced five slash and stab knife wounds, with a stab wound to the heart as the ultimate cause of her death.*
>
> *Everyone in the room cried out in sorrow and disbelief as the doctor's news sank in. I looked over and saw my younger daughter, Bryn, unravelling. Abbe was not just Bryn's only sister; she was her best friend. With my eyes locked on Bryn, my body registered severe, deep grief and debilitating disappointment. Could this really be happening? If it was, how could God allow it? My daughter had been stabbed in the heart. It was unimaginable. A tragic ending for my beautiful baby girl.*
>
> *Only 21 years old, Abbe had tried and tried to get back on her feet from a life marked by intense suffering, tragedy, and ongoing struggles. After giving her life to the Lord and unsuccessfully attempting to heal from years of drug addiction and trauma, how could it end like this? How could something this terrible happen?*
>
> *After hours of crying and trying to absorb what had happened, I went to bed that night, exhausted and numb. There was a void in my soul, the feeling that something precious was ripped from me. My mind raced. Heaviness filled my heart as I thought about my traumatized family and how Abbe was gone forever. Our lives would never be the same.*
>
> *Yet, unexpectedly, I woke the next morning with an incredible and unexplainable peace I attribute solely to the grace of God. I was overwhelmed by the revelation that Abbe was in heaven with the Lord. She was now safe for all eternity with her Father in heaven, His great mercy revealed in her life. A true revelation and the experience of His mercy had produced in me a tangible joy, despite the devastating tragedy that had befallen my family. In His sovereignty, God saw the end from the beginning, and He allowed me to feel the heavenly reality that Abbe was finally home, safe and sound.[2]*

Our loss was immense, but God had given me a compassionate and merciful gift of the revelation and consciousness of heaven's reality that will remain with me forever. Matthew 5:4 says, **"Blessed are those who mourn, for they will be comforted"** (NASB). Regardless of the miraculous peace the Lord gave me, my daughter Bryn experienced a very different reality in the weeks following the murder of her big sister. Bryn was thrown into complete mental chaos, instigated by Abbe's death, past traumas, and ongoing addiction. Immediately following Abbe's funeral, we got word that Bryn was planning on getting "wasted" and had declared that she no longer wanted to live.

Later that evening, as she continued to spiral, we called 911, and the police escorted her to the hospital for a psychiatric evaluation. In hysterics, she left the house screaming every hurtful and cutting word she could muster towards me as an outlet for her rage. I followed her by car to the Canadian Mental Health Centre. When I arrived, the police asked me to leave because Bryn was upset with me being there, and they didn't want to create a disturbance.

I returned home, hoping they would keep her for a few days, praying that God would breathe peace into my troubled daughter's heart. She had already lived through too much for someone so young. Abbe's death was the straw that broke the camel's back.

Just after midnight, I received a call that Bryn had been released, even though we all knew she was still a danger to herself. Digesting this information, my mind began to replay the events of that day. It had started with Bryn in a panic before the funeral, declaring she didn't want to live anymore and threatening to expose me as a terrible parent.

This began early in the morning and continued until I had no time left but to get dressed and rush to the funeral (which I led most of). I had planned on having a quiet morning to think through and emotionally prepare for the service, but the opposite happened. Even still, I was calm, peaceful, alert, and was able to honour Abbe's life well, surrounded by hundreds of friends, family, business associates, and even gang members my daughter had befriended.

Bryn, on the other hand, spent her days leading up to the funeral with a "friend," who we later discovered was still in contact with Abbe's killers. She was afraid of what might happen to her in the wake of Abbe's death and chose to hide away instead of mourning with those who were also grieving. Despite all this, God's mercy and grace strengthened me beyond comprehension. His peace gifted me with rest when anxiety could easily have been my portion. Over the next week, I miraculously slept through each night. It was a supernatural grace response, one not shared by many who walked through this season with us. Each day, I had to surrender my living daughter to God, trusting He would see her through.

I didn't know this then, but I was experiencing the kingdom realm of God, where my experience was not of this world but anchored in the presence of the King of Kings and Prince of Peace, Jesus.

At Abbe's funeral, we chose to worship God amid our pain, and I assumed this would be my family's turning point. I believed that God would intervene and turn Bryn's life around in addition to many other areas of my life that were in disarray. Instead, it was an inception point of the Lord's deep work that was underway.

I went back to the office several weeks after Abbe's murder.

As an engineer, I gravitate to technical businesses and hold several technological patents. My core business, Flō, is an engineering company operating in North America's food retail sector. In the month that followed Abbe's murder, in May 2018, Flō took several financial hits that, on their own, would have been fine but, in conjunction with a symphony of losses and unexpected events, placed cash flow in a precarious position.

In 2017 (one year after I had made Jesus Lord of my life, my King), I attended Flō's board meeting of Christian and non-Christian executives to announce that I was no longer the owner or the majority shareholder.

"Everyone," I announced, "God is now in charge of the ship."

The board went silent. Finally, one man said he had figured as much and wasn't surprised. Such a change had been in the process for some time. Those around me knew my heart and perspective of God had drastically changed. Another inquired how the change would affect our finances and banking arrangements. At the time, I wasn't very concerned with these details. I had given everything over to the Lord. I was focused on becoming a good steward, shepherd, and father rather than just a successful businessman.

And then came the "slash and burn."

Embracing the "Slash and Burn"

After years of family trauma, addiction, multiple divorces, betrayals, and the loss of Abbe, I thought I had finally reached the turning point of my life. Instead, in June 2018, Doug Schneider, the leader of an apostolic council with pastors and marketplace ministers across Canada, came to me apologizing about a prophetic word he was about to give me.[3]

Doug wanted to declare a quick end to the pain and challenges I was facing, but he felt conviction from the Lord that I was about to enter into what he called a "slash and burn" season.

When Doug said, "slash and burn," I knew God was about to do something radical and dramatic to bring forth a new harvest in my life, but it would not be instant or without pain. "Slash and burn" refers to a farming method used for new growth that involves burning all existing growth in a plot of land to prepare the land for regeneration and new life. In the process, everything becomes uprooted, and the land becomes barren for several years before it can return to its original growing capacity.

I wondered what was coming as Doug continued to affirm my identity as a warrior and a worshipper. He said this was not because I had done anything wrong, but to the contrary. He confirmed I would be healed through the process and that God would faithfully restore all that had been lost.

Every area of my life was shaken in the months and years that followed. This word became an anchor for my soul, and I knew God was in charge of the process. He was already in my future. It was God's mercy, goodness, and faithfulness that confirmed what was coming and provided the promise of a beautiful new future following the fire. God provided grace and comfort, day by day and week by week, as I kept my eyes on Him. The enemy was raging, but God's grace was infinitely greater!

So, what does all this mean? If God has determined to stand with us, tell me, who then could ever stand against us?
—Romans 8:31, TPT

If you are in a similar season, remember the storm will eventually pass. Jesus is already in your future, past, and today. No matter what you are facing, keep going. If you submit to Him, you will be overcome by the grace of God.

The Perfect Storm

As 2018 progressed, the slash and burn was in full swing. Everything seemed to be going wrong all at once. Roughly a year after giving the company to the Lord, I faced the harsh reality of unexpected declines plus simultaneous multiple seven-figure losses across a broad array of investments due to a series of unforeseen events and poor decisions. This process of financial shaking would continue to play out over the following years in various areas of my life, including a divorce, my other company, and beyond.

Despite all this, I found comfort in that when we give our lives to God, it doesn't mean we won't suffer. He cares deeply about us. When we choose to die to our flesh (our old sinful nature, pride, carnal or selfish desires, anything that opposes the Holy Spirit within us) and allow Him to sift and refine us, what remains has eternal significance.

In fact, everything in my life was so bad that by August 2018, a group of Christian friends rallied behind me for a month of dedicated prayer over the entire situation.

Moving into 2019, Bryn's struggles with deepening addiction, anxiety, and depression contributed to her dropping down to 90 lbs (significantly below her now healthy 135 lbs weight) in a matter of months. She developed mononucleosis and was continuously sick. She would scream, rip out her hair, throw herself against walls, hit things, and say that she was crazy and insane. Each morning, as she awoke, she screamed in agony that she was still alive. I tried to assure her of her identity and encouraged her we would get through this together.

In September 2019, Bryn and I testified in Abbe's murder pretrial. It was another jolt to our fragile family. To make matters worse, a couple of weeks later, I heard a knock at the door and was served with a million-dollar lawsuit resulting from issues in the forced sale of one of my companies the year prior (which had already resulted in the loss of millions).

Late in October, my third marriage ended. We had married long before my convictions surrounding Jesus became the primary driver of my life. My wife was rightfully exhausted from the years of incredible stress and trauma around the addiction issues with both of my daughters and then Abbe's murder. She was not a Christian and didn't agree with how I had been dealing with the situation, nor with where my deepening faith was headed.

During the divorce, we lost our family home, which was purchased as our "forever dream house." That same month, I put my business on hold to focus solely on Bryn. In fact, the core writing of two of my books occurred amid these events, plus the extreme COVID-19 lockdowns in Toronto, a three-year murder trial, and a corporate lawsuit—all while almost losing my only other daughter, Bryn.

My senior team rallied and came together to support me. I didn't know how long it would take, but they were 100 percent supportive as I continued focusing on my relationship with Bryn and helping her find the deliverance and healing she needed on a special father-daughter inner-heart healing journey.

Looking Back

As Bryn and I dove into the past, many things became clear. The truth was that before I came to know Christ intimately, I prioritized business over family. For decades, family proved to be an immense source of pain. Subconsciously, business seemed like a much easier and safer path for my heart than allowing myself to be vulnerable to the pain I had experienced in my childhood.

When I was just 14 years old, my image of a safe, connected family was shattered by a devastating gun accident that left my brother in a comatose state. My mother dedicated the next 24 years of her life to providing full in-home care for my brother before he eventually passed away.

Following the accident, my family's dynamic became full of unprocessed grief, resentment, and shame related to what had happened to my brother. Our relational ties became strained and slowly unravelled over the years due to ongoing suffering and grief. Ultimately, my father was deeply impacted by sadness and left my mother. He lost his business and relied on alcohol for years before somewhat turning his life around. My other brother attempted suicide multiple times.

Our family was all committed to the Lord for a time; however, my siblings and I drifted away before or while heading to university. As we grew older, we moved further and further away from God. Through it all, my mother believed that God would restore our family. It would take decades for her prayers to come to fruition, but she faithfully began sowing seeds in those early years of our family's heartache.

From my early teenage years into adulthood, after much pain and disappointment, my heart's cry to have intimate relationships shifted to pursuing a life of success and achievement. In a sense, it was easier, and it felt safe. In business, I could rely on what I thought was my strength to succeed, whereas cultivating a healthy family life or walking with the Lord required humility and submission. My desire to be viewed as a strong provider took precedence over establishing a godly foundation in my home. I focused on many charitable endeavours and philanthropy. However, my giving was rooted in a desire to earn God's acceptance rather than out of obedience and the love of God. Although I was achieving higher levels of worldly success, deep down, I was riddled with anxiety whenever storms hit. My trust was in money. My house was not built upon the Rock.[4] My preoccupation with myself and the things of the world left doors wide open for the enemy to attack my daughters.

By the time my girls hit their pre-teens, they slowly fell into the chains of depression and addiction. For a while, I was spending $40,000 per month on in-patient care for my girls, visiting them as often as the addiction centres would allow. As time went on, we learned that both of my daughters had been emotionally and sexually abused by someone close to the family. The abuse opened the door to many other tragedies, including multiple rapes, promiscuous activity, suicide attempts, destructive relationships, etc. Sadly, I missed much of their high school years. Any sense of stability was undermined by the breakup of our family multiple times through divorce, the constant chaos around their lives, and time spent away at treatment centres. Thankfully, from that low point in October 2019, Bryn started to turn around following a deliverance session, after which she gained confidence and new strength in God daily.[5] With the help of some wonderful believers, life coaches, and a lot of hard work on her part, I watched as Bryn was healed, set free, and delivered from spiritual oppression. Her life became a testimony of the redemptive power of the Gospel!

When the Smoke Clears

The fire levelled many things in my life. In many ways, I'm still dealing with challenges and uncertainties that continue to arise from the chaos of those years. Nevertheless, I have experienced incredible transformation throughout the process and see challenges and suffering very differently because of my deepening relationship with the Lord and the work He has and continues to do in my life.

Murder is an unthinkable evil, and it was not God's plan or His destiny for Abbe to die in that way. However, I know that what the enemy intended for evil, the Lord will use for good.[6] In many ways, Abbe's release from this life into heaven was merciful. Though she struggled immensely on this earth, she knew the truth of Jesus. Abbe is now with the Lord and free of all the pain and suffering she experienced daily.

So we are convinced that every detail of our lives is continually woven together for good, for we are his lovers who have been called to fulfill his designed purpose.
— Romans 8:28, TPT

All things work together for good for those of us following Christ, even in the darkest circumstances. All things working together for our good doesn't mean we get what we want or for our comfort. The ultimate good in our lives is sharing the likeness of Jesus, which often involves suffering and being formed by challenges and trials. God can sovereignly counteract the effects of what Satan intended for evil for our good. When we invite the Lord into these situations, everything changes; there is a deepening of faith and relationship with Him, combined with the revelation of many blessings. God is good. The outpouring of love and deep connection He has in store for us is beyond comprehension. Ultimately, the tragedy of Abbe's death brought my family together and gave Bryn and me a second chance to live the lives God had planned for us from the beginning in His kingdom. We embraced the life of glorious freedom Jesus died to give us.[7]

Bryn's life is now fully dedicated to the Lord, and she is committed to sharing the hope of Jesus with this generation and beyond. She served for almost three years as a missionary with YWAM (Youth With A Mission), a far cry from the life she was living just a few years ago. It's incredible to see her transformation. She has shared her testimony multiple times on a global stage, received a biblical studies degree, delivered sermons, and has even written a fantastic book about her testimony called *Dying to Live: Experiencing God's Redemptive Power in the Midst of Tragedy*. She and I are finalizing a joint father-and-daughter book on apologetics that we are eager to release. She has been on various podcasts and co-hosts our father-daughter podcast, "The Father's Pursuit." Together, we started M46 Ministries, dedicated to biblical family restoration. After a life of such wide-scale devastation, pain, loss, abuse, and trauma, Bryn is experiencing an equal amount of wide-scale opportunities to share her testimony for the sake of others and the glory of God. I understand this is not the norm for most people, nor even the highest pinnacle of being a Christian. Following Jesus is about loving and living well daily, simply being faithful.

Bryn's journey unfolds as she grows in faith, navigating challenges contributing to her maturity in Christ. My youngest daughter is vibrantly alive, and our relationship with each other and the Lord deepens daily. God, in His mercy, has delivered us from the pit of hell, in the natural and the spirit. Our relationship is stronger than ever, with its ups and downs, and I can honestly say that God has given us back everything the enemy stole. For the first time, my family has become a place of healing, restitution, and joy.

As I look back over my life, the biblical story of Job has always been a source of strength. Job was a righteous man whom God loved very much, whereas my life was only righteous in my own eyes based on the world's standards. Satan, hearing God's praise of Job, made the case that Job's obedience and love of God were rooted in the incredible blessing God bestowed upon his life. God allowed Satan to test and try Job but not to kill him. Job had misconceptions of God as the source of his suffering rather than Satan. Towards the end of the trials, Job cries out to God to come and explain Himself. God answers Job's cry by taking him on a tour of His created universe of unfathomable complexity. In response, Job was struck with the fear of the Lord.

The fear of the Lord means seeing God rightly in awe, wonder, and adoration, which results in humility. Refining requires fire, which God allows. Ultimately, Job doesn't understand why he went through what he went through but chooses to trust in God's wisdom, decisions, and nature.

The Lord gives blessing, but sometimes He allows it to be removed by Satan. This isn't a punishment; rather, it's a refinement. When the refining process is over, He restores what was lost, plus more! Why? Because the refining process teaches us how to steward *more*. With this in mind, our circumstances don't define us but refine us.

The end of the story? God gave Job another 140 years of life and restored all that Job had lost, but even better than before. This is God's redemption as we yield to Him and learn to trust Him. Job's life had been shaken so that his faith would be unshakable, and his testimony will continue to fuel believers to overcome hardships for thousands of years to come!

We all experience times of testing, which is normal for every human being. But God will be faithful to you. He will screen and filter the severity, nature, and timing of every test or trial you face so that you can bear it. And each test is an opportunity to trust him more, for along with every trial God has provided for you a way of escape that will bring you out of it victoriously.
—*1 Corinthians 10:13, TPT*

We all face times of testing, a natural part of being human. But in every trial, God is faithful, providing opportunity to deepen our trust in Him. Regardless of the source, our Sovereign King not only filters our trials to ensure they are bearable, but also equips us with His grace (strength, wisdom, and peace) to overcome victoriously. His grace empowers us to endure, while growing in character, trust, and faith. Let's avoid complaining or seeing ourselves as victims, recognizing that each trial serves a purpose for our benefit. From my own journey, I've learned that life isn't happening to us, but for us, under the loving guidance and power of the Lord. Our hope rests in the incredible promises of God found in His word!

Find your delight and true pleasure in Yahweh,
and he will give you what you desire the most.
Give God the right to direct your life,
and as you trust him along the way,
you'll find he pulled it off perfectly!
—*Psalm 37:4-5, TPT*

I hope that my testimony and understanding of the kingdom of God will impart hope into your life and help you see the goodness and faithfulness of God in a fresh, new way. In the pages ahead, I pray that you not just read about God's kingdom, but that you experience it yourself. This book is not about ingesting information; it's about taking what God has revealed in Scripture and applying it to our lives. Remember Proverbs 16:24, which says God's Word is sweet like honeycomb. We would be fools to miss out on its goodness.

1. Romans 2:11.
2. Bryan Elliott, *More Than Gold* (Toronto: M46 Publishing, 2023).
3. A prophetic word is a message that reflects God's communication with us. God speaks. He is always speaking. He speaks through creation, dreams, visions, and the church community. God can also speak directly through an individual who receives a special or specific message for us. Of course, like every other spiritual gift, some people abuse, misuse, or fake prophecy. Some try to use "prophetic words" to manipulate and control others, in the same way some teach false doctrines. We test whether a prophetic word (or any other spiritual teaching, including mentoring, sermons, books, podcasts, etc.) is from God in several ways. It should be in line with Scripture. It should encourage and correct rather than tear down or damage. Prophecy should be confirmed as accurate by other believers, your spirit, and the witness of the Holy Spirit.
4. Matthew 7:24-27.
5. "Deliverance" was modeled by Jesus's ministry throughout the gospels. He commanded His followers to do the same (see Mark:16-17-20). It is a term used to describe special prayer ministry employed to "deliver" or "cast out" oppressive spiritual forces (demons) that contribute to physical, mental, or emotional distress.
6. Genesis 50:20.
7. Our story is documented in my first book, *More Than Gold*. If you are a new believer or want to refresh your walk with Jesus, I recommend starting with *More Than Gold* before continuing with *As in Heaven*. See www.m4bministries.com.

WELCOME
TO THE
KINGDOM!

"AT LAST THE FULFILLMENT OF THE AGE HAS COME! IT IS TIME FOR GOD'S KINGDOM TO BE EXPERIENCED IN ITS FULLNESS! TURN YOUR LIVES BACK TO GOD AND PUT YOUR TRUST IN THE HOPE-FILLED GOSPEL!"

KING JESUS
MARK 1:15, TPT

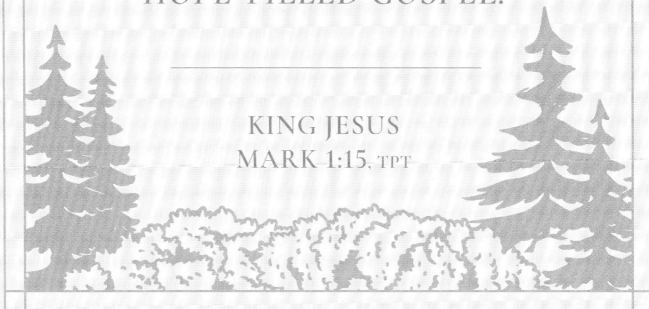

Part 1: Welcome to the Kingdom

"Heaven's kingdom realm is also like a jewel merchant in search of rare pearls. When he discovered one very precious and exquisite pearl, he immediately gave up all he had in exchange for it."
—*Matthew 13:45-46, TPT*

I want you to imagine a King on earth with unprecedented, unmatched, and unlimited power and authority. Imagine a King with unlimited resources whose kingdom is unshakable and eternal. This King rules a kingdom whose government is always increasing with no end.

This benevolent King unconditionally and perfectly loves His subjects. He is a King who is humble and meek. He gave His life for every single person in His dominion.

Imagine a kingdom of honour, a kingdom of family, and a kingdom of heavenly relationships in unity and oneness. This is a kingdom where everyone flourishes, lives abundantly and is governed and defined by love. In this kingdom of righteousness and justice, perfect peace, joy, fun, and celebration always exist.

Imagine a kingdom of hope, destiny, and legacy. A place that provides safety, peace, and provision for all and where all who submit to Him are welcome.

All the citizens here are a royal priesthood under the King of Kings, a kingdom where all its citizens are ambassadors of the King.

Imagine a kingdom where every citizen is asked to steward the unique gifts and abilities the King gave them.

This place has no crime, control, greed, disease, poverty, sickness, or toiling. It is a place bursting with fruitfulness, life, and light. In this kingdom, the King is responsible for the provision and protection of His people and is glorified by their fruitfulness.

Imagine a kingdom whose people share an inheritance with the King as sons and daughters.

Could this promise of a kingdom reality be worth more than gold or be greater than silver?[1] Is it the pearl of great price?[2] Does this kingdom sound like heaven? What if this was available now and not just when you die? What if the answer to all of those questions is "yes"? Would you trade or sell everything to be a part of this kingdom?

This is the gospel of the kingdom of our God and of our Lord Jesus Christ. It is the Father's great joy to welcome you into His kingdom!

"Rescue us every time we face tribulation and set us free from evil. For you are the King who rules with power and glory forever. Amen."
— Matthew 6:13, TPT

The kingdom of heaven is in the spirit realm: established, invincible, eternal, and unshakable. The kingdom of God is the rule of King Jesus. Wherever the King rules, the kingdom of God is at hand, even on earth.

Most agree that the terms "kingdom of heaven" and "kingdom of God" can be used interchangeably. However, for this book, I want to make a slight distinction as a point of clarity.

God is everywhere (life would not exist otherwise), but His kingdom is not yet everywhere. As the kingdom of heaven spreads throughout earth, the kingdom of God is established—His manifest presence comes, revealing and making evident the righteousness, peace, and joy of the Holy Spirit. The invisible kingdom comes into people's hearts and then is manifested on earth and will continue until heaven and earth become one after the return of Jesus. Those who submit to Jesus as their Lord and Saviour, who are adopted into God's family as co-heirs with Christ, are welcomed into the kingdom of heaven. This kingdom reality of living *on earth as it is in heaven* changes everything. The kingdom of heaven will come to earth fully in the future, with the new heaven and new earth. The kingdom of God is how heaven functions. A kingdom is not a democracy. It is a realm of ownership and absolute authority belonging to the King. As Christians, Jesus, our Lord and Saviour, rules *everything*. In the words of Jeremy Treat, Ph.D. and adjunct professor of theology at Biola University, in the kingdom, "God's reign begins in the human heart, but it will one day extend to the ends of earth… The message of the kingdom is not an escape from earth to heaven but God's reign coming from heaven to earth."[3]

I accepted Jesus as my Saviour when I was 13 years old, but I did not make Him my Lord until I was an adult. The word "lord" means "someone or something having power, authority, or influence; a master or ruler."[4] I may have said the words in my salvation prayer, but I didn't know what it meant to submit to King Jesus, nor was my heart ready to do so. Tragically, because I did not understand submission or lordship, I wound up living a worldly and rebellious life for many years. I left the church and lived according to my rules.[5] Though I believed in Jesus and considered myself a Christian, my life looked very similar to non-believers. I justified my behaviour and choices, even though I knew they were not biblical. I knowingly entered into sin, comparing my life to others and not to the Word of God.

"However, your real source of joy isn't merely that these spirits submit to your authority, but that your names are written in the journals of heaven and that you belong to God's kingdom. This is the true source of your authority."
Luke 10:20, TPT

Jesus does more than save us from eternity in hell; He is our Saviour and Lord. The Bible refers to Jesus as "Lord" more than 700 times, which gives us an idea of the gravity of the term.[6] To make Jesus Lord is to acknowledge Him as my owner, my master, the supreme power and authority over my life.

In 2016, I made Jesus my Lord. I submitted everything to Him, which began a new process of surrender and sanctification. I acknowledged that I was bought at a great price by the blood of Jesus. My King died for me! My King's love was so great that He made the ultimate sacrifice for you and me. It is Jesus alone who qualifies us as citizens of heaven!

The kingdom of God is the dominion of God, encompassing any place under the rule and reign of Jesus. For His kingdom to come through us, we must submit to His rule and reign, with Jesus as our Lord! We are called to make the invisible kingdom visible.

Can you see why Lordship is essential for entering the kingdom of heaven? When I decided to dethrone myself and declare Jesus as Lord, a new process began. I started surrendering other areas of my life to His Lordship, embracing the process of the cross where suffering is often necessary. Reflecting on this, I now perceive not only the power of the cross but also its beauty. The cross is meant to strip away all that we were never meant to be, enabling us to become who God designed us to be.

This is the point in my story where I decided to give up the rights to my life and give them to God. Submitting your life to God is living in freedom, not as a robot, but as one who walks with God and experiences the abundance only He can provide. It's the realm of fearing the Lord, where we see Him rightly in reverential awe and wonder. For most of my life, I was an unwise builder whose life was tossed to and fro… but not anymore![7]

The more I learn about God and understand His ways, the more I realize how much He loves and cares for His children. He literally sent His Son, Jesus, to die for our sins so that we could be reunited with Him.[8] If we think of those we love—our children, parents, grandparents, siblings, or even friends who feel like family—then we can imagine (at least to some extent) the unconditional love of our Father in heaven. He knew us before the foundation of the earth. He carefully knit each of us together in our mother's womb and has a beautiful plan for our futures.[9] He knows everything about us—the good, the bad, and the ugly—yet He loves us *unconditionally*. Jesus gave His life so we could have access to the kingdom. He sees *us* as the unique and exquisite pearl of great price.[10]

That's right, the King of Kings and Lord of Lords sees you as a pearl of great price. This perspective changes *everything*.

1. Psalm 19:10, Proverbs 3:14.

2. Matthew 13:45-46.

3. Treat, J. (2019, May 21). *The Kingdom of God in 8 Words*. The Gospel Coalition. https://www.thegospelcoalition.org/article/kingdom-god-8-words/.

4. "Lord," *Oxford Language Dictionary*, accessed October 11, 2023, https://rb.gy/fl1o9.

5. For the sake of clarity, the term "church" is used throughout this book in reference to the physical church. "Church" (capitalized) is used in reference to the body of Christ.

6. Francis Chan, "Is Jesus Your Lord?," *Crazy Love Podcast*, accessed October 11, 2023, https://rb.gy/dlmr4.

7. Matthew 7:24-27.

8. John 3:16.

9. Psalm 139:13, Jeremiah 29:11.

10. Matthew 13:45-46.

Chapter 1: The Kingdom Mandate

To understand the kingdom, we must go back to Genesis and the creation account. In the beginning, God created the heavens and the earth, which is how we know the kingdom of God exists in both dimensions or realms. As such, we must also be active in both the spiritual and natural realms, which we will get into shortly.

Then God said, "Let Us make mankind in Our image, according to Our likeness; and let them rule over the fish of the sea and over the birds of the sky and over the livestock and over all the earth, and over every crawling thing that crawls on the earth."
—Genesis 1:26, NASB

In Genesis, God gave the original mandate for man to have dominion over the earth. The word "rule," or in some translations "to have dominion," comes from the Hebrew word *mamlakah*, which can be translated as "kingdom" or "sovereign" rule. Through mankind (male and female), the earth was to operate *on earth as it is in heaven*. Eden was the original prototype established by God as a visible kingdom to set the example of how Adam and Eve should multiply and expand His kingdom across the entire earth.

Man was literally made to be a physical expression of the invisible God. The very life and Spirit of God was breathed into man, made in the image of God, and man's body was made of the earth. Heavenly and earthly substances came together to create a god-man to rule and reign over the earth and enjoy God and His creation.

As the pinnacle of creation, humans are granted legal access to have dominion (delegated authority) over the earth. God essentially transferred His governorship or rulership to Adam and Eve to establish this mandate, something Satan was aware of. Another way to say it is that God is the sovereign owner and gives us the right of possession or delegated authority. We are to responsibly subdue or manage the resources of the earth as good stewards of His creation.

Adam and Eve were given only one rule, *not to eat of the tree of the knowledge of good and evil*, and they broke that rule:

The Lord God commanded the man, saying, "From any tree of the garden you may freely eat; but from the tree of the knowledge of good and evil you shall not eat, for on the day that you eat from it you will certainly die."
—Genesis 2:16-17, NASB

As a result, their spirits died, and their souls were orphaned. A new system was instituted that was governed by works, which was the consequence of eating from the tree of the knowledge of good and evil. Instead of seeing God rightly, they now had a distorted view of God. Adam and Eve decided they would determine right and wrong for themselves. They traded the pursuit of knowledge for fellowship with God. This is the source of religion, works, the flesh, the curse, and the law. When Adam and Eve sinned and rebelled against God, the relationship shifted as they separated themselves from God and were exiled from Eden (the garden of God). In that moment, the first man and woman also lost their authority and right to rule and reign. They surrendered dominion and leadership on earth to the serpent.[1]

They lost their place in the kingdom of God.

They lost eternal life.

Death and decay entered the world.

Adam and Eve's God-given glory was tainted, and the earth had to endure empty futility, purposelessness, frustration, and chaos with Satan in control of the earthly domain… but God had a plan.

While Adam and Eve lost their ability to fulfill God's mandate, Jesus's victory through the cross restored mankind to God's original intent. By His blood, we are restored from our fallen state to become co-rulers with Christ, sons and daughters of God with the power and authority to, once again, re-establish God's kingdom reign on earth. The Hebrew word for Eden is *edhen*, which means "pleasure" or "delight." Our hearts are the new spiritual "Eden," the new garden of God, and made for God's good pleasure! Like Adam and Eve, our purpose is to tend to the garden of our heart and family. This is how we transform the world!

Once we carried the likeness of the man of dust, but now let us carry the likeness of the man of heaven.
1 Corinthians 15:49, TPT

All About Jesus

Jesus is the Alpha and the Omega, the beginning and the end![2] Jesus is the King. Everything on earth belongs to Him. Remember, Satan is a created, defeated being. We are not in an equal fight between light and dark or good and evil. Jesus has already won! When we remember that we are one with Jesus, the King of Kings, the CREATOR, we will no longer be impressed with the enemy.

Jesus embodies God's love and the centrepiece of God's redemptive plan to restore all things. Now, "…in Him we live and move and exist…" (Acts 17:28, NASB). He is in our past, present, and future! He was there before the beginning and knows the end of the story! We only have breath in our lungs because He wills it! Our lives, gifts, and abilities are all from God. We can't do anything without Him![3] All good that we have is from Him.[4]

Jesus is our life, truth, wisdom, light, way, salvation, righteousness, victory, protector, intercessor, secret place, provider, freedom, deliverer, healer, peace, comfort, joy, love, hope, humility, gentleness, goodness, patience, strength, rest, inheritance, and redemption. All matter and energy are found in Christ, two forms of the same thing that cannot be created or destroyed, all the way down to every atom and subatomic particle. All life is a physical demonstration of Christ. All things, visible and invisible, exist in and through Him! Jesus is in us, and we are in Him.

Jesus preached the kingdom message as the ultimate and perfect solution to all the woes and problems of mankind and the world. Jesus is the perfect example of ruling and reigning altogether void of the oppressive or controlling ways of the world. This is incredibly important as Jesus shows us a new and vastly better way to live. Through the victory of Jesus, the kingdoms of this world will become the kingdom of God and of the Lord Jesus Christ.[5]

Life in the kingdom is only found in Jesus, our All in All. Jesus is the source of everything, and everything finds completion in Him! We were exiled from God's garden, but Jesus brought the garden back inside of us. Jesus has supreme power over everything, everywhere. The amazing news is that for now and all of eternity, God "seated us with Him in the heavenly places in Christ Jesus" (Ephesians 2:6, NASB). This means we are reconciled with God, united with Jesus in Spirit, and share His authority and victory.[6]

All creation eagerly awaits us to become mature sons and daughters and to fill the world with kingdom citizens! Jesus is the blueprint of who we are now and what we will become as we fully awaken to our new creation identity. The world doesn't know how to escape bondage and decay. Our crucifixion with Christ severed the ties to this world and our old life. Jesus is the only way forward; we are in life's union with Him. The minute we enter the kingdom, we are called to take up our calling to restore the world to its original intent, *on earth as it is in heaven*, carrying forward the mission of Jesus. As we progress in our union with Jesus, we become more like Him; all creation will respond, and in the end, every tongue will confess, and every knee will bow.[7]

Kingdom Citizens

The kingdom of God is God's original intent for the world. We subdue the earth with the rule and atmosphere of the kingdom. We do this by the power of His Spirit, learning God's ways, discovering His plans, and obeying His Word concerning our lives, families, businesses, communities, and the world. As we begin to see our circumstances with a kingdom mindset, we can rule and reign in life with Jesus and live *on earth as it is in heaven*.

Our new creation life allows us to bring the unseen heavenly realities into physical reality. The physical realm mirrors the supernatural realm, so what is in the supernatural realm manifests in the natural realm. So often, we hear of Christianity as a religion that has followers waiting to die to go to heaven, but the truth is that we have a heavenly assignment *now*. What we receive in the Spirit, we can translate into the natural. In other words, we are transitioning agents, gateways, or portals to bring heaven to earth now!

It is important to understand "rule" and "reign." God is always ruling. He created the universe, all life, and the systems or guidelines from which everything exists as the sovereign Creator of all. He is supreme, almighty, and omnipotent. He alone is the perfectly righteous judge over all the universe. In heaven, God rules and reigns. On earth, God rules but chooses to reign through His people. We are heirs to God and co-heirs with Jesus.[8] This is why God must work deeply in our hearts to first reign in our life, then our family, and then continue into our sphere of influence. As followers of Christ, we become part of His kingdom family, helping run the kingdom family business (making disciples and bringing healing and freedom to the world). Authority is delegated representative power of the one who sends us: Jesus! We carry the authority of Jesus on earth.

RESTORATION
IS HIS

All creation eagerly awaits the
sons and daughters of God to manifest His:

- Majesty
- Goodness
- Holiness
- Radiant beauty
- Brilliant light
- Splendour
- Nature
- Power
- Creation
- Love
- Joy
- Glory

- Grace
- Mercy
- Faithfulness
- Character
- Justice
- Freedom
- Infinite wisdom
- Wholeness
- Perfection
- Sovereignty
- Vitality

The kingdom of God is the family of God, which is the ultimate purpose behind all creation. The kingdoms of this world are the kingdoms of religion, business, government, education, media, etc. We can all think of examples where these institutions have failed us. We see the damage each one has done in the past or is doing today. Each worldly kingdom has been redeemed but needs to be reclaimed and brought into submission to the kingdom of God.

We often think of the kingdoms of this world as "secular" or *of the world* versus being "sacred" or *of God*. In truth, there is no divide between sacred and secular.

For by Him all things were created, both in the heavens and on earth, visible and invisible, whether thrones, or dominions, or rulers, or authorities — all things have been created through Him and for Him. He is before all things, and in Him all things hold together.
— *Colossians 1:16-17, NASB*

Rather, all is redeemed by Jesus and sacred to God, as seen in the original mission of Adam and Eve to make the rest of the earth like Eden. Our mission is to reclaim what has been redeemed. Scripture reveals that one day, all things will be restored as all things were placed under Christ's rule and reign.[9] This is so that "God may be all in all."[10] One day, God's kingdom will fully encompass the entire earth and beyond. It is all sacred to God.

One distinction between sacred and secular made in Scripture, however, is our role as believers who are called "saints" meant to be salt and light in the world.[11] In other words, we are set apart and called to go into the world and transform all things through the power of the Holy Spirit at work within us. The kingdom of God is where the King reigns in the hearts of man. The kingdom of God is the presence of the King of Kings. Through Jesus, heaven and earth are brought together! Jesus is present within every believer! Wherever we go, the kingdom goes! We must approach all of life with this perspective in mind.

God's kingdom is our inheritance. We have access to the riches of His glory. We are the recipients of His grace and goodness. We see this when looking at our families or across a starry sky as creation declares His splendor and glory![12] This is the glory of a God who is without limit. He is gracious, generous, infinitely loving, and supplies all our needs. To access our inheritance, we must fulfill our mandate by being transformed into the image of Christ and creating disciple-makers who seek His kingdom first. In other words, we must fulfill our mandate by being transformed into the image of Christ and create disciple-makers who seek first His kingdom. Like any good father, there is a time of preparation and maturing before the blessing of the inheritance can be released.

If an inheritance is gained too early in life, it will not be blessed in the end.
— *Proverbs 20:21, TPT*

God's kingdom mandate in Genesis 1:26-28 is as true and important today as it was when it was said thousands of years ago. This is the mandate and purpose of every believer: to have dominion over the earth. We were designed for the kingdom and to rule and reign with Christ. Let me emphasize: We were created for rulership over the earth, but *not over people*. As His hands and feet on earth, we are in the process of bringing about the earth as it is in heaven. What already exists in heaven is our blueprint for the earth.

> *But we are a colony of heaven on earth as we cling tightly to our life-giver, the Lord Jesus Christ, who will transform our humble bodies and transfigure us into the identical likeness of His glorified body. And using His matchless power, He continually subdues everything to Himself.*
> —*Philippians 3:20-21, TPT*

We are here *now* on earth as part of God's divine plan for such a time as this. Heaven, our eternal home, is not meant to be a faraway place! It's supposed to come to earth now and remain until the finale as God's ultimate plan for the future. And to do this, our sovereign God chose to work in and through mankind on earth. We were created to commune with God, live with God as His family, and bring heaven's fullness to earth. However, man's journey of bringing heaven to earth has been challenging.

For most of my life, I've lived my way and on my terms. I was unaware there was so much more. I had a family, but I did not put God first. This left me self-focused, self-reliant, and with skewed priorities. When I decided to live for Jesus, to my surprise, there was a grieving process involving loneliness and sadness as the things of the world lost their grip on me. My priorities began to change, and I noticed that I had much less in common with the people in my old life. Today, as I continue to seek His kingdom before all my other priorities, the realm of the kingdom continues to expand in my personal life, family, relationships, and business. As I align my life with heaven, my family and business also align with heaven.

The Journey Back to Our Inheritance

After Adam and Eve's rebellion and fall, God said that through the seed of woman would come the Messiah (the Saviour, Jesus), who would ultimately crush Satan's head under His feet.

> *"And I will make enemies*
> *Of you and the woman,*
> *And of your offspring and her Descendant;*
> *He shall bruise you on the head,*
> *And you shall bruise Him on the heel."*
> —*Genesis 3:15, NASB*

God chose a special people, His chosen people, the Hebrew people of Israel (Jews), to be an expression of the kingdom of God on earth. They were governed, protected, and provided for according to heaven's blueprint. Israel was intended to be an example to the world of the kingdom of God for other gentile nations to follow.[13] However, the people of Israel ultimately did not fulfill their call to be a light to the nations. They rebelled against God. The Old Testament details the seriousness and consequences of sin and mankind's powerlessness to overcome fallen nature. The chosen people, along with the rest of the world, needed a saviour. In 2 Samuel 7:12-16, the prophet Nathan delivers a message that the promised Messiah will come from the offspring of David to establish His throne and kingdom forever.

In the sixth century BC, Daniel prophesied the coming Roman Empire as a time when the eternal kingdom of God would come to earth.

And in the days of those kings the God of heaven will set up a kingdom which will never be destroyed, and that kingdom will not be left for another people; it will crush and put an end to all these kingdoms, but it will itself endure forever.
—Daniel 2:44, NASB

In the ensuing centuries, empires rose, and empires fell. However, God fulfilled His promise.

But when the fullness of the time came, God sent His Son, born of a woman, born under the Law, so that He might redeem those who were under the Law, that we might receive the adoption as sons and daughters.
—Galatians 4:4-5, NASB

John the Baptist came with the baptism of repentance, preparing the way and announcing the coming of the Messiah, King Jesus. Then Jesus came with the announcement of the kingdom of God and the baptism of the Holy Spirit to be born again to receive His kingdom.

Jesus spoke to the religious leaders of Israel who had not received the kingdom mandate or His message.

"This is why I say to you that the kingdom realm of God will be taken from you and given to a people who will bear its fruit."
— Matthew 21:43, TPT

All that was lost in Adam and Eve, the privilege and blessing of being a son or daughter of God, was restored through Jesus. Jesus is the door into the kingdom of God. He is the restoration power of God that is bringing the world back to God's original design. Out of the greatest act of sacrificial love, Jesus paid the full price for all sin and rebellion of mankind. He gave everything to be reunited with us. We are born into the physical realm, and those with faith in Jesus will be born again into the kingdom's spiritual realm. We can receive the Holy Spirit, the third person of the Trinity, who is God Himself. Believers are adopted as children of God. We have the right to be citizens in the kingdom of God with future heavenly rewards. *This* is the journey back to our inheritance.

"As you passionately seek his kingdom, above all else, he will supply your needs. So don't ever be afraid, dearest friends! Your loving Father joyously gives you his kingdom with all its promises!"
——*Luke 12:31-32, TPT*

1. Genesis 2-3.
2. Revelation 22:13.
3. John 15:5.
4. Psalm 16:2.
5. Psalm 72:8.
6. 1 Corinthians 15:28, Hebrews 12:1-2, John 14:6, John 15:5, Acts 17:28, Colossians 1:15-17, Ephesians 2:6.
7. Philippians 2:9-11.
8. Romans 8:17.
9. Romans 8:22; Ephesians 1:22
10. 1 Corinthians 15:28
11. Romans 1:7; Matthew 5:13-16
12. Psalm 19:1.
13. Isaiah 60:3.

THE KINGDOM MANDATE

Then God said, "Let Us make mankind in Our image, according to Our likeness; and let them rule over the fish of the sea and over the birds of the sky and over the livestock and over all the earth, and over every crawling thing that crawls on the earth."
–Genesis 1:26, NASB

Father, we ask for the grace to embrace the kingdom mandate and fulfill our kingdom calling as ambassadors of Your kingdom!

QUESTIONS FOR REFLECTION

What has the Holy Spirit revealed to you through *The Kingdom Mandate*? How can you apply this to your life?

_____

_____

_____

_____

A kingdom is a form of government or leadership structure. How is the kingdom of heaven similar to governments we are familiar with, and how is it different?

_____

_____

_____

_____

What does it mean to be a citizen of the kingdom of heaven?

_____

_____

_____

_____

Are there areas in your life where you sense God is prompting you to submit to His leadership in a new way? If so, what does that look like?

_____

_____

_____

_____

Notes

_____

_____

_____

_____

_____

_____

_____

_____

_____

_____

_____

_____

_____

_____

_____

Chapter 2: The Kingdom Reality

"Manifest your kingdom realm, and cause your every purpose to be fulfilled on earth, just as it is in heaven. We acknowledge you as our Provider of all we need each day."
Matthew 6:10-11, TPT

As I have grown in my faith, I have deepened my surrender to the Lord, opening myself to become less rebellious, self-reliant, and self-focused by the transformational power of the Holy Spirit. By taking myself off of the throne of my own life, the result is that He is forming Himself in me, making me more truly myself: whole, healed, freed, dependent, and alive for His eternal purposes. I have suffered great tragedy and incredible loss. I have often failed in my walk with God, but over and over, Jesus has proven faithful to His Word and His love for me. Although I would not wish many of the things I have experienced upon anyone, these trials have increased my intimacy and accelerated my journey with the Lord in ways I never thought possible. I am who I am now as a result of the trials I've experienced by the grace of God.

Blessing results from suffering when you are a child of God because God is such a gracious redeemer. He gives us more than enough grace to endure if we are citizens of the kingdom. My suffering has moved me into a place of greater dependency, rest, and faith in God. I am not the same person I was last month, let alone five years ago, and in the process of growth and transformation, I have discovered a kingdom that cannot be shaken and a totally new perspective on life: *the kingdom perspective.*[1]

> We are half-hearted creatures, fooling about with drink and sex and ambition when infinite joy is offered us, like an ignorant child who wants to go on making mud pies in a slum because he cannot imagine what is meant by the offer of a holiday at the sea. We are far too easily pleased.
> — C.S. Lewis[2]

This exemplifies the offer to live as kingdom citizens. How tragic when we are content with salvation alone and live our lives waiting to die to go to heaven, or worse, we live a divided life, still indulging in the things of this world.

The kingdom reality has allowed me to experience **peace above my circumstances**.

Peace is the presence of the Prince of Peace, Jesus. Through Jesus, we have access to peace beyond what makes sense.[3] When I acknowledged Jesus as my King, Lord, and owner, my life started to change, and a peace that I had never experienced began to take hold. It remained regardless of the shaking, trials, and suffering I experienced. This peace is what enabled me to sleep well amid the upheaval after Abbe's death. It is a peace that has persisted regardless of business pressures and financial shaking amid COVID-19 lockdowns, divorce, the sale of my family home, a corporate lawsuit, and a murder trial, all working in tandem. The peace of the kingdom is the gospel of peace, which supersedes everything. This is the peace the world is desperately searching for and is only found in Jesus because peace is a person.

The kingdom reality has allowed me to experience **joy far above my circumstances**.

Joy is a person, and His name is Jesus. I have experienced the greatest joy amid terrible seasons of extreme suffering, tragedy, and loss. I have discovered the blessing of joining in the sufferings of Jesus as He joins in my sufferings. In the same way that I am the pearl of great price Jesus died to save, He is my pearl of great price. Nothing can compare with the joy, comfort, and intimacy of knowing Him. (We choose how close we will come to Him. God is always inviting us to step closer. He is always knocking at the door.)

For our momentary, light affliction is producing for us an eternal weight of glory far beyond all comparison, while we look not at the things which are seen, but at the things which are not seen; for the things which are seen are temporal, but the things which are not seen are eternal.
—2 Corinthians 4:17-18, NASB

I regularly experience peace and joy amid circumstances that would warrant the opposite emotion. The two coming together is what I describe as "calm delight." The more I maintain my focus on God and a kingdom mindset, the more constant this kingdom reality becomes. For example, when I hear bad news or a very negative report, my peace remains as I know God is above everything. He is sovereign, all-powerful, and all-knowing, and my trust is in Him alone. I know things are happening "for me" and not "to me."

So we are convinced that every detail of our lives is continually woven together for good, for we are his lovers who have been called to fulfill his designed purpose.
—Romans 8:28, TPT

The source of our hope is in our salvation, the certainty of our wonderful eternal future with Him, and that nothing can separate us from the love of God. The kingdom reality has allowed me to experience **new forms of wealth that cannot be lost or stolen**. There is no future in evil, only good, as our eternal hope and treasures are rooted in the ultimate justice of God and a glorious eternity. Furthermore, we must remember that while many consider themselves good, only God is truly good. I have tasted and experienced the best the world has to offer. I have experienced the false and fleeting safety and security of money. I have experienced the emptiness, stress, and anxiety of self-reliance. I have lived apart from God and partially with God and have discovered the immense blessing of living my life *all in* for God.

Blessed be the God and Father of our Lord Jesus Christ, who has blessed us with every spiritual blessing in the heavenly places in Christ…
—Ephesians 1:3, NASB

Now the brother or sister of humble circumstances is to glory in his high position; but the rich person is to glory in his humiliation, because like flowering grass he will pass away.
—James 1:9-10, NASB

One skilled in business discovers prosperity, but the one who trusts in God is blessed beyond belief!
Proverbs 16:20, TPT

The longer I live in the kingdom, the more my definition of "success" changes.

But the Lord said to Samuel, "Do not look at his appearance or at the height of his stature, because I have rejected him; for God does not see as man sees, since man looks at the outward appearance, but the Lord looks at the heart."
1 Samuel 16:7, NIV

Money, material items, power, influence, or any other measure of earthly success can vanish at any time. But in the kingdom, everything looks different, upside-down even. For instance, in the kingdom, the last come first, the poor are rich, and the weak are strong.[1] He uses us for His ends, not the other way around. He has a purpose and a plan for every life. True wealth or heavenly riches are spiritual. Eternal life only comes from God. When we claim nothing as our own (humbled and yielded), everything will be given to us. This is the heart position of one prepared to receive the inheritance of God.

The kingdom perspective helped me discover **the power of forgiveness and the grace to forgive when it seemed impossible**.

I received the mercy and forgiveness of my daughter, Bryn, despite my failures as a father. I experienced the power of giving or extending forgiveness amid the horrible wrongs of others against me and my daughters. This includes massive betrayal, sexual abuse, and even murder. Regardless of the positions or opinions of those who have sinned against me, practising forgiveness releases me from the bonds of the sin of unforgiveness and releases God's redemptive power. Giving and receiving forgiveness unites me with the Father as I submit to His authority and embrace the power of the cross.

"Forgive us the wrongs we have done as we ourselves release forgiveness to those who have wronged us."
—Matthew 6:12, TPT

The kingdom perspective has helped me discover **God as my Redeemer and my Protector**.

…for all have sinned and fall short of the glory of God, being justified as a gift by His grace through the redemption which is in Christ Jesus.
—Romans 3:23-24, NASB

I was blind to my pride and rebelliousness for decades. Since I turned to God, after finally recognizing the relentless pursuit of God, I have experienced the gift of redemption and the transformation that occurs as a result of His grace. God has redeemed my life, and I am now His friend and son. I have been saved, forgiven, restored, and filled with hope. And now I get to share it with the world!

1. Hebrews 12:26-28.
2. Dr. Art Lindsley, "C.S. Lewis's Famous Mud Pies: How Imagination Opens the Heart to Truth," *Institute for Faith, Work & Economics*, accessed October 11, 2023, https://rb.gy/8ybdx.
3. Philippians 4:7.
4. Matthew 20:16.

THE KINGDOM REALITY

"Manifest your kingdom realm, and cause your every purpose to be fulfilled on earth, just as it is in heaven. We acknowledge you as our Provider of all we need each day."

–Matthew 6:10-11, TPT

Father, we agree with Your Word and ask that Your will be done on earth as it is in heaven!

QUESTIONS FOR REFLECTION

What has the Holy Spirit revealed to you through *The Kingdom Reality*? How can you apply this to your life?

_____

_____

_____

_____

Where might your perspective need to change so you have a kingdom perspective?

_____

_____

_____

If you have not made Jesus the Lord of your life, what parts of this chapter touched a longing or desire in you for the things of the kingdom?

_____

_____

_____

_____

QUESTIONS FOR REFLECTION *(continued)*

Spend some time reflecting on the Bible passages in this chapter. What thoughts do they bring up? Talk to God about it!

_____

_____

_____

_____

Notes

_____

_____

_____

_____

_____

_____

_____

_____

_____

_____

_____

_____

_____

_____

_____

Chapter 3: Seeking His Kingdom

"But seek first His kingdom and His righteousness, and all these things will be provided to you."
—Matthew 6:33, NASB

What does it mean to seek first His kingdom and righteousness? It's actually pretty simple: It means to consistently make Jesus first in every area of your life. This means we must first take ourselves off the throne of our own life. We lose our life to gain it. This will be an ongoing journey as we enter the process of sanctification, that is, becoming like Christ. When we put Jesus first, we will experience His goodness firsthand.[1] To seek first His kingdom is to seek the presence of God above everything else. It is to live by the Word of God and by His kingdom principles. It means we put the kingdom above our country, government, family, or anything else as we emulate what we worship or hold as the highest priority. We enter the kingdom as citizens and become ambassadors as we reorient our priorities to seek first His kingdom and become about our Father's business. It is in God's kingdom that citizens become ambassadors of His kingdom!

What we focus on expands, which is why our top focus is the kingdom! What we honour, we attract, which is why we first honour the King and His kingdom. Heaven comes as we make God our top priority and our heart's desire. Abiding in Him means to rest, remain, and live in constant awareness of His nearness.[2] It means to engage with Jesus as our friend throughout our day. This is how we enjoy God. The fruit of the Spirit in our lives is the person of Jesus manifesting through the Holy Spirit.

But the fruit of the Spirit is love, joy, peace, patience, kindness, goodness, faithfulness, gentleness, self-control; against such things there is no law.
—Galatians 5:22-23, NASB

When we are filled with God's Spirit, the fruit of divine love in all its various expressions is produced by the Holy Spirit within us, which is for others to enjoy. Our fruit allows others to taste and see the kingdom of God is good.

This is the nature and character of God revealed in His family through the Holy Spirit. The presence of Jesus is THE key to the kingdom and the place where we experience victory in all areas of our lives that need His healing touch and resurrection. When we live as a branch of the tree of life, we are enabled to live above our circumstances! The kingdom comes by Spirit-led living, which comes from friendship with and enjoyment of God.

The kingdom of God is the will of God done on earth, which is always the best will for earth. When we aim to achieve the most noble and highest possible good (His will, the kingdom), our life becomes flooded with purpose and meaning. This is where we realize that everything we do matters because we are making an eternal difference, giving new life to the statement, "When we know the why, we can get through anyhow." By God's design, you were born for such a time as this, on purpose and for a purpose with good works prepared in advance for you to do in expanding His kingdom on earth.[3] With purpose, we gain the strength to endure challenges. As sons and daughters, our focus must first be on His kingdom, for it will continually expand, regardless of what it may look like in the natural realm. We want the physical realm (earth) to manifest the spiritual realm of light (heaven).

Keys to the Kingdom

I received a prophetic word a few years ago that as I take care of the Lord's house, the Lord will show me what it looks like as He takes care of my house. I didn't understand this kingdom principle then, but as I made God the number one focus of my life, He was released to move in my life in an entirely new way. I have seen deep foundations laid in my life, family, business, and beyond. Even at the age of 53, it feels like I am just starting my life with a new sense of awe, wonder, and adoration of God. This is what happens when we seek His kingdom first!

Keys are used to open locked doors. Locks are special mechanisms that keep a door closed. They only open with one specific key. When you have the right key, you can open the door. But the door remains locked if you don't have the right key. Just as we have physical keys that open physical doors, there are spiritual keys that open spiritual doors. These spiritual keys, or kingdom keys, are based on biblical principles. These principles work for *everyone*. However, when we do not follow God's design, chaos and death are the result.

For example, the decentralized free exchange of value, as outlined in the Old Testament, is God's design and is relational and interconnected, promoting unity. However, capitalism has veered away from God's design with more of a transactional model, opening the door to greed, centralizing wealth, and placing the shareholder's profit above all else. Another economic example is communist China, which was forced to introduce some aspects of the free market to keep it from financial collapse. Meanwhile, as Canada and the United States have veered away from their Judeo-Christian foundations, we can observe their descent into darkness and chaos.

Seeking His kingdom and righteousness is impossible without first receiving "the ultimate key" to the kingdom—Jesus![4] Faith in Jesus is the ultimate key to the kingdom. He opened the gates of heaven when He died and rose again to those who receive His forgiveness as Saviour and Lord. However, we are not meant to stop once we pass through the gates (salvation). A kingdom lifestyle of sanctification and holiness is rooted in His love required of each citizen. We are sanctified as we are formed into the image of Jesus by the power of the Holy Spirit.

Every person on earth is given the opportunity to choose faith in Jesus. Faith is God's gift and the key to operating in His kingdom. Salvation faith is given to all but must be exercised. After salvation, faith grows by hearing the Word of God as our trust deepens. Faith remembers what God has done and said. There is also the gift of faith. From experience, life is totally different when we receive the gift of faith! When faith ignites, we come alive. There is a new perspective and a boldness that accompanies this gift. I recently heard a powerful truth rooted in trust: *God is consistent but not predictable*. Faith empowers us to trust and obey God.

The name Yahweh is the name of the God of Israel. It means "I am who I am," or "the One who is" or "the becoming present One." The kingdom is anywhere Yahweh is present. Our holiness was established through grace by our faith in Jesus alone and our new creation life union with Him. It cannot be attained by works. We don't need to be holy and pure to approach God; He draws us closer. His holiness invites us to transform into His likeness, and in this divine encounter, He makes us holy and pure. Holiness, which is Christlikeness in terms of setting ourselves apart for God, is a result of living in proximity to (or intimacy with) the presence of the King and allowing Him to form His character in us through submission and obedience.[5] Doing so results in purity, which is loving what God loves and hating what God hates. It is asking God to create a holy hunger for Him. Living according to biblical principles is living like Jesus. These are the keys to the kingdom and applying them is required to bring heaven to earth. We must take hold of these keys to handle the storms of life that will come, and they will, as well as the victories He has for us ahead.

> *But now, Lord, You are our Father;*
> *We are the clay, and You our potter,*
> *And all of us are the work of Your hand.*
> *—Isaiah 64:8, NASB*

As we journey with the Lord, we learn to trust His process. I have learned that His process is often not what we expect. For example, in mid-2018, I thought I was almost through the worst of the testing and shaking when, in reality, I was only halfway through. Our journey with God is just as much about what we learn and how we grow in the process as it is about the destination. Sometimes, I felt disappointed, impatient, frustrated, and downright fed-up. However, in the process of waiting, God was forming my character.[6] The process is about progress, never perfection. When Jesus is truly our shepherd, we have no wants as we always have more than enough.[7] I am learning to trust God. What I can't see, He can. God is always our provider and our strength.[8]

By default, I used to pray for God to take away trials and tribulations. Now, I pray for His will to be done *on earth as it is in heaven*. I used to pray for God to remove the circumstance quickly, and now I pray for His divine timing *on earth as it is in heaven*. Of course, there are times of attack when we take authority, submit to God, and resist the devil, and the devil flees. This is why we must be led by His Spirit like Jesus.

The Kingdom Mind

> *I pray that you will continually experience the immeasurable greatness of God's power made available to you through faith. Then your lives will be an advertisement of this immense power as it works through you! This is the*

mighty power that was released when God raised Christ from the dead and exalted him to the place of highest honour and supreme authority in the heavenly realm! And now he is exalted as first above every ruler, authority, government, and realm of power in existence! He is gloriously enthroned over every name that is ever praised, not only in this age, but in the age that is coming!
—*Ephesians 1:19-21, TPT*

I have experienced mountains and valleys with God. Through it all, He is always at work, even when it doesn't feel like it. The seeming absence of experiential God moments trains us to trust and experience Him in new ways as God speaks to us through His Word, His still, small voice, and all His creation. Though faith is often forged in times of "not feeling," we learn to walk with Jesus day by day and moment by moment, growing to be unswayed by the things of the world.

The kingdom moves us to fight from the place of victory based on the finished work of Jesus! The name of *Jesus,* the resurrection power of Jesus, the cross, the blood of Jesus, the Word of God, worship, rest, celebration, repentance, forgiveness, mercy, humility, thanksgiving, unity, light, the fruit of the Spirit, the armour of God, and the armour of light are critical weapons of our warfare.[9] Warfare is simply standing true to God, as Satan has no dominion. Therefore, do not give the devil power. We are subjects of the kingdom of light, which displaces evil, the kingdom of darkness. We are not fighting for victory; *we are enforcing a victory already obtained.* In other words, we are always on the offensive, not the defensive. We are not passive but thrusting the kingdom forth, not by our efforts, but through His Spirit.[10] Jesus has given us ALL authority over the power of the enemy.[11] We have all authority; however, we must be aware of God's timing and strategy and move in obedience just as Jesus modelled with the Father, only doing what He saw the Father doing. This is our mandate, *on earth as it is in heaven.*

This kingdom reality has changed my entire outlook and experience with spiritual warfare as I continue to learn to rule and reign on earth. We are made to exercise the power of God made available to us who believe. As we live with the kingdom mindset, we will successfully combat evil through the power of Jesus and living God's way. (More than that, kingdom principles show us how to live in God's will. They are good, pleasing, and perfect! They are *His will,* enabling us to live *on earth as it is in heaven.* In many circumstances, we don't have to ask what God's will is if we are living from His will expressed in these keys.)

As my understanding of the kingdom has deepened, my perception of Satan has significantly lessened. The revelation of the kingdom brings about a fear of the Lord, enabling us to recognize God's supreme and invincible nature, and to see Satan as the defeated foe. The kingdom of God is firmly anchored in the fear of the Lord and expands as we deny ourselves, take up our cross, and follow Jesus. In every aspect of my life, including family and business, where I've wholeheartedly established Jesus as Lord, I've found true freedom and freshness of life.

Freedom From Anxiety: Trusting God as Our Ultimate Source

The opposite of this freedom is anxiety and typically stems from feeling powerless. It is amplified by unresolved past hurt or sin, attachment wounds, neglect, trauma, uncertainty, and even poor diet and lack of exercise. Envisioning the future without God can also be a source of anxiety, and *trusting God* is the antidote. Kingdom citizens are confident of their God-filled future, authority, and power through Christ. Worry leading to anxiety is pride as we are making ourselves our "source." Whereas humility means we cast our cares on the Lord. He is our source. We don't have to carry them by ourselves.

Another source of anxiety is a sense of aimlessness. This is why the Bible tells us to record the vision, make it plain, and write it down (Habakkuk 2:2-3). In addition, Scripture makes it clear repeatedly for us to seek first His kingdom, which ideally will become our highest vision and the greatest aim of our life.

Overcoming Anxiety: Identifying and Addressing Root Causes

When we don't put Him first, we open the door to anxiety, dread, instability, double-mindedness, depression, and an absence of meaning. There are many other causes of anxiety, dread, and depression, such as chemical imbalances or demonic oppression (or a combination of all three). Things that open the door to demonic oppression include:

- Focusing on ourselves, which amplifies our problems and opens the doors to pride;
- Not taking responsibility for our lives or having a vision to work towards;
- Worrying but not talking to God or praying about the circumstance concerning us;
- Making our problems bigger than God;
- Not living by faith;
- Having an orphan mindset, living out of a false identity of self-sufficiency and lack;
- Not renewing our minds with Scripture; and
- Dwelling on what's wrong more than counting our blessings.

We need to spend time with the Holy Spirit to determine the roots of our anxiety. If we choose to give ourselves ultimate authority (which is idolatry), we put ourselves on the slow road to misery and bondage. We have all experienced this, which is why the Christian faith is about dying to ourselves, doing good for others, and renewing our minds. For example, social anxiety is commonly caused by having a hyper-focus on yourself, which is a form of pride. A simple and effective antidote is to practice humility by making others feel known, valued, and comfortable. Doing so naturally takes our eyes off ourselves. As we give, we receive. As we bless, we are blessed. As we sow, we reap.

It is imperative to understand that the more we give into worry and fear, the more pride we have in our lives. Moreover, we worship what we fear, as we've elevated it to the highest place. Why?

Because we are looking to ourselves to "be the answer to our problem" rather than God. When we give God our worries, we lay our pride at the foot of the cross. In a similar vein, when we are thankful, our brains do not register fear. I.e., God made us in such a way that our minds cannot register gratitude and fear at the same time. To seek His kingdom first is to fear the Lord.

A great hack to stop anxiety is to practice controlled breathing. Take two deep breaths in, followed by a slow exhale. Do this several times while thinking about God's peace and giving your worries to Him. Physically, this helps stop anxiety-inducing chemicals in their tracks while helping you refocus on God. Because we are triune beings, body, soul, and spirit, this is an instance where we can use our bodies to help bring our soul into submission to our spirit and, ultimately, to God. Another great hack to stopping anxiety is praying for someone else's needs.

The greatest power known is God's resurrection power, which now works in and through us. As kingdom advancers, we get to appropriate the blood and victory of Jesus into every area of our lives. I have personally been progressively and systematically doing so in all areas of my life since submitting to the Lordship of Jesus. In the simplest of terms, this looks like praying regularly and declaring God's will over my family and business. The more I do, the more I am reoriented to the kingdom lifestyle in submission to my Father in heaven.

From Fear to Faith: A Mother's Journey of Spiritual Warfare

God is on the throne, sovereign and unchallenged. The kingdom of heaven is invincible. Psalm 2:4 tells us that God sits on His throne and laughs at the schemes of the enemy. This reminds me of a recent story where a woman named Rose in my office building accepted Jesus into her heart and life. She and her son were under demonic attack, and she was at the end of her rope. Her 17-year-old son was scared to go into his bedroom, and there was an increasing feeling of evil in her house. As she told me about how dark it was, I excitedly volunteered to go and cleanse the house. When I arrived, the space felt heavy, and the presence of fear was evident. The first thing I did was verbally declare that Satan was defeated and powerless in the light of the supremacy of Jesus. I was playful and light but authoritative. This got others giggling and smiling, which shifted the atmosphere. Then we took care of the Lord's business by anointing each room with oil and blessing the house room by room, dedicating it as the Lord's! The home is now filled with God's peace, and they are taking steps to close any open spiritual door to the enemy.

This mother has turned from fear to faith, from weak to warrior. She is growing in faith, discipling, and praying in power over her son, who also just accepted the Lord. The Lord is building her through the process of growing in Him and fighting for her son, just as He did with Bryn and me. This mother is now on fire and has a powerful testimony to share with the world!

Yours, Lord, is the greatness, the power, the glory, the victory, and the majesty, indeed everything that is in the heavens and on the earth; Yours is the dominion, Lord, and You exalt Yourself as head over all.
—1 Chronicles 29:11, NASB

The war is here on earth between the kingdom of light and love and the kingdom of darkness and fear. Satan is warring for the control of our minds through deception, which is where our personal battle is fought. When we believe a lie or deception, we allow ourselves to be influenced by it. Upon its revelation, we must repent (change our thinking) to align with the truth's influence! There is a war for the souls of men, and we will be in a spiritual war until the return of King Jesus, culminating in the new heaven and new earth.

I make sure I am aware of Satan's ways, as we are not to be ignorant of his schemes, but he is never my focus. Had man not fallen into sin and given Satan a legal right to move on earth since the time of Adam, the outcome of Adam and Eve's time in the Garden of Eden would have been quite different. However, because of their disobedience, humanity's fallen nature continues to provide the enemy a platform from which to wage war on earth.

We are the sum of all the influences we allow in our lives, what we behold. We become what we behold, so we must be aware and glorify God, focusing on the light, not the darkness. The fact that the battle is for our minds highlights why our focus must be on His kingdom and living in victorious kingdom consciousness as kingdom warriors.

These are key truths to internalize as we partner to expand the kingdom. As we rise in unity as the body of Christ, we usher the kingdom of light onto the earth, which displaces all darkness. Darkness is simply the absence of light. We are to storm the gates of hell and are promised to prevail. We are to be offensive, not defensive, constantly expanding the kingdom of God while recognizing our need for one another as the body of Christ.

We are filled with God as Christ's fullness overflows within us. Jesus is over every kingdom and authority in the universe! It is in the battles of our trials, tribulations, and sufferings that our faith is refined like gold, and our sanctification process is accelerated as we go from glory to glory, learning to live in total dependence on God. The sanctified mind opens our spiritual senses.

It is God's grace that empowers us to do what pleases God. What is most dangerous is our flesh or carnal nature, which is why we must die to ourselves or our selfish old nature. Satanism is essentially the glorification of self and indulgence of the flesh. The self is at war with God, so we must yield to the dynamic life and power of the Holy Spirit. The one who has died with Christ has been set free from sin. Humility and sacrificial love are superpowers of the kingdom as we overcome evil with good.

In this you greatly rejoice, even though now for a little while, if necessary, you have been distressed by various trials, so that the proof of your faith, being more precious than gold which perishes though tested by fire, may be found to result in praise, glory, and honour at the revelation of Jesus Christ…
— 1 Peter 1:6-7, NASB

As believers, we often hear people say, "More are for us than against us." We have two-thirds of the angels on our side because only one-third fell into darkness. This is still a gross understatement, as our infinite uncreated GOD is on our side! Satan is nothing compared to God.[12] He has us and gives His angels assignments to assist and protect us. God can continue to create as many spiritual beings as He chooses.

He is the image of the invisible God, the firstborn of all creation: for by Him all things were created, both in the heavens and on earth, visible and invisible, whether thrones, or dominions, or rulers, or authorities—all things have been created through Him and for Him.
—Colossians 1:15-16, NASB

SATAN IS DEFEATED

*Then Jesus made a public spectacle of all the powers and
principalities of darkness, stripping away from them every
weapon and all their spiritual authority and power to accuse us.
And by the power of the cross, Jesus led them around as prisoners
in a procession of triumph. He was not their prisoner; they were his!*
—Colossians 2:15, TPT

*But the one who indulges in a sinful life is of the devil, because
the devil has been sinning from the beginning. The reason the Son
of God was revealed was to undo and destroy the works of the devil.*
—1 John 3:8, TPT

**"I give you the name Peter, a stone. And this rock will be the bedrock foundation
on which I will build my church—my legislative assembly, and the power
of death will not be able to overpower it! I will give you the keys of
heaven's kingdom realm to forbid on Earth that which is forbidden in
heaven, and to release on Earth that which is released in heaven."**
—Matthew 16:18-20, TPT

*Then the devil who had deceived them was thrown into the same
place with the wild beast and the false prophet—the lake of
fire and sulfur—where they will be tormented day and night
forever and ever.*
—Revelation 20:10, TPT

We had an intercessor at a recent conference who observed as everyone in the room shifted into "warfare" mode against the enemy. The guest speaker, a seer, witnessed demons entering the room as the focus turned towards Satan. The more attention the room gave to the enemy's activities, the more demonic activity manifested. The guest speaker intervened, redirected the focus, took authority, and shifted the atmosphere. This raises a question commonly voiced by Kris Vallatton in his sermons: why would we empower an already disempowered enemy? Why not focus on what God is doing instead? Like Jesus, who only did what He saw the Father doing, we are called to align our actions on earth with what heaven is doing – *as in heaven!*

I heard another story about a well-known church that encountered a similar challenge. As they began their worship, they sensed a spiritual heaviness that dampened the atmosphere. Each Sunday, the pastor, a powerful man of God, would address the presence of dark forces, and afterward, the worship environment would return to a heavenly state. However, after some time, the Holy Spirit revealed the true nature of the situation: the enemy desired acknowledgment and glorification. The pastor repented, and the following Sunday, despite the heavy atmosphere during worship, they focused on glorifying God rather than shifting their attention to Satan. The result? *Breakthrough.* This cycle ceased.

Along the same lines, a young entrepreneur I mentor had a pattern of making poor decisions that yielded terrible outcomes. He had a focus on the enemy and would blame his circumstances on Satan, when in truth, he was reaping the harvest of his own unwise choices.

It's easy to magnify Satan's influence and make him "big," a common occurrence in intercessory settings that needs to stop. Similarly, attributing our mistakes to Satan gives him undue attention. Either Satan is defeated, or he is not.

I recently had a conversation with a pastor who is now in the marketplace. He asked me this question: "As your company is a kingdom company and does business with companies who may have very different spiritual influences, how do you engage in spiritual warfare or pray against these forces of darkness?" My answer was simple: we don't. Our focus is on maintaining an "open heaven," which displaces darkness and brings much more joy and peace. This is life in the kingdom of God!

Consider this: darkness cannot infiltrate light; it's impossible. Light always dispels darkness, a truth evident in the natural and spiritual realms. Where the kingdom of God reigns, light prevails, and darkness is displaced. Just as shalom displaces disharmony and love displaces fear.

As believers, we are the leaven in the dough. We permeate our culture with God's victory. It doesn't work the other way around. As we move through the mundane tasks of our days, heaven invades earth. We don't need to worry about or focus too much on the effects of darkness. We can choose to glorify, magnify, and empower God or Satan. As Matthew 9:29 tells us, "We will have what our faith expects."

I know there is a battle. There are times when we must engage in warfare, but it is when God directs us, and He doesn't expect us to dwell there but to return our focus to Him.

When I am in a meeting or conducting inner healing or deliverance or anything significant, *I always cover it in prayer with agreement from our team.* We prefer to take an offensive stance rather than defensive, as Jesus instructs us to take the kingdom where darkness is entrenched. Every morning and every night before bed, I pray the blood of Jesus over my household and recite Psalm 91:1-2. As we "abide" in the shelter of God Almighty, He becomes our fortress and protector, and we get to dwell in His peace, protection, and supremacy.

FOLLOWING HOLY SPIRIT NUDGES

Not long ago, I visited a young couple with two young kids ages nine and 12 who live about an hour and half outside Toronto. I've been mentoring the father, Tyler, for a short time and had only once met his wife, Heather, but I felt a deep sense of love for them both. Over dinner, the Holy Spirit kept highlighting Heather. The feeling was so strong it was distracting to the point where I could not focus on what Tyler was saying. I looked at Heather and said, "The Lord is highlighting you like crazy." Over the next few minutes, she began to open up. For years, Heather had been struggling with paralyzing fear. The gripping fear was so brutal that she had blacked out that morning and came back to consciousness on the floor of the bathroom. She was also being bombarded with ideations of death and other demonically inspired thoughts.

The Lord highlighted Heather again while I was at church the following day in Toronto. I texted Tyler and invited them both to come to my office and finish the ministry time we had begun at their home the night before. They prayed and felt led to come. That afternoon, they showed up at my office, and we spent three hours doing deep inner healing and a few minutes of deliverance over the spirits of abandonment, victimization, death, fear, and a few more. Once the roots had been dealt with and agreement was renounced, deliverance was just a short and simple final step, using the invincible weapons of the power of the Holy Spirit, the power of His Word, the power of His blood, and taking authority in the mighty name of Jesus.

Thank you, Jesus! Earlier in the day, I also felt like the Lord said to give her a specific sum of money, which I planned to do later.

As we were working through inner healing, Heather's need to forgive her father (who rejected and disowned her at age 17) came up. The process of forgiveness was powerful. She went deep into all the specific ways she had been hurt, shamed, and abused by her father and how it made her feel. It was a holy time as she bore her soul and pain, released forgiveness to him, and then blessed him. She told a story of how, a few years ago, the only time her father had given her a sum of money was when they were relying on a food bank. Sadly, he came back three months later and demanded it back. When Heather said the amount of money, it was the exact number the Lord had told me to give her. I was shocked, and she felt deeply seen by the Lord. What amazing redemption on so many levels!

Afterward, I gave her a big fatherly hug as she cried in my arms. (She truly needed a father's embrace.) She was set free and is now on a journey of deeper inner healing. The Lord ministered to her heart in such a way that all the roots were dealt with, never to return. All those places were filled up with the love of God and His light. Her mind was restored to total peace, and all the dark thoughts ceased. A few days later, I had the prayer team pray with Heather, which was also a beautiful experience. Within a week of our time together, Tyler repented for some things he had done in their marriage, and as a couple, they experienced tremendous healing which is still ongoing.

I hope this story inspires you to follow those little Holy Spirit nudges (although this was more than a nudge)! You never know where they will lead! We are more than conquerors through Him who loves us! Love is the superhero of the kingdom! The love I felt for them and the love they felt for me was truly supernatural. I now see them as my spiritual kids, and I can't wait for more God-adventures together.

Heather's Story

When I was 20 years old, my father left my mother, sister, and myself, taking our sense of security with him. For most of the 16 years that followed, I struggled with an anxiety and panic disorder. As the year turned to 2024, I continued to suffer with debilitating anxiety. The morning of the day we were scheduled to have Bryan to our house for dinner, anxiety and fear about money caused me to faint in the hallway outside my bedroom.

God's relentless pursuit of me was made tangible in Bryan's willingness to convey the perfect love of the Father. God knows we need people to represent His love to us. The days that followed were bright with hope, joy, and faith, and were anxiety free. It was as though I had finally shifted into alignment with God's truth and love and was able to experience the fruit of the Spirit. Through all of this, God made it clear that He wants my husband and I to walk with Bryan as a spiritual father to us. Psalm 68:8 says that God sets the lonely in families. These are holy and redemptive relationships! What an absolute kindness and a gift to walk as a spiritual daughter to Bryan. My husband and I are overwhelmed by the beautiful faithfulness of God. The Lord saw that I needed the blessing and covering of a father so that I might walk in the fullness of what He has for me. That is mercy. That is love. God takes our stories of woe and brokenness and changes them into stories of redemption and hope.

Tyler's Story

I did not anticipate that God would use my hunger to learn and grow in my career to bring someone into my life who would help shepherd me into the embrace of the Father and contribute meaningfully to my family's journey of restoration. God knows what we need and is faithful in exceeding our most soaring imaginations! After 16 years of tourment and anxiety, one encounter with God, and now my wife is living in freedom and her faith has never been stronger! God is good!

NAMES OF GOD *Know Our God*

- King of Kings
- Lord of Lords
- Creator of the Universe
- I Am
- Father
- Saviour
- Holy Spirit
- Redeemer
- Jesus
- Christ
- Lord
- Master
- Light of the World
- Emmanuel — God With Us
- Logos — The Word
- Jehovah — God; the Lord
- Adonai — My Lord
- El Elyon — Most High
- El Roi — God of Seeing

- El Olam — Everlasting God
- El Gibhor — Mighty God
- El Shaddai — God Almighty
- Alpha and Omega — The Beginning and the End
- Messiah — Anointed One or Chosen One
- Yahweh — Lord, Jehovah
- Yahweh-Jireh — The Lord Our Provider
- Yahweh-Rapha — The Lord Our Healer
- Yahweh-Nissi — The Lord Our Banner
- Yahweh-Shalom — The Lord Our Peace
- Yahweh-Elohim — The Lord Is God
- Yahweh-Tsidkenu — The Lord Our Righteousness
- Yahweh-Rohi — The Lord Our Shepherd
- Yahweh-Shammah — The Lord Is There
- Yahweh-Sabaoth — The Lord of Hosts

God dwells within us through the Holy Spirit, a gift from Jesus. Now, the kingdom of heaven resides within us!

NAMES OF SATAN *Know Our Enemy*

- Anointed Cherub
- Murderer
- Father of Lies
- Liar
- Adversary
- Lion
- Beelzebub
- The Wicked One
- Accuser of the Brethren
- Tempter
- Thief
- Wolf

- The Devil
- Dragon
- Serpent
- Deceiver
- The Enemy
- The god of this World
- Prince of this World
- Angel of Light
- King Over Children of Pride
- Prince & Power of the Air
- Fowler
- Destroyer

COMPARISON OF ATTRIBUTES BETWEEN GOD AND SATAN

by Kenn Gil

GOD'S ATTRIBUTES	SCRIPTURE REFERENCE	SATAN'S ATTRIBUTES	SCRIPTURE REFERENCE
God is spirit (invisible)	John 4:24	Satan was created	Ezekiel 28:15
God is One, but He exists as three persons: Father, Son, and Holy Spirit	Matthew 28:18-20	His authority is limited by the sovereign rule of God who created him	Job 1:8-12
God is without equal	Isaiah 40:25-26	He wants to be God	Isaiah 14:13-14
God exists everywhere (omnipresent)	Psalm 139:7-12	He is the ruler of this world	John 14:30
God knows everything (omniscient)	1 John 3:19-20	He is the prince of the power of the air	Ephesians 2:1-2
God has all power and authority (omnipotent)	Jeremiah 32:26-27	He is the ruler of darkness	Ephesians 6:12
God is eternal	Isaiah 57:15	He is the prince of demons	Matthew 12:24
God is unchangeable	Numbers 23:19-20	He holds the power of death	Hebrews 2:14-15
God is holy	Revelation 4:8	He is the author of sin	1 John 3:8
God is loving	Ephesians 2:4-5	He is our accuser	Revelation 12:10
God is truthful	John 14:6	He is our tempter	Matthew 4:1-3
God is just	Psalm 89:14	He is our deceiver	Revelation 12:9
God is compassionate	2 Corinthians 1:3	He is the father of all lies	John 8:42-45
God is grace	Romans 5:17	He is a thief of the truth	Matthew 13:19
God judges sin but also offers forgiveness	Psalm 5:3-6 Ephesians 2:8-9	The reality for those who believe his lies	Matthew 7:21-23

Fear the Lord, you His saints;
For to those who fear Him there is <u>no lack of anything.</u>
—Psalm 34:9

Remember, when we fear the Lord, we develop an attitude of reverence. This opens the door to lacking nothing. There is provision power in the fear of the Lord!

Surrendering the Unexpected Outcomes

My life has had many prolonged setbacks, losses, and delays. One time that stands out was the three-year-long murder trial that ended with one of Abbe's assailants (who was charged with first-degree murder) getting off scot-free.

> *"However, I say to you, love your enemy, bless the one who curses you, do something wonderful for the one who hates you, and respond to the very ones who persecute you by praying for them."*
> *—Matthew 5:44, TPT*

Despite my best efforts and continued prayers for justice and mercy through that season, things didn't turn out the way I expected. I surrendered this unexpected outcome to God by once again voicing my anger and sadness to Him and releasing forgiveness. Forgiveness is a powerful way to love our enemies as it releases God's redemptive power into our lives and theirs. Eventually, I was able to bless Abbe's murderers through prayer, knowing justice is the Lord's and not mine.

Another time, after a few years of severe financial losses, I felt a keen sense of disappointment set in. I had expected a much faster turnaround in my businesses. Angrily, I cried out to God and vented my frustrations. It was a raw and honest moment. In the process, God revealed that pride was at the root of my anger and disappointment. I was generally feeling sorry for myself. By focusing on my disappointment, I had shifted my focus from God to myself. Allowing these feelings to fester opened the door to entitlement, bitterness, and self-pity.

> *Confess and acknowledge how you have offended one another and then pray for one another to be instantly healed,*
> *for tremendous power is released through the passionate, heartfelt prayer of a godly believer!*
> *—James 5:16, TPT*

Thankfully, I turned back to Him through repentance and confessed my struggles to my prayer team, which ultimately opened the door to healing. My old mindset of rushing to get things done has not produced good fruit in my life. The Lord had to teach me to wait on Him, to rest, and to trust, knowing that waiting is a process of birthing the new in *His* perfect time. The truth is that God is never in a rush and continually invites us to join Him in rest and silence. It may appear that we are waiting for God, but He is waiting for us. It is a place of freedom and respect for God. We all must learn to be honest and relational with God while living out the ways of the kingdom. As the Spirit leads us, we experience the fruit of the Spirit of patient endurance, self-control, and hope that will never disappoint because it relies on the certainty of God's promises and His power.

Struggles expose what is hidden deep in our hearts. In the suffering of disappointment, my trust was tested. I had shifted my focus onto my own experience and the wrestle of emotions within my heart, which caused me to lose sight of the goodness of God. The revelation of God's goodness and greatness enables us to praise above our circumstances. I was learning to lean into God, His Word, and the support of other believers in spite of my circumstances. I learned to live as unto the Lord and not unto myself. I learned to release my expectations or judgment of "good" and "bad," knowing God's ways are higher than mine and He is infinitely good. He is King. Not me. I replaced my expectations with the antidote to entitlement: thanksgiving. My trust returned, and I saw God rightly once again.

God's plans, processes, and timings are perfect. In this season, God was teaching me to give up my right to understand and helped me yield to a new level of abandonment, which naturally leads to contentment. He was training me to rule and reign by living above my circumstances. This mindset shift opened doors to His peace, thankfulness, joy, and faith. The doors to the flesh were closing as I leaned into the Spirit's leading. A fruit of His Spirit is patient endurance, another description of hope!

Unbelief puts our circumstance between us and God, but faith puts God between us and our circumstances.[13]

These are just a couple of examples of setbacks or letdowns in my life, but there have been many others. Through them all, God revealed that when living in the kingdom, existing worldly structures and mindsets must come down. In other words, God had to shake the "hell" and the world out of me. Much of this shaking answered my prayers for "more at all cost" and for freedom. Some of the shaking resulted from attacks of the enemy, and some from the judgments and mercy of God. I have learned that none of this is happening to me; it's happening *for me* as I walk it out with God. God is far above Satan and even uses what the enemy intended for evil for our good.[14]

Abundant Life: Embracing God's Provision and Kingdom Stewardship

"The thief comes only to steal and kill and destroy; I came so that they would have life, and have it abundantly."
—*John 10:10, NASB*

As I acknowledge daily that everything good comes from God, I recognize I am merely a steward of God's resources. By surrendering to Jesus as my King, embracing stewardship, and growing in the journey of sonship, I gain access to heaven's resources as a co-heir. I know that my heavenly treasures can never be stolen. I know that God will provide all I need as I seek His kingdom. By grace, I yield my life daily as a living sacrifice. Satan has nothing to kill, as my life is the Lord's. I have God's eternal, unshakable kingdom within my heart, which cannot be destroyed. Faith is our victorious power that overcomes evil, and it is the anointing of God that breaks the yoke of the demonic. Evil expresses itself through deception and lies. We must fill ourselves with truth, align our thoughts with Christ, and break agreements where we have come under deception. Jesus is our covering and our strength. Unity in the body of Christ serves as a primary defence against the attack of the enemy and releases the blessing of the Lord.

Pastor and teacher Dr. David Jeremiah was struggling with fear early in his life and was given this word by a friend who helped him change his thinking:

God's man in the center of God's will is immortal until God is finished with him.[15]

This helped him see that Jesus reigns above it all and allowed him to live in the joy of the Lord. He keeps this line written in the front of his Bible to this day. The apostle Paul was a prime example of this quote as he endured stoning, rods, beatings, lashes, imprisonment, being bitten by a deadly snake, shipwrecks, and more. Nevertheless, he continued on his mission by the grace of God until God's appointed time came.

It is important to remember the battlefield of life is in our minds.[16] The mind can hinder or propel us forward in our walk with God, which is why renewing the mind with the Word of God is the key to transformation. I have experienced times when my mind reverts to self-reliance, usually out of fear. This results in hasty decisions made out of frustration and stress.

For the mind set on the flesh is death, but the mind set on the Spirit is life and peace…
—Romans 8:6, NASB

When I am intentional about spending time with God in prayer and reflecting on what God has already done in my life, my response to challenging situations looks much different. Instead of fear and panic, my actions come from a place of peace and trust, filled with expectancy for what God will do. The mind set on the Spirit is life and peace.

Our spirit is reborn when we accept Jesus as our Lord and Saviour. However, our mind still needs to be renewed by the power of the Holy Spirit. As believers, the process of renewing our minds will continue for the duration of our time on earth. As faith comes from hearing the Word of God, we can declare the truth of His Word aloud. We can always learn to be more like Jesus! As long as we are still breathing on this earth, we will never "arrive." There will always be another level of humility, enabling more profound connections and a deeper expression of love available to us as we mature. Love is the ultimate mark of maturity, progressing in our union!

We cannot experience God's best if we still hold onto "lesser things." Salvation is just the first step into the kingdom. His tests and trials awaken and purify us while forming our characters, ultimately preparing us for the increase and co-reigning with Christ—short-term pain for eternal gain.

In the same way that gold and silver are refined by fire, the Lord purifies your heart by the tests and trials of life.
—Proverbs 17:3, TPT

Harvest of Kingdom Seeds: Transitioning Into God's Reality

Doors are gateways or transition points. In the spirit realm, this looks like transition points into new realities for God or Satan. Before I was a committed follower of Jesus, I had many open doors in the spirit realm to the enemy. These included moral compromise, ungodly soul ties, ungodly beliefs, generational curses, unhealed traumas and hurts, and more. I had sowed ungodly seeds throughout much of my life. Because of this, I endured a bitter harvest of my choices even as Jesus restored and redeemed my life.

Jesus is the door to eternal life and the door into the kingdom. When I made Jesus my Lord, I began to sow different seeds. I did this by applying biblical keys. However, it took time to produce a new godly harvest. In the transition period, the immediate fruit was from my past, but gradually, a new harvest emerged. In God's grace and mercy, He used the suffering of this transition period to continue to form and shape me. God was restoring me and the blessing to my generational line.

God will never be mocked! For what you plant will always be the very thing you harvest. The harvest you reap reveals the seed that you planted. If you plant the corrupt seeds of self-life into this natural realm, you can expect a harvest of corruption. If you plant the good seeds of Spirit-life you will reap beautiful fruits that grow from the everlasting life of the Spirit. And don't allow yourselves to be weary in planting good seeds, for the season of reaping the wonderful harvest you've planted is coming! Take advantage of every opportunity to be a blessing to others, especially to our brothers and sisters in the family of faith!
—Galatians 6:7-10, TPT

When we sow kingdom seeds, we reap a kingdom harvest.

It is the greatest joy of my life to hear that my children are consistently living their lives in the ways of truth!
—3 John 1:4, TPT

Since Bryn's turnaround at the end of 2019, I have experienced this verse repeatedly. As I mentioned previously, she and I launched a podcast called "The Father Pursuit" on January 4, 2023. One day, I vividly remember walking into my company's building as I listened to my daughter on one of the episodes through my headphones. The harvest of good seeds planted was so apparent at this moment. I was filled with such overwhelming gratitude, peace, and joy that when I arrived at my office, I lay face down on the floor and cried. I said to the Lord, "I am starting to believe!" I was moving into a higher realm of faith, seeing the kingdom more clearly with a deeper understanding of our new creation life. Seeing her place God first in her life and develop a godly character within has been incredible.

While we should certainly be proud of our children when they succeed in sports, school, or work, the truth is that all worldly accomplishments are temporary. Furthermore, they do not result in the ecstatic joy described in 3 John 1:4 and other scriptures. I can now emphatically state, through experience, that *the greatest gift and the most powerful way to honour our parents is to follow Jesus.*

What God did for me and Bryn, He can do for you and your family. Over the last few years, the two of us have "died" to ourselves in so many areas. We are being resurrected in Christ as we submit everything over to Him. God planted us as seeds, and we burst forth with more life and good fruit than we could ever have imagined. In the same way, the seeds we plant now are bearing great fruit in the lives of others. God is a faithful gardener!

Every day, I am learning that it is not so much about what I do, but about *who I become*. We cannot reproduce what we are not and cannot take people where we have not gone. I steward the life of Jesus in me to honour Him so that I can play a role in reproducing Jesus in others. I have discovered the joy of obedience and the freedom of leaving outcomes to God. My story is not over; it is just beginning. My life is now an epistle, a declaration, a testimony of Jesus.

We cannot rely on calling ourselves "Christians" or believing that it is enough to consider ourselves "good people." Redemption comes from surrender and yielding to God's will and authority. No matter what you face, God offers glorious freedom. However, to experience it now, we must chase after the pearl of great price, that which is worth more than gold and is greater than silver, spiritually, emotionally, and in our character and actions. I have discovered that if we have God, we have everything.

1. Psalm 34:8.
2. John 15.
3. Esther 4:14, Ephesians 2:10
4. Matthew 6:33.
5. Holiness means living a set-apart life dedicated unto the Lord and as a living sacrifice.
6. Romans 5.
7. Psalm 23.
8. Philippians 4:12-13.
9. Ephesians 6:10-18, Romans 13:12.
10. Zechariah 4:6.
11. Luke 10:19.
12. Galatians 4:8, TPT.
13. "F. B. Meyer Quotes," *AZ Quotes*, accessed October 11, 2023, https://rb.gy/x8z62.
14. Genesis 50:20.
15. David Jeremiah, *Twitter*, accessed October 11, 2023, https://rb.gy/2ltlx.
16. Romans 12:2.

SEEKING HIS KINGDOM

Yours, LORD, is the greatness, the power, the glory, the victory, and the majesty, indeed everything that is in the heavens and on the earth; Yours is the dominion, LORD, and You exalt Yourself as head over all.
—1 Chronicles 29:11, NASB

Father, thank You for the grace to seek first Your kingdom daily!

QUESTIONS FOR REFLECTION

What has the Holy Spirit revealed to you through *Seeking His Kingdom*? How can you apply this to your life?

_____

_____

_____

_____

Consider a time you had to forgo your own agenda in order to seek first God's kingdom? What was the outcome?

_____

_____

_____

_____

How can you sow seeds towards a good harvest in God's kingdom?

_____

_____

_____

_____

QUESTIONS FOR REFLECTION *(continued)*

Is there an area in your life where you are experiencing the fruit of a negative choice? If so, take time to reflect on that experience with the Lord and ask for His perspective and redemptive plan working it for your good.[15]

Notes

[15] Romans 8:28.

Chapter 4: The Kingdom of God Is at Hand!

From that time Jesus began to preach and say, **"Repent, for the kingdom of heaven is at hand."**
—*Matthew 4:17, NASB*

Welcome the King of Glory, for He is about to come through you.
—*Psalm 24:7, TPT*

Repentance: Gateway to Kingdom Living and a Renewed Mindset

Jesus began His public ministry by telling people to repent. Jesus came to bring the wonderful news that His kingdom has arrived, and we get to participate in its coming! The door to enter this glorious kingdom is to turn away from sin and towards Jesus to experience an entirely new reality. This is repentance, and the gospel of salvation opens the door to the kingdom of God. In other words, the gospel of salvation is just the beginning. Jesus preached the gospel of the kingdom of God, not the gospel of salvation.

The revelation of the gospel of the kingdom is not understood by the intellect of man but by those who come welcoming the truth like children. Jesus invited the world into an entirely new reality. The presence of His kingdom of righteousness convicts, not condemns, our hearts to turn back to Him, and His kindness leads us to repentance. What is repentance?

- Repentance means to turn from sin and to turn towards God or to return home.
- When we accept Jesus, by grace, our spirits are born again as entirely new creations. Repentance is not a result of the flesh but God moving in our hearts, calling us back to who we truly are as new creations.
- Repentance means to change the way we think, from the Greek word *metanoia*, which means "to have a transformed heart." It results in a profound change of perspective, changing how we behave.
- Heart-level repentance feels genuine sorrow for sin, turns away from sin, and turns to God, seeking to reorient one's entire life and follow Jesus.
- Repentance releases the power of God to transform. A transformed mind and soul results in changed behaviours.
- Repentance is the fruit of God's grace in our lives.
- Repentance opens the realm of the kingdom as it is the antidote to sin, which places a barrier between God and us.

Consider the following quotes from Bill Johnson:

> We have repented enough to be saved, but not enough to see the kingdom.[1]

> The renewed mind is sustained repentance.[2]

These two statements encapsulate the power of repentance to live from kingdom realities. Salvation is just the beginning of our changed thinking. We are continually being transformed by changing how we think by filling our minds with the truth of the Word of God. The renewed mind or mind of Christ formed through repentance awakens us to our new reality as citizens of His kingdom.

The Asbury revival of 2023 started as a college student began to confess sins and repent.[3] Such behaviour is meant to be a part of our regular daily walk as followers of Christ. Daily repentance is what it takes to live in daily revival. The more we are aware of our brokenness and mourn over our sins, the more we are aware of His forgiveness. The deeper the level of repentance, the greater the release of power and blessing! In Asbury, the realm of the kingdom superseded the physical realm, and those who participated experienced a uniquely beautiful peace and joy.

Without the shedding of blood, there is no forgiveness of sin. Since Jesus is our sin-bearer, God looks to Jesus as our perfect sacrifice and never to our works to atone for our sins. In the Old Testament, the lamb was always inspected to be an acceptable sacrifice, never the person. Positionally, we are born again, forever alive and forgiven of sin. We are eternally holy, safe, and secure based on the finished work of Jesus. Practically, we are in a process of sanctification while on earth. We are continually being renewed into the likeness of Jesus. Our part, to freely confess our sins to be cleansed from all unrighteousness, is ongoing.[4] When we repent, we lose our life as we know it to follow Him and commit to a radical countercultural lifestyle. When we repent, our sins are forgiven. When we confess our sins to trusted believers, we find healing. The wages of sin is death, which can be spiritual, emotional, or physical. It can also look like the death of dreams, purpose, vision, or relationships. Our sin can destroy goodness in all areas of life, for ourselves and others. Ultimately, the gift of God is everlasting life through Jesus!

Embracing Kingdom Realities: The Power of Repentance and Trust

Repentance is the antidote to sin and leads to sustained change in how we think, which changes how we behave. Sin can distance you from the Word of God, yet the Word of God has the power to keep you from sin and transform your thinking to align with God's will. His truth makes us understand how much we need His grace. The kingdom of life and vitality swallows the kingdom of death and decay! No wonder the gospel of the kingdom is so important! The change in thinking that emerges from repentance opens us to kingdom realities, which will radically change everything in our lives.

Serving the Anointed One by walking in these kingdom realities pleases God and earns the respect of others.
—Romans 14:18, TPT

As we discover our kingdom mandate, we can move into our God-given callings wherever God has planted us. He not only has a book of good works for our lives, but He also supplies the grace and the gift of the Holy Spirit to accomplish it together. Consider this passage:

We have become his poetry, a re-created people that will fulfill the destiny he has given each of us, for we are joined to Jesus, the Anointed One. Even before we were born, God planned in advance our destiny and the good works we would do to fulfill it!
—Ephesians 2:10, TPT

According to *The Passion Translation's* notes on this verse, "Although implied, these good works make up our destiny. As we yield to God, our prearranged destiny comes to pass, and we are rewarded for simply doing what he wanted us to accomplish."[5] Yielding is a posture of the heart. It trusts God. Trust is the foundation of faith that endures! Faith is anchored in trust. Faith is an expression of dependency. Faith is the currency of heaven!

In the World, Not of It: Embodying Kingdom Principles in a Temporal Realm

We will always reflect the nature of the world we are most aware of.

—Bill Johnson[6]

We are *in* the world, not *of* this world, and we are here to change the world. But what does that actually mean? This phrase is often repeated by believers, putting into perspective our role on earth. It means this earth, as it is today, is not our ultimate dwelling place; therefore, our decisions should not be influenced by things of this world, referring to the lust of the flesh (sexual immorality), the lust of the eyes (covetousness), and the pride of life (boasting or arrogance, self-focus, worldliness). Heaven on earth is our ultimate and eternal dwelling place! It means our lifestyle, character, and decisions should reflect the ways of heaven and the kingdom of God as we do our part to show unbelievers the truth of Scripture through God's love. We are to be conformed to the patterns of heaven, as seen in the scriptures reflecting the nature and character of God. We are not to be conformed to this world (materialism, self-focused lifestyles, and the pursuit of temporal pleasures).

And do not be conformed to this world, but be transformed by the renewing of your mind, so that you may prove what the will of God is, that which is good and acceptable and perfect.
—Romans 12:2, NASB

The kingdom of God has come to earth once again, and we have been restored as children of God, recovering all that was lost in Adam (if we choose it). As God originally intended before the fall, we can once again assume dominion (God's delegated authority) to rule and reign as ambassadors of Jesus. As an ambassador of His kingdom on earth, we carry the presence and authority of Jesus and represent Jesus everywhere we go. Like an earthly ambassador with the authority and backing of the nation they represent, their role is to speak on behalf of their nation according to their policies, not their personal opinions or preferences. They prioritize their nation's business, and the nation provides for their individual needs. We are now God's family and ambassadors. We are His sons and daughters. Because we are co-heirs with Jesus, the King of Kings, we are royalty. We represent His kingdom by expressing His love, mercy, goodness, power, principles, nature, and ways in and through us.

> **"I am not asking You to take them out of the world, but to keep them away from the evil one. They are not of the world, just as I am not of the world."**
> —*John 17:15-16, NASB*

In the Old Testament, God's presence dwelt first in the Tabernacle, which could be moved around as needed, and later in the temple.[7] Today, through the power of the Holy Spirit, *we* are God's dwelling place. As God's family, we are created to rule and reign in life on earth. The resurrection of Jesus was the greatest display of power. Through Jesus, God's power and authority within allow us to fulfill our original kingdom mandate from Genesis.

> *…and what is the boundless greatness of His power toward us who believe. These are in accordance with the working of the strength of His might which He brought about in Christ, when He raised Him from the dead and seated Him at His right hand in the heavenly places…*
> —*Ephesians 1:19-20, NASB*

God transforms us from glory to glory as we yield to Him and encounter His love. God gives us the power to find hope in the darkest times and to overcome sin, temptation, and trials. He gives us the power to perform miracles. His power brings beauty from ashes. His power working in us transforms our hearts and lives. His immeasurable power is available to us by faith. We are the hands and feet of Jesus on earth, and Satan is under our feet! We are more than conquerors, as Jesus has already defeated the enemy. We will have trouble and suffering in this world but take heart and be courageous. Jesus has overcome the world, and we are His representatives. Our job is to enforce His victory.

The Triune Being: Understanding Our Three-part Makeup and Divine Purpose

> *Or do you not know that your body is a temple of the Holy Spirit within you, whom you have from God, and that you are not your own?*
> —*1 Corinthians 6:19, NASB*

God created us in His image as three-part (triune) beings. We have a body, a soul, and a spirit meant to operate in triune integration and wholeness. We are spiritual beings with a body, enabling us to have an earthly experience. Like God, who is one in three, three in one, we have a great purpose to live as a multidimensional creation with the ability to bring heaven to earth. We are to embrace the totality of our three-part being. We are to embrace the fullness of our makeup. Jesus became fully human so that we, who are fully human, could become like Him.

Like Jesus, we are the meeting place between heaven and earth; we are the light of the world because we are in life union with Him. God is sovereign because He created all things, upholds all things, and governs according to His divine purposes. There is a mystery or holy tension between

His sovereignty and our stewardship, as we are made in His image and have been granted sovereignty over our lives. From this position of sovereignty, we have the freedom to choose to yield to our glorious Creator. Doing so allows us to bring all things under Christ's rule, as every aspect of life is sacred and waiting to be reclaimed.

Reclaiming Dominion: Rediscovering Humanity's Authority on Earth

By His sovereign design, God chose to work through people primarily. Originally, Adam and Eve had legal rights on earth. However, they lost their authority to Satan in the fall, giving the enemy rule and reign in and through mankind, creating demonic systems. Now, the enemy uses technology, governments, the media, etc., to expand his reach and advance evil in people's minds. Satan's strongholds reach across the earth and are in every sphere of society, including parts of the church. As the enemy gains our agreement, he is empowered to move on earth. However, *it all starts with our minds.* Jesus won a total victory, and now we are back in our rightful place as stewards of the earth, taking the victorious kingdom to where darkness is entrenched!

The heavens belong to our God; they are his alone, but he has given us the earth and put us in charge.
—*Psalm 115:16, TPT*

…for the weapons of our warfare are not of the flesh, but divinely powerful for the destruction of fortresses. We are destroying arguments and all arrogance raised against the knowledge of God, and we are taking every thought captive to the obedience of Christ, and we are ready to punish all disobedience, whenever your obedience is complete.
—*2 Corinthians 10:4-6, NASB*

Ruling and reigning on earth includes ruling and reigning over our body and soul. Our souls are our minds, wills, and emotions. Our hearts are the gateway between earth and heaven. The mind, the gateway to the heart, is where the battle is fought. The mind can be the problem or the solution, depending on where we set our attention.

Battling Strongholds: Unveiling the Lies and Embracing Truth

For as he thinks within himself, so he is…
—*Proverbs 23:7a, NASB*

This is why Satan, the father of lies, is battling for control of our minds. The battle is between truth and lies; strongholds are his primary weapon. Evil is expressed through deception. A stronghold is a thinking pattern in the heart that is not aligned with God's truth. We are typically unaware of the lie, as it is part of our belief systems. Once a stronghold is discovered and dismantled with truth, there needs to be a period of processing the truth regularly for 30–40 days. This changes the neurology of our brain as we allow the revelation of the truth to penetrate our hearts. Our external reality manifests our internal reality as seen in our health, families, relationships, finances, etc. It is important to regularly reflect and inventory our external realities to provide insight into our belief systems. As for me, I also have trusted people who offer insight into my blind spots (after all, I can't see them). These people call me out on my pride, poor judgment, or ungodly beliefs. They also raise my awareness when I am impacted or triggered by unresolved hurts or traumas that cause me to act out of a destructive pattern.

Our renewed minds, surrendered wills, and healed emotions enable us to live abundantly. As God gave us emotions, emotional health is key to spiritual maturity. To start, when we are emotionally wounded, there is always demonic oppression. We can think of our emotional capacity as a cup. When we have wounds and unprocessed emotions, our cups fill with pain. When full, even a minor event or stress is amplified as there is no space in the cup. When the cup overflows, we get emotionally dysregulated, and the logical part of our brain is temporarily compromised. As we heal and process our emotions, our cup empties, and we have a greater capacity to deal with life's hardships while staying emotionally connected. Emotional health is essential for strong relationships. Being emotionally available and having spiritual and mental resilience in the face of challenges helps us love and have compassion to care for and serve others. This allows God's light from the heavenly realm to flow into the physical realm, the convergence between the seen and unseen. In the words of Bill Johnson, "You know your mind is renewed when the impossible looks logical." [8]

Living Naturally Supernatural: Embracing Kingdom Reality

The Beatitudes describe what the posture of our hearts should be to receive the kingdom. Our spirits are what gets born again as a new creation. We are a spirit! The key to entering the secret place is allowing God to remove everything that is not pleasing to Him in a lifestyle of repentance, which sanctifies our minds. This lifestyle of repentance and intimacy, making God our number one, pursuing Him with all our heart, opens us to the secret place. This place is our source of abundant life.

Our imagination is also a bridge between the spiritual and physical. Our inner worlds manifest on the outside through our physical bodies. Our spirits are meant to communicate instructions from the invisible realm to our minds through imagination and ideas. We can clearly see the manifestation of the kingdom of God through the lives of godly men and women on earth. We also see the manifestations of the demonic using people as pawns to establish demonic systems on earth. We see this in the fruit of people's lives all the way to the fruit of nations. It is reflected in the culture and spheres of society.

Our spirits are seated with Jesus in the heavenly realms—right now! This is the greater realm, as everything in the physical realm was created in and through the eternal spiritual realm, which is the world behind the physical world. All things were created by Jesus and for Jesus. We experience the kingdom of God as we commune with the Holy Spirit, spirit to Spirit.

Our bodies give us legal rights on earth, enabling us to engage in the physical realm and manifest the invisible into the visible. It is our body that allows us to change the world. Good health enables us to run the good race in the fullness of our destinies. The body was created to serve, worship, and glorify God. We are not our own. Our physical body, soul, and spirit has been bought with an infinite price, the tears and blood of Jesus.[9] With that in mind, our spirits must lead our souls, and our souls must lead our bodies. In other words, the body must be submitted to the soul, and the soul must be submitted to the spirit, which results in divine alignment and well-being. As we are a spirit, living naturally supernatural allows for the light and revelation of His truth to become our kingdom reality. God wants to flood our entire yielded being with His Spirit. To live abundantly, we live in rest, well-being, and with resilience, and are enabled to overcome the tests and trials of life.

Someone living on an entirely human level rejects the revelations of God's Spirit, for they make no sense to him. He can't understand the revelations of the Spirit because they are only discovered by the illumination of the Spirit.
—1 Corinthians 2:14, TPT

The mature children of God are those who are moved by the impulses of the Holy Spirit.
—Romans 8:14, TPT

For most of my life, I was ruled by my soul, which was wounded. I was also ruled by the desires of my flesh. I lived in rebellion and was blind to it. As I began the process of healing, yielding to God, and becoming a lover of His Word, a new alignment occurred. My spirit began to strengthen, my inner world quieted, and the promptings and leading of the Holy Spirit began to emerge. My selfish behaviours and sinful desires continually declined. I truly began to love what God loves and hate what God hates. Even still, my soul needs ongoing sanctification. It tries to take charge. This often requires an intentional pause to move back to a place of rest before making a decision. Having others around to hold me accountable and give honest feedback has also been incredibly important in this ongoing process of maturing.

The Power of the Heart: Navigating the Gateway to the Invisible

Keep your thoughts continually fixed on all that is authentic and real, honourable and admirable, beautiful and respectful, pure and holy, merciful and kind. And fasten your thoughts on every glorious work of God, praising him always.
—Philippians 4:8, TPT

Our hearts are where our spirits, souls, and bodies converge. It's where Jesus takes up residence when we submit to His Lordship. To make Jesus Lord is to make Jesus our owner. Our King. The heart is the gateway between the invisible and the visible, and the mind is the gateway to the heart. Eyes are also a gate; therefore, what we watch matters because it affects us. Ears are a gate, so what we choose to listen to matters. Bodies are a gate, so what we do with or to our bodies matters. Everything we ingest impacts our hearts. Therefore, we must be intentional about receiving heavenly instruction and daily guidance from the Word and the Holy Spirit. We are what we take in. We are what we think, as what we think dictates what we do.

For as he thinks within himself, so he is…
—Proverbs 23:7a, NASB

Proverbs 23:7a implies that we create our realities based on our thoughts. How we steward our hearts has a physical expression on earth. We hold beliefs in our hearts, which form our thoughts, which become actions, which eventually form our behaviours. For example, as I hold love in my heart towards a person, there will be an expression on earth as my thoughts, intentions, and behaviours towards that person become rooted in love. As we hold the Word of God in our hearts, our realities will conform to the Word and will have expression on earth. My entire world changed as I filled myself with the Word of God.

Watch over your heart with all diligence,
For from it flow the springs of life.
—Proverbs 4:23, NASB

We are told to guard our hearts, which is the job of our renewed minds. It's not surprising that the most dangerous battlefield we will face in life is the one in each of our minds. The key to winning the war against ungodly attitudes and thought patterns is to renew the mind by dwelling on the Word of God, allowing the Holy Spirit, the Spirit of truth, to lead us to all truth.

We are destroying arguments and all arrogance raised against the knowledge of God, and we are taking every
thought captive to the obedience of Christ.
2 Corinthians 10:5, NASB

What we hold in our hearts has an expression on earth. Some time ago, Bryn and I were having father-daughter relational issues. Chantal, who leads our prayer team, asked me, "What are you holding in your heart towards Bryn?" As I considered her question, I realized that while my words and actions were important, what she was receiving and responding to was based on the position of my heart. Examining my heart towards Bryn revealed I had hidden expectations of her being like me. In prayer, I began to truly appreciate that she is beautifully, uniquely made, and very different from me. I realized I was holding her to an unrealistic standard rather than appreciating her personal growth journey. As a result, I carried judgment, disappointment, and dishonour in my heart towards her, which made my words empty and my ability to connect futile. Because of this, she resisted my guidance and closed the door on our conversations in certain areas.

Once I realized this truth, I repented and shifted my heart to a place of peace, love, and honour. I also repented to Bryn, and within days, she opened up about her struggles and challenges, which I had been insensitive to due to my judgments and wrong assumptions. Curiosity and compassion replaced judgment. Once repair had been made, we collaborated again and set off on a new path of growth and relationship! Since I cannot change anyone else, the change had to start with me. By changing my heart position, I was able to shift the external relationship.

Disciple-making: Empowering Kingdom Carriers

We are made in the image and likeness of God. We represent His values, nature, and culture and are tasked with implementing His heavenly rulership through making disciples. To make a disciple means to "make a follower of Jesus." This is done through teaching, training, mentoring, and parenting believers in the faith with Jesus as our model and guide. We all need to make disciples and be discipled. We also get to encourage those we are discipling to begin discipling themselves. We must bring others up behind us and learn from those who have gone before us. As my hunger for the Lord grew, I continually sought out mature Christians, learning as much as I could from them. My journey continued as God connected me with a spiritual father who provided a deeper level of relationship to experience the Father heart of God, spiritual covering, and relational discipleship as a father and son, which accelerated my journey of sonship and supercharged my love of God's Word and disciple-making.

As iron sharpens iron, So one person sharpens another.
—Proverbs 27:17, NASB

I am constantly learning and growing on the journey of life. The prayer team at Flō and my corporate team are places of growth and learning as iron sharpens iron. I have close friends who are mature in Christ. We build up, pray, and encourage one another. My spiritual father and founder of Ripple Effect Ministries, Kenn Gill, has made an enormous difference in my life and has accelerated my journey. The more I progress into greater levels of sonship, the more my ability to be a father to others increases. God has connected me to many young adults and earthly fathers whom I can pour into in many different areas of life and business. As God pours into me, I pour out to others so that they can pour out to others, and so on. This is the way of the kingdom and the purpose of this book!

Believers are called to preach the wonderful news of the kingdom and disciple nations (the Great Commission) in the understanding and application of kingdom principles. The principles of the kingdom of God span the entire Bible, with the kingdom impacting every sphere of society, the entirety of human life, and encompassing the earth and cosmos. As the gospel of the kingdom is preached, people will discover a life of faith filled with hope, honour, love, and more. As a person is discipled, they mature and prepare for their boundaries or jurisdiction to be increased. At the most basic level, a disciple is one who hears and obeys the voice and Word of God to become the hands and feet of Jesus.

Jesus continued, **"It has been written by the prophets, 'They will all be taught by God Himself.' If you are really listening to the Father and learning directly from Him,**

you will come to Me. For I am the only One who has come from the Father's side, and I have seen the Father!"
—*John 6:45-46, TPT*

The Leaven of the Kingdom: Impacting Society Through Discipleship

Think about it like this: The kingdom is the leaven working in and through His people to impact the entire loaf, the earth. It is not a top-down hierarchy as in an organization, but a dispersion of His people into society. As kingdom citizens disciple nations in the teachings of Jesus, the nations will manifest His kingdom to be progressively made into the image of heaven on earth. Good leaven keeps on reproducing! Jesus is our model with His three disciples in His inner circle, then the 12 disciples, and then the 70 others He sent out to the towns and places He was about to go.[10] As a person is discipled into becoming a kingdom citizen, they can then create a kingdom family. Kingdom families come together to form kingdom communities, kingdom communities form kingdom cities, and eventually, the kingdom expands across the earth! It is worth noting that bad leaven can spoil the loaf, so be aware of what you let grow.

No man or woman is an island. We are all called to live within a believing community, the family of God. This is whether or not we marry and have children. God's kingdom and nature are made visible in the family, which is the cornerstone of His kingdom. In terms of kingdom priorities, God and your relationship with Him must be first, and family, as the cornerstone of society, should be second. Although not called out specifically in Scripture, your community, church family, and business dealings come after God and immediate family.

Go ahead, build your career and give yourself to your work. But if you put Me first, you'll see your family built up!
Proverbs 24:27, TPT

…But as for me and my house, we will serve the Lord.
—*Joshua 24:15b, NASB*

Jesus's mission, which is our mission, is to grow God's family and establish His kingdom on earth. We all start as spiritual orphans separated from our Heavenly Father. By God's design, through Jesus, we are adopted as sons and daughters.[11] He is our good and perfect Heavenly Father.[12]

A father of the fatherless and a judge for the widows, Is God in His holy dwelling. God makes a home for the lonely; He leads out the prisoners into prosperity, Only the rebellious live in parched lands.
—*Psalm 68:5-6, NASB*

"I will not leave you as orphans; I am coming to you."
—*John 14:18, NASB*

Discipleship begins in the family to teach, train, and bless our children and our children's children. As families are discipled and transformed, nations are discipled and transformed. Families are meant to be a place of safety and provision to experience God's love. A man and a woman coming together to become one flesh jointly represents the nature of God.[13]

The family is designated as the primary environment for profound impact and influence on children. Parents bear the ultimate responsibility and accountability for modeling, teaching, and training their children in the ways of the Lord.[14] While public schools or social media may present challenging influences, they cannot be to blame for issues that arise with children.

Parents also get to model a life honouring God and His Word to the younger generation. Marriage and family are two of God's primary methods of teaching us sacrificial love or how to put others ahead of ourselves. As Jesus said in John 15:13, **"Greater love has no one than this: to lay down one's life for one's friends."** By His grace, we demonstrate our love for God by surrendering our lives to His will and laying our lives down in marriage. A husband must die to himself for his wife daily as Christ died for His Church. To submit is to lay down our desires and to put the other ahead of ourselves. To do it well, we must practice! This applies to those without children as well, as Jesus models in the following passage:

And He took a child and placed him among them, and taking him in His arms, He said to them, **"Whoever receives one child like this in My name receives Me; and whoever receives Me does not receive Me, but Him who sent Me."**
—*Mark 9:36-37, NASB*

Family Foundations: Nurturing Children in the Ways of the Lord

God makes the importance of children clear throughout Scripture. We can see the level of godliness in a culture reflected in how they treat their children, including the unborn. Not only are we to care for them and model Christ to them, but we are to actually become *like* children so that we might enter the kingdom of God.[15] No matter what our stage or season of life, God commands us to care for the young, widowed, and marginalized.

The nature of the Father was replicated in the Son, Jesus, the first sent to proclaim and establish God's kingdom on earth. We begin as converts to Christ, then grow as disciples of Christ, and then as apostles (or "sent ones") for Christ. As fathers and mothers, we are called to establish the kingdom of God through our children and families. Family is the cornerstone of society and His kingdom mandate, jointly representing the nature of God. Jesus's mission is to grow God's family through adoption. We also get to be fruitful and multiply to expand and establish His kingdom on earth.

Train up a child in the way he should go [teaching him to seek God's wisdom and will for his abilities and talents], Even when he is old he will not depart from it.
—Proverbs 22:6, AMP

Rediscovering Biblical Parenthood: Restoring God's Design for Families

Earthly fathers are the spiritual heads of the household and provide spiritual covering for the family. They are to disciple, teach, be an example, train in the ways of the Lord, bless, establish identity, and declare destiny over their children. Fathers are to be the prophets, priests, kings, and leaders of their households. As prophets, we get to encourage, envision, and speak words of life to our children. As priests, we get to intercede for our families and teach the Word of God. As kings, fathers are to lead, honour, protect, provide, govern, discipline, and provide clear and healthy boundaries. As leaders, fathers serve, carry burdens, and make sacrifices for their families. Men are to demonstrate authority by the sacrifice of serving and laying down their lives for their families, as we only have authority with those we are willing to love and honour through our service to them.

While fathers are tasked with the privilege of showing their children the love of our Heavenly Father and leading them to live lives that are honouring to God, mothers are also charged with great responsibility throughout Scripture. The Bible clearly outlines a mother's role, rooted in a unique type of love that implies caring, nurturing, and embracing their children. Mothers are to be present, daily influencing their children's lives, much like the Holy Spirit comforts and guides us, teaching the Word of God and training and disciplining accordingly.[16] Their lives are to be a model of godly living. Their role is complementary to a father's role; together, they represent the fullness of the nature of God, both the feminine and masculine, the two becoming one flesh. We must defer to Scripture on the roles of men and women and not to popular culture or opinions, as Satan is trying to distort and deceive what we believe in this area and many more.

Embracing Divine Partnership: Men and Women in God's Design

Genesis 2:18 tells us that Eve was made to be a helper for Adam. The word "helper" is the Hebrew word *ezer*, which conveys the idea of someone who supports or provides aid. It is important to note that this word is also used in Scripture to describe God as our *ezer* or helper. Men and women are partners who have different and complementary roles. God created divine order in the family unit, with men charged to lead, guide, and direct their families in the ways of the Lord. Men and women are equal in value but different in function, which is no different from the five-fold ministry roles; all are equal, but each role varies in function.

WOMEN IN THE BODY OF CHRIST

Women have had many powerful positions in the Old Testament and the body of Christ. Men and women are both meant to be "Jesus on the earth" as vessels of God. Scripture declares a divine order and different roles established for men and women. However, men and women are spiritually equal (Galatians 3:28) and essential in bringing the kingdom of God to earth. Consider these women from Scripture: Miriam was a prophetess, Esther risked her life to save the Jews, and Deborah was a prophetess and a judge. Jesus exercised redemptive equality. He was counter-cultural in His time and greatly honoured women. He welcomed both women and men as followers (which was revolutionary). Jesus had female disciples, such as Mary Magdalene and Joanna. He defended the adulterous woman and respected the marginalized and outcasts of society. He performed miracles on women. In the early church, Anna was a prophetess, Pricilla was a teacher, Phoebe was a minister, the Samaritan woman at the well was the very first evangelist, Mary Magdalene, along with other women, was the first to see the risen Christ and instructed to preach the gospel making her a central figure of the Christian faith.

In addition, the word *paraclete* is of Greek origin and typically refers to the Holy Spirit. It means "one who comes alongside" or "advocate." The Holy Spirit is our comforter, helper, advocate, supporter, and empowerer.

Mothers and fathers use their authority to consistently hold their children accountable, which eventually leads to developing responsibility. Parents have the privilege and duty to see their children reach their God-given potential. As we commit our children to the Lord, we get to partner with Him in faith to see our children grow up as healthy adults.

As parents, we are to regularly speak blessings and declare the promises of God over our children. Write out these powerful promises from Scripture and make a covenant with God to confess and give thanks to Him. Don't quit, as God is faithful!

My mother continued to pray for me, and at age 46, I fully gave my life to the Lord. We get to create a multi-generational kingdom legacy and establish generational blessing with our words and actions. Our responsibility is to share the ongoing testimony of God in our lives, to instill a kingdom worldview, and to equip our children with kingdom values and principles to live a kingdom lifestyle. This makes the family an apostolic training hub or a time of preparation to be sent out to expand the kingdom. This is not just for Sundays. It should be seven days a week. The whole family can go out and reproduce in others what has been produced in them. Disciple-makers produce disciple-makers who love God with every part of their beings. This is how we teach our children to seek first His kingdom, and it's one of the most powerful ways we can expand the kingdom here and now.

*   *   *

If you want to journey deeper into God's design for the family, check out the following on the M46 Ministries Blog:

- Family Foundations: A Biblical Model For Family
- Family Foundations: Defining The Family
- Family Foundations: Building A Strong Family
- A Father's Blessing
- A Mother's Blessing

*   *   *

Reigning in the Kingdom: Empowering Families to Fulfill Their Divine Mandate

"Hear, Israel! The Lord is our God, the Lord is one! And you shall love the Lord your God with all your heart and with all your soul and with all your strength."
—Deuteronomy 6:4-5, NASB

These words, which I am commanding you today, shall be on your heart. And you shall repeat them diligently to your sons and speak of them when you sit in your house, when you walk on the road, when you lie down, and when you get up. You shall also tie them as a sign to your hand, and they shall be as frontlets on your forehead. You shall also write them on the doorposts of your house and on your gates.
—Deuteronomy 6:6-9, NASB

These verses are separated for a reason. Typically, we hear them cited separately… but go back and read them again *together*. God designed families as the template of heaven on earth. The blueprint of the kingdom is family! We have all the rights and privileges as family members of the household of God. Our mandate is to teach our children to love God! We must first seek the kingdom of God and His righteousness for our families, which brings transformation and healing. If we don't actively disciple and guard our children's hearts and minds, the world will do it for us, but in all the wrong ways. If your family isn't in order from a biblical perspective, don't expect anything else in your life to be ordered correctly. There is an order to the ways of the kingdom, and as I mentioned before, I have learned the hard way that family must come before business or even church. Your family is your first ministry.

Entering the kingdom community through repentance is to experience an entirely new way of life. It allows us to exercise dominion and authority over the earth under the kingship of Jesus. We have been reestablished as rulers over the physical realm. As believers' hearts are united into His family, God's will and purposes will be established on earth. The outcome is that God's people will be the most prosperous on earth in body, mind, spirit, family, relationships, and beyond. This comes as we live life God's way, the better way.

> The kingdom is God's reign through God's people over God's place.
> —Jeremy Treat[17]

The kingdom of God is love expressed in and through the family, as family is the fundamental social construct on earth. In family relationships, we can live out the values and principles of God's kingdom. By God's design, we are adopted as children of God and grow into mature sons and daughters. Again, it is God who puts the lonely in families.

Restoring Fatherhood: A Journey from Brokenness to Redemption

He will turn the hearts of the fathers back to their children and the hearts of the children to their fathers, so that I will not come and strike the land with complete destruction.
—Malachi 4:6, NASB

Keep in mind, just a few short years ago, my heart was not turned to my Heavenly Father or my children. I loved my daughters, Abbe and Bryn, and did my best to raise them. However, unresolved childhood trauma, my own father issues, and living under the consequences of my sin did not exactly make me the father of the year.

A father's role is to disciple, instill identity, provide vision, and create a safe environment. I failed on all four accounts. The presence of discipleship was not in my home. I was replicating a pattern that I had learned in my family. As a result, I did not disciple my children. Much of what I learned growing up in my Baptist church, I chose to ignore, choosing instead to live life my way. I was not living a godly life, so my role in character development was also lacking. I could not instill identity because my identity was not established. I did a poor job helping my girls discover their God-given talents, gifts, and passions. And I did not provide a safe environment because I was emotionally unavailable, and my priorities were not in order. I was not operating as a son of God and didn't know God as my Father. In short, I couldn't give what I didn't have.

I was rebellious and selfish and mostly checked out. Honestly, I thought of myself as a good person with a healthy dose of self-righteousness. I called myself a Christian, though the life I lived was according to my own standard, not Jesus's. The result was three failed marriages and both my daughters becoming trapped in a destructive cycle of addiction.

I was also doing yoga multiple times a week until God gave me a dream of the kundalini serpent in my bed, which caused me to research the demonic nature of yoga, literally meaning "yoke" to or in union with brahman, a false god. Yoga is completely anti-biblical and part of the new age. Some might say that yoga is just exercise. They are wrong. Yoga is a spiritual exercise, and you can't separate the spiritual from the physical (we are body, we are a soul, and we are a spirit). The poses literally yoke you to a Hindu god. (For more on this topic, check out the M46 Ministries Blog, *Yoga: The Yoke Of Sin*.

As a parent, I loved my girls, was involved, and did my best, as do most parents, but I was emotionally unavailable and prioritized work over genuine connection. Parents often try to do their best, but because of their own wounds, they end up falling short and wounding their children. I was blind to the damaging impact of my past unhealed traumas on others and was more broken than I realized.

For the eyes of the Lord move to and fro throughout the earth so that He may support those whose heart is completely His…
—2 Chronicles 16:9a, AMP

The Power of Fatherhood: Embracing Sonship for Family Restoration

By God's grace, in 2016, things started to change. I was the prodigal son returning home to my Heavenly Father after 28 years of compromise and rebellion.[18] He relentlessly pursued me, awaiting me with open arms for my return. As I repented and made Jesus Lord of my life, my heart began to burn for God, for my heart to be completely His. I began to read the Bible. I started caring for my heart and discovered the power of inner-heart healing. I learned about generational curses and iniquities, discovering the ungodly alliances in my life that provided a legal basis for darkness to invade. I began to grow in prayer and intimacy. I began to practice living in constant awareness of God. I began to study godly perspectives on science and continually increased in awe and wonder of our glorious Creator.

I engaged in deliverance and began to dissolve my ungodly beliefs with the truth of the Word of God. I learned about the power of parental blessings and the role of a godly father. (Check out the M46 Ministries Blogs: *A Father's Blessing* and *A Mother's Blessing*.)

I began making God my number one priority, followed by my family, work, church, and friendships.

The transformation was not instant; however, a new journey with the Lord began. As a father, caring for my heart was necessary for healing to come to my family. This process led to writing a series of books and, eventually, a podcast. Each shares the details of my life story with vulnerability. Because of what God has done in my life, I am compelled to share the good news. Please keep in mind that God has a unique story and role in His kingdom for each of us; all parts of His body are necessary. My journey into a deeper relationship with God has led me to a new life of freedom and peace in the Holy Spirit that I couldn't believe was possible. It ultimately revealed that before I could be established as a father, I needed to be established as a son. I have discovered that what I carry is a powerful weapon as it permeates into my family and beyond. As a father, I get to be a living example as I follow Jesus.

This began a beautiful process of restoration and wholeness in me and, eventually, in my family. As I began to walk out my faith by the grace of God, my daughter began to see the changes I was making. For the first time, my life started to look different from the world, and Bryn noticed.

I have lived through extremely unhealthy family dynamics, and yet I know that God loves families and is always involved in the hearts of mothers and fathers. It is God who turns the hearts of parents to their children and the children to their parents. This is the process of restoration of the family by the redemptive power of Jesus!

1. Bill Johnson, "The Renewed Mind is Sustained Repentance," *Facebook*, accessed October 13, 2023, https://rb.gy/khy0a.

2. Bill Johnson, "Bill Johnson, Quotes, Quotable Quotes," *Good Reads*, accessed October 13, 2023, https://rb.gy/k0som.

3. Greg Gordon, "Asbury Revival: Will Believers Recognize Its Legitimacy?," *Thinke (Think Eternity)*, accessed October 13, 2023, https://rb.gy/7ol5f.

4. James 5:16.

5. "Ephesians 2:10," *YouVersion: The Passion Translation*, accessed October 13, 2023, https://rb.gy/eu472.

6. Bill Johnson, "We Will Always Reflect the Nature of the World We Are Most Aware Of," *Facebook*, accessed October 13, 2023, https://rb.gy/bpkwp.

7. The Tabernacle was a mobile place of worship, like a tent (though God gave very specific instructions about how it should be set up). After the Israelites settled in the Promised Land, King Solomon built a more permanent structure; this was the first temple. The Babylonians destroyed this temple as the Israelites were taken into captivity. Once released, Ezra and Zerubbabel led the construction of the second temple. It was destroyed by the Roman empire in the first century.

8. Bill Johnson, "The Supernatural Power of a Transformed Mind," *Bill Johnson*, accessed October 13, 2023, https://rb.gy/pdqns.

9. 1 Corinthians 6:19-21.

10. Luke 10:1 (some translations say 72).

11. Ephesians 1:5.

12. Matthew 5:48, Psalm 18:30.

13. Genesis 2:24.

14. For more information, see "The Father's Blessing," on the M46 Blog, https://m46ministries.com/a-fathers-blessing-part-2/.

15. Mark 10:13-16.

16. Deuteronomy 4:9, 5:15, 6:6-7, Psalm 78:5-6, Proverbs 1:8-9, 6:20, 13:24, Ephesians 5:1-2, Isaiah 66:13, 49:15.

17. Treat, J. (2019, May 21). *The Kingdom of God in 8 Words*. The Gospel Coalition. https://www.thegospelcoalition.org/article/kingdom-god-8-words/.

18. Luke 15:11-31.

THE KINGDOM OF GOD IS AT HAND

From that time Jesus began to preach and say, **"Repent, for the kingdom of heaven is at hand."**
–Matthew 4:17, NASB

Father, we ask for the grace to take up the call to disciple our families and those around us!

QUESTIONS FOR REFLECTION

What has the Holy Spirit revealed to you through *The Kingdom of God is at Hand?* How can you apply this to your life?

_____

_____

_____

_____

In what ways have parents, mentors, and friends contributed to your discipleship walk?

_____

_____

_____

_____

How can you intentionally encourage others in their faith journey?

_____

_____

_____

_____

What key truths are we called to pass on to others?

_____

_____

_____

_____

Notes

Chapter 5: Kingdom Identity

He has rescued us completely from the tyrannical rule of darkness and has translated us into the kingdom realm of his beloved Son. For in the Son all our sins are canceled and we have the release of redemption through his very blood.
—Colossians 1:13-14, TPT

Choosing Kingdom Over World: Embracing God's Values

For years, I lived a life where I called myself a Christian but was living no differently than non-believers. I experienced no transformation, and my choices produced much bad fruit.

You have become spiritual adulterers who are having an affair, an unholy relationship with the world. Don't you know that flirting with the world's values places you at odds with God? Whoever chooses to be the world's friend makes himself God's enemy!
—James 4:4, TPT

While this scripture may seem harsh, it is ultimately for our good. The "world" refers to the systems and values that oppose God's Word. Partnering with the world results in a mind governed by the flesh, which works against God. In the school of hard knocks, I have discovered there is no way to live both *in the world* and *in the Word*. This is why Jesus compassionately tells us to seek first His kingdom.

Jesus, our King, took our place and died for us as the ultimate and eternal sacrifice for our sin on a brutal cross to reconcile all of humanity back to Himself.

"For God so loved the world, that He gave His only Son, so that everyone who believes in Him will not perish, but have eternal life."
—John 3:16, NASB

Redemption Through Faith: Finding Eternal Life

Through His grace, if we choose to enter the process, God heals every hurt and broken part of our souls and sanctifies us so we can be the person He created us to be. As we enter the process of being restored to His original intent, we join Him in the process of restoring the earth to His original design.

But He was pierced for our offenses, He was crushed for our wrongdoings; The punishment for our well-being was laid upon Him, And by His wounds we are healed. All of us, like sheep, have gone astray, Each of us has turned to his own way; But the Lord has caused the wrongdoing of us all To fall on Him.
—Isaiah 53:5-6, NASB

Faith is how we have a relationship with God. By faith, we live according to His Word. In other words, faith pleases God. We are saved by faith; without it, God is restricted from operating in our lives. We are to live by faith, not by experience. Faith is a gift from God that we get to exercise and grow in.

But the one who doubts is condemned if he eats, because his eating is not from faith; and whatever is not from faith is sin.
—Romans 14:23, NASB

For the wages of sin is death, but the gracious gift of God is eternal life in Christ Jesus our Lord.
—Romans 6:23, NASB

Confession, Repentance, Salvation: The Journey to Redemption

No matter how good you think you are, you still have a measure of sin. All fall short of God's standard. Everyone needs a saviour. Jesus owed us nothing but gave us everything. He took the full punishment for what we deserved. For you and me and all of creation, He endured the cross. Then, through the power of His resurrection and the blood of the Lamb, He gave us everything only *He* deserved: eternal life by faith through grace alone, with our names written in the journals of heaven. When we receive salvation, some people say, "Hell lost another one," but it's so much more than that! The kingdom gained a new citizen!

…If you confess with your mouth Jesus as Lord, and believe in your heart that God raised Him from the dead, you will be saved.
—Romans 10:9, NASB

What's our part? We must admit that we are sinners who need a saviour, repent for our sins, and believe in Jesus, making Him the Lord and Saviour of our lives. There is nothing we can do to save ourselves. We are justified by grace through faith and never by our good works. The above scripture says that when we believe with our hearts and confess with our mouths that "Jesus Christ is Lord," we will be saved. This is worth repeating as I didn't experience transformation until I made Jesus the Lord of my life, the greatest confession of my life. My life was no longer my own, and I fully belonged to Jesus. I don't want you to miss out on this opportunity.

Lordship is a key principle of the kingdom, beginning with our entrance into the kingdom and how we live for all eternity—lordship results in obedience. When we are submitted to the Lordship of Jesus, our lives are built on the Rock (Jesus) to stand firm in the storms of life.

For God made the only one who did not know sin to become sin for us, so that we might become the righteousness of God through our union with Him.
—2 Corinthians 5:21, TPT

NEW CREATION
LIFE IN JESUS

God chose and commissioned us to go into the world to
bear fruit. (John 15:16, TPT)

God chose us before He laid the foundation of the universe!
(Ephesians 1:4, TPT)

Love is a choice, and choice is the foundation for relationships. Jesus
chose to love. He chose us while we were His enemy; He died for us. This
is proof of His commitment. (Romans 5:8, John 15:16)

Jesus relentlessly pursues us. He unconditionally accepts and loves us and
waits for us to respond to His invitation. (John 6:44)

Jesus invites all those who are weary and burdened to receive His rest.
(Matthew 11:28-30)

Jesus didn't come to judge the world but to save it, for people to come to Him as they
are. (John 3:17)

Now, if anyone is enfolded into Christ, he has become an entirely new person. All
that is related to the old order has vanished. Behold, everything is fresh and new.
(2 Corinthians 5:17)

Through Jesus, sinners are made clean and become sons and daughters of the most
high God. (Luke 7:36-50)

Because of Jesus, the weak say I am strong and the poor say I am rich.
(Joel 3:10, 2 Corinthians 12:10)

Through Jesus, murderers and thieves are forgiven to become kings and
priests. (1 John 1:9, Revelation 1:5-6)

Through Jesus, the voiceless and beaten down become His ambassadors.
(2 Corinthians 5:20, Ephesians 6:19-20)

Through Jesus, you and I were sinners, no different from any
other, and are now saints, made pure, set apart in Jesus.
(1 Corinthians 1:2)

Through Jesus, we are all carriers of the glorious kingdom
of God. (Matthew 5:3, Colossians 1:13)

Redemption and Renewal: Embracing the Work of Grace

In the kingdom, the repentant murderer who gives His life to Jesus may still get a life sentence in the natural world, but in the kingdom, he gets eternal life and becomes a co-heir with Jesus.[1] In the kingdom, identity is received, not achieved as in the world. Grace, God's riches at Christ's expense, is divine enablement. It is getting a reward or blessing we don't deserve. Because of the work of the cross, we have been justified by faith alone. That is grace. Jesus delivers us from sin consciousness and brings us into grace consciousness as our minds are renewed. Our spirit is fully redeemed, and our soul is now in the process of redemption or sanctification. We now get what Jesus deserves as God regards us as He regards Jesus. When we sin, we run back to Him to be made holy and pure. He continually draws us to Himself to conform us into His image.

Remember, Jesus invites people to come as they are, in their brokenness and sin, and He will work on them from the inside out as they get to know Him. It is God who does the changing! As children of God, let's be Jesus-focused and not sin-focused. Sin is a dethroned monarch, and God's grace is our divine enablement to walk in the light and to do what pleases God. Grace does not ignore sin; it empowers us to live in dependence and righteousness.

Transformed Perspectives: Seeing Through the Lens of Heaven

Before I walked with God daily, I saw myself through the lens of the world. This is where we all start before receiving the revelation of our identity as God's children. My view was limited and short-sighted, focused more on my accomplishments and earthly value than on my true identity as a son of the Father. I lived as an orphan, striving for worth that can only be found in Jesus. For better or worse, I claimed to be:

- A business owner (this was my primary focus, an area I did well in, a safe place)
- A father, husband, and son (I tried and did my best, but was more broken and wounded than I realized)
- An athlete (basketball was my passion and a big part of my identity growing up and in university)
- Generous (a value I learned from my family, but with misplaced motives)
- Wealthy (I believed I was defined by what I had and what I accomplished)
- A victim of tragedy (my traumas had never been healed; I had yet to overcome them)
- Not enough (a lie that my external success failed to correct)
- A good person (I was blind to my compromise and self-righteousness, which is a sin)
- Self-reliant (I was self-help-focused and had an independent, distant, and guarded mindset)

Jesus said in John 16:7 that it was better for Him to leave as He was just one man on earth, but upon His leaving, we would receive the Holy Spirit, allowing us to spread Jesus throughout the earth. Through Jesus, we receive the Holy Spirit and become co-heirs with Jesus, the King of Kings over all creation. As soon as we are born again, we are no longer citizens of this world but citizens of heaven, *and this is how we must see ourselves*. People are saved to impact the world in the area God has placed them, using the gifts and abilities He has given them. This is God's way of loving others through us, as the hands and feet of Jesus (i.e., from what would Jesus do to what is Jesus doing). These interactions are relational, immediate, and intimate. One doesn't have to look far for opportunities to love others well. We are called to serve those around us and those whose paths we intersect. This is the kingdom.

How we see God and see ourselves impacts everything. We are set free when our thoughts and perspectives align with the truth. The truth is our new reality in Christ, in His kingdom. Our "position" in Christ is complete; however, our "condition" is a process of awakening, remembering, and returning to the fullness of this glorious truth.

Embracing True Worth: Displacing the Big Three Lies

When we believe in a lie, we give power to the enemy. This is why we are told to take our thoughts captive and make them obedient to Christ; having His truth displaces the enemy's lies. There are many lies that people believe, but here are the big three lies that impact our core identity:

1. I am not enough.
2. I am not lovable.
3. I am unworthy.

These are the lies that dwell in the orphan's heart and create barriers to receiving God's love. The lie "I am not enough" plagued me throughout my life. It often made me feel like an imposter, leading me to disqualify myself, my opinion, and my voice. Growing up, I was taught to be independent and not ask for help or communicate my needs, which resulted in shame when I needed others. Whenever I encountered disrespect, although rare, I was quick to take offence, which was my deep insecurity triggering pride. It was like hitting a raw nerve.

Early in my life, I was extremely shy, not understanding this was a form of pride. My shyness resulted from living in the fear of man, powered by lies. Once this was broken, there remained a natural and healthy element of quiet reserve meant to promote meekness and protect from arrogance. I lived as a spiritual orphan for so much of my life, not knowing I had access to a totally different and new identity through Jesus. In my adult life, I often became a "rescuer" rather than providing healthy support to others. This ultimately positioned other people around me as powerless victims, making me feel better about myself in the immediate. Feeling like a hero quieted the torment in my mind, but it didn't change anything. This wound up creating an even bigger problem. If you want to understand this more, search "drama triangle" online. I also recommend checking out my daughter Bryn's M46 Ministries blog, *Victim Vs. Victor Mindset*, excerpted from her book, *Dying to Live*.

Keep in mind that I wasn't aware of this lie until light shone into the darkness. From the eyes of the world, my life looked ideal. I was a leader, rich, successful, tall, fit, lived in one of the wealthiest neighbourhoods in Toronto, had my own company and all the trappings of this world… but until my issues were addressed, my pain remained, sometimes dormant, sometimes active. Ongoing inner healing has been vital in my ability to connect heart-to-heart with people. In the process, which is ongoing, Jesus transformed many memories with His presence and enabled me to have a context for these experiences within a larger perspective. Before I could connect with others, I needed to connect with myself and God. We are designed to need one another and live in interdependence, but engaging others in this way takes humility and courage.

Because I lived in a mode of self-reliance, I have discovered that it is easier for me to be vulnerable about my past, shortcomings, and struggles rather than express my immediate needs and ask for help. This is something I am still working on. We are designed to need one another and live in interdependence, but it takes humility and courage to engage others in this way.

As I fill my mind with truth, lies that once burdened or tormented me are now laughable. I remember a time when I received truth in place of a lie, and Satan tried to come back a few times to test the truth, but it was now so obvious. I literally laughed out loud, and that was the end of Satan's attempt to use it against me. The truth sets us free!

God is less concerned with how much money I have or what job I do and more concerned about how I submit everything I have and everything I am to Him. Do I model a lifestyle of worship with my actions, or am I living for my own gain? Am I giving from a sacrificial place of love for the Father and His children, or am I just trying to be a "good person?"

The Picture on the Box: Understanding a Kingdom Worldview

Everyone has a worldview, or the lens used to understand and process reality. A worldview answers the big four questions:

1. Who am I?
2. Why am I here?
3. Where am I going?
4. Does life have any purpose?[2]

While most worldviews fall into seven main categories (theism, monotheism, atheism, pantheism, panentheism, deism, finite godism, and polytheism), each person's worldview is influenced by many factors including where they were born, which family they were born into, life experiences, social influences, etc. For a worldview to be accurate, it must align with reality, therefore, only one proper worldview exists: a kingdom worldview.

A kingdom worldview is a transformative lens aligning our perception with heaven, revolutionizing every aspect of life! In a world filled with complexities, diverse information, and cultural debates, many form their worldview haphazardly, drawing from various sources without a coherent foundation. Imagine life as a puzzle—your morals, values, and perspectives as pieces, with the box top representing your worldview. Knowing the picture on the box simplifies fitting each piece where it goes. An incomplete or misaligned worldview is like assembling a puzzle with the wrong image. With only one life to live, investing time in shaping a kingdom worldview becomes a meaningful pursuit. So, what's your worldview? Is it a kingdom one or a worldly one? What "picture" are you trying to create with your puzzle pieces? Could it be that some pieces are not fitting because you are modeling your life on the wrong image?

THE TRUTH
OF THE MATTER

Every person is significant and designed for kingdom impact on earth! *Jesus and the Father are one, and we are one with Jesus.* Through Jesus, we receive the gift of the Holy Spirit to be His hands and feet on earth. This means:

◊ We are temples of the Holy Spirit, the house of God. (1 Corinthians 3:16)

◊ We are the crowning jewel of creation. (Psalm 8:5)

◊ We are a gateway between heaven and earth. (Psalm 24:7)

◊ We are a body (seen realm), a soul (seen-unseen gateway), and a spirit (unseen realm). (1 Thessalonians 5:23)

◊ We are multidimensional creations living in the natural and spiritual realms. (Genesis 1:26-28, Galatians 5:25, Romans 8:11)

◊ We are God's family. (1 John 3:1)

◊ We are united as one body of Christ, one mind, and one heart. (Ephesians 4:4)

◊ We are beloved sons and daughters of God. (Romans 8:15)

◊ We are new creations in Christ, one with Him and seated with Him in heavenly places. (2 Corinthians 5:17, Ephesians 2:6-7)

◊ We are Jesus on earth — His body, hands, and feet. (1 Corinthians 12:2)

◊ We are citizens of heaven. (Philippians 3:20)

◊ We are ambassadors of Jesus. (2 Corinthians 5:20)

◊ We are ambassadors of the Gospel. (Ephesians 6:20)

◊ We are kings. (Revelation 1:6)

◊ We are priests. (1 Peter 2:9)

◊ We are heirs through God. (Galatians 4:7)

◊ We are co-heirs with Jesus. (Romans 8:17)

◊ We are brothers and sisters of Jesus. (Hebrews 2:10-12)

◊ We are here to bring heaven to earth and glorify God as a light in the world. (Matthew 5:14-16)

◊ We are God's treasure! (1 Peter 2:9-10)

◊ We are carriers of the kingdom of God of righteousness, peace, and joy in the Holy Spirit. (Romans 14:17-19)

Discovering True Identity: The Path to Sonship and Destiny

He predestined us to adoption as sons and daughters through Jesus Christ to Himself, according to the good pleasure of His will, to the praise of the glory of His grace, with which He favored us in the Beloved.
—Ephesians 1:5-6, NASB

Our greatest need is for belonging, relationships, and connection as we are made in the image of the triune God who exists in perfect relationship and unity. Sonship is eternal belonging and connection. To belong, we must be fully known, loved, and accepted. Only God knows us fully, from every thought to the number of hairs on our heads.[3] God will never love us more, and He will never love us less. Our belonging is truly and completely found in God. It is the Holy Spirit who leads us to the Father through Jesus. As mind-blowing as this sounds, we receive our identity as sons and daughters with Jesus as *our older brother.*

It is important to understand that the orphan spirit cannot be simply cast out like a demon but must be displaced in the journey of sonship as we grow in the revelation of our true identity. This is why it is important to become a student of sonship.[4] The orphan spirit (aka the spirit of slavery, the spirit of bondage) is rooted in religion, motivated by following a written code. In truth, we have been fully released from the power of the law. Co-buried with Jesus, we are dead to the law, which awakens sinful desires. Now, we live in freedom and new life, co-resurrected with Jesus through the power of the Holy Spirit.[5]

We are no longer governed by the law but by the reign of God's grace through faith alone. We are free to live, not according to the flesh, but by the dynamic power of the Holy Spirit.

An orphan's life is marked by performance and self-reliance. They see God as a punisher, a false view of God, because of unhealed traumas, especially mother and father wounds, and ungodly beliefs. These cement lies around identity. Religion says, "God is good, you are bad; try harder to be good enough." Remember, identity is received, not achieved, and destiny flows out of identity. As we heal and replace lies with truth, darkness is displaced with light, and we begin to experience the true love of God as our Father. We are gradually set free as God displaces the orphan spirit, and we live in the revelation of the truth. Our true identity is revealed through the renewing of our minds.

The mature children of God are those who are moved by the impulses of the Holy Spirit. And you did not receive the "spirit of religious duty," leading you back into the fear of never being good enough. But you have received the "Spirit of full acceptance," enfolding you into the family of God. And you will never feel orphaned, for as he rises up within us, our spirits join him in saying the words of tender affection, "Beloved Father!" For the Holy Spirit makes God's fatherhood real to us as he whispers into our innermost being, "You are God's beloved child!"
—Romans 8:15-16, TPT

For me, the lie "I am not enough" gave root to my false identity as an orphan. Once I submitted my life to Jesus and started to see myself as a son, God began to reveal how this lie played out in my life. This presented me with the opportunity to renounce these lies, one by one, slowly renewing my mind to the will of God. Remember, the process of sanctification (becoming like Christ) is both immediate and ongoing. His sanctifying grace enables us to take on the character of Jesus. The journey to maturation is ongoing and spans our lifetime, so be patient. I have discovered and experienced that a sound mind is a mind full of truth illuminated by the Spirit and a mind that is anchored on Jesus. This is a mind at peace, the mind of Christ.

Kingdom Revelation: Seeing Life Through the Eyes of Sonship

The Father set the bar when He said to Jesus in Matthew 3:17, "...'This is My beloved Son, with whom I am well pleased'" (NASB). God said this to Jesus before He had even started His public ministry. That is before He did anything to earn God's love (which is impossible— He already loves unconditionally).

These are the Father's words to all of us. *You are my son. You are my daughter. I love you unconditionally. I am well pleased with you. I like you because I made you to be you.* In other words, He loves you because you are family. He loves you simply because you exist. You are home, and your heart is His home. There is nothing to earn and or prove, as God has the same love for us as He does for Jesus, our brother. You are home, in Christ, in the Father, safe and secure for now and all eternity. This is the Gospel!

We are all sons growing with our Heavenly Father. As I have progressed in my journey of sonship, I have grown in the revelation of the kingdom of God, as the kingdom resides in our hearts, not our heads. Sonship and the revelation of the kingdom are mingled as sonship allows us to see from the perspective of heaven, whereas orphans see God from Satan's perspective. Dependency and the ability to rest are key indicators of sonship. The more I see myself as a son, the more I progress in the revelation of the goodness of God and the fear of the Lord. The fear of the Lord produces humility, awe, wonder, and adoration, leading to curiosity and continuous learning. It is primarily relational. When we fear the Lord, we seek not to let anything come between our relationship with our Heavenly Father. As sons, we would not want to do anything that might hurt His heart.

I have seen the truth about how perspective shifts reality. This played out with our prayer team at Flō. As we have grown personally and in our ministry, our hope, passion, and joy have increased. Our focus is on His presence, promises, and the victory of God and less on Satan. We see God in a new light, burning with a new intensity with a passion for prayer and moving in the authority and government of God.

> Royalty is my identity. Servanthood is my assignment. Intimacy with God is my life source. So, before God, I'm intimate. Before people, I'm a servant. Before the powers of hell, I'm a ruler with no tolerance for their influence.
> —Bill Johnson[6]

As sons and daughters, we are representatives of our Father and are about our Father's business, the family business. Like any family, mature sons possess authority. Mature children learn to live and function in this authority. We are designed to self-govern, to rule from within, and not be "ruled over" from the outside (i.e., the world, our flesh). Jesus is in charge. He is the head. The rest of us are equals, though our functions may be different. The kingdom has no hierarchy, although there is structure and order. Each one of us is needed as a member of the body.

The journey of sonship is a journey into our true identities. We become secure and stable when we are convinced of our value and God's love for us. With any journey, we can have ups and downs, times of orphan mindsets, and times of sonship mindsets as our minds are renewed. The mindset of sonship involves healing and learning to live from our life union with Jesus so that we can fully receive and live in the spirit of adoption and the fullness of God's kingdom.[7] We discover that we already have everything we need for life and godliness through our union with Jesus. We receive sonship through the finished work of Christ and not by any work of our own. We bring nothing to the table except our choice to exercise the faith He placed within us. It is all by grace! Jesus came to build His house with living stones (people), not buildings (although we are called to gather), and to bring heaven to earth *now*, co-ruling with Jesus and going into all the world preaching the gospel of the kingdom.

Embracing Spiritual Parenthood: The Impact of Spiritual Fathers and Mothers

I honour my father, Kenneth Elliott for doing his best. When we were young, he actively participated in our sports, even coaching our teams. He consistently tried to take our family camping and on special trips. Dad, known for his gregarious laugh, was a dedicated and hardworking entrepreneur and was generous to those in need. Although Dad was private about his faith, he prioritized taking us to church every Sunday, which established our family in faith. Sadly, following my brother's accident, a lifetime of tragedy and unhealed traumas took a toll on his life and our family.

In God's grace and mercy, when God brought my spiritual father along years after my father's death, his name was also Kenneth – Kenn Gill. One of God's greatest confirmations regarding Kenn becoming my spiritual father occurred after he invited me to a conference at a large church in Alberta. I usually sat in the back, but Kenn sat up front. During worship, I entered a profound experience with my heavenly Father. In this vision, I felt the Lord putting His arms around me like a dad would hug his son. At that moment, Kenn (who had walked back to where I was) put his arms around me. The timing was truly supernatural and rocked me. My experience in the supernatural realm collided in perfect time with my experience in the physical realm. I am so grateful for Kenn and his wife Cheryl's role as spiritual parents in the years since that moment. God knows exactly who we need to parent us (no matter how old we are) to become who He created us to be.

Having Kenn Gill as my spiritual father has greatly accelerated my journey of sonship, along with his wife Cheryl as my spiritual mother. This is by God's design. Spiritual fathers and mothers bring wisdom, counsel, accountability, and correction. It is a lifelong journey, a two-way relationship of honour and support. Spiritual fathers provide someone to answer questions and support growth in a place of safety. They do not replace our birth fathers, but they will help strengthen our family relationships. Setting realistic expectations on both sides and maintaining open communication with our spiritual parents is critical, just like we would with any good and intimate friendship. To avoid any manipulation or control, it is always advisable for the spiritual child to pursue their spiritual parents. This was difficult for me, as I have always been self-reliant, but it was worth pushing through my pride and insecurities to vulnerably ask to be fathered and then submit my life! We become a people of authority by being under authority. The benefits of having spiritual parents to help us mature in the faith cannot be emphasized enough!

That is what it means to be saved. You declare that you belong to another system of things. People point to you and say, "Oh, yes, that is a Christian family; they belong to the Lord!" That is the salvation that the Lord desires for you, that by your public testimony you declare before God, "My world has gone; I am entering into another."[8] The kingdom of God expands as fathers and mothers raise sons and daughters who understand that they are heirs of the kingdom. This allows people to live as free sons and daughters of God (rather than those under the yoke of bondage to the law). I love the following quote, "Religion says: I messed up. My dad is going to kill me. The Gospel says: I messed up. I need to call my father."[9]

The journey into sonship and expanding the kingdom is the calling of every person who accepts Jesus as their Lord and Saviour. Sadly, many Christians stall out at salvation. This is like saying "I do" to your spouse at the wedding ceremony but not going on to live the rest of your lives together, building a family, and enjoying children and grandchildren. Of course, the gospel of salvation is important! We need to help people get to "I do." However, what's the point of getting married unless you will enjoy life together, sharpening each other to become more like Christ in the process? That is the gospel of the kingdom! One is not complete without the other.

Jesus *once* mentioned the need to be born again in His conversation with Nicodemus (a Pharisee). However, He spoke about the kingdom more than 100 times in the Gospels.

> *Jesus answered,* **"Truly, truly, I say to you, unless someone is born of water and the Spirit, he cannot enter the kingdom of God."**
> *John 3:5, NASB*

When we are born again, we become new creations by the power of the Holy Spirit, which is how we enter the kingdom. It is also the Holy Spirit who connects us to the Father. Jesus made the way! He continually preached about the kingdom of God. Salvation is the critical first step towards partnering with God, but salvation alone does not transform the world. If we want to fulfill our God-given purpose, we must step into the glorious work of the kingdom to manifest the glory of God on earth. It is only through the power of the Holy Spirit that we are empowered to bring heaven to earth, partnering with God to manifest the eternal, spiritual realm of the kingdom into the physical.

The next step of obedience after choosing to follow Jesus is to be baptized, identifying with Jesus's death and resurrection. Through our public declaration of faith through our water baptism, we are entering into the co-crucifixion and co-resurrection with Christ, which is also an accelerant in the process of sanctification and moving into continuing deeper levels of kingdom realities.[10] In baptism, our old nature dies, and we begin to replace our old thinking patterns with the truth. His grace divinely enables sanctification. It is also possible to receive deliverance during baptism, as many have experienced as they came out of the water. This is how we can live "in eternity," even while journeying through our appointed days on earth.

We become kingdom citizens when we are born again. Baptism, by water and by the Spirit, thrusts us into the realities and power of His kingdom! These kingdom realities empower us to build and enjoy family life in the kingdom.

In November 2019, Bryn and I were baptized in water. This act declared our total dedication to following Jesus, dying to our old natures, and a fresh filling of the Spirit (an ongoing process). We always have the Holy Spirit, but we need an ongoing infilling of the Spirit to overflow into the world for others. I remember Bill Johnson was asked why we needed continual infilling, and his answer was simple yet profound: "Because we leak." We are to be led by the Spirit, with God's presence continuously empowering our lives. This is what life in God's kingdom is all about!

1. Luke 23:43.
2. Norman Geislar and William Watkin, Worlds Apart: A Handbook on Worldview (Wipf & Stock Publishers; Reprint edition, 2003).
3. Matthew 10:30.
4. I recommend John Alley's *The Spirit of Sonship*, which offers a free download on peace.org, and Jack Frost's *Slavery to Sonship*.
5. Romans 6:34, 8:4.
6. Bill Johnson, "Bill Johnson Quotes," *QuoteFancy*, accessed October 13, 2023, https://rb.gy/2y7s7.
7. Romans 8:15.
8. Watchman Nee, "You're 'Good News' Partners!," *Power Packed Promises*, accessed October 13, 2023, https://rb.gy/hszlx.
9. Quote originally attributed to Ruth Graham.
10. For more on the power of baptism in the Spirit, see "Spirit-led and Empowered" and "Let Go" in *More Than Gold*, pp. 135–138.

KINGDOM IDENTITY

He has rescued us completely from the tyrannical rule of darkness and has translated us into the kingdom realm of his beloved Son. For in the Son all our sins are canceled and we have the release of redemption through his very blood.
—Colossians 1:13-14, TPT

Father, we ask for the grace to fully grasp our true identity as Your sons and daughters, bought with the precious blood of Jesus.

QUESTIONS FOR REFLECTION

What did the Holy Spirit reveal to you through *Kingdom Identity*? How can you apply this to your life?

_____

_____

_____

_____

How has God personally expressed His love to you?

_____

_____

_____

_____

What questions do you have for God regarding your identity? Questions can be a great way to begin a transformational conversation with God.

_____

_____

_____

_____

QUESTIONS FOR REFLECTION *(continued)*

Have you considered asking for a spiritual mother or father? Who is the Holy Spirit bringing to mind? This is a key to the expansion of the kingdom. This prepares you to do the same for others, creating other mothers and fathers.

Notes

Chapter 6: Kingdom Living

"Now wherever you go, make disciples of all nations, baptizing them in the name of the Father, the Son, and the Holy Spirit. And teach them to faithfully follow all that I have commanded you. And never forget that I am with you every day, even to the completion of this age."
—*Matthew 28:19-20, TPT*

"And as you go, preach this message: 'Heaven's kingdom realm is accessible, close enough to touch.' You must continually bring healing to lepers and to those who are sick, and make it your habit to break off the demonic presence from people, and raise the dead back to life. Freely you have received the power of the kingdom, so freely release it to others."
—*Matthew 10:7-8, TPT*

Jesus ministered from place to place throughout all of the province of Galilee. He taught in the synagogues, preaching the wonderful news of the kingdom and healing every kind of sickness and disease among the people. His fame spread throughout all Syria! Many people who were in pain and suffering with every kind of illness were brought to Jesus for their healing—epileptics, paralytics, and those tormented by demonic powers were all set free. Everyone who was brought to Jesus was healed!
—*Matthew 4:23-24, TPT*

Love as the Weapon: Combating Evil with Good

Jesus came to destroy the works of the devil.[1] I have discovered that the only way to successfully combat evil is by living, thinking, and acting in union with Jesus. The best way to combat evil in the day-to-day is to love people. Why? Because the Word says we combat evil with good.[2] God continually brings people across my path who need hope, encouragement, deliverance, healing, or sometimes just a compassionate ear to listen. I love identifying strongholds in my life and replacing them with truth (I also love helping others do the same). I regularly share the Gospel. I have gone into hospitals to pray for people. I have gone into people's homes to bring the light of God when there is demonic oppression. These sorts of practices enforce the victory of Jesus through our obedience. I have walked with people going through hardships, sharing in their burdens. I regularly pray in authority to bind darkness and release the light and power of God, depending on the situation. Combating evil by displacing it with the kingdom of God is a great adventure!

HIS MISSION IS
NOW OUR MISSION

Jesus came to proclaim the gospel of the kingdom of
God and heal every disease and sickness among the people.
(Matthew 4:23)

Jesus came not to be served but to serve. (Matthew 20:28)

Jesus came to model a life of gentleness and humility, totally
submitted to the Father. (Matthew 11:29)

Jesus ransomed many with His life. (Mark 10:45)

Jesus discipled and baptized young believers. (John 4:1-2)

Jesus came to reveal the Father. (John 14:9)

Jesus came in grace and truth. (John 1:14)

Jesus came full of compassion, mercy, and loving-kindness. (Matthew
9:36, Luke 6:36, Ephesians 2:4)

Jesus came as the solution to the problem that all have fallen short
of the glory of God. (Romans 3:23)

Jesus went about the Father's business, establishing His will
and His kingdom *on earth as it is in heaven.* (Luke 2:49)

Jesus taught the principles of the kingdom and
demonstrated the kingdom on earth. (Mark 1:14-15)

"So if the Son sets you free, you really will be free."
—*John 8:36, NASB*

Living in Freedom: Making Jesus Lord of Every Area of Life

Freedom is rooted in knowing the Son personally. Every area in our life that we make Jesus Lord, there is freedom. The truth is that we are not our own; we have been bought at a price. As we know the truth, we live from a new reality, a kingdom mindset, and we will be set free. We receive the truth through intimacy with Jesus, received as revelation in our hearts by the Holy Spirit. This sets us free from ourselves and the world to live from the fullness of our life union with Jesus.

We are called to serve, give our lives, go about the Father's business, disciple, baptize, and establish His will and kingdom on earth. Just like Jesus, we are to proclaim the gospel of the kingdom of God. The gospel of the kingdom starts when the door of salvation opens. The kingdom is moving towards the restoration of all things to God's original purposes. It is a concept encompassed by the words of Jesus in Revelation 21:5, **And He who sits on the throne said, 'Behold, I am making all things new...'"** (NASB).

Jesus entrusted us with the great responsibility and privilege of joining Him in His mission for the world and the entire cosmos. A life with Jesus is a life bursting with purpose, adventure, and unimaginable potential!

Then he taught them another parable: **"Heaven's kingdom can be compared to yeast that a woman takes and blends into three measures of flour and then waits until all the dough rises."**
—*Matthew 13:33, TPT*

Leaven of the Kingdom: Transformative Influence in Everyday Actions

In the kingdom, things start small and gradually expand. It only takes a small amount of leaven (the inception point of the kingdom, which symbolizes the power of the kingdom to bring transformation) to permeate the entire loaf once the presence of Jesus shows up. Said another way, seemingly small acts of faith and kindness can have a significant impact and influence to bring about transformation. My friend Derk Maat says, "Every act of kindness is an act of discipling the nation." When we see a need and meet that need, we are sowing small seeds. We will see what God does over time as we bless others. When we understand the small things are as important as the seemingly big things, everything takes on significance. Just because something starts small doesn't mean we should expect it to stay small.[3] We are to be faithful and present to the opportunities God reveals. As we move in love, share the Gospel, bless, and serve, we are destroying the kingdom of darkness, little by little, and ushering in the kingdom of God.

On earth as it is in heaven means that all forms of poverty are continually reduced as we align each area on earth with heaven.[4] Moving into spiritual, material, motivational, and relational well-being and prosperity of spirit, soul, and body are manifestations of living under an open heaven. As kingdom citizens, we are granted rights, privileges, and power to live above our circumstances, living in the absolute authority of God's Word. This is incredible news!

The premier social indicator that transformation has occurred is the elimination of systemic poverty. I seek to dislodge systems within my sphere of influence that keep me and others poor spiritually, relationally, materially, and motivationally.[5]

Jesus said in Mark 14:7, **"For you always have the poor with you, and whenever you want, you can do good to them; but you do not always have Me"** (NASB). However, as God's kingdom expands, poverty is gradually alleviated. Ed Silvoso defines the four aspects of systemic poverty as material, relational, spiritual, and motivational. As we meet one another's needs in these four areas, systemic poverty in every form <u>will be alleviated</u>, as in the early church of Acts. When new kingdom systems are progressively implemented, systemic poverty will continue to decline. God's solutions and ways align earth with heaven.

As we seek first His kingdom, God promises that He will supply all our needs. 3 John 2 says, "Beloved, I pray that in all respects you may prosper and be in good health, just as your soul prospers" (NASB). This is God's will for us. The more we seek His kingdom, the more we experience the abundance of His presence. Why is this? Because the more we seek His kingdom, the more we live from our life union with Jesus, and the closer we move to our highest calling and purpose to bring heaven to earth.

> In the world, we rejoice because we are happy. In the kingdom, we're happy because we rejoice.
> — Bill Johnson[6]

The abundant life revealed in healthy relationships between unified believers is one place where we experience the goodness of God. God uses relationships to channel resources, create new partnerships, and build networks. Relationships are the foundation of unity. Therefore, I encourage you to think inter-connectedly. Together, we can reach our God-given purposes.

Jesus proclaims the kingdom of heaven as he quotes Isaiah 61 in Luke 4:18-21:

"The Spirit of the Lord is upon me, and He has anointed me to be hope for the poor, healing for the brokenhearted, and new eyes for the blind, and to preach to prisoners, 'You are set free!' I have come to share the message of Jubilee, for the time of God's great acceptance has begun." *After he read this He rolled up the scroll, handed it* *back to the attendant, and sat down. Everyone stared at Jesus, wondering what He was about to say. Then He added,* **"Today, these Scriptures came true in front of you."** *(TPT)*

Furthermore, Acts 2:44-46 gives us the perfect model of living and working together as a community of believers. In this passage, the early believers had everything in common and sold their possessions to share with those who needed them. They met together daily in the temple and shared meals in each other's homes. They were joyful and generous.

Imagine a world where this is the norm. Instead of living in silos, managing our resources, struggling to get by, or waiting for the government to intervene for others or ourselves, we, the church and body of Christ, came together to care for each other and worship together. It's not that this doesn't happen today. In fact, many churches and believers give generously and devote significant resources to those in need, including time, money, tangible gifts, and a heart of service. But this is the bare minimum God calls us to.

Heavenly Treasures: Embracing the Inheritance of God's Kingdom

"Nevertheless do not rejoice at this, that the spirits are subject to you, but rejoice that your names are recorded in heaven."
—Luke 10:20, AMP

Once I made Jesus my Lord and King, my life began to change. What I valued shifted from worldly things to heavenly things. I couldn't articulate or explain what was happening, but as the things of this world started growing strangely dim, I felt pulled to something other-worldly. Over time, this new way of living became my love and passion. Paul describes it perfectly:

But whatever things were gain to me, these things I have counted as loss because of Christ. More than that, I count all things to be loss in view of the surpassing value of knowing Christ Jesus my Lord, for whom I have suffered the loss of all things, and count them mere rubbish, so that I may gain Christ.
—Philippians 3:7-8, NASB

Paul understood this reality. Jesus is the ultimate treasure of heaven, and we experience the realm of heaven as we realize the great price Jesus paid for us.

- Through Jesus, His Father is now our Heavenly Father; Jesus is our eternal treasure chest filled with the riches of His glory.
- Through Jesus, we are united with the family of God.
- Through Jesus, His authority becomes ours as we are seated with Him in heavenly places. We have received a glorious heavenly treasure of the eternal, unshakable, eternal kingdom.
- Through Jesus, we are made right with God, which produces peace and joy. It is the love of God that releases His joy within us.

Heavenly treasures come as we live with heaven in mind and set our affections on the things above.[7] Heavenly treasures are of the Spirit and are eternal. The Father of Glory imparts the riches of the Spirit of wisdom and revelation to know Christ through deepening intimacy. Salvation, eternal life, love, joy, peace, hope, and faith are all included in the unfathomable inheritance of Jesus and God as His sons and daughters. When we recognize our dependence on God, we partake in humility, a form of kingdom riches. When we can rejoice in even the worst moments of life, we know we have found the true treasure of heaven. I have experienced this in the face of murder, murder trials, significant loss, and ongoing suffering. It doesn't mean I don't suffer emotional pain, but it does mean I can have joy and hope amid difficult times. The joy of the Lord is our strength, which leads to hope far beyond any circumstance.[8]

This is why the Scriptures say: Things never discovered or heard of before, things beyond our ability to imagine these are the many things God has in store for all his lovers.
—1 Corinthians 2:9, TPT

Kingdom Living: Investing in Eternal Riches and Spiritual Legacy

Whatever earthly riches we accumulate are only temporary and can be lost or stolen. However, God gives us the opportunity to trade earthly riches for heavenly riches, eternal rewards that will never be lost, as we submit to Him daily. This is the power of living in the kingdom while still on earth. We do this by seeking first His kingdom, which means being generous to those in need and using our resources for the betterment of others.

As a dad, living for the kingdom of heaven means honouring the ways of God, discipling my daughter, and leaving a spiritual legacy for my family. As an entrepreneur, this means building a kingdom company, starting a charity to build up and empower children and families living in poverty, starting a family restoration ministry, and living below my means so that I can give generously. By using the gifts, people, and resources the Lord has entrusted me with to expand His kingdom, each endeavour that started in seed form continues to grow.

A good person leaves an inheritance to his grandchildren,
And the wealth of a sinner is stored up for the righteous.
—Proverbs 13:22, NIV

I always thought of this only in terms of earthly wealth, as my reality was earthly. Although the transfer of wealth and wisdom to the next generations is essential, I now believe the greatest wealth is the spiritual wealth to leave a godly legacy. *This* is far more valuable than gold. Priceless, in fact.

"For where your treasure is, there your heart [your wishes, your desires; that on which your life centers] will be also."
—Matthew 6:21, AMP

BIBLICAL FEASTS AND REDEMPTION

By Matt Davis, *The Jewish Road*

The invitation to a deeper faith often starts with a simple realization: We're part of a much larger story, one that spans not just years, decades, or even millennia, but all eternity. We have these pivotal moments etched into the narrative, moments designed by God to draw us closer to Him. They are the biblical feasts, known in Hebrew as *moadim* (םידעומ), or "God's appointed times."

Spring feasts like Passover and Pentecost focus on what Christ accomplished during His first coming: His crucifixion, resurrection, and the sending of the Holy Spirit. They're our roots, the foundation of our faith.

Unlike the fulfilled promises of Spring, the Fall feasts, such as the Feast of Trumpets (Yom Teruah), the Day of Atonement (Yom Kippur), and the Feast of Tabernacles (Sukkot), point us to what is still to come—the return of Jesus and our eternal life with Him.

It's easy to linger in the familiarity of the New Testament and lose sight of the rich context provided by the Old Testament. That gap between the two is like a missing chapter in our family history. It separates us from our Jewish roots and, perhaps, from fully understanding the heavenly rhythm Jesus invites us into.

Zoom in on one of these appointed times, the Feast of Tabernacles or Sukkot. Rooted in the Old Testament, God instructed the Israelites to build little booths known as *sukkahs*. These serve as living memories, signifying God's faithfulness during their 40 years of wilderness wandering. Roll that insight into the New Testament, where John shares that Jesus "dwelt" among us. Jesus didn't just show up; He tabernacled with us, making the Old Testament tradition of Sukkot incredibly relevant for every believer today. God's glory is literally among men.

In our family, as Messianic Jews, we bring this feast to life every year by building a sukkah, a backyard tabernacle. It's not just a tradition; it's a hands-on way to tell the story of God to the next generation and anticipate the kingdom now and not yet. Sitting under the palm-branched rooftop, we're part of something bigger—a narrative that spans past, present, and future. It's an annual reminder of God's consistency, His everlasting promises, and the future we have with Him.

So whether you're new to the faith or have walked this path for years, paying attention to the full spectrum of God's appointed times can deepen your understanding and enrich your spiritual journey. Paul reminds us in Colossians 2:16 that observing these feasts isn't a requirement, but understanding their depth enriches our faith.

The invitation stands. Dive deeper into the whole story of God's relationship with us, spanning from the Spring feasts that remind us of His first coming to the Fall feasts that awaken us to His return. Our God is a God of promises—past, present, and future. By engaging with these feasts, we align ourselves with His eternal plan, living here on earth with hearts set on the heart of heaven.

A Note from Bryan

God says that those who bless the nation of Israel will be blessed. In Genesis, God said, *"And I **will bless those** who **bless you**, And the one who curses you I will curse. And in you all the families of the earth **will be blessed**"* (12:3, NASB). Great ways to bless Israel include praying daily for the peace of Jerusalem and the safety of Israel's borders, donating to native-Israeli ministries, and fighting Antisemitism at home and abroad. Educate yourself on Israeli politics and prophetic significance in the end times, as well as the role of God's chosen people today. I recommend these resources to get started:

◇ Christians United for Israel (CUFI.org)

◇ The Faithful Galileans (FaithfulGalileans.com)

◇ Tikkun Global (TikkunGlobal.org)

Future rewards root us in the ultimate eternal justice of God, which is the source of our hope. Welcome to the kingdom of hope! While we have access to His treasures or "storehouse," Jesus also tells us we can make deposits into this treasury.

> **"Do not store up for yourselves treasures on earth, where moth and rust destroy, and where thieves break in and steal. But store up for yourselves treasures in heaven, where neither moth nor rust destroys, and where thieves do not break in or steal; for where your treasure is, there your heart will be also."**
> —Matthew 6:19-21, NASB

He tells us to "store up" treasures in heaven. This is another example of the upside-down Gospel where our work is not for personal gain or momentary satisfaction but an investment into our future in heaven by first seeking His kingdom. We may not see the fruit now, but we can be confident of our inheritance as sons and daughters of the King of Kings. As we sow our resources into kingdom activities, we lay up treasures in heaven. Interestingly, Isaiah 33:6 in NKJV states, "The fear of the Lord is His treasure." It is the fear of the Lord that inspires us to show God reverence and awe, and ultimately, what inspires holiness. It is worth spending a few minutes meditating on how the fear of the Lord is a treasure!

Our relationship with Jesus is not dependent on the deposits we make, yet God does speak of rewards, crowns, and treasures in heaven for those who do His will and live in union with Him and His priorities. Children enjoy the pleasures and privileges of living in their father's house, and the father delights in their presence. As children mature, they begin to take up responsibilities in that household, leading them to become fully mature adults. They have the opportunity to partner with their father and contribute to the household treasury. In the same sense, we get to partner with Jesus in His kingdom work.

God doesn't look at things the way people do. People look at the outward appearance of things, but the Lord looks at our hearts.[9] No matter how "good" our accomplishments might seem on the outside, our inner motives matter most. In Hebrews 11, we learn about the "heroes of the faith" (Abraham, Isaac, Jacob, Moses, Samuel, David, etc.) who died steadfast in their faith without seeing the completion of all the promises God gave them in their lifetimes. We have the benefit of seeing in Scripture and our lives just how massive their investments were for the kingdom.

> *You love Him passionately although you have not seen Him, but through believing in Him you are saturated with an ecstatic joy, indescribably sublime and immersed in glory. For you are reaping the harvest of your faith—the full salvation promised you—your souls' victory!*
> —1 Peter 1:8-9, TPT

The kingdom is about people as it is built relationally with spiritual fathers, mothers, sons, and daughters. We store heavenly treasures when we lead others to salvation, love, bless, serve, and disciple others, and care for widows and orphans.

As we serve and meet the needs of others, God backs it with His power. We cannot reproduce what we are not and lead people where we have yet to go. As such, spiritual fathering can only go as far as you have become a son to the Father. One of the greatest kingdom investments is a father's investment in sons and daughters, as this is how the kingdom of God is expanded: through heirs.

Sons become fathers who then deposit their incredible treasures into sons and daughters, making this an investment that keeps producing long after you leave earth. Jesus said that those who follow His commands and teach them to others would be called great in the kingdom of heaven.[10] As we are discipled and grow, we multiply by discipling and helping others grow. In the words of Ann Voskamp, "When you help others live better - it's your life that gets better."[11] As a kingdom investor, I daily choose to stand in faith. I know I will eventually reap a harvest by playing the long game!

> *"And whoever gives a cup of cold water to one of my disciples, I promise you, he will not go unrewarded."*
> —*Matthew 10:42, TPT*

Even the simplest acts of kindness, such as giving a cup of cold water, will not go unrewarded. We are here on earth as mist in the air, here for such a short time within the view of eternity.[12] I encourage you to cherish these days. Hold them as sacred. This is our opportunity to embrace the love of Christ, even when it's difficult and we experience trials and suffering. What a privilege it is to love God by loving others!

* * *

One day, we will face the judgment seat of Christ as we give an account of our lives and receive our eternal rewards and assignments. The crowns given, referred to in Revelation, refer to the eternal rewards of living for Jesus.[13] Pause and grasp the enormity of this statement—what you do now impacts your eternal positioning within the kingdom. This is our proving ground. As I ponder, these questions come to my mind:

- Is there enough oil in my lamp for the bridegroom's return?
- Am I prepared for the coming of the most important appointment in my life?
- Am I living for God?
- Am I answering the call of God for my life?

The finish line of this race is our last breath on earth. Fight the good fight![14] Run the good race![15] Consider the words from a poem Jim Caviezel, actor and Christ-follower (most known for his role as Jesus in *The Passion of the Christ*), recited:

God's Hall of Fame

Your name may not appear down here
In this world's Hall of Fame,
In fact, you may be so unknown
That no one knows your name;
The Oscars and the praise of men
May never come your way,
But don't forget God has rewards
That he'll hand out someday…

This crowd on earth, they soon forget
When you're not up at the top,
They'll cheer like mad until you fall
And then their praise will stop;
Not God, He never does forget,
And in His Hall of Fame,
By just believing on His Son,
Forever—there's your name.

I tell you, friend, I wouldn't trade
My name, however small,
That's written there beyond the stars
In that celestial Hall,
For all the famous names on earth,
Or glory that they share;
I'd rather be an unknown here,
And have my name up there.[16]

Jesus is our eternal treasure chest filled with the riches of His glory for now and for all of eternity. We must remember, no matter what we "do," if we have not loved, we have nothing![17]

Living within you is the Christ who floods you with the expectation of glory! This mystery of Christ, embedded within us, becomes a heavenly treasure chest of hope filled with the riches of glory for his people, and God wants everyone to know it!
—Colossians 1:27, TPT

1. 1 John 3:8.

2. Romans 12:21.

3. Zechariah 4:10.

4. Matthew 6:10.

5. "Our Core Values," *Transform Our World*, accessed October 14, 2023, https://www.transformourworld.org/our-core-values/.

6. Bill Johnson, @bethel.

7. Colossians 3:2.

8. Nehemiah 8:10.

9. 1 Samuel 16:7.

10. Matthew 5:19.

11. Ann Voskamp, "35 Quotes to Make You Smile," The Simplicity Habit, https://www.thesimplicityhabit.com/smile-quotes-for-instagram/, accessed January 10, 2024.

12. James 4:14.

13. Revelation 4:9-11.

14. 1 Timothy 6:12.

15. Hebrews 12:1.

16. "Jim Caviezel-Christian Poem," *YouTube*, accessed October 13, 2023, https://rb.gy/5o0yg.

17. 1 Corinthians 13:1-3.

KINGDOM LIVING

Living within you is the Christ who floods you with the expectation of glory! This mystery of Christ, embedded within us, becomes a heavenly treasure chest of hope filled with the riches of glory for his people, and God wants everyone to know it!
—Colossians 1:27, TPT

Father, we ask for the grace to discover the joy of life in Your kingdom continually!

QUESTIONS FOR REFLECTION

What did the Holy Spirit reveal to you through *Kingdom Living*? How can you apply this to your life?

Are you spending more time storing up earthly treasure or kingdom treasure? Explain.

In what ways do you need to realign your values and time with the kingdom?

What does kingdom treasure look like in your life? What does investing in that treasure look like?

_____

_____

_____

_____

Notes

_____

_____

_____

_____

_____

_____

_____

_____

_____

_____

_____

_____

_____

_____

THE KINGDOM OF GOD IS...

1. **The kingdom of God** is a central theme in the Bible, representing God's reign and sovereignty made manifest on the earth through His kingdom citizens.

2. **The kingdom of God** is not confined to a physical place but is a spiritual reality of righteousness, peace, and joy in the Holy Spirit.

3. **The kingdom of God** is a realm where God's will is established.

4. **The kingdom of God** is a source of healing and restoration, breaking the chains of sin and sickness.

5. **The kingdom of God** is a source of hope, as His kingdom is both now and more to come as we move towards the full realization of God's reign in eternity.

6. **The kingdom of God** is advanced through acts of kindness, compassion, and selfless love.

7. **The kingdom of God** is the supernatural made natural, practical, and tangible.

8. **The kingdom of God** is love in action.

9. **The kingdom of God** is proclaimed through the preaching and demonstration of the gospel of the kingdom, calling people to repentance and expansion of the kingdom.

10. **The kingdom of God** is a transformative influence on culture and society, partnering with God to bring heaven's solutions to the world's problems.

11. **The kingdom of God** is likened to a banquet, where people from every nation gather to partake in the joy and fellowship of God's kingdom.

12. **The kingdom of God** is a source of grace, wisdom and authority, empowering believers to live according to God's divine principles.

13. **The kingdom of God** is a reality that empowers believers to be salt and light in the world, influencing it positively.

14. **The kingdom of God** is proclaimed through signs and wonders, showcasing God's supernatural intervention in the natural world in and through His kingdom ambassadors.

15. **The kingdom of God** is a source of spiritual discernment, guiding believers to distinguish between right and wrong, making wrong things right through prayer and action in the power of the Holy Spirit, leading to peace and joy.

16. **The kingdom of God** is advanced through the Great Commission, where followers of Jesus are called to make disciples of all nation by sharing the fullness of the gospel of the kingdom.

17. **The kingdom of God** is a realm of faith where grace abounds, obliterating sin and offering a path to redemption and freedom.

18. **The kingdom of God** is a source of unity, breaking down barriers of cultures, nationality, denomination, and social status.

19. **The kingdom of God** is proclaimed through acts of love, justice, mercy, forgiveness, and humility, as seen in the teachings and life of Jesus.

20. **The kingdom of God** is a realm where the Spirit of God empowers believers to live righteous and holy lives partnering with God to bring heaven to earth.

21. **The kingdom of God** is a reality that transcends temporal circumstances, offering an eternal perspective and divine solutions to the problems in the world.

22. **The kingdom of God** is proclaimed through the testimony of believers, sharing the transformative power of God's grace in their lives.

23. **The kingdom of God** is proclaimed through the teachings of Jesus, unveiling divine mysteries to those with ears to hear.

24. **The kingdom of God** is being about our Father's business, establishing His will *on earth as it is in heaven*. It is a realm where the Spirit of God empowers believers to bear fruit and glorify God.

25. **The kingdom of God** is a reality that calls for radical love for our enemies, reflecting the unconditional love of God.

26. **The kingdom of God** is proclaimed through the transformative work of the Holy Spirit, bringing about new birth, renewal, and reformation.

27. **The kingdom of God** is the family of God, which is the ultimate purpose behind all of creation.

28. **The kingdom of God** is a place of endless joy, where laughter and celebration reflect the Father's happiness with His children, who experience joy in simply being with Him.

Part 2: The Kingdom Constitution

In my first book, *More Than Gold*, I wrote the following:

> God made the earth and the entire universe function according to His Word and His ways. This system allows humanity to demonstrate the dominion of God on earth. God created all, and therefore, everything is subject to Him. He has eternity in mind. No matter what it looks like on earth, you can trust in His eternal plan.[1]

A constitution is a system of fundamental rules, principles, and ordinances for the government of a nation and, in God's case, His kingdom. The kingdom of God is God's perfect design for the earth, as it is already established in heaven. We carry the kingdom and the presence of God within and can operate and rule in His authority. God's Word is eternal and unchanging. Whatever His constitution says, King Jesus is obligated to fulfill it!

All Scripture is inspired by God and beneficial for teaching, for rebuke, for correction, for training in righteousness; so that the man or woman of God may be fully capable, equipped for every good work.
—2 Timothy 3:16-17, NASB

When I started reading the Bible in 2016, it was hard to understand and difficult to engage. Can you relate? Now, I absolutely love the Word of God! I receive more and more as I read, ponder, and reflect on Scripture. It brings such life, peace, and joy to my life. It is an anchor to my soul and is my foundation. I love the ways of God and the wisdom of God found in the scriptures.

There are times when I like to read longer passages of Scripture. There are other times when I take a more contemplative approach and read a short section of Scripture, ruminating there for weeks, just soaking it in. This eliminates the need to *do*, and instead, I can just *be* with the Word of God to receive His revelation. In other words, by digesting God's Word at a slower pace, any sense of "duty" is removed. Reading the Bible isn't a task to be crossed off my list of to-dos; it's a sweet time of resting in God's presence and enjoying Him as He teaches me through His Word.

The Word of God needs to penetrate our hearts. It needs to be worked into our entire physiology. It needs to move from knowledge to true revelation. We are to actively participate with the living Word just as we do in close, personal relationships. This quote from *A Tale of Three Virtues* gives beautiful insight into this area as we slow down and enter into the Word with our sanctified imagination active and emotions heightened, allowing our senses to engage and come alive:

> The epicenter of the "nature" on which we base our art is in the life of Christ. He is the Word perfected, at full strength, flawless and fully expressed. So start (and end) by looking at Him as intently as possible. Notice His every gesture. Try to hear the inflection of His words. Spotlight the potency of His every action. Watch for the reaction of those around Him. Stare down His adversaries. Check out every participant in His encounters with

publican, Pharisee, leper, scribe, beggar, fallen woman, disciple, multitude, lawyer, corpse, mother, governor. Try to climb into the scenes. Feel the weather; touch the faces, sense expectations, danger and suspense; imagine Christ's emotions. And always, always, relate your impressions to the whole person you are trying to know.[2]

Scripture interprets Scripture, meaning we are to seek the full counsel of the Word of God, not just individual verses. Lone scriptures can easily be taken out of context. Embracing and investigating the full Word of God is how we keep ourselves in the truth as the scriptures explain themselves. The scriptures are much more than a collection of stories, principles, and keys. They are the revelation of God and a place to get to know and encounter Him. If you still struggle to understand or see God's Word in this light, I encourage you to press in more. Read more, ask more questions, and seek counsel and wisdom. I promise you that the more you show up, the more opportunity God has to reveal Himself to you. The hungry get fed!

The Bible reveals God's story of His love and pursuit of us. It is also the constitution of God's kingdom. Like a nation's constitution, which establishes all rules, systems, and authorities, the Bible lays out the laws of the universe. God's Word contains His principles, plans, and purposes for creation.

Today, many believers are unwilling to accept every point described in God's constitution. Some pick and choose what they believe, while others try to justify passages that don't align with what the world says is true. Still, many deny it altogether. Just as earthly kingdoms have privileges and consequences, the kingdom of God is the same. God is the King, and He makes the rules. His authority is absolute. His Word is law. God is not subject to our opinion. What we feel about His Word, the Bible, is irrelevant. His kingdom is not a democracy! If we are going to thrive in the kingdom, we need to learn God's ways and unlearn the world's ways. The laws of the world's governments are ever-changing, but the laws of God do not change.

Honour God's holy instructions and life will go well for you. But if you despise his ways and choose your own plans, you will die.
—Proverbs 19:16, TPT

God releases blessings, and His kingdom is brought into the earth as we follow and implement His wisdom and principles. The world has to learn the principles by trial and error, but we have them in the Bible! God's Word is full of examples of people who got it right and those who suffered the consequences of their bad choices. All it takes is looking to the Proverbs for wisdom, the Gospels for what it means to live in the kingdom, and the Old Testament to understand our struggle with sin, to receive ancient wisdom, and how to embrace the goodness of God. God's Word is the ultimate "how-to" guide that eliminates the need to experiment with ideas the world says will help us live full lives.

God designed everything under the sun to operate according to His Word. We are designed to live out the principles of God from our union with Jesus, seeking first His kingdom and a relationship with Him. We can follow His Word as a religious rule book or joyfully participate in the relationship that comes from knowing Jesus intimately and following Him. Apart from Jesus, the principles will still bear good fruit because they are innately good and are God's design. When we apply a principle, we are exercising faith and placing a demand on the resources of heaven. Scripture tells us that everything good is a gift from God.[3]

However, God will bless non-believers who practice His principles to fulfill His Word because He is just. Plainly and simply stated—biblical principles work.

The more we know and implement God's principles, the more we will glorify God in our abundant living and expand His kingdom. It is God's power that fulfills His kingdom principles. Everything changes as we learn how the kingdom of heaven works and apply it on earth. We must never forget that everything is by grace in God's kingdom, and faith is our title deed!

The Sermon on the Mount

Most earthly constitutions are not considered, spoken, or written from a place of joy. Rather, they are written by a legislative body seeking to protect and guarantee the interests of the stakeholders/shareholders. God's constitution is written for righteousness, peace, and joy in the Holy Spirit, inaugurated by the King. Knowing God's principles allows us to live in God's design. The kingdom of God is not merely a set of rules or principles but experiencing the guidance, presence, and transformative nature of the Holy Spirit. The kingdom introduces a stewardship model of living where we love not our own lives because we belong to the King.

The Sermon on the Mount has been described as a condensed "kingdom constitution," where Jesus defines kingdom living and the necessity of making His kingdom our top priority. The Beatitudes invite us to see the world differently so that we can thrive.

> *"Listen to the truth I speak: Whoever does not open their arms to receive God's kingdom like a teachable child will never enter it."*
> —Mark 10:15, TPT

The Beatitudes

The Sermon on the Mount begins with the Beatitudes, a guide to living a righteous life and enjoying the nine blessings of Jesus outlined below. This was totally countercultural, as the Jewish leaders believed that God only blessed the males who were holy, righteous, and wealthy. In contrast, Jesus invited all, including the lost and broken, to enter His kingdom and be blessed. Jesus is the door to His kingdom, which comes by simply recognizing our need for a saviour and choosing to believe. As we go beyond the door and enter His kingdom, we go from citizens to ambassadors, from children of God to sons and daughters.

The Beatitudes describe the heart position and life of mature sons or daughters of God who are prepared to receive their inheritance as heirs of God and co-heirs with Jesus, for theirs is the kingdom. The Beatitudes are meant to be put into practice and demonstrate the mature heart condition of a truly blessed and joyful person who is humble in spirit, aware of their need for God, grieved and repentant over their sins, and meek (gentle, strong under control, lowly, long-suffering). In other words, our weakness becomes a resting place for His peace and His power. It takes God to see God as Jesus, as it is Jesus who makes us pure. They hunger for righteousness, resulting in the fruit of flourishing in the blessings (invocation of divine favour, God's empowerment to prosper) of joy, comfort, contentment, refreshment, spiritual prosperity, and peace.

In essence, the Beatitudes reflect the heart of those utterly dependent on God for everything. Mature sons and daughters epitomize the longing for His kingdom to manifest now — *on earth as it is in heaven*. This profound hunger for the kingdom, both present and yet to come, characterizes the truly blessed. These individuals not only recognize their need for God but also actively seek the realization of His promises in the present.

THE BEATITUDES

MATTHEW 5:1-12, AMP

When Jesus saw the crowds, He went up on the mountain; and when He was seated, His disciples came to Him. Then He began to teach them, saying,

"Blessed [spiritually prosperous, happy, to be admired] are the poor in spirit [those devoid of spiritual arrogance, those who regard themselves as insignificant], for theirs is the kingdom of heaven [both now and forever].

"Blessed [forgiven, refreshed by God's grace] are those who mourn [over their sins and repent], for they will be comforted [when the burden of sin is lifted].

"Blessed [inwardly peaceful, spiritually secure, worthy of respect] are the gentle [the kind-hearted, the sweet-spirited, the self-controlled], for they will inherit the earth.

"Blessed [joyful, nourished by God's goodness] are those who hunger and thirst for righteousness [those who actively seek right standing with God], for they will be [completely] satisfied.

"Blessed [content, sheltered by God's promises] are the merciful, for they will receive mercy.

"Blessed [anticipating God's presence, spiritually mature] are the pure in heart [those with integrity, moral courage, and godly character], for they will see God.

"Blessed [spiritually calm with life-joy in God's favor] are the makers and maintainers of peace, for they will [express His character and] be called the sons of God.

"Blessed [comforted by inner peace and God's love] are those who are persecuted for doing that which is morally right, for theirs is the kingdom of heaven [both now and forever].

"Blessed [morally courageous and spiritually alive with life-joy in God's goodness] are you when *people* insult you and persecute you, and falsely say all kinds of evil things against you because of [your association with] Me. Be glad and exceedingly joyful, for your reward in heaven is great [absolutely inexhaustible]; for in this same way they persecuted the prophets who were before you."

For just one day of intimacy with you is like a thousand days of joy rolled into one!
Psalm 84:10, TPT

In the words of C.S. Lewis, "Joy is the Serious Business of Heaven."[1] My mentor, Kenn Gill, studied joy for one year straight, giving over 40 messages titled "Unleashing Joy" during that time. His messages' central theme was that Jesus is the source of all joy. He also explained to me that the word for "blessed" is translated from the Greek word *makarios*, meaning "from a place of joy, a place inside, or a place of spiritual prosperity." As a helpful exercise, try replacing the word "blessed" in Matthew 5:1-12 with the words "from a place of joy" and read the Beatitudes out loud. The kingdom is a kingdom of joy that flows from living out of our inheritance in Christ.

I was listening to a live spontaneous worship set by Cageless Birds, and these words really hit me deeply:

I used to think that I have joy, but now I know that joy has me.[5]

The Gospel Is the Good News of Great Joy

This is the glad message of our happy God. Joy has us because joy is a person! Jesus came so that His joy may be ours through our life union. As we set our affections on Jesus, our experience of joy increases. This sounds crazy, but it's true, and I wouldn't say it if I hadn't experienced it repeatedly. As we deny ourselves and take up our cross, the result is joy! Jesus is our joy, and He has us. Joy is rooted in what we hold dearest and flows from our union with Him. By God's design, we find fulfillment and deep inner joy as we live in service to others and not for ourselves. By faith, joy is always available, even in times of sorrow or losing what we hold dear or significant. Joy allows us to stay in relational connection amid suffering, as joy is more than just an emotion. It is an attitude, a mindset, something that can be cultivated as a value and a manifestation of the kingdom.

Joy is rooted in believing that God will never leave or forsake us. It is a deep or calm delight rooted in what we consider dearest and cherish as most valuable or significant, such as Jesus or a loved one. Joy is a gentleness, a sweetness, and a tenderness. Joy is not fleeting like feelings, circumstances, or happiness. It is a result of living an authentic life, embracing our identity, using our God-given talents to serve others, and living in connection with others and God. When we are authentic, we have nothing to hide and can live in freedom and joy, carefree like a child. Joy is living by faith in the expectation of God's goodness towards us. Living in joy is a great service to God and the world. The joy of the Lord is truly our strength, as His joy is our joy. Joy is the essence and atmosphere of the kingdom expanding within and through us. By faith, we can access this joy from our permanent union with Jesus! Delighting in the Lord and the joy of the Lord are massive weapons of warfare as they usher in the kingdom and displace darkness, resulting in life and vitality. This is how we live above our circumstances as a Spirit-led life.

From Paul, Silas, and Timothy. We send our greetings to you, the congregation of believers in Thessalonica, which is in God the Father and the Lord Jesus Christ. May God's delightful grace and peace rest upon you.
—1 Thessalonians 1:1, TPT

Paul says in 1 Thessalonians 1:1, "May God's delightful grace and peace rest upon you." The usage of *charis*, "grace" in ancient Greek, carries a connotation of something that awakens joy and pleasure. The study notes for this verse in *The Passion Translation* describe how the Greek concept of grace imparts delight, often attached to a strong emotional element.[6]

Laughter and Creativity

Research shows that humour and laughter directly affect creativity. In an article in *Psychology Today* by Moses Ma, we learn that "[laughter] can help people solve problems that demand creative solutions by making it easier to think more broadly and associate ideas/relationships more freely. Recent research shows that people in a lighter mood experience more eureka! moments and greater inspiration."[7]

Laughter is also the business of heaven. Laughter is good medicine and embodies the culture of the kingdom. This is one of the reasons the scriptures state that whoever becomes like a child will be the greatest in the kingdom of heaven. On average, a child laughs 300 times daily, while an adult laughs only 17 times daily.[8]

George Land, Ph.D., was a brilliant general systems scientist. In 1968, he conducted a study to test the creativity of 1,600 three- to five-year-old children using the same test he had created to help NASA select innovative engineers and scientists. The children were retested when they turned ten and once again at 15. The results were astounding. When the children were first tested, 98% were deemed creative. By age ten, that number had dropped to 30%. By age 15, only 12% tested as creative. Finally, when the test was given to 280,000 adults, only 2% tested as creative. "What we have concluded," wrote Land, "is that non-creative behavior is learned."[9]

Lesson: If we want to be innovative, creative adults, we need to embrace the childlike joy of the kingdom.

Conflict of Values

There is a divine tension at play as we enter a kingdom full of power and authority with a posture of dependency and humility. Jesus embodied this from His birth in the humblest of locations, to growing up in Nazareth, working as a carpenter, then riding into Jerusalem on a donkey, and finally, dying a criminal's death nailed to a cross. Everything in the kingdom starts small, like the tiny mustard seed.[10] Starting small is the way of the kingdom, slowly growing and expanding throughout the earth. We let God grow our seeds by His Spirit, in and through us, not by our own efforts. His kingdom is an inside-out, upside-down, last-is-first kingdom, and we have been chosen to be a part of it!

"She has been forgiven of all her many sins. This is why she has shown Me such extravagant love. But those who assume they have very little to be forgiven will love Me very little."
—Luke 7:47, TPT

The above scripture captures the end of an incredible story in the Bible about a Jewish leader inviting Jesus to his house for dinner. During the meal, a woman noted as a sinner enters the house with an alabaster jar filled with expensive perfume equivalent to one year's wages. She kneels at Jesus's feet and immediately begins to weep over His feet. She dries His feet with her long hair. She anoints Jesus with the costly perfume. In response to the judgmental attitudes of the others at the dinner, Jesus responds with the words quoted above.

There was a clear conflict of values present among those at the dinner. The Pharisee was upset to see this woman "wasting" such precious treasure on Jesus. He couldn't see the whole picture. He had no idea that this moment was a prophetic act preparing Jesus for burial and a proclamation of Jesus as the ultimate treasure of far greater worth than silver or gold.

The woman knew she was undeserving. She was deeply in touch with her brokenness and need for forgiveness, while the "good people" in the room were distant and cold. She understood what it meant to truly worship because she knew what it meant to love and be loved by the Son of God. The others kept Jesus at a safe distance. She recognized the beauty and worth of Jesus. They saw just another rabbi. She experienced God in the flesh. They witnessed another guest (a sinner nonetheless) come for dinner. She traded a year's wages for something much more valuable.

No person is considered righteous.[11] Only Jesus is worthy! He is the treasure of heaven, poured out for the undeserving and ungodly, which is each and every one of us. A holy and perfect God died in our place. This is the scandal of the gospel of grace!

Stormie Omartian, a Christian author and musician, explains Jesus's response to our sins as follows:

> I had to understand that God loves my mother as much as He loves me. He loves all people as much as He loves me. He loves the murderer, the rapist, the prostitute, and the thief. And He hates all of their sins as much as He hates ours. He hates murdering, raping, whoring, and stealing as much as He hates pride, gossiping, and unforgiveness. We may sit and compare our sins to other people's and say, "Mine aren't so bad," but God says they all stink, so we shouldn't worry about whose smell[s] the worst. The most important thing to remember when it comes to forgiving is that forgiveness doesn't make the other person right; it makes you free.[12]

All have sinned and fallen short of the glory of God. Those who assume they don't have much to be forgiven for will not experience the fullness of joy of their salvation and the resulting extravagant love and thankfulness for Jesus's forgiveness. Like the sinful woman, we are to pour out our lives on the feet of Jesus. Doing so is the appropriate response to the forgiveness of sins and a sweet-smelling sacrifice of praise.

If you were in the room with the religious leaders of the day, what would you have felt when the woman with the alabaster jar displayed her extravagant love for Jesus? Is there anything in your heart that would keep you from pouring out a gift on Jesus worth a year's wages? What would an extravagant offering to Jesus look like in your own life?

This woman discovered that Jesus was so good, true, righteous, and worthy of it all that she gave an unthinkably extravagant sacrifice. She knew that the good life is only found in Jesus, our All in All, the author of our faith.[13] Have you discovered that Jesus is so good, true, righteous, and completely worthy of it all? Have you tasted and seen that the good life is only found in Him? Have you experienced the author of your faith? If not, it's time to take Him up on His invitation to step into something deeper, sweeter, and more intimate: real relationship and abundant kingdom life.

The Upside-down Kingdom

The Roman Empire valued power and strength alongside immorality, hedonism, and violence. Living with mercy, purity, gentleness, repentance, meekness, and humility was radically counterintuitive to their way of thinking. Jesus raised the bar on sin and exposed the fallen human condition and the problems of the unredeemed human heart. Jesus's solution to a desperate and bankrupt world was not religion but the kingdom of heaven.

Israel was expecting a mighty messiah to overthrow the Roman Empire. They expected a king riding on a white horse. Jesus came on a donkey. They expected a king on an earthly throne, but Jesus chose the cross. They rejected the suffering servant who sacrificed His life for the salvation of mankind and for His kingdom to come to the earth. Those of the kingdom of darkness, the religious leaders of the day, saw Jesus as a threat to their power and had Jesus crucified to save themselves. On the cross, mercifully and with great compassion, Jesus asked the Father to forgive His killers because He knew they were unaware of what they were doing.[14]

In Luke 17:20-21, Jesus tells the Pharisees the kingdom of God had come to earth and was in their midst because the person and presence of Jesus was in their midst. His kingdom was coming in the changed hearts of men. They expected a mighty kingdom invasion, but Jesus came to bring His kingdom forth, one transformed heart at a time. They could not see the kingdom as they had not yet been born again into the kingdom of God through faith in Jesus.

Unlike the kingdoms and systems of this world, Jesus used broken, messy, and seemingly weak people like the 12 disciples, the woman at the well, and others to spread the Gospel while simultaneously rebuking the "righteous" religious leaders whose hearts were cold.

When we come face-to-face with our brokenness, we are at the point where we recognize our sinfulness, spiritual emptiness, and desperate need for forgiveness. Here, we acknowledge that we cannot save ourselves. We can instead choose to turn to God in surrender and dependence. In return, we receive His glorious grace and mercy.

The Beautiful Ways of the Kingdom

In his second letter to the Corinthian church, Paul describes a kingdom not of this world.

> *We may suffer, yet in every season we are always found rejoicing. We may be poor, yet we bestow great riches on many. We seem to have nothing, yet in reality we possess all things.*
> *2 Corinthians 6:10, TPT*

The essential message of the constitution of His kingdom is this: When we can rejoice in even the worst moments of life because we know that Jesus is worth it all, then we have taken up residence in the kingdom. That is where we embrace righteousness, peace, and joy. It is where we receive God's goodness as we go to Him like children, yoking ourselves to King Jesus and not religion.

> **"Come to Me, all who are weary and burdened, and I will give you rest. Take My yoke upon you and learn from Me, for I am gentle and humble in heart, and you will find rest for your souls. For My yoke is comfortable, and My burden is light."**
> *— Matthew 11:28-30, NASB*

We are training to rule and reign now, not just in the afterlife. He provides what we need for life and godliness.[15] In Jesus, we have all authority.[16] In Jesus, we will do even greater things than He did on earth.[17]

God is merciful and gives good gifts to the undeserving. As followers of Jesus, we have access to all things in the kingdom and move into the fullness of our inheritance as we mature. Our journey is progressive as we choose daily to walk in holiness and purity, being shaped into the image of Christ by the power of the Holy Spirit. As we do, we will progressively receive the fullness of life.

THE UPSIDE-DOWN KINGDOM IN SCRIPTURE

We die to live. (John 12:24 and Matthew 10:39)

We are in the world but not of the world. (John 15:19)

Those who lose their life will find it. (Matthew 10:39)

We are saved by grace through faith. (Ephesians 2:8-9)

He who humbles himself will be exalted. (Luke 14:11)

When we give, we receive. (Luke 6:38)

When you claim nothing as your own, everything will be given to you. (Matthew 5:5; 6:33)

We receive freedom to the degree we yield or surrender. (Galatians 5:13-14, Romans 6:22, 1 Peter 2:16)

The greatest is the least. (Luke 9:48)

The first shall be last. (Matthew 20:16)

The greatest is the servant of all the others. (Matthew 20:26)

His power is made perfect in our weakness. (2 Corinthians 12:9-10)

The world's wisdom is foolishness to God. (1 Corinthians 3:19)

The wisdom of God is foolishness to the world. (1 Corinthians 1:25-27)

The one who loves his life loses it, and the one who hates his life in this world will have eternal life. (John 12:25)

The narrow gate leads to eternal life. The wide gate and road lead to destruction. (Matthew 7:13-14)

We live and make decisions by our faith, not by what we see. (2 Corinthians 5:7)

In suffering and pain, we experience His comfort. (2 Corinthians 1:3-7)

Jesus gave up all honour to be gloriously honoured. Jesus gave up all authority in obedience to the Father to receive all authority. Jesus gave up His life to receive eternal life for all who believe. (Philippians 2:6-11)

We are to seek His kingdom first and His righteousness, and then we receive His blessing, health, healing, provision, peace, love, joy, family, power, and authority made available only because of His grace and mercy. (Matthew 6:33, Romans 6:23, Ephesians 2:8)

A LIVING SACRIFICE

St. Francis wrote some of the most poignant words describing what a living sacrifice looks like and how to war from the opposite spirit (if we receive hate, we respond in love). He understood the inside-out, upside-down kingdom! He was a man who sought first God's kingdom and lived under its authority:

The Peace Prayer [1]

Lord, make me an instrument of your peace,
Where there is hatred, let me sow love;
where there is injury, pardon;
where there is doubt, faith;
where there is despair, hope;
where there is darkness, light;
where there is sadness, joy;

O Divine Master grant that I may not so much seek
to be consoled as to console;
to be understood as to understand;
to be loved as to love.
For it is in giving that we receive;
it is in pardoning that we are pardoned;
and it is in dying that we are born to eternal life.
Amen.

I prayed this prayer with Abbe often before bed when she was little. Today, as I read these words, I am reminded of what a living sacrifice looks like as a life fully yielded.[2] Jesus only did what the Father did, which is a perfect model for how we should live.[3] Seek Him, find Him, know Him, and become like Him, a living sacrifice, pure and holy, tried and true. *Father, we ask for the grace to live an abundant kingdom life!*

---

[1] "Peace Prayer," *Loyola Press*, accessed October 13, 2023, https://rb.gy/0483d.
[2] Jeremiah 29:13, 2 Chronicles 15:2, Romans 12:1.
[3] John 5:19.

We are made holy by God's grace. His divine enablement allows us to live behaviorally holy lives exhibited by purity. What is purity? Purity is freedom from sin or that which separates us from God and healthy relationships. Pure water is free from contaminants, just as gold is refined so that it contains no imperfections. Though only God is truly pure, our love of righteousness and purity will make us stand out in a dark world. The more we pursue God and embrace the kingdom, the more we will be refined and made pure. Our lives will reflect His in thoughts, words, and actions. This is one of the reasons we all need to ask for the baptism of fire *daily*. His fire is what separates us from lives of sin and propels us towards lives of holiness.

> *"As for me, I baptize you with water for repentance, but He who is coming after me is mightier than I, and I am not fit to remove His sandals; He will baptize you with the Holy Spirit and fire."*
> —*Matthew 3:11, NASB*

Jesus died so we may live. We cannot be pure without Him. We cannot be lifted up unless we go low. We cannot be forgiven unless we forgive. The list goes on and on, but at the end of the day, as we seek first His kingdom, we take the focus off ourselves and put it back onto Jesus.

Following Jesus is costly. What are you willing to give up to follow Him? What are you *not* willing to give up? What parts of your life have you not surrendered? I can say from experience that every worry, stress, fear, and sin I have released to God has resulted in supernatural peace and restoration. Even all the "good" things I've given up for the sake of the cross or simple obedience have been worth the cost. In the end, they weren't worth as much as I thought. However, He really is worth it all. But, as I have discovered, there is still much to unlearn from my years living in the world's kingdoms.

In March 2021, God gave me a word to "simplify and streamline" my life and remove anything "extra" to create space and capacity. This season of obedience ended up being an incredible gift of freedom. Much of what I said "no" to was good, but it was not what God had for me in this new season. For example, I made significant shifts in my company, like hiring a president, to narrow my active role and remove myself from the day-to-day business activities. I also made minor changes, like unsubscribing from emails, to minimize distractions. In short, I put my house in order. Life is about simple obedience and intimacy with the Lord, as He always knows best.

*   *   *

Father, we ask for the grace to live surrendered lives and release everything back to You with open hands!

1. Bryan Elliott, *More Than Gold*, (Toronto: M46 Publishing, 2023), 227.
2. Steven R. Mosley, *A Tale of Three Virtues*, (Sisters: Multnomah Publishers, 1990), 236.
3. James 1:17.
4. C.S. Lewis Book Club, "The Serious Business of Heaven," *C.S. Lewis Book Club*, accessed October 13, 2023, https://rb.gy/hwc2c.
5. Cageless Birds, *YouTube*, accessed October 14, 2023, https://rb.gy/pi0aw.
6. "1 Thessalonians 1:1," *YouVersion: The Passion Translation*, accessed October 13, 2023, https://rb.gy/89ssy.
7. Moses Ma, "Humor and Laughter Support Creativity," *Psychology Today*, accessed October 16, 2023, https://rb.gy/okycw.
8. Carol Whipple, MS, "Connecting Laughter, Humor and Good Health," *University of Kentucky College of Agriculture, Food and Environment: Cooperative Extension Service*, accessed October 13, 2023, https://rb.gy/mrxc3.
9. Linda Naiman, "Can Creativity be Taught? Here's What the Research Says," *Creativity at Work*, accessed October 13, 2023, https://rb.gy/ounnn.
10. Matthew 17:20.
11. Romans 3:10.
12. Stormie Omartian, "Praying to Forgive Yourself, God, and Others," *FaithGateway*, accessed October 13, 2023, https://rb.gy/qmc5s.
13. Hebrews 12:2.
14. Luke 23:34.
15. 2 Peter 1:3.
16. Matthew 28:18-20.
17. John 14:12-14.

GOD
LOVES YOU

In love, our Heavenly Father picked us

before creating the world.[1] Jesus is in us.[2] The

apostle Paul simply and powerfully reveals the essence of

our life with God in Acts 17:28 where he says, "for in Him we

live and move and exist..." (NASB). He is Immanuel, God with us![3]

We are God's dwelling place. His life is now ours, and His love

is our love. Just like joy, love is also a person. "I used to

think that I had love, but now I know that love

has me."[4]

---

[1] Ephesians 1:4.
[2] Romans 8:10.
[3] Matthew 1:23.
[4] Cageless Birds, *YouTube*, accessed October 14, 2023,
https://rb.gy/pioaw.

Chapter 7: The Greatest Kingdom Principle: The Law of Love

We have come to know [by personal observation and experience], and have believed [with deep, consistent faith] the love which God has for us. God is love, and the one who abides in love abides in God, and God abides continually in him.
—1 John 4:16, AMP

I will never forget an encounter I once had with the Lord. I saw Him on the cross, his head hanging down on his chest near death. His eyes met mine, and I heard Him say, "For you." Jesus died for every single one of us. He died for me and for you.

This encounter left me changed forever. The kind of love Jesus has for us is beyond comprehension. As Jesus said in John 15:13, "**Greater love has no one than this: to lay down one's life for one's friends**." By His grace, we demonstrate our love for God by surrendering our lives to His will, embodying His profound love through our actions, which is *agape*, sacrificial or selfless love.[1]

"So this is my command: Love each other deeply, as much as I have loved you. For the greatest love of all is a love that sacrifices all. And this great love is demonstrated when a person sacrifices his life for his friends."
John 15:12-13, TPT

Love: The Essence of the King's Domain

The King's domain is the realm of love, and we enter this realm of love by faith! With people, there are physical and emotional expressions of love, but God is Spirit; therefore, our love for Him is expressed in the spiritual realm by faith. The Holy Spirit reveals the Father and His love to us. The more we know Him, the more we love Him. We can have faith that He is continually expressing His love and that He is good and faithful, which is always true regardless of encounters and feelings. The more we love Him, the more we trust Him. The more we trust Him, the more we can yield to Him. Humans cannot define love. Only Jesus, who is love, can define love.

The kingdom of God is simple, full of adventure, purpose, and, of course, love. Love is the greatest force in the universe, as it is the essence of God. We receive the Holy Spirit through faith in Jesus, and the Holy Spirit connects us to receive the love of the Father. Jesus lived a life of love on earth and is the perfect model to follow. God created the world so His love could flow in and through His citizens. His banner over us is love, the canopy of heaven.[2] The new command of Jesus is love, which is the ultimate expression of Jesus and His kingdom. We are loved because we exist! There are no conditions or strings attached. As believers, we must activate ourselves as the hands and feet of Jesus and learn practical ways to love Jesus and love *like* Jesus on earth. We are invited to become the beauty of God on earth.

What we carry in our hearts will have expression on earth, so we must guard our hearts.[3] It is important to let God search our hearts regularly for unforgiveness, bitterness, impure motives, offence, etc., so we can quickly repent and return to our Father's open arms for our love connection to be fully restored.[4] To guard our hearts is to not allow them to grow cold or be influenced by the world but to burn from our life union with Jesus as our heart's desire.

Trusting Love: Building Intimacy with God and Others

Love depends on intimacy. Trust is required for intimacy. Without trust (in God or anyone else), we will hold back a part of ourselves. God is 100 percent trustworthy. He will never betray, hurt, or throw us under the bus. He always has our best interest at heart, even amid the fires of suffering. Because He is completely trustworthy, we don't have to withhold anything from Him. We can love Him and be intimate with Him with total vulnerability. Proverbs 3:5 tells us to trust God with ALL our hearts. Love demonstrates itself in trust. We must learn to trust God in our earthly relationships, knowing we can and will sometimes be hurt, lied to, and betrayed. God is always working in relationships, as the kingdom is all about relationships. We are both hurt and healed in relationships, but we grow and become stronger and wiser with every healing. (If you want to know more about love, go read the Song of Songs!)

As we grow, we become rooted and established in love so that we can be sent out. As we grow, we are becoming a conduit of God's love. We become bridge builders of trust with others based on integrity, consistency, and perseverance through challenges together. Trust is the foundation of relationships, and relationships are built at the speed of trust. Orphans find it very difficult to trust as they have a distorted view of God, whereas sons are filled with trust, knowing their good and perfect Heavenly Father. Sonship demonstrates dependency on God, which requires trust. Pastor and speaker Brian Orme often says, "Faith is dependency on display." It is moving out of our strength and into His.

Kenn Gill teaches that faith and trust are a two-sided coin. We need both, as it is our trust in God that allows us to live out our faith. The Bible serves as the foundation for trust, as God never changes. Agape love is the motivating force behind our works, and trust activates our faith. As we choose to trust, the grace of God comes. When we focus on what we will get rather than on the King, it is easy to be slowly pulled in the wrong direction. This is why Jesus made it very clear that we are to seek first His kingdom and His righteousness, and then we are granted access to the riches of His glory.[5] And what should be in our hearts?

*   *   *

Father, we ask for the grace to love you!

Love! Love is our greatest weapon! Love, love, love! Love loves to love!

God is love!

WHAT IS LOVE?

God is love, and His love for us is everlasting.
(1 John 4:8 and Jeremiah 31:3)

Our Father gave His only Son as a perfect love sacrifice to
restore our relationship with Him for eternity. (John 3:16)

Jesus demonstrated His love for us by sacrificing Himself for you and
me. There is no greater love than to lay down one's life for his friend.
(John 15:13)

The Holy Spirit demonstrated His love for us by choosing to make His home
within us. (1 Corinthians 6:19-20)

Jesus commands us to love others in the same way He loves us. (John 15:12)

We demonstrate our love for Jesus by keeping His commandments.
(John 14:15)

The first fruit produced by the Holy Spirit within you is love.
(Galatians 5:22-23)

We are to abide in faith, hope, and love; *but the most
important is love.* (1 Corinthians 13:13)

If you don't love, you don't know God. (1 John 4:8)

As you delight in Him, there is a natural flow of His river in you that will eventually flow out of you to others. He loves you. He created you. He did a great job! Enjoy God. Zero pressure. Loving others is not about pleasing God or needing to fulfill a religious obligation. While Jesus commands us to love others, it is also a privilege. We get to love others by partnering with God as His sons and daughters.

And may the Lord increase your love until it overflows toward one another and for all people, just as our love overflows toward you.
—1 Thessalonians 3:12, TPT

I used to think the opposite of love was hate or indifference, but it is selfishness (self-focus). What gets in the way of love? Ungodly beliefs, unhealed wounds, and areas needing deliverance can all lead to guarded or hardened hearts towards God and others. As humans, we love others the way we have been loved, which is why experiencing the perfect love of Jesus is life changing. It is the revelation that we are loved by God that casts out all fear and helps us love righteously.[6]

When Love Is Sin

Believe it or not, love can be sin. When? First, when we love something created in an idolatrous way. Second, when we love the world's ways. And third, when love arises from "the desires of the flesh, the desires of the eyes, [and] the pride of life."[7] If we love objects, people, or habits in a way that deviates from Scripture, we find ourselves in a form of love that is sin. As God is love, He alone can help us love righteously. Any other sort of love or source of love is an open door to sin because God will never go against His word.

Sinful love always leads to death. Pure love always leads to life. Tragically, if we do not humble ourselves and our will to God's ways and repent, He will eventually give us over to the lusts of our flesh.

The love of Jesus is agape, which is God's sacrificial, unconditional love for us. The source of all agape love is God. It is God who increases our love to overflow into the world as a fruit of the Spirit. We primarily love Jesus by following the new command.[8] By loving one another, everyone will know that we are His disciples, especially when we show love when we don't feel like it! In the war against darkness, love is our most powerful weapon—love wins because love never fails![9]

The Generosity of Love: Embracing Others-focused Living

We do not become less self-focused by trying to be less self-focused but by changing our focus to meet the needs of others, the fruit of a surrendered life. Those motivated by the flesh only pursue what benefits themselves, but the mind set on the Spirit finds life, our source of love.[10] As we love others, particularly when it is difficult, we love Jesus and naturally become less self-focused and more God-focused. We take up our cross as we choose this others-focused sacrificial love. In return, the love of Jesus is directly and indirectly poured back on us through His Spirit and others. The key to connecting with people is to care for them, which happens through relationships. The word "communicate" is of Latin origin, meaning "commune-I-care." To have friends, one must first be friendly. This loving care begins with the gift of being fully present, a rare gift of honour, and a practice of actively noticing everything about that person. As I naturally have a high sense of urgency, I need to be even more aware of distraction or being ruled by hurry as a strength overplayed becomes a weakness. Presence is a practice of love.

Think of the woman who poured perfume at Jesus's feet. Her gift was an outpouring of the love she had received from Him. The more we receive the love of Jesus, the more love we have to pour out on others and the more love we experience. We can only give what we receive from Jesus. The more we open ourselves and walk in His ways, the more He will pour out through us. We do the loving, God does the changing!

When we act with forgiveness, generosity, mercy, etc., we will receive the same in return. This gives insight into the golden rule from Luke 6:31, **"Treat people the same way you want them to treat you"** (NASB). What we do for another comes back to us, multiplied, good or bad. Can you see how the kingdom of God powerfully expands as these truths are embraced and lived out? The greater overcomes the lesser. Light overcomes darkness. Love overcomes fear. Always, completely.

Practical Steps to Love Like Jesus

When we experience God's love, we naturally love others the way He loves us. The source of our love is our life union with Jesus. When we do not love others, it means we have temporarily lost connection with the vine, Jesus! Remember, we are all branches of one vine, and the branches are totally and utterly dependent on the vine (the position of sonship). Jesus, the vine, is our source of life and love, our All in All. The branch does not toil to produce fruit. Fruit is the result of being connected to the vine, and love is the primary fruit of the Spirit.

God mainly works through people and the prayers of His people. We can love Jesus directly by loving other people who have received Jesus. As believers, we are to be the hands, feet, and voice of Jesus to demonstrate love to all the world. When we receive His Son as our Lord and Saviour, we become living gateways for the King of Glory to come through our lives through love. God chose to make His home within us, transforming us into the Holy of Holies by the power of the Holy Spirit. The government of God is love, and our authority (rule and reign *on earth as it is in heaven*) is in the realm of love. Our love for others is rooted in thankfulness as a response to God's love. I like to say that faith is the currency of heaven, and faith expresses itself through "boots-on-the-ground" love.

Love never stops loving…
—1 Corinthians 13:8, TPT

BOOTS-ON-THE-GROUND LOVE

As ambassadors of Jesus, we are to make the supernatural love of Jesus practical and tangible. "Boots-on-the-ground" love looks like this:

◊ Spending time with Jesus and knowing Him so that you can be Jesus to others

◊ Being truly present with yourself and others

◊ Loving others without an agenda or trying to change them (leave that to God)

◊ Carrying one another's burdens

◊ Caring for people in practical ways

◊ Enjoying life (happiness is a gift to others) and prioritizing the well-being of others

◊ Being open and approachable

◊ Creating human connection through vulnerability

◊ Moving in compassion and mercy

◊ Loving Jesus by loving other believers

◊ Providing for those in need as the hands and feet of Jesus

◊ Practising humility and kindness by thinking of others before yourself (Remember, God always comes first!)

◊ Honouring others well, recognizing and calling out their unique makeup, value, and gifts

◊ Discover peoples' love languages and apology languages

◊ Communicating our needs to set up others for success to serve and love us well

◊ Making time for people

◊ Inquiring and listening to discover the needs of others to bless and love well

◊ Releasing grace, forgiveness, and blessing to those who hurt us

◊ Showing love by setting boundaries to provide clarity, safety, and security

◊ Being slow to anger, quick to forgive, and blessing those who have mistreated us

◊ Overlooking an offense (excluding abuse) and blessing them

◊ Believing the best about others

◊ Refusing to engage in gossip or slander

◊ Being aware to let others see Jesus through you because Christ lives within you

◊ Looking into the mirror and gazing into the eyes of Jesus

◊ Asking Jesus to shine within you

This is living in God's kingdom—NOW! If people can grow in love like this, imagine how much more the perfect love of Jesus is for us! When we follow Jesus's command to love one another deeply, our emotions will eventually follow.

God never stops loving because He *is* love. When we feel love, we are feeling God through the person of the Holy Spirit. When God puts someone in our hearts with a feeling of compassion or love, however subtle, He has something for us to deliver to them. When someone comes to my mind, I no longer ignore it as a random, meaningless thought. The Lord will reveal He wants me to give my time, encouragement, wisdom, or provision for a need. Sometimes, He wants me to pray for the person. As I become more aware and more intentional towards listening to these prompts from the Holy Spirit, I can feel myself more automatically turning my love switch "on."

There are times when I feel a wave of God's compassion or love and am prompted to send a text or voice recording or to call or arrange a meet-up. Every time I move in obedience and let God's love flow through me, I am amazed at what He does, not just for the person but for me! Whenever I love others, I am filled by God's love. It is a gift that goes both ways. Now, when I may feel a little down, I love to ask God, "Who can I bless?" As He brings people to mind, I send notes of blessing or encouragement, and by the end of the day, my spirits have lifted. Blessing others ultimately blesses us.[11] I have discovered that as I encourage others, I am encouraged, and as I strengthen others, I am strengthened. This is the kingdom of God!

If our devotion is to the cause of humanity, we will be quickly defeated and broken-hearted, since we will often be confronted with a great deal of ingratitude from other people. But if we are motivated by our love for God, no amount of ingratitude will be able to hinder us from serving one another.[12]

The Honour to Love Others

Loving others the way He loves us is not an obligation but an honour. We *get* to obey Him as we are now His friends. We obey because we trust Him. We yield because we trust Him. The more we get to know Him, the more we want to know Him. It's why we were created as His family, to be loved and to love. To know Him and to make Him known. Now, don't get me wrong, I have chickened out many times when it comes to following through on the promptings of the Holy Spirit to love others the way He wants me to. It takes courage, trust, and vulnerability to do what is uncomfortable. As we grow in sonship, we become more like Jesus, who perfectly obeyed the Father. Jesus faced much rejection, but He was rooted and established in the love of our Father. Thankfully, the more you obey, the more courageous and bolder you will become. It is like a muscle. The more you love, the easier loving becomes.

We may feel the compassion and love of God for a stranger when walking down the street. You may be reading, brushing your teeth in the morning, at work, or reading in a coffee shop when God highlights someone. When He does, there is always a purpose in it. As we practice listening to the Holy Spirit, we learn to become sensitive to His prompting (just as Jesus immediately did what the Father directed).[13]

When I am travelling and out of my normal element, I tend to be more sensitive to the leading of the Holy Spirit simply because my awareness is heightened to my surroundings. Routine and familiarity tend to lull us into complacency, and we can lose our awe and wonder of all of God's creation. We can grow in being intentional about how we live and engage in life so we can raise our awareness.

I start almost every day in silence with the Lord and often ask, "What do You want to do today? Who is in Your heart?" I am learning to leave "margin" in my life, making time and space by simplifying my schedule and regularly prioritizing time with the Lord. My heart position allows me to take time with the Lord, respond to whatever adventure He has planned for me that day, and live from a place of rest.

Recently, Bryn and I went to church with one of Bryn's friends, who (unbeknownst to me) has been struggling and trying to turn her life around. Bryn has slowly and patiently been loving her back to life. After church, the three of us decided to have lunch together.

On the way to lunch, I felt a sense of compassion and love from God for Bryn's friend. The Lord gave me three specific ways He wanted me to bless her. One of the ways was to stop at a cash stop and get $500. After lunch, I passed her the money, and she instantly began to sob, which, from my perspective, seemed like an extreme response. However, I continued to present the other two blessings from the Lord. These included setting up an investment opportunity to give her hope for the future. I also offered to cover the cost of going through an inner healing program as she was visibly struggling deeply.

Later that day, Bryn told me that her friend was incredibly stressed as she didn't have all the money for rent (which happened to be exactly $500 short) and, earlier in the morning, was praying to God for help when an unexplainable peace came over her. When Bryn told me this, we both started to laugh and give thanks to God. I finally understood the reason for her reaction to the gift. God is good! Though I had no context for what Bryn's friend was going through prior to my offerings, my obedience to His prompting was a blessing to God, myself, and, of course, Bryn's friend.

Over the last few years, I have learned to move when God stirs my heart because, in those moments, I know God has a specific job for me to complete with Him. God wants us to be a channel of His love. A channel is not a container. It is a conduit for a river. HE is the RIVER, the source of all life. So, jump in His river and let the water flow through you!

Then the angel showed me the river of the water of life, flowing with water clear as crystal, continuously pouring out from the throne of God and of the Lamb. The river was flowing in the middle of the street of the city, and on either

side of the river was the Tree of Life, with its twelve kinds of ripe fruit according to each month of the year. The leaves of the Tree of Life are for the healing of the nations.
Revelation 22:1-2, TPT

Embracing the Trinity of Love

The government of God is founded on love. Love is the royal law of heaven. God dwells within us, and His love moves through us in the fullness of the Trinity (the Father, Son, and Holy Spirit). The Trinity is not a term used in the scriptures but emerged as early theologians attempted to express the triune nature of God. It is used to describe the Godhead, as God is three distinct persons in one: the Father, the Son, and the Holy Spirit.

So often, the Father, Son, and Holy Spirit are a total mystery and will always be to a certain extent. However, as I wrote these sections, I received new clarity on how I interact with each member of the Trinity. When I am engaged in inner-heart healing, it is Jesus who shows up and engages with me in places of past pain or current confusion. When journaling with the Lord in the morning, I often hear the Father whispering messages to my heart. And as I live, write, and work, I sense the Holy Spirit continually with me, highlighting things, guiding, comforting, giving ideas, and more. Have you experienced each member of the Trinity? Take some time to reflect and consider your relationship with the Father, Jesus, and the Holy Spirit.

God is always speaking through His unique language in and through life. God is always present. Why? Because God is love.[11] The gift of our living, loving God is that we get to encounter His love through His presence every minute of every day.

Your calling is to fulfill the royal law of love as given to us in this Scripture: "You must love and value your neighbor as you love and value yourself!" For keeping this law is the noble way to live.
James 2:8, TPT

We can experience the love of the Trinity in the simple things of life. I recently had a weekend where I prepared a great dinner and turned on good music with the intent of setting aside time to enjoy God. I was filled with gratitude for the blessings of the food and time with Him. I always joke that food is my love language, so getting into the zone was easy. It was a time of great peace and joy, talking with and experiencing the Lord's powerful and life-giving presence.[15]

Jesus invites us to bring Him our burdens so we can fully experience His goodness and life more abundantly. In times of suffering, my experience of the Trinity has been different. I have suffered with Jesus, where I enter His suffering and He into mine. When we go to Jesus in difficult times rather than indulge in false or unhealthy comforts and distractions, we are blessed with His comfort. It makes all the difference when we choose to trust in our good and perfect Heavenly Father, knowing He is sovereign and loves us more than we could ever imagine. We can trust that He is producing gold in us through the process.[16]

Love is the ultimate way to experience God! Where there is love, there is God. The King of Glory, the Creator of the universe, the Maker of heaven and earth, is always available and continually drawing us into a loving relationship. The King is love and His kingdom is relational. The kingdom of God is the presence of Jesus and Jesus will be where He is desired and adored. You are the object of His affection. He wants to be your friend. He wants you to know His heart and to enjoy Him before anything else. This is exactly what we were created for, and it is the key to an abundant life on earth. This should blow your mind! Thank you, Jesus!

Love Is the Answer in Good Times and Bad

In my life, I've learned more about love in the darkest of times than in the happy times. Life is messy, and God often does His best work amid our messes, pains, and sufferings. That is when we become most desperate for Him. After my oldest daughter was murdered, my younger daughter, Bryn, continued on a very dark path and was almost impossible to connect with. She was depressed. Anxious. Addicted to many different drugs. Mentally ill. Suicidal. It was the most challenging season of my life (and hers), and I leaned on the Holy Spirit like never before.

As I experienced the Father's love for me, I was able to give it to Bryn, regardless of her responses. Like in the parable of the Prodigal Son, I was able to await with arms open wide at every opportunity, continually inviting her into my life.[17] There were ups and downs and times of deep discouragement. There were times when I didn't represent the Father's heart well, but God showed up anyway. I didn't realize the deep work God was doing until we were out of the darkness, and she chose to start living her life for Jesus. Entering into the sufferings of Jesus transforms us as we experience God's love through it. God uses everything for our good![18] God has infinite ways to answer prayer, but He often uses people. Many times, as entitlement has gripped my heart, I have prayed for a heart of gratitude. Almost immediately, God puts me in touch with people who vulnerably share their deep life struggles, which promptly snaps me out of the fog.

Is your heart open, sensitive, and willing to be an answer for someone? Are you willing to let God use your voice, hands, and feet? Are you willing to be empowered by the Holy Spirit? When you feel the love of God, you can be assured God is on the move and ready to move through you. This turns every day into an adventure with God. We don't need to be perfect to be used by the Holy Spirit. God only needs our "yes," our obedience, and our devotion. You've probably heard it said: "God doesn't call the qualified, but He qualifies the called." He is looking for a living sacrifice. Out of a place of dependence and surrender, we get to put God on display to the world, in and through our lives. We get to glorify God in our weakness and brokenness.

I have been crucified with Christ; and it is no longer I who live, but Christ lives in me; and the life which I now live in the flesh I live by faith in the Son of God, who loved me and gave Himself up for me.
—Galatians 2:20, NASB

How can you be an answer to prayer?

- Be sensitive to God's love and respond accordingly.
- Show up when you feel the Holy Spirit prompting you to show up.
- Choose the most excellent way, the path God has laid out for you, and in love.
- The principle of love empowers us to live out the rest of God's principles. Through Him, we become love in action to the fullest. We all have been given a measure of love.

We love, because He first loved us.
1 John 4:19, KJV

As we receive more of the love of God, the principles become natural as we become increasingly heavenly-minded. I encourage you to pray daily, "Lord, enlarge my heart to receive Your love, baptize me in Your love, and for the grace to love well." Remember, love never fails.[19]

1. *Agape* is a Greek word used in the New Testament to describe love in its highest form. Agape love is sacrificial, costly, unconditional, puts others above ourselves, and brings healing, just as the love Christ displayed on the cross brings redemption.
2. Song of Solomon 2:4.
3. Proverbs 4:23.
4. Psalm 139:23-24.
5. Matthew 6:33.
6. 1 John 4:18.
7. 1 John 2:16.
8. John 13:34.
9. 1 Corinthians 13:8.
10. Romans 8:5-6.
11. Genesis 12:2.
12. Oswald Chambers, "The Determination to Serve," *My Utmost For His Highest*, accessed October 13, 2023, https://utmost.org/the-determination-to-serve/.
13. John 5:19.
14. 1 John 4.8.
15. It doesn't take much investigation in Scripture to see how much God values food and feasting together with His people. Check out Luke 14 for a few examples.
16. 1 Peter 1:6-7.
17. Luke 15:11-32.
18. Romans 8:28.
19. 1 Corinthians 13:8.

BLESSING YOUR SPIRIT

Often, our souls are overfed and become dominant, overshadowing our neglected spirits. This hinders us from being guided by the Spirit and fulfilling God's will. According to God's design, our bodies are meant to submit to our souls, and our souls are meant to submit to our spirit, which is in union with Jesus. This alignment allows the fruit of the Spirit to flourish in our lives, benefiting others by bringing heaven to earth. This process accelerates healing and restoration as we grow in our true identity and become aware of our completeness in Christ, free from wounds, lies, and deception. Satan works through deception, and when we believe a lie, we come under its influence. However, as our spirits soar in truth and revelation, and as we yield fully to God, we release the life of Jesus into the earth.

I first discovered the practice of "Blessing Your Spirit" through Arthur Burke and Sylvia Gunter's book, *Blessing Your Spirit: With the Blessings of Your Father and the Names of God.* Their ministry offers various tools and resources. They provide a rich collection of truth and blessings for our spirits, which instill identity, legitimacy, purpose, and sonship, among other key elements of who God calls us to be.

Ultimately, "Blessing Your Spirit" is designed to bring healing, restoration, and empowerment, facilitating a life of faith, hope, and love in deeper connection with God. We have the power to bless our spirits or the spirits of others, whether in person or not. We can even bless a baby's spirit while still in the womb, and we can nurture and empower our children's spirits, especially those facing challenges, even if we are not physically present with them. This practice can be engaged face-to-face with spouses, friends, and family or during solitary prayer times empowering everyone to shine!

One of the greatest signs of the kingdom is celebration! Sometimes, during my quiet time with the Lord, I join with the kingdom and simply call forth my daughter's spirit and celebrate her. I speak words such as, "I celebrate the day you were born. God absolutely loves what He created, and so do I. I celebrate being your father and honor you as my daughter. I love how you engage and love people. I celebrate your unique gifts and abilities and appreciate the way you apply them at work or in making others feel seen and cherished on special occasions, etc."

THE GREATEST KINGDOM PRINCIPLE: THE LAW OF LOVE

Love is not just a principle among many. It is *the* fundamental principle that empowers believers to live out the other principles of God's kingdom. The kingdom of God is a realm of love, and we enter this realm by faith expressing itself through love.

Father, we ask for the grace to receive Your love and to love others!

QUESTIONS FOR REFLECTION

What did the Holy Spirit reveal to you through *The Greatest Kingdom Principle: The Law of Love?* How can you apply this to your life?

_____

_____

_____

_____

How have you experienced God's love in your life?

_____

_____

_____

Who is God calling you to bless with a demonstration of His love today?

_____

_____

_____

QUESTIONS FOR REFLECTION *(continued)*

Who has God used recently to display His love towards you?

_____

_____

_____

_____

Notes

_____

_____

_____

_____

_____

_____

_____

_____

_____

_____

_____

_____

_____

_____

_____

_____

Chapter 8: The Kingdom Principle of Thanksgiving

You can pass through His open gates with the password of praise. Come right into His presence with thanksgiving. Come bring your thank offering to Him and affectionately bless His beautiful name! For Yahweh is always good and ready to receive you. He's so loving that it will amaze you—so kind that it will astound you! And He is famous for his faithfulness towards all. Everyone knows our God can be trusted, for He keeps His promises to every generation!
Psalm 100:4-5, TPT

Living in Thankfulness: Nurturing Connection with God and Others Through Gratitude

Thanksgiving is present throughout the Bible. It is a powerful kingdom key for us. It infuses us with strength and encourages us in every way, every day. We can be eternally thankful that we are now and forever kingdom citizens. We have the privilege of living in victory above our circumstances. As we give thanks for our daily needs being met, we seek first His kingdom by acknowledging God as our provider and Lord. Thankfulness is the gateway to the awesome presence of God! Even the word "praise" can be translated as "thanks to God." The more we lift our thanks to the Lord, the more our hearts open to receive all He is and all He has for us.

In everything give thanks; for this is the will of God for you in Christ Jesus.
—1 Thessalonians 5:18, NASB

When we learn to give thanks in all circumstances, hope and gratitude fortify our hearts. What you carry in your heart has an expression on earth. A grateful heart produces humility and generosity while destroying pride and fear of lack. A grateful heart guards against entitlement, self-pity, and victimization. A grateful heart invites the presence of God (the wellspring and source of all life) and opens our creative thinking and creative expressions on earth.

"Whoever exalts himself shall be humbled, and whoever humbles himself shall be exalted."
—Matthew 23:12, NASB

God exalts the humble, and it is the humble who receive the promises of God. To humble oneself is to live a life of love, a life of self-sacrifice in service to others. God created us physiologically to be grateful. Giving thanks produces oxytocin, a hormone that helps us bond with whom we are thanking.[1] We bond with the object of our affection. As we give thanks to the Lord, we are literally bonding to our Creator. The greater the thankfulness in our hearts, the greater our revelation of God's goodness, the greater our thankfulness, and so on.

When we are in a state of gratitude, we activate the relational part of our brain, which allows us to form connections. Unsurprisingly, this is why so many inner healing sessions begin with gratitude to usher us into an awareness of Emmanuel, God with us. Practising awareness is key. Knowing that God is always present, we become more sensitive and in tune with all the ways God communicates and reveals Himself constantly.

Encountering God Everywhere: A Journey of Divine Awareness

Recently, my daughter Bryn and I were asked to submit answers to a few questions for a TV show. We intentionally answered and submitted them separately.

One of the questions was: Where and how do you experience God?

> **Bryn's answer:** *I experience God in everything I do. Whether that's talking to friends or in prayer, focusing on Him. I see God in believers and unbelievers. I see God in families and in children. I see God in nature and in beautiful things. At this point in my walk with the Lord, it would be hard for me not to see Him. He literally made everything and everyone. Even people who feel they are far from God can teach us about the heart of God in different ways. Seeing different cultures and expressions of diversity shows me God. You can learn about God through anyone, anytime. Not just mature believers.*

> **Bryan's answer:** *Jesus is All in All. Literally everywhere. The Word of God is alive and active. His Word is a place of encounter. Jesus is the living Word, the Word made flesh. His kingdom is within, our indwelling God. His kingdom is at hand. My office is a place of encountering the Lord. A place of worship and prayer (with a prayer room) and regular time with the Lord create a place of His presence. Observing His creation. Living in constant awareness of God, seeing Him in people, hearing His voice, a recent multi-week Holy Spirit adventure, experiencing Him in the good times and in suffering, the highs and lows of life. In Him, we live, move, and have our being. Where there is life, there is God. Where there is love, there is God. In the suffering, there is God. In all of creation, there is God! To be still and know that I am Lord, stillness, especially in the early morning. Friendship with the Lord of the universe, thankfulness, listening to the birds, watching the sky, sunrise, and sunsets, being by the water and in all of nature, living in awareness of Him and all His creation, billboards, journaling, listening, talking with Him, encounters, seeing Him in others regardless of who they are. Simply talking with God as my friend.*

I was pleasantly surprised at how similar our answers were and the broadness of our awareness of His presence. We have simply been practising living in awareness of His presence. Of course, we both go through times when we don't sense or feel Him in our daily walk, but the truth is that God is always present. We can enter into an experience with God anytime. He is always speaking, but we must be attuned to His voice.

The Language of God: Recognizing His Voice in the Diversity of His Creation

> *"My sheep listen to My voice, and I know them, and they follow Me."*
> —John 10:27, NASB

Voice can also be translated as "language," meaning God can speak in the still, small voice or the "language of God" in many ways using all of creation. He will speak in ways that are unique and meaningful to each person because He knows everything about you.

God's life and presence permeate all creation. He is omnipresent as He is everywhere, all the time. However, much more is available; the Holy Spirit and His manifest presence are transformational and life-giving! The kingdom of God is an inside-out process where internal transformation paves the way for external renewal.

With the presence and guidance of the Holy Spirit, we experience the righteousness, peace, and joy of His kingdom, which is beyond mere rules. For believers, the Spirit of God is never distant. He is living inside of us, and He is our friend. Our ability to see and hear Him is a process within us that is continually unfolding. Sometimes, we call seasons of His seeming silence "wilderness seasons." Such seasons reveal the illusion of separateness and expose what needs to change in our lives. Separateness does not exist. However, God can be silent in how He typically communicates with you, but He is still present (remember, He is always present through His Word, the Bible). When God seems silent, I typically stay on the same path and reflect on what He has said before because He may have already spoken. Once again, He is always speaking in His Word! There are always great purposes in the ways of God. Thinking God is far away when we don't experience Him with our physical senses is a sign of our carnal desires. We are to live by faith. The truth is that God is always closer than any person could ever be. Our relationship with God is spiritual, not fleshy or selfish, but focused on God. Intimacy with God cannot be based on encounters or feelings, but on faith. You are never alone!

We are meant to have divine encounters and incredible spiritual experiences filled with awe and wonder, entered into by faith and love. We are called to be Spirit-led, inviting Him into our thoughts, imagination, and daily moments, and to continually encounter God, living in awareness of His presence in every detail of life. This is life in God's kingdom *now*. They are also practical, as God designed us to co-labour with Him in everything, all the time. When we hunger for more, it is the Holy Spirit working in us. By our renewed minds, we are enabled to grow in the truth of God and the faith to live in awareness of Him in our daily lives. This is the awakening of our spiritual senses as we begin to see things from God's perspective. We are designed to live in heavenly realities.

For in Him we live and move and exist.
—Acts 17:28a, NASB

God wants our faith to grow continually. He wants us to live aware of His presence. He wants us to have faith that He loves us, that He will never leave us, that we live in Him. He wants us to walk in a faith that has us continually talking to Him and listening to Him. This is an unshakable foundation that we can build. In this place of faith, we can experience God and know Him better.

By repenting, changing the way we think, turning from our sins, and placing our faith in Jesus, we receive the gift of salvation by faith alone. This is the greatest gift of unimaginable proportions. We've been offered eternal life with heaven as our eternal home! This understanding provides the foundation for our thankfulness. God's great mercy that holds back what we do deserve and the great grace that gives us what we don't deserve are both incredible reasons to give thanks.

Your spiritual roots go deeply into His life as you are continually infused with strength, encouraged in every way. For you are established in the faith you have absorbed and enriched by your devotion to Him!
—Colossians 2:7, TPT

The footnotes to this verse in *The Passion Translation* say that the word "devotion" in the original Greek means "overflowing with gratitude."[2] Other translations say "abounding" with thanksgiving. When we understand that all we are and all we have come from God alone, thankfulness is the only natural response.

Ultimately, thankfulness reminds us of whom we depend on. If we continue to stay in a thankful, calm, meditative state, our entire brain lights up and becomes active.[3] In addition, when we are in this calm state, the energy field from the heart changes dramatically, and our heartbeat decreases and becomes steady.[4] All this to say, when we choose gratitude and love, even the photons (a fundamental particle of light) emanating from our being dramatically increase, just like turning up the volume.[5]

Finally, as our gratitude increases, our joy increases. Many studies have shown living in gratitude promotes health and well-being by improving our immune system, reducing inflammation, and increasing our ability to rest.[6] In fact, it is impossible to be happy without being grateful.[7]

Overflowing with Gratitude: Strengthening Our Bond with God and Others

As we continue to give thanks, we are naturally strengthening our bond with God and growing in awareness of our communion or oneness with Him! We deserved eternal separation from God—but Jesus! We had a problem that was infinite and eternal, impossible to overcome—but Jesus! God sacrificed His one and only Son, who suffered in our place, took the full penalty for our sins and died on our behalf to reconcile us with the Father. EVERYTHING we have that is good is from our Heavenly Father, the Father of lights. When someone smiles at you, shows you compassion, gives you a gift, or you create a special memory with a friend, receive it as a gift from your Father.

Every good thing given and every perfect gift is from above, coming down from the Father of lights, with whom there is no variation or shifting shadow.
—James 1:17, NASB

EVERYTHING good involves the Father. We are to overflow with gratitude constantly and abundantly. Thankfulness is a lifestyle. It's not a moment or opportunity. Giving thanks is like building muscle. We start small and work out to expand thanksgiving in our lives as we live, as we work, in times with family, at meals, in nature, and in quiet. When someone does something for us or loves us, it is from God. When something good happens, it is from God. It is much more difficult to pray if we are not grateful. However, the more we give thanks, the more reasons we see to be thankful. Thankfulness begets thankfulness!

It is hard to compare or envy a person when we are grateful for them. It is much more difficult to feel or experience lack when we are thankful for the little things. It is much easier to care for our bodies when we are thankful for them. Thankfulness shifts us into fruitfulness! God designed us for gratitude and praise.

Sacrifice of Praise: Embracing Gratitude in the Midst of Challenges

Be faithful to pray as intercessors who are fully alert and giving thanks to God.
— Colossians 4:2, TPT

At Flō, a group of believers who gathered to pray each morning started to declare "Praise the Lord!" whenever good news or bad news came. We did so to consciously declare our trust and faith in God, as both are inextricably connected. Not long ago, we had a stretch of challenging situations that we met by praising the Lord despite negative news, or what believer and author Barry Maracle often refers to as "circumstantial evidence in the temporary realm." When we finally received positive news, one team member shouted, "Praise the Lord!" Another said, "It's great to be able to praise Him for good news for a change," and everyone laughed. Shouting out "Praise the Lord!" literally changes the atmosphere and brings His joy and peace, regardless of the challenge. We were learning to unlock the power of prophetic thankfulness, transforming circumstances with praise.

Now faith is the certainty of things hoped for, a proof of things not seen.
— Hebrews 11:1, NASB

The atmosphere of faith, the *certainty of things hoped for and the proof of things not seen,* rises as we choose to praise and give thanks in all circumstances. When circumstantial evidence in the temporary realm is painful, difficult, or not as we expected, we can trade our expectations for thanksgiving and offer a sacrifice of praise that glorifies God. When suffering, we get to make a sacred offering, a sacrifice of praise, knowing that God is producing something for eternity. Our praise is always anchored in the goodness of God. When we read about Paul and Silas in Acts 16:25-44, who were in prison and had just been beaten, we can take courage. These two men were giving thanks and singing hymns of praise despite their temporary circumstances. They actively released the power of God. In the end, not only were they freed, but the jailor and His entire household were saved.

Prayer with thanksgiving helps keep our motives pure and in alignment with the will of God. This is how we acknowledge our trust in God and activate our faith before seeing the answer to our prayers. One way we can do this is by giving thanks in advance for the promises of God we find in the Bible. Giving thanks in alignment with His Word and nature is a prophetic and powerful form of prayer. Jesus demonstrates the power of a thankful heart in prayer in Matthew 14:18-21. With the five loaves and fish, Jesus gave thanks. Externally, this made no sense. What was there to give thanks for? A boy's lunch when thousands were hungry? However, by faith, He chose to give thanks for not enough, trusting that God would provide. Just as the loaves and fish were multiplied to feed the crowd, our resources are multiplied for the benefit of others.

Directing Our Soul: Cultivating Thankfulness in Every Circumstance

> Praise God from Whom all blessings flow
> Praise Him all creatures here below
> Praise Him above ye heavenly host
> Praise Father, Son and Holy Ghost[8]

Thankfulness is a choice more than a feeling. God made us in such a way that our subconscious focus and feelings follow our conscious choices to give thanks, which is backed up by neuroscience. When we declare truth or thankfulness, an instruction is sent to the subconscious mind to make it a reality as what we focus on expands.[9]

> *Bless the Lord, my soul, And all that is within me, bless His holy name.*
> —*Psalm 103:1, NASB*

God gave us emotions to express and experience life. King David understood these principles. He experienced many trials and freely expressed his feelings and hurt to God in the Psalms. However, he learned to direct his soul (mind, will, and emotions) to praise God. Following his example aligns our perspective with God's perspective. Thankfulness also produces humility, which allows us to gain new perspectives. We begin to see and experience life differently, with a thankful heart in humility and peace. In thankfulness, we use our will to exercise our choice to live with gratitude, even when it's hard.

Pause, take a moment, and give thanks.

Is it free-flowing, or is it difficult?

The Joy of Repentance: Rediscovering Thankfulness in God's Presence

If giving thanks is difficult, ask the Holy Spirit to reveal what is in the way. For me, at times, entitlement or comparison may be the thankfulness thief. There are other times when I've focused on what I don't have, what I've missed out on, what I've lost, or even on my good goals, which have stolen my awareness of my present blessings and what I do have. These thankful thieves also steal our peace and joy. When revealed, I repent (change my thinking) and return to the arms of my Heavenly Father, and thankfulness bubbles up again. For others, unforgiveness, bitterness, self-pity, victimization, or the ugly and exhausting chains of the spirits of legalism and performance may be blocking thankfulness. I love the wonderful lifestyle of repentance. So simple. So powerful. So freeing!

I encourage you to remember all the things God has done for you. God is the source of every good thing. He is never the problem or the source of trouble. The saints of old gave thanks in trials and persecution as they knew it was producing gold as refined in the fire. They understood that ease and comfort are greater threats to progress than persecution and trials. Our life circumstances are temporary, but God's Word and promises are eternal. The fires and testing are used to refine us and create testimonies of His goodness, both for His glory and for the benefit of others. As we live a lifestyle of repentance, it produces peace and joy. When I notice that I am not experiencing the kingdom in these ways, I first check if I've lost my gratitude.

Transformed by Gratitude: The Power of Thankfulness in Our Lives

Thanksgiving activates the blessings and promises of God.

Thanksgiving opens us to the atmosphere of heaven.

Thanksgiving guards our hearts and results in new levels of wholeness.

On the other hand, murmuring, complaining, and ungratefulness not only grieve and quench the Holy Spirit but also quench the power of God in our lives and sicken our hearts. Ingratitude quenches the fire and passion within us, leaving us lukewarm and useless. It causes us to take our blessings for granted and plants seeds of unbelief.

From Limitations to Increase: Embracing a Lifestyle of Thankfulness

> An unthankful heart is imprisoned by limitations. A thankful heart is positioned to see increase… The absence of thankfulness is self-trust.
> —Bill Johnson[10]

Thanksgiving is a kingdom key, resulting in a fruitful life. Thankfulness produces a grateful heart, an attitude of gratitude from which our words and actions flow. Let's enter His presence with thanksgiving today and every day! His presence is our love. His presence is our peace. His presence is our joy. His presence is everything. God is infinitely good. It is impossible to exaggerate the goodness of God. He is infinitely loving. Infinitely compassionate. Infinitely kind. Infinitely perfect. Infinitely powerful. Infinitely great. Infinitely righteous. Infinitely just. Infinitely Holy. He is our good and perfect Heavenly Father! He is eternally worth thanking! All we have is only by the grace of God!

1. Rita Watson MPH, "Gratitude Sparks Oxytocin and Love: Study Points to CD38: Gratitude may be the secret to a harmonious relationship and lifelong love," Psychology Today, accessed October 14, 2023, https://tinyurl.com/ms9adce7.

2. "Colossians 2:7, TPT Footnote V7," *LifeBible*, accessed October 14, 2023, https://lifebible.com/bible.

3. Rita Watson MPH, "Gratitude Sparks Oxytocin and Love: Study Points to CD38: Gratitude may be the secret to a harmonious relationship and lifelong love."

4. Ibid.

5. Ibid.

6. Ibid.

7. Ibid.

8. From the hymn, "Praise God From Whom All Blessings Flow."

9. Madhuleena Roy Chowdhury, BA, "The Neuroscience of Gratitude and Effects on the Brain," *PositivePsychology.com*, accessed October 14, 2023, https://tinyurl.com/2s2d5j9n.

10. Bill Johnson, "Bill Johnson Ministries," *Instagram*, accessed October 14, 2023, https://www.instagram.com/p/Cxn0VcJMo3/.

THE KINGDOM PRINCIPLE OF THANKSGIVING

Thanksgiving within the kingdom is more than a ritual; it's a heart posture that acknowledges God's generosity, goodness, faithfulness, sovereignty, and unmerited grace, leading to a deeper intimacy with Him. True thanksgiving transcends circumstances, encouraging believers to give thanks not only in times of abundance but also in trials, trusting that God works all things together for good.

Father, we ask for the grace to be marvelously thankful in all circumstances!

QUESTIONS FOR REFLECTION

What did the Holy Spirit reveal to you through *The Kingdom Principle of Thanksgiving*? How can you apply this to your life?

_____

_____

_____

_____

Are you truly thankful? If not, how does ingratitude affect your daily life and relationships?

_____

_____

_____

_____

Practice thankfulness today by consciously thanking God for who He is and what He has done verbally or in writing. As an extra challenge, try thanking Him for something every half-hour by setting a timer on your phone.

_____

_____

_____

QUESTIONS FOR REFLECTION *(continued)*

Whom are you personally thankful for? Consider a way to tell them today.

_____

_____

_____

_____

Notes

_____

_____

_____

_____

_____

_____

_____

_____

_____

_____

_____

_____

_____

_____

_____

_____

_____

Chapter 9: The Kingdom Principle of Peace

And the God of peace will swiftly pound Satan to a pulp under your feet! And the wonderful favor of our Lord Jesus will surround you.
—Romans 16:20, TPT

Victory in Divine Peace

The warfare in the spirit realm is a battle over our peace as we seek to hear, see, and obey God. The more we obey His commands (His constitution, i.e., the Bible) and embrace a kingdom lifestyle, the more peace we will experience. We may still experience trials and sufferings, but we can know and embrace a heavenly realm of peace that comes only from God every single day, no matter what we are going through. This makes me think of my walk home from the funeral home after Abbe's murder. Though I should have felt a stinging pain from her tragic end and the loss we all felt, I was completely overwhelmed by God's peace! So much so that I chose to walk home just so that I could sing God's praises at the top of my lungs without confusing or hurting family and friends who might not understand. While I greatly mourned her loss and still do, I know that God uses all things for good.[1] Then, I knew Abbe was safely at home with Jesus. And now, I see how much God has used that event to draw myself, my daughter, and so many others to Him.

When we seek first His kingdom, all that we need will be added to us. As we first seek His kingdom, the result is a peace that is added unto us. His kingdom is peace. Jesus is the Prince of Peace, and peace is an expression of love. Peace is a person: Jesus. We have peace when we understand that we have been made right by God. We have peace when we understand His righteousness is ours. We have the peace that surpasses understanding when we give up our right to understand and choose to trust God.

As we look to God in our circumstances as our provider, protector, and redeemer, God will cause our circumstances to work together for our good.[2] Even if we make mistakes, God will ultimately turn it into a blessing if we turn our hearts to Him. The ultimate truth is that we never have a reason to worry or give into anxiety because life is a journey of deepening trust in God as He redeems the hurting parts of our souls. As we live continually in peace, God, the source of love and peace, will be with us. Essentially, we are creating a place for His manifest presence, which is His kingdom of peace, to rule and reign.

Peace as Rest

As sons and daughters, we have the incredible blessing, privilege, and gift of rest because we trust in the sovereignty of God, the complete victory of Jesus, and the knowledge of who we are in Christ. Yieldedness is humility, being dependent on God. Trust is a posture of our hearts that allows us to yield to God, and from this place, we can truly rest. The principle of lordship (or yielded to the King) is key. In a kingdom, the king is responsible for the safety and protection of his people. God's kingdom is the presence of King Jesus. Protection and safety are found in abiding in His presence, which is the place of rest. Rest is of the Spirit which is how we are able to work from rest, being led by the Spirit and functioning from the overflow of His Spirit. We rest because we trust. Rest is a powerful weapon in the kingdom. Peace is the result of a transformed heart, which ushers in the presence of the kingdom of God. If we align our lives with the truth of His Word, take care of our hearts, and stay close to Him, we will be covered. Peace is the byproduct of this lifestyle!

Don't be pulled in different directions or worried about a thing. Be saturated in prayer throughout each day, offering your faith-filled requests before God with overflowing gratitude. Tell Him every detail of your life, THEN God's wonderful peace that transcends human understanding, will guard your heart and mind through Jesus Christ.
—*Philippians 4:6-7, TPT (emphases added)*

Notice the "then" emphasized at the beginning of Philippians 4:7. The key to living in kingdom peace is to offer our faith-filled requests to God with a heart of gratitude and walk in relationship by telling Him every detail of our lives. God loves details!

In Matthew 6:25-34, Jesus tells us never to worry about provision, what we will eat, drink, or wear. This is the opposite of what the world tells us. Jesus refers to the lilies of the field and how He clothes them and the sparrows and how He feeds them. He tells us we are much more valuable than flowers or birds. Our Heavenly Father knows what we need even before we ask, so we can rest assured that He will provide for our needs as we first seek His kingdom. It is the will of God to bless and prosper us as our King is glorified in the prosperity of His people.

Faith is not based on what is seen but on what is unseen. When we see something, faith is not required. As my faith increases, terrible news in the world and bad reports or life circumstances have less and less of an effect on my emotions because the reality of the kingdom is constantly growing inside of me. There was a time when everything was going wrong in my business (financially speaking) just after Abbe had passed. Then came time for our quarterly board meeting, and I was presenting the situation. One board member said that there was no way to contingency plan for a storm hitting the company this broadly. Another, surprised by how emotionally and mentally stable I was, said, "I have no idea how this guy is even still standing." I will tell you how… the supernatural grace and peace of God.

"For My yoke is comfortable, and My burden is light."
—*Matthew 11:30, NASB*

Embracing God's Peace Through Casting Cares

When we choose to worry, we are exalting our cares or problems above God, which creates anxiety. God instructs us, in humility, to regularly cast our cares and burdens on Him, as we are not meant to carry them. Jesus promises us his burden is light. Whenever you're burdened, verbally and physically, as a prophetic act, give your cares to God (prophetic acts release the power of God).

Not only can He handle them, but He *wants* to handle them. His grace is sufficient. God also uses His people, the hands and feet of Jesus on earth, to lighten and carry one another's burdens.

Remember, when we don't give God our burdens, we are forced to carry them ourselves. This leaves an open door to the enemy. But as soon as we cast our cares on Jesus, the power of God's peace is released over our circumstances. It's His peace that crushes Satan under our feet. We close the door to chaos and welcome peace every time we choose to give Jesus our stress, trouble, confusion, and pain. In the kingdom, there is no room for worry or anxiety, as our King is perfectly faithful to fulfill His Word. Knowing this empowers His kingdom of peace to rule and reign in our hearts over any circumstance, destroying the authority attached to chaos. Shalom!

Because we are in the world, we have problems, and we suffer. But, we can take courage because He has overcome the world. The kingdom of light displaces darkness every time, as darkness is simply the absence of light. Jesus is always victorious! As we abide, rest, and stay in peace, heaven is activated on our behalf. We can do this daily by remembering:

- Jesus is the source of our life.
- Jesus is our secret place.
- Jesus is our dwelling place.
- Jesus is our righteousness.
- Jesus is our peace.
- Jesus is our joy.
- Jesus is our protection.
- Jesus is our armour.
- Jesus is with us in pain, grief, and suffering.
- Jesus is our comfort and strength in times of trouble.
- He is Emmanuel, God with us!

Your crucifixion with Christ has severed the tie to this life, and now your true life is hidden away in God in Christ.
—Colossians 3:3, TPT

We have incredible eternal security NOW, as stated in Colossians 3:3 above. My life is in God AND in Christ! When He died, we died. When He rose, we rose. We belong to God. We are eternally safe and secure! But there is so much more than mere safety. We are His. We have been claimed by God as His inheritance. God no longer sees our old selves, but our new creation lives with the power of sin eternally broken. We are the blueprint of Jesus. As He is, so are we because of our oneness with Christ.[3]

Shalom: The Multidimensional Peace of God's Kingdom

If you know me, you know that I will often say "*Shalom!*" when I greet people or say goodbye (or even to end most emails). When I truly discovered the weight of this word in Scripture, I couldn't help but make it a part of my regular vernacular. The Hebrew word *shalom* is best translated as "peace," but it is so much more.

Shalom is one of the key words and images for salvation in the scriptures. The Hebrew word refers most commonly to a person being uninjured and safe, whole and sound. In the New Testament, shalom is revealed as the reconciliation of all things to God through the work of Christ… Shalom, when experienced, is multidimensional, complete well-being—physical, psychological, social, and spiritual; it flows from all of one's relationships being put right—with God, with(in) oneself, and with others.[4]

After reading that description, how can you NOT crave true shalom? Shalom encompasses all that is peace, harmony, wholeness, completeness, and security. Shalom is the fruit of abiding in His presence. Shalom is living in divine prosperity and order, a place of true flourishing in the reality of God's kingdom of righteousness, peace, and joy in His Holy Spirit.[5] Shalom!

The kingdom is God's perfect design for everything, which brings divine order or shalom. The kingdom is the realm of shalom. Romans 16:20 reveals that shalom is also a weapon because God is seen as crushing the enemy under our feet! We are not called to be peacekeepers; we are called to be *peacemakers*. The difference is that peacekeepers take on a passive role, while peacemakers take on a very active role. As believers, we are called to engage in the war for peace, and shalom is our weapon. Peacemakers are blessed![6] It's been said, "I used to think that I had peace, but now I know that peace has me."

Bryn and I were just talking and reflecting on our "old lives." Looking back at what we once considered "normal," we now clearly see it as chaotic due to the peace and tranquility we currently experience. With both Abbe and Bryn struggling with addiction, our lives were marked by a whirlwind of stress, chaos, and drama. Today, I know our self-focus has been greatly reduced, which has a massive calming effect. Our choice of friends, activities, priorities, and Bryn's use of drugs and alcohol have all completely changed. We have experienced God's kingdom bringing order to chaos. God has changed so much in our lives and continues to do so! Bryn and I have discovered that the safe and secure place is in following the lead of the Holy Spirit, trusting in the infallible Word of God, and living in close proximity to the King!

Now, may the Lord himself, the Lord of peace, pour into you his peace in every circumstance and in every possible way. The Lord's tangible presence be with you all.
—2 Thessalonians 3:16, TPT

1. Romans 8:28.
2. Romans 8:28.
3. 1 John 4:17.
4. Timothy Keller, "The Meaning of Shalom in the Bible," *New International Version*, accessed October 13, 2023, https://www.thenivbible.com/blog/meaning-shalom-bible/.
5. Romans 14:17.
6. Matthew 5:9.

BE FILLED WITH PEACE!

*There is such a great peace and well-being that comes to
the lovers of your Word, and they will never be offended.*
–Psalm 119:165, TPT

*When you abide under the shadow of Shaddai, you are hidden in
the strength of God Most High. He's the hope that holds me and the
stronghold to shelter me, the only God for me, and my great confidence.*
–Psalm 91:1-2, TPT

*When we live our lives within the shadow of God Most High, our
secret hiding place, we will always be shielded from harm. How then
could evil prevail against us or disease infect us? God sends angels with
special orders to protect you wherever you go, defending you from all harm.*
–Psalm 91:9-11, TPT

The LORD will fight for you while you [only need to] keep silent and remain calm.
–Exodus 14:14, AMP

*Finally, beloved friends, be cheerful! Repair whatever is broken among you, as your hearts are
being knit together in perfect unity. Live continually in peace, and God, the source of love and
peace, will mingle with you.*
–2 Corinthians 13:11, TPT

*When you live a life of abandoned love, surrendered before the awe of God, here's what
you'll experience: Abundant life. Continual protection. And complete satisfaction!*
–Proverbs 19:23, TPT

*Every promise from the faithful God is pure and proves to be true. He is a
wraparound shield of protection for all His lovers who run to hide in Him.*
–Proverbs 30:5, TPT

*The character of God is a tower of strength, for the lovers of
God delight to run into His heart and be exalted on high.*
–Proverbs 18:10, TPT

*"No weapon that is formed against you will succeed; And every tongue that
rises against you in judgment you will condemn. This [peace, righteousness,
security, and triumph over opposition] is the heritage of the servants of
the LORD, And this is their vindication from Me," says the LORD.*
–Isaiah 54:17, AMP

*Watch where you're going! Stick to the path of truth,
and the road will be safe and smooth before you.*
–Proverbs 4:26, TPT

THE KINGDOM PRINCIPLES OF PEACE AND PROVISION

The kingdom of God is a realm of divine order, peace, and provision. It is a place where we experience eternal security in Christ. The kingdom is God's perfect design for *everything*. As we live in this reality, we discover that true shalom is the fruit of abiding in His presence — true flourishing in righteousness, peace, and joy.

Father, we ask for the grace to follow and to live in Your perfect peace!

QUESTIONS FOR REFLECTION

What did the Holy Spirit reveal to you through *The Kingdom Principles of Peace and Provision?* How can you apply this to your life?

_____

_____

_____

_____

What would happen if you used worry as a signal to pray?

_____

_____

_____

_____

Take time to recall a moment when you experienced God's peace in the midst of a stormy situation. What emotions does this memory bring up?

_____

_____

_____

_____

Where do you need to experience shalom in your life?

_____

_____

_____

_____

Notes

_____

_____

_____

_____

_____

_____

_____

_____

_____

_____

_____

_____

_____

_____

_____

_____

Chapter 10: The Kingdom Principles of Honour and Humility

Be devoted to tenderly loving your fellow believers as members of one family. Try to outdo yourselves in respect and honour of one another.
—Romans 12:10, TPT

Show respect for all people [treat them honourably], love the brotherhood [of believers], fear God, honour the king.
—1 Peter 2:17, AMP

Honouring the Intrinsic Worth of all People

The world gives honour based on wealth, status, success, fame, and power, but the kingdom is very different. Every person on earth is deserving of honour, not as a result of actions, as we are all imperfect, but simply because they are made by and in the image of God.[1] This allows us to see people as God's people and not objectify them into any category, denomination, or faction that dehumanizes them. Honour means to revere or to fix a valuation. As the body, all are equal in value but different in function. We are in need of one another by design.

The size of God's sacrifice, His one and only Son, Jesus, and the sufferings of Jesus demonstrate the immensity of God's love and value for each person on earth. The price paid for something indicates its value, making every person of infinite value regardless of the state of our lives or our past. Each and every person is worth the highest price ever paid for anything in the history of the world. Love Himself died for us. When we are able to receive the revelation of honour, we can finally be fully ourselves when we understand our worth, which opens us to quality connections with others.

Honour is an act of God's grace. God has greatly honoured us by creating us in His image and in His great sacrifice for us. We have been honoured as Jesus first chose us; we didn't choose Him.[2] God shows us honour by trusting us to steward His creation. God honours us with the incredible privilege of being sons and daughters in His family. Honour has been extended to us as everything we have, whether honour, faith, love, or even life itself, is a gift from God. As we freely receive, we freely give.[3]

But when the kindness of God our Saviour and His love for mankind appeared, He saved us, not on the basis of deeds which we did in righteousness, but in accordance with His mercy, by the washing of regeneration and renewing by the Holy Spirit.
—Titus 3:4-5, AMP

Honour is love and respect made visible. Honour always flows from love, and love is made visible by serving. The blessing of honour is a core principle of the kingdom. Honour builds people up and creates personhood or a person of inherent unique individual value. We show honour when we treat others with reverence and respect, demonstrating that we recognize the weight of someone's words, positions, or behaviours. The same is also true of the opposite.

Remember when I had judged Bryn and held dishonour in my heart towards her? My heart position and wrong expectations resulted in my words and actions dishonouring her. As a result, I experienced dishonour from Bryn, which has been rare in our relationship. However, I know now that her response was only the fruit of my own seeds of dishonour. As I repented and honoured Bryn, the relationship shifted to one of healthy, mutual respect. Now that I understand the impact of honour, I try to be more sensitive and mindful to hold honour in my heart, as what we carry in our hearts has an expression on earth.

Insult your Creator, will you? That's exactly what you do every time you oppress the powerless! Showing kindness to the poor is equal to honouring your maker.
— Proverbs 14:31, TPT

As we honour God, He will honour us. As we honour others, God will honour us. As we carry the spirit of honour, it elevates not only us, but our families and future generations.

The kingdom of God is anchored in the biblical concept of authority, where submission is not merely an obligation but a reflection of our reverence for God. Submission is holy and beautiful. It is to place our desires beneath the desires of Jesus and His commands, making Him Lord. In Scripture, we are called to submit to earthly authorities with a spirit of obedience and respect, embodying the larger principle that all authority is ultimately derived from and accountable to God.

Scripture tells us over and over that in obedience, we are to submit:

- To God
- To our parents when we are young
- To elders
- Healthy, Christlike leaders who are watching over our souls (pastor, mentor, etc.)
- Wives to their husbands
- To the government
- To each other in Christ

Honouring God: Moving Beyond Obedience to a Higher Call

According to Scripture, obedience is good. But when we honour God, we go far above and beyond obedience. Honour is a higher call. It's more than just "doing what's right." It's doing what's right with the right heart. Slaves obey. Sons and daughters honour.

HOW DO WE HONOUR GOD?

◊ Seeking first His kingdom as our top priority

◊ Acknowledging the authority of God

◊ Surrendering our lives and desires to the Lord, embracing a lifestyle of sacrificial or selfless love

◊ Working as unto the Lord with godly character

◊ Obeying His commands

◊ Honouring our parents, His people, and all of creation

◊ Living in awareness of God in awe and reverence

◊ Showing kindness to the poor, widows, and orphans

◊ Living with thankfulness, knowing that every good gift is from God

◊ Stewarding well whatever God places in our hands

◊ Choosing joy, abiding in His kingdom of righteousness, peace, and joy

◊ Seeking His will, loving His Word, agreeing in prayer, and partnering with God in life

◊ Honouring God with our words, decisions, and actions

◊ Honouring God with our bodies as temples of the Holy Spirit by maintaining health and purity

◊ Loving others as ourselves

◊ Showing hospitality and compassion for others

◊ Becoming like a little child before Him

◊ With our finances, faithfully stewarding and giving generously with a cheerful heart

◊ Honouring those in authority

◊ Praising Him in all circumstances, especially in suffering, knowing He is always good and always with us

Honour your father and your mother, so that your days may be prolonged on the land which the Lord your God gives
you.
—Exodus 20:12, NASB

In the above verse from Exodus, God tells us to honour our mothers and fathers. This command is repeated in Deuteronomy 5:16. Paul repeats it again in Ephesians 6:2-3. Interestingly, it is the only commandment that comes with a blessing.

Honour (respect, obey, care for) your father and your mother, as the Lord your God has commanded you, so that
your days [on earth] may be prolonged and so that it may go well with you in the land which the Lord your God
gives you.
— Deuteronomy 5:16, AMP

What does this tell us? God loves honour. And God loves when we honour according to His heaven-on-earth plan, even when it doesn't make sense to us. Honour is required for strong families. Strong families create thriving communities.

He will turn the hearts of the fathers back to their children and the hearts of the children to their fathers, so that I
will not come and strike the land with complete destruction.
—Malachi 4:6, NASB

Honour places things in their proper order. As parents turn their hearts to God, He turns their hearts to their children to love and honour them, which results in God turning the hearts of their children towards their parents in love and honour. This is the foundation and heart of M46 Ministries, the ministry I co-founded with my daughter Bryn based on Malachi 4:6.

Honour empowers God to work in our families. Children should honour their parents, or parents become peers. We are called to honour those in authority over us and those whom we have authority over, or there will be chaos.

Now, all of us have questions at times about what it means to honour those in authority over us when things are complicated. Some have abusive parents or an abusive spouse… what does honour look like then? Others experienced abusive church leadership… what does honour look like then? What about when our government is enforcing evil instead of good… what does honour look like in this situation? (If you are experiencing abuse within your marriage or other relationships, I encourage you to seek counsel from a pastor or spiritual mentor.)

Honour doesn't mean we will always agree with those over us or under us, but it does mean that we will treat them with kindness and respect. This might mean respectfully disagreeing at times.

As Malachi 4:6 warns, if Satan can break down the family and its legacy, then there could be *complete* destruction. This is why we are seeing such a great attack against families. The good news is that family reconciliation is made possible by turning our hearts to God and to one another *by the power of the Holy Spirit.* We are not alone in this!

Sometimes, especially in cases of abuse or neglect, it can be very difficult to honour our parents, particularly when it is necessary to remove oneself from the situation (or perhaps did long ago). In this situation, honour will look different and may include a combination of private forgiveness, inner healing, prayer, and being intentional about what you hold in your heart towards that parent. In this case, reconciliation may not be wise or possible, but our hearts must always be reconciled to Christ.[4]

All people (parents included!) are flawed. We don't honour our parents because they are perfect, but because of their position and because they are made in the image of God. We would not be alive without our parents. As children, we honour our parents by obeying them and by giving weight to or valuing their input in our lives. As we mature, we honour them by respectfully listening to their words, taking care of them, and loving them to the best of our abilities. The greatest way we can honour our parents is to give our lives to Jesus!

Dishonour vs. Honour: Understanding the Spiritual Impact

Do you remember the story of Ham, who was the son of Noah? He dishonoured his father, received a curse, and consequently, the generations of Ham became slaves.[5]

As we honour our parents, we honour God. However, we must understand the opposite is also true. Satan was the first to dishonour God and, as a result, was cast out of heaven and made separate from God. This is not the fate we desire. We must never partner with and empower the demonic spirit of dishonour because when we do, we are inviting the evil of Satan into our lives. Jesus is clear: We are not to dishonour our parents.[6]

And He answered and said to them, **"Why do you yourselves also break the commandment of God for the sake of your tradition? For God said, 'Honour your father and mother,' and, 'The one who speaks evil of father or mother is to be put to death.'"**
—*Matthew 15:3-4, NASB*

The above passage declares that death is the penalty for dishonour, which shows the seriousness of dishonour and the importance of honour. The opposite of honour is to revile, to address with offensive language, and to treat with disrespect. In *The Passion Translation,* the phrase used in verse 4 is "Whoever abuses or insults his father or mother," and in the NIV, the phrase used is "Anyone who curses their father or mother is to be put to death." Dishonour results in a curse.

"The one who receives a prophet in the name of a prophet shall receive a prophet's reward, and the one who receives a righteous person in the name of a righteous person shall receive a righteous person's reward."
—Matthew 10:41, ESV

The general principle is when we honour someone, we are positioned to receive what they carry, a reward for the breakthrough and the glory of God. However, when we dishonour someone, we are closed off from receiving the thing that we need that they carry.

Therefore the Lord God of Israel declares, "I did indeed say that your house and the house of your father was to walk before Me forever"; but now the Lord declares, "Far be it from Me—for those who honour Me I will honour, and those who despise Me will be insignificant."
—1 Samuel 2:30, NASB

As we honour others, we receive the blessings of honour into our lives through the principle of reciprocity or sowing and reaping.

Do not be deceived, God is not mocked; for whatever a person sows, this he will also reap. For the one who sows to his own flesh will reap destruction from the flesh, but the one who sows to the Spirit will reap eternal life from the Spirit. Let's not become discouraged in doing good, for in due time we will reap, if we do not become weary.
—Galatians 6:7-9, NASB

There are very few reasons not to submit to authority. There are times for civil disobedience when certain authorities command us to do evil or require us to live in direct violation of God's commands, but this is a topic beyond the scope of this book. In these cases, remember that the authority of God and His revealed will in Scripture are always our highest forms of authority and the ones we will be called to account for on Judgment Day. We can, however, always become active in supporting new godly government leaders and laws.

THE GREATEST AMONG YOU WILL BE
THE ONE WHO ALWAYS SERVES OTHERS.
REMEMBER THIS: IF YOU HAVE A LOFTY
OPINION OF YOURSELF AND SEEK TO
BE HONORED, YOU WILL BE HUMBLED.
BUT IF YOU HAVE A MODEST OPINION
OF YOURSELF AND CHOOSE TO HUMBLE
YOURSELF, YOU WILL BE HONORED."

-MATTHEW 23:11-12, TPT

1 Philippians 2:5-8.

2 John 5:19; Mark 10:45; Romans 8.

3 Matthew 20:28.

4 Matthew 16:24.

5 John 13:4-17.

6 John 15:13.

7 Matthew 16:25.

8 Colossians 1:15.

9 Matthew 10:39.

And they took offense at Him. But Jesus said to them, **"A prophet is not dishonoured except in his hometown and in his own household."** *And He did not do many miracles there because of their unbelief.*
Matthew 13:57-58, NASB

This above passage describes a tragic chapter in Jesus's life. He had just returned from doing countless miracles. But, because of the lack of honour in Nazareth, He did not display His usual wonder-working miracle power there.

Not showing honour demonstrates a lack of belief, which Jesus called "unbelief." Sadly, those in Nazareth had cut off the power of Jesus to work in their lives by closing the door as they were unwilling to receive Him.

Childlikeness and Humility: Keys to Kingdom Greatness

Acknowledging we are sinners in need of a saviour begets humility. This heart position of humility was our entry point into the kingdom by grace through faith. It takes humility and obedience to God's commands to honour those in authority over us. It takes humility to know who is in authority. Why? Because humility always precedes honour.

We can choose humility, recognizing God as our source. We have Jesus as our ultimate example of perfect humility. After all, when Jesus described His character and nature, He used the words "gentle and humble."[7] The fear of the Lord produces humility. The fear of the Lord is awe and wonder, which is why the scriptures tell us to become like children to enter His kingdom. Sadly, many people love Jesus but continue to compromise as *they do not fear the Lord.*

Childlikeness is playful, joyful, and imaginative and allows us to dream. Do you remember reading about the study on children and creativity earlier in the book? Science shows that childlikeness is a state of openness and wonder, causing us to be fully present and alive.

Childlikeness allows us not to take ourselves or life too seriously. Childlikeness is a state of mind that keeps everything novel and deepens our love of life. Childlikeness embraces uncertainty, disconnects us from "self" consciousness, and opens us to full dependency and trust in our Heavenly Father. Childlikeness is a key to humility, which is why the scriptures tell us that becoming like a little child is to become great in the kingdom.

This weekend, there was a young man who was heavily demonized, greatly suffering, and in need of deliverance, so he and his mother came to see me and a couple of other believers. We prayed for him and blessed him. Then the Holy Spirit gave me a picture of him on my back, which I shared with him. He was resistant at first, saying he was too old and big for a piggyback ride in public. Finally, he jumped on, and I ran with him, jumping on rocks, spinning, and going up and over things. He turned into a little child and was laughing, saying how much fun it was. This was deliverance as play and love displaced the heaviness, orphanhood, and darkness. I had the honour of representing our Father in a new way in a simple act of obedience.

"Whoever continually humbles himself to become like this little child is the greatest one in heaven's kingdom realm."
—Matthew 18:4, TPT

For My hand made all these things, "So all these things came into being," declares the Lord. "But I will look to this one, At one who is humble and contrite in spirit, and who trembles at My word."
—Isaiah 66:2, NASB

*   *   *

Father, we ask for the grace to be childlike and for a contrite heart!

Father, we ask for the grace to live in humility and receive a fresh baptism of the fear of the Lord to be filled with reverence.

May we delight in the fear of the Lord so that our hearts become saturated with awe-inspiring presence. Let us tremble with awe, reverence, and adoration as we gain a fuller understanding of Your supreme holiness, wisdom, power, authority, and the infinite depths of Your love and goodness.

*   *   *

WHAT IS BIBLICAL HUMILITY?

◇ Humility is yieldedness.

◇ Humility is selflessness.

◇ Humility is the fear or awe of the Lord.[1]

◇ Humility allows us to see ourselves and God rightly.

◇ Humility is the fruit of a transformed mind by the power of the Holy Spirit.

◇ Humility exposes pride, is the antidote to pride, recognizes weakness and sinfulness, and leads to repentance.

◇ Humility precedes submission and acknowledges God's authority.

◇ Humility precedes gratitude, and gratitude promotes humility.

◇ Humility precedes honour.

◇ Humility puts others first, valuing oneself less.

◇ Humility is marked by a willingness to serve.

◇ Humility precedes unity.

◇ Humility precedes wisdom.

◇ Humility precedes presence (holiness) and holiness precedes purity.

◇ Humility precedes glory.

◇ Humility is like a superpower and is a key to the kingdom.

◇ Humility is a virtue that enables us to steward the power and authority of the kingdom and reveal Jesus's life as we go about our Father's business.

---

[1] Proverbs 22:4.

Humility is a result of seeking God and is rooted in the admiration of God, living in awareness of Him as almighty, sovereign over all, and utterly beyond ourselves. To be humble is to be dependent on God for everything. It is humility that displaces pride and selfishness as our identity becomes rooted in something much greater than ourselves. This is why we have the popular saying, "The door is in the floor!" When we go low and tremble at His Word, it is God who will raise us up. As we understand that ALL we have is by grace, the realm of humility expands within us.

> *The reward of humility and the fear of the Lord are riches, honour, and life.*
> *—Proverbs 22:4, NASB*

When we see God rightly, in awe and wonder, we gain heaven's perspective. We see ourselves rightly. Humility is the result.

> *Therefore, having these promises, beloved, let's cleanse ourselves from all defilement of flesh and spirit, perfecting holiness in the fear of God.*
> *—2 Corinthians 7:1, NASB*

When we live in awe of God, we honour His creation. When we live in awe and wonder of God, we are open to receiving His wisdom and live in obedience, prayer, and worship. When we live in awe of God, we create a place for His glory. The source of revelation and knowledge is found as we fall in surrender before the Lord. We cannot expect to see the *shekinah* glory until the Lord sees our sincere humility.[8] In the footnotes of *The Passion Translation* for Proverbs 15:33, it notes that the word *kabod* is translated as the English word "glory" 156 times in OT.[9] Humility leads to honour, which results in God's glory, His manifest presence.

As we mature, a powerful way to honour God is to die to ourselves, our self-focus, pride, and rebellion. We do this by embracing the cross, denying ourselves, and loving God. It's the flesh that keeps us from loving others. It's the flesh that holds onto pride, which is the source of dishonour.

> *I have been crucified with Christ; and it is no longer I who live, but Christ lives in me; and the life which I now live in the flesh I live by faith in the Son of God, who loved me and gave Himself up for me.*
> *—Galatians 2:20, NASB*

If pride is the sin of all sins, humility can be described as the virtue of all virtues. God exhorts the humble and resists the proud. It is humility that is the antidote to pride. It opens our awareness of how little we actually know. It makes us teachable. Humility allows us to truly listen, learn, grow, and receive. Humility transforms us. When we are humble, we see people as people. When we no longer see people as objects, we avoid disastrous results. We can approach others with curiosity and honour. We can learn from them and develop a relationship with them, which is what the kingdom is all about. In business, while attempting to move forward quickly, I have definitely treated people as objects or doers without considering the impact on them. In those instances, I put the mission above the people. However, the more I have embraced humility, the more God has opened my eyes to change this and other behaviours. He's inviting me to better love and honour others through my actions by the power of the Holy Spirit.

> *"Listen to the truth I speak: Whoever does not open their arms to receive God's kingdom like a teachable child will never enter it."*
> —Mark 10:15, TPT

Honour is manifested in love. It is in doing things for the benefit of others.

> *Do nothing from selfishness or empty conceit, but with humility consider one another as more important than yourselves; do not merely look out for your own personal interests, but also for the interests of others.*
> *Philippians 2:3-4, NASB*

Paul reminds us here that honour elevates and dishonour tears down. If you want to experience God's presence, life, and blessings in the kingdom, a great place to start is by incorporating the principles of honour and humility into every relationship in your life. Even if honour is not returned by the person you are honouring, God will honour you. Honour begets honour!

1. Genesis 1:27.
2. Ephesians 1:4.
3. Matthew 10:8.
4. To reconcile a relationship would be to make amends with the person who hurt you, to come to an agreement or win them over. This is not always possible as it would imply re-establishing a relationship. If a person is unsafe, this would be an unwise decision, unless completely led by the Holy Spirit and attempted in an open, supportive, Christian community. However, being reconciled to Christ means your heart is free from unforgiveness and bitterness towards the person who hurt you, while maintaining healthy boundaries to protect your safety.
5. Genesis 9:20-28.
6. 1 Peter 3:7 also tells us that we are to honour our wives so that our prayers will not be hindered. Honour is a key to answered prayer!
7. Matthew 11:29.
8. The Hebrew word *shekinah* means "dwelling" or "one who dwells."
9. "Proverbs 15:33," *YouVersion: The Passion Translation*, accessed October 13, 2023, https://www.bible.com/bible/1849/PRO.15.TPT.

THE KINGDOM PRINCIPLES OF HONOUR AND HUMILITY

Humility and honour intertwine in the kingdom of God. This creates a harmonious atmosphere where people, motivated by love, prioritize serving others while recognizing and celebrating the dignity of every person.

Father, we ask for the grace to be humble and to honour others well!

QUESTIONS FOR REFLECTION

What did the Holy Spirit reveal to you through *The Kingdom Principles of Honour and Humility*? How can you apply this to your life?

_____

_____

_____

_____

How can you demonstrate honour to others?

_____

_____

_____

Who has shown you honour, and how has it impacted your life?

_____

_____

_____

Ask the Holy Spirit if anything is in the way of you becoming like a little child before the Father. How is childlikeness related to humility?

Notes

Chapter 11: The Kingdom Principle of Sowing and Reaping

God will never be mocked! For what you plant will always be the very thing you harvest. The harvest you reap reveals the seed that you planted. If you plant the corrupt seeds of self-life into this natural realm, you can expect a harvest of corruption. If you plant the good seeds of Spirit-life, you will reap beautiful fruits that grow from the everlasting life of the Spirit. And don't allow yourselves to be weary in planting good seeds, for the season of reaping the wonderful harvest you've planted is coming! Take advantage of every opportunity to be a blessing to others, especially to our brothers and sisters in the family of faith!
—Galatians 6:7-10, TPT

It is obvious in the natural realm that if you sow mustard seeds, you get a mustard tree. If you sow pumpkin seeds, you get pumpkins. If you sow corn seeds, you get corn. The same applies to the spiritual realm and the eventual manifestation in the physical realm. You grow what you sow. We must all realize that we don't get away with anything. This is the law of reciprocity for which the golden rule, the essence of the law of love, talks about. The kingdom is an "others-focused" kingdom based on serving, blessing, and faithfulness, with its principles meant to be lived out. Lives become the evidence of a transformed heart that glorify God in their families, work, communities, and those who cross their path. God rewards us with reaping more of what we sow so that we can do even more good! God rewards and promotes the sowing of love in all of its forms. What we sow, we reap. As we sow things of the Spirit, it reaps 100 fold. There is great increase when we sow in the Spirit.

Growing in the Natural and Spiritual Realms

Before 2016, I sowed many seeds of self-life (the flesh) as I was living life on my terms. This dramatically changed as I dedicated my life to God and looked to honour Him with everything I did and all that I had. I began to sow more and more Spirit-life seeds of prayer and biblical study, which moved me from one who would never pray out loud to awkwardly muttering a prayer, to gaining a prayer language, to absolutely loving prayer! Now, when I have the honour to pray, I am excited to move as the Holy Spirit leads and to release the Word of God that now dwells richly within me.

In the natural realm, a seed reproduces after its own kind.

"In everything you do, be careful to treat others in the same way you'd want them to treat you, for that is the essence of all the teachings of the Law and the Prophets."
—Matthew 7:12, TPT

What we choose to do and say matters as we are constantly sowing seeds. When we are Spirit-led, we naturally manifest the fruit of the Spirit, which will yield an eternal harvest.[1] We begin to dispense our new creation life as leaven of the kingdom as a ripple effect across the earth! The fruit of the Spirit is the key to living above our circumstances and living in the kingdom!

Law of Reciprocity

This is sometimes called the "law of reciprocity." In essence, the law of reciprocity encourages positive behavior by highlighting the interconnectedness of human relationships and the idea that our actions have consequences. It's a principle that promotes empathy, compassion, and understanding, recognizing that our actions not only impact others but also shape the kind of world we live in.

In the natural realm, the condition of the soil is important for the plant to live and flourish.

> *"But what is sown on good soil represents those who open their hearts to receive the message and their lives bear good fruit—some yield a harvest of thirty, sixty, even a hundredfold!"*
> *—Mark 4:20, TPT*

Spiritual soil is the condition of our hearts. As we yield our hearts to the Lord and allow Him to work, our hearts are softened to receive by the power of the Holy Spirit. Humility, repentance, and forgiveness are the keys that allow the soil of our hearts to bear good fruit. I have made inner-heart healing an ongoing part of my journey as wholeheartedness is our design—to love God with all of our hearts and to be totally free in the spirit.

Small Beginnings, Great Impact: Embracing the Seed of God's Kingdom

In the natural realm, all living things start small, in seed form. Then they grow.

> *Then Jesus taught them another parable:* *"Heaven's kingdom can be compared to the tiny mustard seed that a man takes and plants in his field. Although the smallest of all the seeds, it eventually grows into the greatest of garden plants, becoming a tree for birds to come and build their nests in its branches."*
> *—Matthew 13:31-32, TPT*

The most common way the Lord chooses to answer our "big prayers" is to give us the seed to the answer. The Lord often chooses to give us the acorn instead of the oak tree we prayed for because the process of caring for the acorn develops the character in us to contain the answer once it's given so that the answer will not destroy us.[2]

Kingdom life is a journey, and God builds us in the process. Ultimately, the kingdom seed is within and continuously expanding to become a mighty tree. Everything begins with the first step of faith. We are constantly sowing seeds. The mustard seed in the passage above represents a beginning that is small, humble, seemingly insignificant, unimpressive, and appears powerless but gradually grows into a mighty tree, representing profound impact, transformation, and influence by the power of God. God's process most often starts small and slowly progresses as He builds the foundations of character and maturity in us. We hear stories of those who have been promoted quickly because of a unique spiritual gift, only to crash when the weight of the position and responsibility becomes too much, as their character has yet to be established.

In 2013, I got a call from my mother, who has always had a heart for the down and out, to come to Saint John, New Brunswick, a city 20 minutes away from where I grew up. She wanted me to come and see the poverty of which I was unaware. As I began to explore these areas and see into the lives of those I encountered, I felt a righteous indignation coupled with compassion.

Though I was an engineer with no true understanding of poverty, God led me to partner with a 26-year-old saleswoman who was passionate about solving systemic poverty in Saint John. We first began by trying to reform and reinvigorate an existing organization in the child poverty space. This venture turned out to be a total failure, but we got to see the problem up close and meet many suffering families. This fired us up to press on. To put it lightly, we were both in over our heads, but felt a call to do *something*. With my resources and her tenacity, we made a plan and drew on the wisdom of many.

This mustard seed sown by my mother is now a growing organization called Bee Me Kidz that serves over 2,000 parents and children in high-priority neighbourhoods (highest need) with high concentrations of multi-generational poverty and new immigrants. Today, Bee Me Kidz is in the process of expanding across the province. We started with seeds of love, hope, and honour, which have grown and become the foundation of the organization.

Another seed that started small but is currently growing was planted when I honoured a close friend and worship leader named Chantal by promoting her to be a key member of my company and to lead our prayer team. When we release honour to specific people, we receive what they carry. In this case, we gave Chantal a voice and a platform. At first, she wasn't sure what she could bring to a business. However, she began to bloom and flourish in marketplace ministry! Her diligent work started an entirely new life trajectory of peace and prosperity within our business and personal lives. Because of her willingness to lead in her place of gifting and anointing, we are all changed.

> God gives us things in seed form but because we expect for God to give us an oak tree instead of an acorn, we have very little value for what has been given to us and end up aborting the miracle in its development stages.
> —Rhoda Gayle[3]

Flō started with a $20,000 loan from my parents. I walked into the unknown world of business at age 28, having just left a stable job with lots of student loans, loads of insecurities, a shaky marriage, and a new family. In other words, I had little to offer, but a small seed of hope in the form of my parents' investment in my future. Though $20,000 might seem like a lot of money, and it is, this was my small beginning.

Zechariah 4:10 tells us not to despise small, seemingly insignificant beginnings. Today, Flō operates across North America, serving food retail chains. Though it feels like we are at the beginning of a grand new adventure with God, we can look back and attest to how far we have come.

Another fun small seed that has gone on to reproduce began when my mother discovered an organization called Compassion International many years ago. Through Compassion, my mother and I were able to financially support children in a poor town about three hours outside Lima, Peru. The six-, seven-, and eight-year-old children we originally blessed are now adults. Many still write my mother letters and remember her many visits to Peru. Today, these children have miraculously become professionals and pastors. In fact, our relationship with the believers in Peru has grown so deep that our partner church in Lima allowed us to build an extension to their building to honour my late brother Mark as a surprise gift to my mother. God works in mysterious and wonderful ways.

In the natural realm, the grain of wheat must die to experience life and produce a great harvest.

> *"Let me make this clear: A single grain of wheat will never be more than a single grain of wheat unless it drops into the ground and dies. Because then it sprouts and produces a great harvest of wheat—all because one grain died."*
> — *John 12:24, TPT*

Jesus is the ultimate example of this principle as He died, went into the ground, and was resurrected to produce a great harvest. When we get baptized, we experience a co-death and co-resurrection with Jesus, which yields an eternal harvest. As we daily die to our self-life, we truly live. When we live a Spirit-led, kingdom life, there will be a great harvest.

My own flesh and blood, my precious daughter Abbe, who was murdered on May 23, 2018, went into the ground. Yet, through the redemptive power of Jesus, many around the world have been impacted in ways I never could have imagined through her death. God is good! M46 Ministries was launched four years to the day Abbe went to be with the Lord. Remarkably, this was not planned. It was the result of God's divine orchestration. The Lord gave me the above scripture shortly after Abbe's death as a promise, and here He was fulfilling it! In addition, Bryn's book *Dying to Live: Experiencing God's Redemptive Power in the Midst of Tragedy* was released on the same day as our ministry's launch. So much life from the ashes of death.

One example of inner-heart healing happened just after we began M46 Ministries. I had an unexpected Malachi 4:6 vision or encounter in the spirit.[4] In this encounter, I was walking with Jesus and holding His hand in a meadow alongside a brook. As I walked, I got smaller and smaller until I was about a five-year-old boy. Then I turned and wrapped my arms around Jesus's neck in a beautiful embrace of a son and his Heavenly Father. Then I turned and saw my earthly father. As I looked at him, he became smaller until he was a child. He was crying, and I could see the hurt and brokenness that had impacted his life and ability to connect and be a father. Compassion, mercy, love, and healing filled my heart. Suddenly, I embraced my father, kid to kid, son to son. I held him with such love as he sobbed in my arms. Next, I turned and was 52 again. My daughter, Bryn, was a child. She wrapped her arms around my neck in a restorative, loving embrace, safe and secure. This vision was a true picture of generational restoration!

In the natural realm, there is time between planting, seedtime, and harvest, where much development happens before a plant can bear fruit.

While the earth remains, Seedtime and harvest, Cold and heat, Summer and winter, And day and night Shall not cease.
—Genesis 8:22, NASB

Embracing the In-between: Finding Purpose in the Waiting

We live in a destination and outcome-obsessed culture! However, the place of "in-between" is where we spend most of our lives, in the small and mundane, in the waiting. The time between seedtime and the harvest is when we have the most opportunities to glorify God. It is a time of preparation, growth, and maturing. It is a time of moving, step by step, towards the promise, vision, harvest, or outcome. When you have done everything and don't see the fruit yet, you can be sure something is happening below the surface. Stand firm in faith. Remember, love is patient and patience is a fruit of love! God is love and He is always working! The "in-between" is also a potential place of disappointment and discouragement. It is when our expectations are unmet that hope deferred can set in. In the in-between, our trust is anchored in the goodness and faithfulness of God, and patience is the fruit of the Spirit as we fix our eyes on Him. I have discovered that God will not meet "my" expectations, but He will always live up to His Word.

In the middle of the season, before the breakthrough… before the light at the end of the tunnel, I choose to praise Him because He is good. Thankfulness is our weapon in the middle. Our faith is displayed in our dependence on Him in the middle. In the middle, when our trust is in God, we will never be disappointed. In the middle, I have chosen to trust in God, regardless of how I may feel.

I have discovered that hope deferred is never an issue with God. He is never surprised and infinitely faithful. Rather, the issue is my level of faith, focus on myself rather than God, and lack of thankfulness. Based on my history with God, knowing He is always with me, I also see "bad" or difficult events as temporary problems or setbacks that will be overcome as there are always solutions or a new and better way ahead. Once I express my emotions of grief, frustration, or anger, I can then release the outcomes and timing to God. I can choose to marvel at His infinite goodness and supreme greatness, which anchors me in thankfulness and trust. As I dwell in these truths, I know that God's got me. The outcomes are His, working all things together for our good.

Success is defined by my "yes" to Him. This is the point where I choose to walk by faith and not by sight, knowing that the delay is often my time of preparation. Hope that the world gives (an expression of uncertainty) is very different from our hope (an expression of certainty) the joyful assurance and expectation in the goodness of God and His promises for our future. Our hope is an essential element of our faith, which is rooted in the promises and faithfulness of God! Our level of hope is a reflection of the level of truth we carry in our hearts. When our hope is low, it is an indicator that we are believing lies. In fact, any circumstance that is void of hope indicates the presence of a stronghold, a hidden lie, or lies built into our belief system. When we believe a lie, it must be revealed and then displaced with truth. Truth always brings freedom and hope. Again, we provide faithfulness, and God will provide the eventual fruitfulness. When we are led by His Spirit, hope and patience are limitless. God is teaching us to be led by His Spirit.

> **"What delight comes to you when you wait upon the Lord! For you will find what you long for."**
> *Matthew 5:4, TPT*

> *For the Scriptures encourage us with these words: "Everyone who believes in him will never be disappointed."*
> *—Romans 10:11, TPT*

From Seedtime to Harvest: Navigating the Journey of Promise

One of our prayer team members at Flō recently heard a phrase that went something like, "Idols are mostly fashioned by impatience." We must resist the natural impulses of impatience and control to embrace the time between seedtime and harvest. Remember, the seed dies, the roots go down, the plant matures… and only then does it bear fruit.

> *So, dear friends, don't let this one thing escape your notice: a single day counts like a thousand years to the Lord Yahweh, and a thousand years counts as one day. This means that, contrary to man's perspective, the Lord is not late with his promise to return, as some measure lateness. But rather, his "delay" simply reveals his loving patience towards you, because he does not want any to perish but all to come to repentance.*
> *2 Peter 3:8-9, TPT*

If we receive a promise in the form of a prophetic word, we must steward the word to attain the promise, to be a doer of the word and not just a hearer. I knew a man who had received a powerful prophetic word saying, "God is giving me a million-dollar business." This man was literally waiting for something to fall into his lap, whereas God was prepared to work with him to bring this vision into reality. He was literally doing nothing other than agreeing with God to bring this word to fruition. Even after others had encouraged him to take the initiative, he resorted to reaching out for financial support while waiting passively for the promise. The end of this story, as you can imagine, was not good. God can obviously do financial miracles, but He put us in the physical realm to work *with* Him.

God will typically put a problem or a desire in your heart that He has a solution to bring to the world through you. We can stand and activate our faith in the natural realm by agreeing in prayer, building our skill sets to be able to steward the promise, learning to follow and lead, listening to God, and building relationships. All of these things can be part of stewarding the Word and proving ourselves faithful. God created us to partner with Him and to live interdependently (and intergenerationally) with others to serve and live out our destiny.

The time of waiting (waiting on the Lord is often translated as *entangled with the Lord*), growing roots, and preparation to bear fruit is a gift. It is a time of learning how to steward life in the promised land.

Remember, we tend to focus on the destination and often miss much of the present. A large part of the God journey is embracing the mystery and the adventure and releasing the demand for certainty and outcomes to God. This time of growth is also one of preparation for harvest so that we will be ready to move into action and release the labourers into the fields.

And don't allow yourselves to be weary in planting good seeds, for the season of reaping the wonderful harvest you've planted is coming!
—Galatians 6:9, TPT

It's worth asking yourself the following questions: Have you faithfully prepared yourself to steward the promise? What skills or knowledge need to be developed or gained? Are there areas of your character that need formation or pruning? Are you in alignment with the Holy Spirit in every relationship, mindset, or habit? If not, what is the Lord asking you to do about it?

In the natural realm, a tree is known by its fruit.

"You'll never find choice fruit hanging on a bad, unhealthy tree. And rotten fruit doesn't hang on a good, healthy tree. Every tree will be revealed by the quality of fruit that it produces. You will never pick figs or grapes from thorn trees. People are known in this same way. Out of the virtue stored in their hearts, good and upright people will produce good fruit. Likewise, out of the evil hidden in their hearts, evil ones will produce what is evil. For the overflow of what has been stored in your heart will be seen by your fruit and will be heard in your words."
—Luke 6:43-45, TPT

"You can spot them by their actions, for the fruits of their character will be obvious. You won't find sweet grapes hanging on a thorn bush, and you'll never pick good fruit from a tumbleweed."
Matthew 7:16, TPT

Bearing Abundant Spiritual Fruit

A cherry tree doesn't need to try to produce cherries; it just does (so long as it is a healthy, mature tree). This is the same with the fruit of the Spirit. When we are Spirit-led and filled with His Word, the fruit of the Spirit (love, peace, joy, patience, etc.) naturally manifests in our lives. Good trees produce good fruit. Unhealthy trees produce unhealthy fruit. I have experienced a lot of bad fruit in my life. Thankfully, as the Lord has healed me from the inside out, my life has been greatly simplified, and now I carry the wonderful peace of God. My life is now a joy to live, full of creativity and possibility with good fruit everywhere. It is hard to imagine what my life was like just a few short years ago. Glory to God!

In the natural realm, there is multiplication, as the harvest will produce much seed for the next season of sowing and reaping. As I live for God and saturate my life in His presence and His Word, the resulting harvest is a gift of thanks to God working in and through my life. The greatest and most joyous harvest in life is seeing lives change.

My daughter Bryn is my most precious harvest, who is now impacting lives all over the world. I also have the honour and privilege of spending time with many young entrepreneurs and have seen them grow, flourish, and begin to reproduce, sowing more and more good seeds into the world. In my company, I am seeing a transformation in people, which in turn impacts every area of their lives.

We must remember: When we sow into lives, the impact is broad, not only on their families and spheres of influence, but also on future generations. Everything we do now matters! This is the great harvest and why Jesus has called us to share the Gospel and to be disciple-makers who produce disciple-makers unto discipling the nations! As Jesus is, so are we now on earth!

"Go therefore and make disciples of all the nations [help the people to learn of Me, believe in Me, and obey My words], baptizing them in the name of the Father and of the Son and of the Holy Spirit, teaching them to observe everything that I have commanded you; and lo, I am with you always [remaining with you perpetually—regardless of circumstance, and on every occasion], even to the end of the age."
Matthew 28:19-20, AMP

The Patience and Perseverance in Sowing and Reaping

God's principle of sowing and reaping produces long-term, incremental, and lasting change. Keep in mind that there is always a tension between perseverance and patience as the harvest is ripening.

This is a time to be still and a time to learn to receive the guidance of the Holy Spirit and become sensitive to His gentle nudges. Every tree bears fruit in God's timing. From a seed, a papaya tree can start to product fruit in 6-9 months, a banana tree in 9-12 months, a fig tree in 1-2 years, citrus trees in 2-6 years, and the Brazil nut tree, 10-30 years. Each of us are a unique one-of-a-kind creation, in God's divine process, according to God's divine timing. Each type of seed we sow is in God's timing. Let's be patient and hungry, for if we continue to do good and not grow weary, we will certainly reap a harvest.

There will be multiplication and a harvest of the kind of seed sown; the choice is ours. Will you choose faith or fear? Will you choose God's ways or the ways of the world? Will your belief system be godly or ungodly? Will you be self-led or abide and be Spirit-led? These choices will impact your thoughts, words, actions, and, ultimately, the harvest in your life. You will be known by your fruit.

God's undeserved grace is not limited by human actions. God loves to bless us where we haven't "sown" because of His extravagant generosity and mercy. Let us be vessels of God's grace and mercy on earth with acts of kindness, generosity, and blessing towards others. By helping others reap where they haven't sown, they may be brought to repentance and freedom.

The Pathway to Extraordinary

In closing, let's consider the story of the loaves and fishes, which illustrates the principles of generosity, sowing, thanksgiving, active faith, and God's abundant, more than enough provision. It all started with a young boy generously giving his five loaves and two fish. Jesus received them and first gave thanks to the Father. He then instructed His disciples to go and distribute what they had. As they went, active faith released the miracle of multiplication so that the 5,000 (plus women and children totalling more than 10,000) were fed, plus twelve baskets of surplus.[5]

We sow so that the kingdom can increase, others can be blessed, and for God to be glorified. However, things don't always occur linearly in the kingdom, and we have to trust God to bring the fruit where He wants it. This is the kingdom of God, not the prosperity gospel. We take care of His kingdom, and all lesser things will be added unto us. As we release control and surrender our loaves and fishes (our time, money, abilities, etc.) to God, God will use the little or ordinary to perform the extraordinary.

Remember, it is God who provides the seeds and empowers us to steward them well.

This generous God who supplies abundant seed for the farmer, which becomes bread for our meals, is even more extravagant towards you. First, He supplies every need, plus more. Then He multiplies the seed as you sow it, so that the harvest of your generosity will grow. You will be abundantly enriched in every way as you give generously on every occasion, for when we take your gifts to those in need, it causes many to give thanks to God.
—2 Corinthians 9:10-11, TPT

1. Galatians 5:22-24.
2. Bill Johnson, "Bill Johnson Ministries," *Instagram*, accessed October 13, 2023, https://tinyurl.com/43ikhejv.
3. Rhoda Gayle, "God is Answering Our Prayers by Giving us Seeds," *GodTV*, accessed October 13, 2023, https://godtv.com/god-answering-prayers-seeds/.
4. M46 Ministry's name and mission comes directly from Malachi 4:6.
5. John 6:1-14.

THE KINGDOM PRINCIPLE OF SOWING AND REAPING

The principle of sowing and reaping is a divine economy, illustrating that our choices and actions have consequences. God's faithfulness multiplies the seeds of righteousness sown in obedience. God is the sower, depositing the seed of the kingdom into the soil of a believer's heart, which if receptive and nurtured, allows the kingdom's transformative power to be released within.

Father, thank You for multiplying Your seed in our lives!

QUESTIONS FOR REFLECTION

What has the Holy Spirit revealed to you through *The Kingdom Principle of Sowing and Reaping*? How can you apply this to your life?

_____

_____

_____

_____

Is there a particular area of your life that is barren where you would like to see good fruit? Ask God, "What seeds can I sow to produce a harvest in this area?"

_____

_____

_____

_____

In what areas of life have you witnessed a good harvest? Reflect on these and give thanks.

_____

_____

_____

_____

Notes

Chapter 12: The Kingdom Principles of Forgiveness and Mercy

Bearing with one another, and forgiving each other, whoever has a complaint against anyone; just as the Lord forgave you, so must you do also.
—*Colossians 3:13, NASB*

The Command of Forgiveness: Love's Gift

Forgiveness, as you know, is difficult for most people. However, forgiveness is not a suggestion for a Christian. It is a command for our good *and* the good of His kingdom. We receive it from God and get to release it to others. Forgiveness is also a great love gift from God that we must not take lightly as it *required the suffering and death of God. God's grace can be called aggressive forgiveness, in which sin doesn't have a chance!*[1]

Those who are forgiven much, love much. When we begin to grasp the enormity of the forgiveness we have received from Jesus, it's not uncommon for our hearts to soften towards others. In fact, this is exactly what God calls us to! What we have freely received, we are to freely give unto divine multiplication.[2] However, forgiveness is an action that flows from our own free will. We make the choice to forgive.

To forgive means to cancel a debt and release whoever hurt you to God. It doesn't necessarily mean you trust them again or that you have to be in their lives. It does mean that you can, honestly and sincerely, bless them to move on and sincerely choose to "let them off your hook." They no longer "owe" you. You won't make them pay their debt to you because Jesus already paid the debt that they owe us. This opens our hearts to more freely forgive and move in grace.

The Redemptive Path of Forgiveness

One of the most important reasons we are called to forgive is because unforgiveness is an open door to the enemy to have access to our lives. When we don't forgive, we give bitterness, pride, offence, resentment, and bondage legal access to us. These flesh-driven emotions are not allowed in the kingdom of heaven as they are of the kingdom of darkness. Forgiveness is the key to removing those emotions and strongholds that do not belong in God's kingdom. Forgiveness brings healing, wholeness, and freedom.

It is sometimes very difficult to forgive, especially in cases of extreme injustice, abuse, and slander. Hurt people hurt people, which gives insight into (but does not excuse) bad behaviours. Regardless, God says we must forgive. I have received healing and freedom as I moved in forgiveness towards those who murdered my daughter, those who raped my daughters, the person who emotionally and sexually abused them at a young age, and those who betrayed my family and business and beyond as He leads. In fact, Bryn and I recorded a podcast titled "When Forgiveness Feels

196

Impossible" to describe what we went through and the process of forgiveness around these types of horrible events.[3]

> It's the hardest to forgive [the people who have hurt us the most]. I think getting the Lord's heart for other people and understanding that, even just understanding the Lord's grace — that it's not just for people who are trying or people who love the Lord back. His grace is for everyone.[4]

Forgiveness is NOT an option. It is a profound gift! When you do not want to forgive or feel that you cannot forgive, I give you this word of caution: It is not for us to debate or provide our opinions about why we think something is unforgivable. God's Word is absolute. He is the ultimate judge, and He will enact justice in His perfect timing on our behalf because He is just![5] But that doesn't change the fact that God says we must forgive.[6] There are consequences of sin; they are often delayed, but they will come. God will not be mocked.[7] While only Jesus can provide the atoning payment of forgiveness of sins, we must forgive those who sin against us for many amazing kingdom reasons.[8]

The Grace to Forgive the "Unforgivable"

If we put our hurt or loss above the redemptive power of God, we are guilty of idolatry. I have found that when a big loss first happens, I am often tempted to put my pain in God's place. I literally need to strengthen myself in the Lord, lean on other believers to speak truth and life over the circumstance, cast my cares on the Lord, repent, and reorient myself with the promises of His kingdom.

Jesus tells us that we receive forgiveness as we forgive. In fact, if we don't forgive, we won't receive forgiveness.

> *"For if you forgive other people for their offenses, your heavenly Father will also forgive you. But if you do not forgive other people, then your Father will not forgive your offenses."*
> *—Matthew 6:14-15, NASB*

> *"Do not judge [others self-righteously], and you will not be judged; do not condemn [others when you are guilty and unrepentant], and you will not be condemned [for your hypocrisy]; pardon [others when they truly repent and change], and you will be pardoned [when you truly repent and change]."*
> *—Luke 6:37, AMP*

As we release our debtors from their debts to us, our debts to God are released. We receive Jesus's payment, which is far superior to any payment a human could make. Jesus wants us to be fully and completely free from any fleshly chains connected to unforgiveness. He wants to wash and heal our hearts completely from wrongs done against us. If we want to experience the full benefits of

Jesus's forgiveness of our sins, the physical, emotional, and spiritual healing of our diseases, and the joy of living without bitterness, vengeance, or ill-will towards others, we must begin by forgiving others.

As we forgive those who have sinned against us, we demonstrate the kingdom. This is a way to love our enemies as forgiveness is a beautiful demonstration of sacrificial love. As we forgive people, even the seemingly unforgivable ones, we are allowing them to experience the Gospel. Through forgiveness, we release the redemptive power of God's love into the lives of the ones who harmed us. We are declaring and demonstrating the healing and redemptive power of Jesus, who is able to save and deliver them.

I was recently in an interview when the host commented, "You have experienced so much loss." Without thinking, I responded instantly, "There is no loss in the kingdom." We all know there is loss in the earthly realm. Much of my loss came from betrayal and injustice. Some losses came from bad decisions, which are always learning opportunities. I needed to mourn my loss.

We all need to mourn at times. Forgiveness was a huge part of my process and kept my heart soft as I was learning to be dependent on God, knowing He is my provider and His supply is infinite. As I did, God invited me to experience true joy and comfort in His presence. God redeems all! Though we may not always see redemption on earth, we can be confident that ALL is redeemed in the supernatural realm. And one day, the two will be brought entirely together... no longer divorced.

As we declare and continue to believe in God's eternal promises, seeking first His kingdom, regardless of our natural circumstances, God's pullback is underway in preparation to be launched. The loss in the temporal realm becomes a pullback of the string of a bow, and we become the arrow that will go even further when released by God. Remember, the kingdom of God is always expanding despite the circumstantial evidence in the temporary realm. Joseph went down to the prison, maintaining His faith and maturity, and was eventually "shot" all the way to the top position in Egypt's government.[9] From the promise as a boy to the palace was a long process of preparation. God is faithful!

> *"Rather love your enemies and continue to treat them well. When you lend money, don't despair if you are never paid back, for it is not lost. You will receive a rich reward and you will be known as true children of the Most High God, having His same nature. Be like your Father who is famous for His kindness to heal even the thankless and cruel."*
> —*Luke 6:35, TPT*

One way to love our enemies is to forgive and bless them. Remember the law of sowing and reaping? What we sow we will reap, so let's choose love and forgiveness rather than bitterness and resentment. I can say from experience, the process of forgiveness grows easier with practice.

Here are some practical steps you can take. First, be specific. Write out what the person who hurt you did and how it made you feel. When you forgive him or her, release forgiveness for what they did AND how it made you feel. It is important to truly feel the emotions to release them. The next step is key: Pray for and bless the person, as prayer and blessing for those who hurt you are acts of sacrificial love.

> *"But I say to you who hear, love your enemies and do something wonderful for them in return for their hatred. When someone curses you, bless that person in return. When others mistreat and harass you, accept it as your mission to pray for them."*
> *Luke 6:27-28, TPT*

Consider the words of Jesus on the cross.

> *[But Jesus was saying,* **"Father, forgive them; for they do not know what they are doing."** *And they cast lots, dividing His garments among themselves.*
> *—Luke 23:34, NASB*

With forgiveness, love, and mercy in His heart, Jesus asked God to forgive His killers. Jesus is our example of forgiveness!

Oh Lord, Have Mercy

> *"How blessed you are when you demonstrate tender mercy! For tender mercy will be demonstrated to you."*
> *—Matthew 5:7, TPT*

Mercy is closely linked to forgiveness, and like forgiveness, it is also not a suggestion. According to Oxford Languages, mercy is to show "compassion or forgiveness towards someone whom it is within one's power to punish or harm."[10] I like to say that "mercy is holding back what we deserve, and grace is getting what we don't deserve." His grace is what empowers us to do what pleases God. The sun shines and the rain falls on both the righteous and the wicked as a demonstration of God's goodness and mercy. However, there is a difference between being impartial and the eternal implications of faith. Author Randy Alcorn says in his book *Heaven*, "For Christians, this present life is the closest they will come to Hell. For unbelievers, it is the closest they will come to Heaven."[11]

> *Who is a God like You, who pardons wrongdoing*
> *And passes over a rebellious act of the remnant of His possession?*
> *He does not retain His anger forever,*
> *Because He delights in mercy.*
> *—Micah 7:18, NASB*

God delights in showing mercy. In fact, His mercies become new each day as we arise.[12] I have experienced God's mercies more times in my life than I can count. We have all received great mercy, and in response to the great outpouring of His love, let us purposely live with an ever-increasing awareness of this incredible gift!

The Lord has instructed me by speaking to my heart to show mercy in the literal forgiveness of debts. Sometimes, it has been based on simple generosity, and other times, it has been based on gross injustices. I have lent money to people whom, when they came to propose a repayment plan, I blessed with forgiveness of the loan as a seed in their lives. I have also had seven and eight-figure financial injustices where God led me to drop the legal proceedings, instead choosing to forgive and pray for mercy for the perpetrator.

The first time I faced betrayal and gross financial injustice was before I made Jesus Lord in 2016. I was determined not to lose the battle, regardless of the cost. Thankfully, God used my advisory board to convince me to settle and move on, keeping my pride at bay. Years later, I did move in forgiveness, but that was not where my heart was before Christ became my Lord!

To repeat, what we have freely received, we are to freely give. Our mercy comes from God. As we extend mercy, we receive mercy. All this is unto divine multiplication. God grants mercy so we can be merciful to others. We are simply passing on what we have received from Jesus as we love our neighbours as ourselves.

Forgiveness, Mercy, and Judgment

And remember that judgment is merciless for the one who judges others without mercy. So by showing mercy, you take dominion over judgment!
—James 2:13, TPT

"Do not judge by the outward appearance, but judge with righteous judgment."
—John 7:24, NASB

When Jesus came to earth 2,000 years ago, He didn't come to judge but to find and rescue the lost.[13] When He ascended to heaven, that baton was passed to us. His mission is now our mission. Our ministry is one of reconciliation, not condemnation or criticism. Jesus will eventually return as judge at the end of the age. Judgment is not our job. It's His. Only God knows the entire story. Only God can truly and righteously discern what is in men's hearts.

"Do not judge, and you will not be judged; and do not condemn, and you will not be condemned; pardon, and you will be pardoned. Give, and it will be given to you. They will pour into your lap a good measure—pressed down, shaken together, and running over. For by your standard of measure it will be measured to you in return."
—Luke 6:37-38, NASB

God is THE judge. The judgments of God can be severe but are always for our good and to destroy evil. As the ekklesia (see Chapter 15 for more on this subject), we administer the government of God on earth, allowing and disallowing on earth what is allowed and disallowed in heaven. This is a form of judgment, administering the will of God on earth. We are to *hate* evil and *love* people. God hates sin. We are to bring people to freedom, which means calling out sin for believers and speaking the truth about the nature of sin.

Not judging others does not mean we are not supposed to use good judgment and discern between good and evil. We are not to tolerate evil as what we tolerate expands. God calls us to be wise in all of our relationships! God also draws attention to the fact that there is a difference between judging those inside the church and those outside the church. Those outside the church don't know better. They are not called to the same high standard. Those inside the church who are acting in ways damaging to themselves or the body must be lovingly corrected and, if they are unrepentant, put outside the congregation. Paul makes this point known.

For what business is it of mine to judge outsiders (non-believers)? Do you not judge those who are within the church [to protect the church as the situation requires]? God alone sits in judgment on those who are outside [the faith]. Remove the wicked one from among you [expel him from your church].
– 1 Corinthians 5:12-13, AMP

We, the church, have been guilty of hypocrisy, pointing to others' sins (believers and non-believers) before dealing with our own issues.[14] When we live our lives in repentance with our eyes on God, we live out the Gospel for others to see and experience God's goodness and kindness, which leads them to repentance. Consider the following scripture regarding those who "will not inherit" the kingdom of God as the road is narrow. This is meant to be sobering for all of us, in the fear of the Lord, as God always honours our free will. However, we get to live in grace consciousness and not sin consciousness (as His sin conquering grace is always sufficient when we embrace the beauty of repentance, simply returning to our good and perfect Heavenly Father).[15] When we see someone veering away from God, we can declare John 10:28-29, that no one will snatch them from our Father's hand as we continue to pray.

Surely you must know that people who practice evil cannot possess God's kingdom realm. Stop being deceived! People who continue to engage in sexual immorality, idolatry, adultery, sexual perversion, homosexuality, fraud, greed, drunkenness, verbal abuse, or extortion —these will not inherit God's kingdom realm. It's true that some of you once lived in those lifestyles, but now you have been purified from sin, made holy, and given a perfect standing before God all because of the power of the name of the Lord Jesus, the Messiah, and through our union with the Spirit of our God.
—1 Corinthians 6:9-11, TPT

Mercy triumphs over judgement! The plumbline of Scripture is for everyone's good, calling people up and encouraging them. Removing the plumbline only causes harm and is not merciful. We are to couple our mercy with the fear of the Lord to love well and to not fall into giving unsanctified mercy.[16] Many have lived far from the kingdom for decades. There is a measure of patience required for new believers as Jesus works in their hearts, removing the bonds and old patterns of sin in their lives. Jesus does not call those who are *sinless* to come to Him; He says come as you are and be transformed through daily walking with Him. Let's never forget, the good news Gospel is about justification by faith alone by the grace of God and never about our works.

A good rule of thumb is when we discern that something is not of God, we must address the situation with honour and great care, knowing that God is the ultimate judge and that we only see in part. The goal of using good judgment and discernment is to bring life, not death, freedom, not bondage. The enemy is the enemy, not people; the enemy uses people as pawns in his plans. Therefore, we must first address the issue in the spirit realm in prayer. Sacrificial love and humility are our superpowers!

Let's never forget the words of Jesus in John 8:7, **"…He who is without sin among you, let him be the first to throw a stone at her"** (NASB). We are to be quick to first search our own hearts in repentance to gain the perspective of God.

*   *   *

Father, we ask for the grace to forgive, to be merciful, and to discern right from wrong.

*   *   *

The greatest characteristic of a saint is humility. As evidenced by being able to say honestly and humbly, "Yes, all those, as well as other evils, would have been exhibited in me if it were not for the grace of God. Therefore, I have no right to judge."[17]

Receiving Forgiveness and Mercy

If you cover up your sin you'll never do well. But if you confess your sins and forsake them, you will be kissed by mercy.
——Proverbs 28:13, TPT

I used to think freedom came from forgiving myself, but we cannot forgive our own sins. Only Jesus can forgive sin (though we do have the power to forgive those who sin against us). What we do have a say in is whether we will agree with condemnation and shame or agree with forgiveness. It's less about "forgiving ourselves" and more about receiving and agreeing with the forgiveness Jesus already offers.

It should be noted that agreeing with condemnation is idolatry or grasping at control, which is counter to God's Word. For example, often, when we are dealing with shame, particularly in inner healing sessions, we are presented with the opportunity to release the burden of judgment we are holding over ourselves. This can feel like "forgiving ourselves," but really, it's about releasing (giving to God) the shame and guilt we're using to keep control and protect or punish ourselves. It's about leaving our shame and guilt at the cross. When we receive forgiveness from Jesus, we experience healing and freedom. Only God's forgiveness heals and frees us! Even if we have to deal with the natural consequences of sin (which we will), His grace enables us to do so well.

1. Romans 5:21, MSG.
2. Matthew 10:8.
3. E8, S1, *The Father Pursuit Podcast.*
4. Ibid.
5. Psalm 50:6.
6. Colossians 3:13.
7. Galatians 6:7-8.
8. Luke 11:4.
9. Genesis 39-41.
10. "Mercy," *Oxford Languages,* accessed October 13, 2023, https://tinyurl.com/mwpszcsr.
11. Randy Alcorn, *Heaven,* Goodreads.com, accessed April 9, 2024, https://www.goodreads.com/work/quotes/36257-heaven.
12. Lamentations 3:22-23.
13. Luke 19:10.
14. Matthew 7:5.
15. Consider James' warning to believers in James 5:19: One's soul falls into death by knowingly entering into sin without repentance, which is evidence of a seared or corrupted conscience.
16. Jude 22.
17. Oswald Chambers, "The Unchanging Law of Judgment," *My Utmost for His Highest,* accessed October 13, 2023, https://utmost.org/the-unchanging-law-of-judgment/.

THE KINGDOM PRINCIPLES OF FORGIVENESS AND MERCY

The kingdom of God is a realm where forgiveness and mercy flourish, reconciling people to God and to one another.

Father, thank You for giving us the grace to forgive and demonstrate mercy.

QUESTIONS FOR REFLECTION

What has the Holy Spirit revealed to you through *The Kingdom Principles of Forgiveness and Mercy?* How can you apply this to your life?

_____

_____

_____

_____

Recall a specific time when God extended His mercy to you or someone you know. Is there someone around you who you can show mercy to? How?

_____

_____

_____

_____

Pause and ask for the Father's heart and love for someone who has hurt you. How will this change your perspective, motives, and actions towards this person?

_____

_____

_____

_____

Notes

Chapter 13: The Kingdom Principle of Sabbath

In Exodus 19-20, God reveals Himself to Moses on Mount Sinai in the third month after the Israelites had left Egypt. He goes on to list the Ten Commandments or laws the people should follow in order to remain pure and not sin. Among these commandments, God establishes the Sabbath:

Remember the Sabbath day, to keep it holy. For six days you shall labor and do all your work, but the seventh day is a Sabbath of the Lord your God; on it you shall not do any work, you, or your son, or your daughter, your male slave or your female slave, or your cattle, or your resident who stays with you. For in six days the Lord made the heavens and the earth, the sea and everything that is in them, and He rested on the seventh day; for that reason the Lord blessed the Sabbath day and made it holy.
—Exodus 20:8-11, NASB

Sabbath, known as *shabbat* in Hebrew, means to "cease" or "desist."[1] Practically speaking, the Sabbath is a day of rest or a day when no work is done. According to this passage and tradition, the seventh day of every week is meant to be set apart as a holy day of rest, a day when we cease from our regular work. In Jewish culture, the Sabbath typically begins at sundown on Friday and lasts until sundown on Saturday. In Christian culture, the Sabbath is often reserved for Sundays, though many choose to practice on a different day of the week due to alternative work schedules. The day we actually celebrate as Sabbath is not the point, although God worked this issue out with me personally, which I will share later in this section. Rather, God commands us to rest one day a week from our labour.

The Faith to Rest

So we conclude that there is still a full and complete Sabbath-rest waiting for believers to experience. As we enter into God's faith-rest life we cease from our own works, just as God celebrates His finished works and rests in them.
—Hebrews 4:9-10, TPT

God loves and rewards faith that chooses to rest. Sabbath rest is the strategy of heaven. Rest is something that God modelled for us in creation since God Himself rested on the seventh day.[2] The Sabbath requires surrender. It requires *faith*. Specifically, faith that God will take care of everything when we turn our attention to Him. The Sabbath allows God to bring our work to completion and releases us from chains, exhaustion, and toiling. Our bodies, minds, and spirits need one day a week to recover. Adequate rest is necessary to stay physically, mentally, and spiritually strong.

In Exodus 23:11, God commands the Israelites to allow even the land to rest for one year out of every seven. Giving the land time to rest allowed it to be *more* productive. In fact, letting a field rest is scientifically proven to be beneficial to farmers. Forcing your land to work or produce non-stop leads to major man-made disasters like the Dust Bowl in the 1930s. During this unusual chapter in history, American prairies used for farming were depleted of nutrients necessary to support life that only come during seasons of the soil "lying fallow." As such, crops refused to grow. When the rains did not come, there was no growth to keep the soil from turning into dust and blowing away. Tragically, thousands of farmers were affected, contributing to economic disaster and exacerbating the impact of the Great Depression. However, if farmers had let the land rest as God had commanded, a great deal of loss and pain would likely have been avoided.

In early 2023, our ministry released a podcast episode called "The Faith to Rest." Matt Davis, my co-host and great friend, opened with these words:

> Sabbath is not dependent upon our readiness to stop. We do not stop when we are finished. We do not stop when we complete our phone calls, finish our project, get through this stack of messages, or get out this report that is due tomorrow. We stop because it is time to stop.[5]

The Sabbath requires us to surrender everything. If you've lived any amount of time on earth as an adult, you know that life doesn't stop. It slows, but only when we submit our time, schedules, and responsibilities to the Lord. When we do, He promises to carry us and provide for us as we pause to spend time in His presence. The Sabbath is an act of obedience and trust. It does not depend on whether we've crossed every task off our list or made peace with the cleanliness of our house. The Sabbath eliminates urgency and frees us from the need to "finish" what's before us.

Whenever and whatever God instructs us to do produces life. When I reflect back on my life and the bad decisions I've made, most of them were made with haste and not from a place of rest. They were made in times of my life when I was moving too fast and in my own strength. Rest positions us to slow down, hear God, and make wise decisions from a position of stillness, not striving. As the place of rest is of the Spirit, to rest is to submit all things to God. It is to embrace the peace of His presence that only He can offer. Rest can look like taking a day off of work where you wake up early to enjoy God's Word over coffee, play catch with your kids, and savour a good meal, but it is also a state of mind and heart that results from a Sabbath lifestyle. In other words, rest can be active; it is working from a place of rest and creativity in the Lord.

Poor is one who works with a lazy hand,
But the hand of the diligent makes rich.
—Proverbs 10:4, NASB

Rest is not an excuse for laziness, as we were created to co-labour with God. Laziness reveals itself in a lack of engagement in life, whereas rest is a place of active engagement with God and life. We are made to work hard (glorifying God, working as unto the Lord) and also rest well, delighting in the goodness of God. In the realm of calm, quiet, and stillness, we become aware, sensitive and responsive to our spirit. This is a principle we cannot live without! God created us to flourish, and the Sabbath is part of His plan.

Consequently, there remains a Sabbath rest for the people of God. For the one who has entered His rest has himself also rested from his works, as God did from His. Therefore let's make every effort to enter that rest, so that no one will fall by following the same example of disobedience.
—*Hebrews 4:9-11, NASB*

Adam and Eve were made on the sixth day of creation, and their very first day in the kingdom was the seventh day, a day of rest. The kingdom is in a constant state of Sabbath rest. Those who dwell in the kingdom have their eyes constantly on Jesus, and He, in turn, gives them supernatural peace and rest and guards and protects their work from the strain of toiling. In the long run, this gives kingdom dwellers greater longevity and more productivity than those who work themselves to the bone without stopping. God made us to rest, and when we do, the quality of our lives and work greatly improves.

Jesus freed us from "works" for salvation by grace. Justification is through faith alone. He wore the crown of thorns to break the curse and release us from toil. Jesus is the Lord of the Sabbath and is the Lord over our work. As sons and daughters, we are commanded to choose to rest and then work from the place of rest for the remainder of the week, understanding work is worship as unto the Lord.

I know that when I am tired, worn out, distracted, striving, or operating in my own strength, life is very difficult. Even little challenges seem big. Creativity wanes. Toiling, fear of lack, and stress set in. Peace vacates. This is a callback to the secret place with God, back to the place of rest and faith! We can place our burdens and cares back on God where they belong. The reality of the nearness and the abundance of His kingdom returns when we do. From this place of rest, God has carried me through the most immense challenges of life in His grace and peace. I've come out transformed and with a greater revelation of the supremacy of God and His kingdom.

"Come to Me, all who are weary and burdened, and I will give you rest. Take My yoke upon you and learn from Me, for I am gentle and humble in heart, and you will find rest for your souls. For My yoke is comfortable, and My burden is light."
—*Matthew 11:28-30, NASB*

A Sabbath Lifestyle

Resting as God instructs us will always result in producing more fruit, even if that means having seasons that look "fallow." I personally believe it is important to rest daily during times of Bible study, prayer, and reflection, as well as weekly during the Sabbath. (Note: I didn't say to rest FROM these things, but actually *during* these times.)

For me, this looks like starting my day early in silence with the Lord. This helps me approach my day from a place of rest. The more I choose to be *with* God before attempting to do *for* God, the more peace and joy I experience in life. God is never in a rush. This has required me to create margins and simplify my life. For example, in this particular season of my life, I have adopted a minimalist lifestyle, which gives me great flexibility and capacity with few things to manage.

Because I have a propensity for action, embracing the Sabbath and Sabbath lifestyle is still a work in progress for me. The ability to rest is a good indication of our progression in receiving the truth of our identity, revealing whether we are operating from an orphan mindset (always working for approval and survival) or from a child of God mindset (receiving His good gift of rest and provision).

> Joy is peace dancing and peace is joy at rest.
> —F.B. Meyer[1]

Refraining from doing regular work does not mean that we don't take care of ourselves or others. In fact, Jesus and His disciples harvested grain to eat on the Sabbath when they were hungry. This was against the interpretations and additional rules the Pharisees had around Sabbath laws.[5] Jesus even healed a man's hand on the Sabbath.[6] Again, it appeared this was against Sabbath laws. However, there are laws and higher laws. Jesus knew better than the Pharisees. The law of love ultimately trumped their man-made laws. While the law of religion was provided for our benefit, the law of love is the greatest law.[7] It enables us to live in freedom in the spirit of the law and avoid legalism. The higher law of love always says to do good and protect life. When Jesus explained this to the angry Pharisees, they had no response.

The Lord of the Sabbath

> *Jesus said to them,* **"The Sabbath was made for man, not man for the Sabbath. So the Son of Man is Lord even of the Sabbath [and He has authority over it]."**
> —*Mark 2:27-28, AMP*

Ultimately, the Sabbath is a day to remember what God has done for us through Jesus's death, resurrection, and ascension. Jesus is our Sabbath rest, our eternal rest from works and labouring. Jesus is our place of rest. Jesus is our secret place.

*　　*　　*

Father, we ask for the grace of the Sabbath.

*　　*　　*

For the vast majority of my life, I didn't really know about the Sabbath, much less honour it. I lived in self-reliance, felt weary, and operated out of a high level of stress. Then, a few years ago, I began to live in the awareness of the Sabbath, but didn't stop my activities. I often engaged in business or whatever came to the surface on the day I had "set apart." It's taken much practice and revelation through God's Word and guidance from brothers and sisters in Christ to help me embrace the Sabbath.

Today, I like to do things that are different on my Sabbath to distinguish it from my usual activities. Many find it beneficial to plan for the Sabbath, so all meals are ready, and there is little thought required on that day. For me, I usually start with early-morning quiet time, journaling or writing, having coffee before church, spending time with family, enjoying walks, a nap, a quiet afternoon reading, great food (feasting is always a must), games, hiking, biking, etc. Sabbath will look different for everyone as what brings each person life and rest will vary. Sabbath should be practised out of obedience to God and should never invoke shame or the idea that we will do it perfectly. It is for our good and not to invoke condemnation. It is a practice that improves over time and is filled with grace.

I have to be strategic to make sure my Sabbath rest doesn't get tainted or overpowered by my natural inclination to do and produce. Because I have lots of ideas and things flowing through my mind at all times, I have instilled a system that I call a "parking lot." As ideas come, I "park" them by writing them on a list to be revisited the following day. As I write the ideas down, the thoughts are released from my mind, and I can continue with my Sabbath.

Recently, a friend of mine was reading a draft of this book and asked, "Does God set the timing and seasons, or do you?" I stopped and reflected, then began to laugh (because of revelation, not a sour religious response). I felt fresh conviction and revelation in my heart towards the Sabbath and realized how simple and clear God's instructions are for the Sabbath. So, I finally decided to receive the gift of rest, not on Sunday (which worked better for my schedule), but on the traditional Friday night through Saturday night. This decision was not made out of legalism, but rather as a response to something the Holy Spirit put in my heart. Ultimately, the Sabbath is not about convenience. It's about obeying God's commands and abiding in His presence. My Sabbath is now Friday sundown to Saturday sundown! This is the process of wrestling with God unto revelation. If we approach the Sabbath only based on knowledge and adherence to the law, all we have is religion, like the Pharisees. Jesus is Lord of the Sabbath!

I am now doing much better with this practice and actually have an excitement for this day of rest and connection. God is always shifting us into the fullness of His plans (heart-level revelation) and is gracious in the process. Sabbath really is a practice, and the more we do it, the more we reap the fruit of rest. As you can see, rest is a powerful weapon in the kingdom.

1. The Editors of Encyclopedia, "Sabbath: Judaism," *Britannica*, accessed October 13, 2023, https://www.britannica.com/topic/Sabbath-Judaism.

2. Genesis 2:2.

3. Matt Davis quoting Wayne Muller, "Faith to Rest," *The Father Pursuit*, accessed October 13, 2023, https://thefatherpursuit.podbean.com/e/faith-to-rest/.

4. F.B. Meyer, "F.B. Meyer Quotes," *QuoteFancy*, accessed October 16, 2023, https://tinyurl.com/2s3mxma6.

5. Matthew 12:1-2.

6. Matthew 12:9-13, Mark 3:1-6, Luke 6:6-11.

7. Matthew 22:36-40.

THE KINGDOM PRINCIPLE
OF SABBATH

In the kingdom of God, the Sabbath is a weekly divine appointment to rest and remember that God is the ultimate sustainer of our lives. Every Sabbath is an invitation into a deeper relationship with Him.

Father, thank You for helping us step into Sabbath rest!

QUESTIONS FOR REFLECTION

What has the Holy Spirit revealed to you through *The Kingdom Principle of Sabbath*? How can you apply this to your life?

_____

_____

_____

_____

What does the rhythm of labour and rest look like in your life? Have you established "margins"?

_____

_____

_____

_____

What tools/habits can you implement to help you honour the Sabbath?

_____

_____

_____

_____

Notes

Chapter 14: The Kingdom Principle of Transformational Suffering

Everyone in the world suffers, so you're never alone in your grief. Suffering without Jesus almost destroyed my life and my family. Suffering *with* Jesus changed everything.

In my first book, *More Than Gold*, I dedicate the last quarter of the book to the subject of suffering. Today, God continues to put suffering in my heart to share in my writings. I am more convinced than ever before that He will give our suffering great purpose if we surrender it to Him. As you read this section, remember to never compare your suffering with anyone else's, as everyone's journey and capacity are unique. What's traumatic for one person may simply be uncomfortable for someone else.

Get ready. This is a difficult subject and a very dense section meant to challenge our thinking about suffering. I have discovered that God is with me in everything. As I accept the reality that life is hard and embrace the redemptive purpose of pain when submitted to God, the more I am aware that things are happening *for me* and not *to me*. My life is the Lord's, and He is working all things together for my good. This mindset prepares me to move in trust and grow as a result of my obstacles and challenges. A life is fulfilled in the overcoming of challenges, not in the pursuit of comfort. I have also discovered that as I choose to embrace uncertainty, my openness to learning increases, and so does my ability to truly live in the present, becoming more alive and aware of each moment. God asks us to be a people who know how to suffer. Consider suffering the "grace path" to the heart position of the Beatitudes. If we suffer well, it has the power to turn our world upside down, allowing the kingdom to explode in and through us.

It is grace that changes us, and all change involves suffering. In this process, we become a light to the world as we take up our cross and follow Jesus. With this in mind, suffering becomes a badge of honour based on how we position ourselves before the Lord in the midst of the fire. Life circumstances, pain, and shame do not define us, rather, they refine us. We never need to feel shame about suffering. This refining process prepares us to receive our inheritance as co-heirs with Christ, teaching us how to steward blessing and preparing us to rule and reign with Him. Suffering is the gateway to walking out the fullness of life in the kingdom.

The Origin of Suffering

The foundation of suffering (and our faith) is our belief in the absolute, unchanging nature of God's infinite goodness and knowing that His plans for us are always and only good.

"For I know the plans that I have for you," declares the Lord, "plans for prosperity and not for disaster, to give you a future and a hope."
—Jeremiah 29:11, NASB

Suffering in itself is not of God, though He can and does use it for our good and His glory. Rather, suffering is the direct result of the enemy's plans and man's sin. When God created the heavens and the earth and made man to steward them, He gave mankind free will, which permits both good and evil. This was an act of love and established our ability to have a relationship with both Him and others. Remember, God said each aspect of creation was "good" (with the exception of man being alone, so He created woman).[1] There was no evil on earth until man made the choice to go against God's will when he ate from the Tree of Knowledge of Good and Evil. This was the first sin that opened the door to suffering.

Mathematician, bioethicist, and believer Dr. John Lennox explains it this way:

> Could God have created a world without suffering? Yes, He could have, but you and I would not live in it because it would empty the world of something most precious to our humanity, and that is the capacity to love, and our capacity to love, hinges on our capacity to choose.[2]

On this earth, we will suffer in small and mighty ways. We will suffer physically, emotionally, and spiritually as we reap the consequences of sin in this world, including the sins of others as well as our own sins. It's important to remember that God is always compassionate about our suffering. In the midst of this horrible reality, the greater truth is that God (who is love and the source of abundant life) can redeem anything and is always with us.

> *To grant those who mourn in Zion, Giving them a garland instead of ashes, The oil of gladness instead of mourning, The cloak of praise instead of a disheartened spirit. So they will be called oaks of righteousness, The planting of the Lord, that He may be glorified.*
> *—Isaiah 61:3, NASB*

We are urged to respond to Satan's attacks by rising up with righteous anger and partnering with God to enforce the victory of Jesus. We know that while we are on this side of eternity, there will be suffering.[3] There are mysteries we may never understand. There are many "Why, Lord?" questions we will only understand when this part of our existence has passed away, and we are with the Lord in glory. However, when we know the circumstance is an attack by Satan, we are called to submit to God and actively resist the devil so that he will turn and run![4] We know God will ultimately use what the enemy meant for evil for good.[5] He is all-powerful and can take our pain and turn it into beauty, gladness, and praise because He is good![6] He is the great redeemer!

Suffering Invites Redemption

I grew up with the expectation that I would live a life of comfort. Blessing was what happened when you accepted Jesus into your life; therefore, I assumed suffering was simply "bad." However, God sees the big picture, and He knows the end from the beginning so we can rest in His sovereignty and goodness. While this may be controversial, I believe that we cannot label suffering as simply "evil" or "bad," as so much good can come from it. The more we are aware of God at work in the in-between moments of our life, the more we will recognize Him at work when times of suffering and hardship come.

> **"These things I have spoken to you so that in Me you may have peace. In the world you have tribulation, but take courage; I have overcome the world."**
> *—John 16:33, NASB*

As believers, it is imperative that we understand we are in a battle. As we walk in righteousness to advance His kingdom, the more opposition from darkness we will face. We must go through the darkness and tribulations so that we can be overcomers. It is a beautiful and difficult natural part of the process of maturation. When we go through darkness and tribulation, we have an opportunity, in a radical way, to practice experiencing God on the inside, which is greater than anything we will face on the outside. We demonstrate the faith to overcome as we walk through darkness. The one who overcomes will receive the many promises in the Book of Revelation!

> Don't doubt in the dark what God has told you in the light.
> —Daniel C. Juster[7]

Do you remember the prophetic "slash and burn" word I received in the middle of the fire in June 2018? There was another aspect to the message. Doug said the slash and burn was not because I had done anything wrong, but quite the opposite. Rather, it was because of the position of my heart and the declaration of my life as belonging to God. It was God's mercy, letting me know what was to come, and it was His grace that sustained and transformed me in the process. Because I had said "yes," God was separating me from the things of the world so that I would discover myself and Him as He refined, formed, shaped, and matured me. In fact, both *More Than Gold* and *As in Heaven* are the result of what God has done for me. He has given me a passion to share His message with the world.

Jesus is the originator and perfecter of our faith.[8] He tells us plainly that discipleship demands sacrifice. There is suffering in sacrifice. I have experienced a little of what it means to sacrifice for my faith. I honour those around the world and throughout history who have experienced unimaginable loss and pain to follow Jesus through the power of the Holy Spirit.

Remember, you are a doorway for Jesus so that the King of Glory may come through. I have opened this door and have personally experienced the power of Christ overcoming the world in my own life and heart. In times of darkness, God is my light. Because of what I've been through, Jesus has given me the opportunity to compassionately reach out to those around me who are also suffering and suffer along with them. Following Jesus is easy when we are comfortable, but our true commitment is tested in the trials that expose what is in our hearts.

Because Jesus flipped suffering on its head through His death and resurrection, something that once led to death now leads to abundant life and resurrection life. The sacrifice and suffering of perfect and holy Jesus in place of undeserving sinners was a full display of God's nature, His goodness, His faithfulness, His grace, and His glory. Based on the absolute victory of Jesus, we can take heart as Jesus has overcome the world, and we are in Him.

Jesus absorbed the curse entirely, taking it upon Himself in our place, and thereby restoring the blessing of Abraham. While suffering remains part of our human experience, through Jesus, our suffering becomes redemptive, drawing us closer to God.

The Blessing of Suffering

I recently read an article titled "How Does Suffering Help the Believers?" where the authors describe ten blessings that come from suffering. According to the article, suffering:

1. "Contributes to the eternal glory by purifying, refining, and sanctifying the character.
2. Cultivates trust and dependence on the Lord.
3. Exerts a purifying influence upon the mind.
4. Humbles pride, subdues self, and is often the way of bringing the will of the believer in line with God's will.
5. Tests the believer's faith and the truthfulness of his profession as a follower of Christ.
6. Gives a place for the exercise and perfection of faith. For faith is strengthened by exercise.
7. Helps the Christian to see things in their true value.
8. Creates in the Christian a fitness for glory. He finds it easier to set his affections on heavenly things.
9. Proves the foolishness of human wisdom by placing the believer in difficult positions, where his own helplessness and need of the Lord becomes clear.
10. Consecrates human relationships. Nothing contributes more to [the] understanding of others and having kindness towards them than do suffering, trial, and affliction."[9]

However, the blessing of suffering comes only when our hearts are postured towards Jesus and when we invite Him into our suffering. When we are one with Jesus, He comes into our suffering through the spirit and through others who are also one with Jesus.

We will not avoid suffering in this world. In fact, suffering is promised.[10] Life is hard, and there is nothing we can do to change that, but we will be okay with Jesus! It is foolish to pretend we can get through life without experiencing pain or that it can be avoided by some effort of our own. If we are willing and able to turn and face it, pain can act as a thermometer, a compass, or a guide to show us what is injured or misaligned inside of us and reveal beliefs and situations that we need to remove ourselves from.

In many cases, pain can be a helpful indicator as it points us to a problem. However, if we don't feel and process our emotions in painful situations, they will come back later, continuing to inflict pain and suffering until they have been processed.

For the majority of my life, I tried to bypass or ignore my pain, which resulted in unhealed wounds, invulnerability, a lack of authentic connections, relational issues, a narrowing of my emotional range, and a general heaviness or tiredness. I now understand that tears are a gift from God that frees our souls and releases our emotions.

Jesus, the only one who was sinless and perfect, took on the greatest suffering and punishment unto the greatest victory. He took on the fullness of physical, emotional, and spiritual pain for you and me. When we suffer, we can go to Jesus, knowing He understands our pain and can comfort us like nothing else the world has to offer. Not only that, but because of Jesus's sacrifice, we can leave our suffering at the foot of the cross, knowing it is His burden to carry.

NOT A PUNISHER

God never brings sickness, disease, or punishment, as proven by the life of Jesus. These are part of the system of the world that was put into play when Adam and Eve rebelled against God. By doing so, they relinquished their dominion over the earth to Satan. We see the results on earth and the entire cosmos in the manifestation of death and decay. When we suffer, we must remember that God is not a punisher—that is Satan's view of God. Rather, Jesus's life was the ultimate revealing of our Father's good and perfect nature.

I will never forget when a particularly difficult season of my life was under intense fire, from my family life to my businesses. Everything that could go wrong was going wrong, and as time went by, it just kept getting worse. I called it my "slash and burn" years. Throughout this period, I consistently received an image of Jesus holding my heart and comforting me amid the fire.

Later, a prophet I respect received a word from the Lord that he saw Jesus holding my heart in the midst of the enemy coming with the fire to destroy what I held dear. The prophet described Jesus's hands forming a kiln around my heart to form, shape, and protect me. The fire of the enemy was intended to burn and destroy me; however, Jesus's comfort and protection shielded me from the destruction. It was a classic scenario of God taking what the enemy meant for harm and using it for my good and His glory. The message continued that the fire I was experiencing was used to mold me and make me more like Jesus. This was such a beautiful confirmation of what I knew to be true while not diminishing the reality of my suffering. Rather, it reminded me that there was a light at the end of the tunnel, and God's plans would ultimately triumph over the enemy.

We suffer as we enter the narrow doorway into God's kingdom: As we yield our lives to Jesus and allow His character to be produced in us, we will be asked to make sacrifices. These sacrifices, which are always for our good, will look different for each of us as we reorient our lives to the kingdom. These sacrifices may involve lifestyle changes, including relationships, priorities, finances, fleshly desires, etc. There is always a cost to things of great value! For example, salvation, although a free gift, costs us our lives in exchange for His.

> **"Anyone who comes to Me must be willing to share My cross and experience it as his own, or he cannot be considered to be My disciple. So don't follow Me without considering what it will cost you. For who would construct a house before first sitting down to estimate the cost to complete it?"**
> —*Luke 14:27-28, TPT*

We suffer when we are being disciplined: We suffer when the Father (the gardener of our garden, our internal world) prunes, cleans, or "disciplines" the worldliness/sin/unfruitfulness off of us so the good fruit of the Spirit can grow and we can bear a great harvest.[11] We are disciplined primarily spiritually through His Word and His Spirit living within us.

> *"For whom the Lord loves He disciplines, and He punishes every son whom He accepts."*
> —*Hebrews 12:6, NASB*

We suffer in times of earthly lack, which is a reality on earth but not in the kingdom: This helps us learn to be thankful and content in all circumstances. It points us to depend on Jesus as our source for all things in the spiritual and in the physical. Suffering from lack also reminds us to lean on the church and fellow believers as we participate in and receive from the body of Christ.

We suffer as a result of our sins and the sins of others: We suffer unnecessarily when we make decisions that we know are wrong and go against our conscience. Much suffering is of our own making when we reap the natural consequences of our choices. Alternatively, we may suffer because of someone else's sin.

We suffer as we pass through trials of disappointment, delays, and discouragement: The discipline of delay has been used again and again in my life as God continues to form my character, producing patient endurance or perseverance and a refusal to give up in the waiting. During these trials, we can learn to encourage ourselves in the Lord and receive hope that never disappoints based on the futuristic certainty of God's promises.

We suffer as we experience seasons in the wilderness: The wilderness can make us feel separate from God. However, learning to press in beyond our feelings when we seemingly get nothing in return for our devotion is essential. The goal of the wilderness is that we would come up out of it leaning on our Beloved. God is always present and available, no matter how alone or isolated we feel. How we experience God will vary. However, our life union or oneness with God is the greatest truth. Satan expresses himself on earth through deception. God is using the journey through these things to form and mature us as overcomers who place God first above everything, at the very core of our lives and far above our feelings and emotions.

We suffer as we learn obedience: Jesus fully submitted Himself to God and limited Himself to the human experience of learning and growing. I have been an entrepreneur for 25 years, able to make my own decisions and live my way. When I finally yielded my life to God, I faced much opposition from friends and family who didn't understand what I was doing. Even still, I went through my own process of yielding my will to His. As I matured, my love of God progressed, and I learned to live more sacrificially. What was painful at first became natural over time. *"Although He was a Son, He learned obedience from the things which He suffered."* — *Hebrews 5:8, NASB*

We suffer when we learn to fast: Fasting is the practice of denying ourselves so that we teach and train our bodies to hunger for God and fast for God, reacting to suffering in prayer and in the Word, especially during meal times. This sensitizes our spirits to recognize Emmanuel, God with us, address unbelief, and recognize God as our source, sustainer, and Creator. Delayed gratification results in a greater outcome. Biblical fasting typically refers to denying oneself food, though some people today choose to fast from electronics or specific foods. Keep in mind that this is not about dieting or losing weight, though healthy eating requires self-control to deny our unhealthy desires, which is a form of suffering. Fasting consecrates our desires. In order to grow, we need to stretch out of our comfort zones and into the unknown, *which requires suffering*. A diamond is produced under great pressure. A pearl is created through irritation. Gold is refined in fire. Things of value are costly.

We suffer when we let go of the past and step into the new: We grieve the loss of loved ones, jobs, relationships, seasons of life, etc. Regardless of how positive the "new" is, we naturally grieve what was. For example, getting married or moving to a new city for a job promotion, while positive in nature, might cause someone to grieve the independence of their single life or the comfort of their hometown. Remember, grief is only temporary, as it is a transitioning emotion that moves us out of the old and opens our hearts to receive the new. After a while, what once seemed like suffering gives way to a new and better way of living. Suffering, in its many forms, acts as an accelerant as it causes us to press into God for relief, answers, and reconciliation. Suffering wakes us up to change.

Suffering Is Personal

When you are punished severely, you learn your lesson well —for painful experiences do wonders to change your life.
—Proverbs 20:30, TPT

In my case, I have often learned things the hard way. Much of my previous suffering was caused by my own sin for which I felt unconvicted, unrepentant, and blind for much of my life. But that was due to the nature of my flesh (self-life) and a testament to the depth of my blindness. I have discovered that continuing with inner-heart healing has been an incredible accelerant in bringing an end to selfishness, allowing me to yield or surrender more fully. Ultimately, it is the Spirit of God that displaces darkness and the self-life within us.

Let me emphasize this: As you yield to the dynamic life and power of the Holy Spirit, you will abandon the cravings of your self-life. When your self-life craves the things that offend the Holy Spirit you hinder Him from living free within you! And the Holy Spirit's intense cravings hinder your self-life from dominating you! So then, the two incompatible and conflicting forces within you are your self-life of the flesh and the new creation life of the Spirit. But when you yield to the life of the Spirit, you will no longer be living under the law, but soaring above it!
—Galatians 5:16-18, TPT

The enemy can use others to inflict evil and pain on us. Sometimes, we have open doors of agreement or legal rights in our lives for Satan to come through. This could be as simple as watching TV shows or movies that are not honouring the Lord. It may be from involvement in the occult, unhealthy relationships, unresolved anger, or negative soul ties. But sometimes circumstances just go wrong. Regardless of the source of the trial, we can be assured Jesus's plans are good, and He will use everything for our good and His glory if we keep our eyes on Him! I know that God loves me too much to leave me as I am. Change can be painful, but when we suffer and come to the end of ourselves, seeking God as our source and strength, we learn obedience and how to seek the well-being of others above ourselves.

Jesus Is With Us in Suffering

The afflictions of the righteous are many, But the Lord rescues him from them all.
—Psalm 34:19, NASB

Jesus is present with us in our suffering. He feels our pain. He mourns with us. But He also takes action to save and redeem. In suffering, we experience our comforter, the Holy Spirit. God also uses Christians as the hands and feet of Jesus on earth to come alongside and carry our burdens and strengthen us in the faith.

Your pain is not wasted when submitted to Jesus.
—Bryan Elliott, More than Gold[12]

We are never alone. God is with us, and many of the saints around the world are also suffering. This brings me comfort, although I would never wish suffering on anyone; I know that trials are part of life on earth. It is a common experience, and I am not alone in the process. Life can be hard, plain and simple—but we are not alone, and we will be okay!

God's comfort is power. It's not meant merely to make us feel better. It's meant to make us more like Jesus.
—Rosaria Champagne Butterfield[13]

The absolute key to suffering well is to dwell in the revelation of the goodness of God! This is the source of our praise above and through any circumstance. Even in our suffering, through Jesus, we can offer a sacrifice of praise to God. We can fix our eyes on Him. We can stand in faith. It is God's grace that empowers us to not only endure but to overcome. This brings us into a greater place of intimacy with Jesus, experiencing His kingdom of peace and joy in the midst of our earthly trials. It is the reality of the kingdom of Jesus that enables us to not only endure suffering, but to be transformed in the suffering. The Christian life is a life of self-denial and picking up our cross. The process of transformation involves dying to self so that we can be living sacrifices, holy and pleasing to God. In dying to self (to sin, our fleshly desires, and our old man through patterns of this world), we put on the new man (the mind of Christ) and reveal Jesus to the world.[14]

"For whoever wants to save his life will lose it; but whoever loses his life for My sake will find it."
Matthew 16:25, NASB

Here is another kingdom principle that is totally counter to the ways of the world: If we focus only on ourselves, we slowly wither and die, whereas when we forget ourselves in the service of others, we flourish by God's design. The cross, a symbol of brutal and bloody execution, is the symbol of Christianity for good reason. To carry a cross (your own instrument of death) is to endure the most humiliating and painful death imaginable. The cross reminds us of the suffering of Christ and His willingness to endure the most excruciating agony in order to bring life to the entire world.

To enter the kingdom involves a process of taking up our own cross and following Jesus's example, dying to our flesh and denying ourselves in order to be transformed into the image of Christ. We lose our lives to gain true life. We die to live. This process of transformation (through dying to ourselves) is what prepares us to follow Jesus and live out His teachings as His hands and feet on earth.

> Do not insult the work of the cross by complaining about your problems. Welcome trials, for they teach you what you are and lead you to renounce yourself, and yourself is, of all possessions, the most dangerous… All that should concern you is glorifying God.
> Jeanne Guyon[15]

The Choice to Suffer

For all who choose to live godly as worshipers of Jesus, the Anointed One, will also experience persecution.
—2 Timothy 3:12, TPT

As Scripture shares the life of Jesus, it is clear that the world hates Jesus, and it will hate His godliness within us. If we are to advance His kingdom, we will face suffering. In 2 Timothy 3, Paul speaks to Timothy as a father to a son with the promise of suffering for those who want to live godly lives. Paul himself experienced a long list of suffering, including 39 lashes five times, jail, stoning, and shipwrecks.[16] Through it all, he praised God. In addition, at least ten of the 12 disciples, those closest to Jesus, were tortured and murdered for their faith.[17] If Paul or any of the apostles chose not to engage in the public arena preaching and teaching, they might have lived more "normal" lives with less suffering. Imagine, though, what would have happened if they had stayed within the four walls of the church? Look closely at the scripture below and the word "provided" that is highlighted.

And since we are His true children, we qualify to share all His treasures, for indeed, we are heirs of God Himself. And since we are joined to Christ, we also inherit all that He is and all that He has. We will experience being co-glorified with Him provided that we accept His sufferings as our own.
—Romans 8:17, TPT (emphasis added)

Ultimately, we enter into His sufferings and experience His suffering as our own as we move in the truth of our co-crucifixion and co-resurrection with Jesus unto new creation life. We are treasures of His great grace!

We consider living to mean that we are constantly being handed over to death for Jesus's sake so that the life of Jesus will be revealed through our humanity. So, then, death is at work in us but it releases life in you.
—2 Corinthians 4:11-12, TPT

The death of our flesh happens in the refining fire of God. We can only die to the flesh by the Spirit as our old self is slowly displaced by our new identity in Christ. In reality, it's our flesh that causes us to suffer. The more we yield to God's process of sanctification and refinement, the freer we are to respond to the will of God, making the fullness of our union with Jesus and new creation life a reality. The way we experience suffering changes exponentially the closer we get to the Father. The more we are self-reliant, independent, willful, and determined to hold onto our "stuff," the more the suffering will hurt. Alternately, the more we step into our true identity as sons and daughters of God and draw near to Him, yielded to His plans and purpose no matter what, the less the fire of God will feel like suffering. We lose our lives to find life!

They conquered Him completely through the blood of the Lamb and the powerful word of his testimony. They triumphed because they did not love and cling to their own lives, even when faced with death.
—Revelation 12:11, TPT

John's words in Revelation 12:11 demonstrate the power, grace, love, and victory of the cross. But we cannot stop there. There are two sides to the cross. Death *and* resurrection. Suffering *and* joy. The crucified life is one that dies daily and simultaneously lives every minute in the newness of a resurrected life. When we lose our life, we gain it. When we die, we live. When we suffer with Jesus, we experience deep joy and peace in every circumstance. This is clearly how the Apostle Paul was able to go through such horrific suffering and still maintain a positive attitude, his eyes fixed on Jesus![18] He knew that everything he was going through was for God's glory, the encouragement of the church, and his own character growth. He (nor any one of us) can go through such suffering without the empowering grace of God to carry us through.

I used to be in awe of the martyrs and wonder if faced with losing my life for the sake of Christ, would I stay strong? Now, I know that I could not, and neither could they, without God's empowering grace in the face of suffering. I no longer fear death for the sake of Christ, because if and when that day comes, it's His grace that will carry me through. More importantly, it's His supernatural ressurection power that will burst forth defeating death, whenever that day comes.

Be strong and courageous; don't be terrified or afraid of them. For it is the Lord your God who goes with you; He will not leave you or forsake you.
–Deuteronomy 31:6, NIV

With that, I want to encourage you that when you "lose your life" and feel that everything is falling apart, you will fall right into God's grace if Jesus Christ is your Lord and Saviour.

I can do all things [which He has called me to do] through Him who strengthens and empowers me [to fulfill His purpose   I am self-sufficient in Christ's sufficiency; I am ready for anything and equal to anything through Him who infuses me with inner strength and confident peace.]
— Philippians 4:13, AMP

Our suffering unto life begins with our bold "yes" to Jesus. I clearly remember giving my life to Jesus, making Him my Lord, and praying many times for "more at all costs" with fear and trembling. My mother remarked that it was a dangerous prayer. What she meant was that the prayer invited the flames of God's purification and the fire of His holiness. This results in shaking everything that can be shaken, so that what remains is unshakable. To be clear, this does not include evil, although God will also use evil for our good. Please never forget that God has all of eternity to make up for our present sufferings, and ultimately, He will ensure there is perfect justice for every wrong. Praying for *more at all costs* was dangerous to my way of life as I knew it. Regardless, I knew the process would yield eternal benefits, no matter how much I "lost" in the process.

Our suffering is an invitation to find Jesus. I have experienced great suffering and great love. I experienced life in the kingdom during the days and weeks following Abbe's murder like never before. The peace and supernatural joy in the middle of the worst, high-stress, extremely painful, and confusing weeks of my life can only be explained by the presence of Jesus in my suffering. During this season, God gifted me with the consciousness of heaven, which will always strengthen me. This peace continued through the ongoing trials in my family, personal life, and business. It was never in my own strength. Other believers continued to strengthen me throughout the years of intense shaking. I am a very different man of God because of the trials and suffering, especially in regard to my relationship with Bryn. God did not deliver Bryn at once, but over many months; He made it into a process for both of us, with many ups and downs. The process involved learning to love, learning how to war, and learning to press into Him to win the battle. I remained vulnerable with others and regularly leaned on some of my closest brothers and sisters in Christ to strengthen and encourage me. God used the fire as a time of acceleration to create deep foundations for both Bryn and me.

> *But even if you happen to suffer for doing what is right, you will have the joyful experience of the blessing of God. And Don't be intimidated or terrified by those who would terrify you.*
> *—1 Peter 3:14, TPT*

A Fresh Perspective on Suffering

A close friend of mine, Charles Zimmerman, had some very deep comments on how my daughter Bryn's book *Dying to Live* changed his perspective on pain and suffering. It bolstered his faith and trust in God for whatever may come his way.

In the book, Bryn shares her history of trauma, abuse, addiction, rape, rebellion, and the severe grief she experienced when Abbe was brutally murdered. Through it all, by the power of the Holy Spirit and the grace of God, Bryn was empowered to overcome the enemy to experience a life transformed by the Saviour.

As Charles read Bryn's story, he couldn't help but ponder what he would have felt if he was in *my* shoes. He told me he would have been praying fervently for Bryn's pain and trials to come to an end (as well as the pain I experienced as a result). He also thought that he would potentially have become angry with God for being seemingly absent from the heartache.

The truth is, as I watched Bryn and Abbe suffer, I suffered. I felt helpless at times and couldn't understand how or why everything was happening. I fought for them. I pressed on and, by the grace of God, never gave up. God met me in my pain and used it to refine me. Though there were times I desperately wanted God to answer my prayers for a breakthrough—*and fast*—He was more concerned with who I (and Bryn in her own process) was becoming.

The Father's heart is always full of love, and His commitment to bring us out of death and into life is absolute. This often occurs through painful processes. Rather than exercising my need to control and understand, I gradually chose to trust in His goodness and in His process. By entering into the sufferings of Christ, a crushing or a death process with God began. As a result, He formed something beautiful within me and within Bryn. He wants the same for you, too. Our redeemed lives are the reward for the sufferings of Jesus.[19]

Looking back, if I had seen the end from the beginning like God does, I would have thanked Him in the midst of it all in a much deeper way. God can only accomplish certain things in the furnace. In my seasons of suffering, when I faced discouragement and disillusionment, I leaned on others in the body of Christ and chose to stand in faith regardless of how weak I may have felt. I learned that when I am disillusioned, I am believing in an illusion. I discovered that when my hope lessens, I am believing a lie. I learned that my never-changing and eternal foundational belief is in the absolute goodness of God! The more I pressed in, the more He revealed Himself to me in new ways that can only be found in the trials of life. God's grace carried me in ways I can hardly explain.

Suffering Leads to Jesus

When my girls were growing up, I failed to keep them safe and protect them when they were younger by unknowingly allowing a child predator into our home. This resulted in years of sexual abuse. When they were teens, they were both raped and abused multiple times. Abbe attempted suicide *multiple* times. I am fully aware that God is not the source of this suffering; it was Satan. As a result, they suffered from depression, anxiety, mental illness, and suicidal tendencies in addition to the bondage of addiction from pot all the way to cocaine and heroin. I became desperate and was willing to do anything to save their lives, but I was spiritually blind in many areas. I was emotionally broken and not equipped to lead my family well. In 2016, I gave my heart to the Lord, which ignited a flame and began a new process of yielding, growing, and healing in my life. I was no longer the ruler of my life. God was.

The Lord is close to all whose hearts are crushed by pain, and He is always ready to restore the repentant one. Even when bad things happen to the good and godly ones, the Lord will save them and not let them be defeated by what they face. God will be your bodyguard to protect you when trouble is near. Not one bone will be broken.
Psalm 34:18-20, TPT

How we look at suffering requires discernment and an ability to see from God's perspective. We do not want to interrupt the deep work God wants to accomplish as we enter into the suffering of Jesus. As a parent, sometimes we have to, with discernment, allow our children to struggle so that they will grow. Experiencing the natural consequences of our behaviour is a powerful way to learn. Bryn, after trying everything from drugs to rehab to therapy, endured much suffering before turning to Jesus, who was her last resort. She finally came to the end of herself, broken, desperate, and sickly, to the point of death, before opening herself to deliverance and Jesus. She is now a beautiful trophy of God's marvellous love and grace. The mercy of God can feel severe, but it is His mercy that leads to salvation and life.

When Abbe and Bryn were struggling with addiction, I spent whatever was required on various rehab centres and did whatever I could to get them help and keep them safe. For a period of time, it worked. However, whenever they came back to the real world, they would fall back into their destructive lifestyles because true inner healing had not been achieved.

There was one particular time I remember praying for a breakthrough for Bryn as I watched her plunge into darkness. Her behaviours were causing great pain to herself and those of us who watched her struggle. Her suffering became my suffering and caused me to press into the Lord in new ways. I learned dependency, to press into the Lord deeply, to fight for my family, and to love sacrificially.

As I went deeper with the Lord, my heart was being transformed by the power of the Holy Spirit. This is what Bryn ultimately responded to, not the repeated attempts at correction or discipline, which didn't work because I was (unknowingly) trying to get outward conformity first. The change in me allowed me to love her and invite her into transformation. All transformation is an inside-out process. My new way of living invited Bryn into health and wholeness. When parents don't know what to do, I suggest they take a look at the condition of their heart, which is the catalyst for change. We can't change our kids, but we can change ourselves.

> God whispers to us in our pleasures, speaks in our conscience, but shouts in our pains; it is his megaphone to arouse a deaf world.
> —C.S. Lewis[20]

Be greatly encouraged! When Jesus redeems, He makes it better than it would have ever been otherwise. He makes all things new! If you knew the glorious plan of God, who is already in your future and knows the good plans He has for your life, what would your response be in the midst of the trial?

> There are measures of His presence you can only find in "the valley of the shadow of death." They're not on the mountaintop of victory. They're in the dark place, where you abandon yourself to His purposes. It's dark to us, but it's completely light to Him... Nothing works outside of His capacity to redeem and restore.
> —Bill Johnson[21]

*   *   *

Jesus, we thank You for always being with us amid our suffering.

We ask for Your grace to endure as Your glory saturates and is revealed within us because of our oneness with Jesus. Help us seek You with all of our hearts, to know You, and reflect You more each day. Please help us remember that You are always with us, and Your grace is sufficient.

*   *   *

The Buffalo Approach

All of us experience storms in life. The question is how and when do we respond to those storms? In January 2024, my company, Flō, celebrated 25 years in business and hosted *A Better Way*™ team event in Miami. Our keynote speaker, Matt Davis, educated us on one of the most fascinating characteristics of a buffalo – how it reacts when a storm is coming. While cows, their close relatives, huddle together and try to avoid the storm, buffalos take the storm head on and charge directly into its path. They run at the storm and by doing so, they can run straight through it. This reduces the amount of time, frustration, and exposure they have in the storm itself, and it gives them access to the best vegetation once they are through it. Are you more like a cow who is fearful of the storm approaching, or are you more like a buffalo who knows a storm is coming and faces it head-on?

Throughout life we are either anticipating the coming storm, we are in the middle of the storm, or we are experiencing life after the storm. We don't get to choose whether we have storms, we only get to choose how we are going to respond. Charging into the storm and leaning on God all the way through it gives us access to the best stuff in life. Living "A Better Way" requires courage in the face of the storm. So, instead of being fearful and resisting the storm, be like the buffalo.

This approach encourages us to embrace adversity, seeing it not as a barrier but as a catalyst for growth and breakthrough. It's in these trials that we learn to depend on others and discover our deepest strengths and capabilities. Never forget, life does not happen to us, it happens for us! As a company, we've adopted the "buffalo" mentality, knowing that we are called to be a light in the darkness and to meet the needs of others. In fact, we sent a small buffalo figurine to every employee to have on their desk. When there is a storm, with a smile, they hold up the buffalo for others to see and we charge the storm together.

We took the "buffalo" approach with Gavin (*See Enter Into Suffering on the following page). We ran towards him when everyone else ran away. To bring the kingdom of God to places that have been entrenched in darkness means that we will sometimes have to enter dark places with the courage that comes from God alone. Interestingly, buffalo are also animals that stay in herds. If we are isolated, we become easy prey. But, together (as a company and as the church) we are strong.

When we don't face our problems, we open ourselves to worry or anxiety, and we are commanded not to worry. Our suffering is most often magnified in our minds, leading us to replay worst-case scenarios that rarely materialize. So much of our suffering is self-inflicted. However, when we shift our mindset, courage replaces worry and problems become opportunities, ruling and reigning in life by God's design, providing opportunities for God to show Himself strong.

Because the King is with us, there's nothing we cannot face with confidence. In my own life, I've been through so many different storms with the Lord that very little phases me. Because I've walked through troubled waters with Jesus, the storms of life no longer look as scary as they used to, which allows me to walk alongside others in their storms.

ENTER INTO SUFFERING

by Gavin Walters

I knew Jesus as my Savior and practiced following after Him in obedience and laboring for Him. I saw challenges and overcame them, failures and grew from them. There was abundant fruit and prosperity, for which I gave thanks. As a creed, I would claim axioms like "I would rather choke on greatness than nibble on mediocrity" and "Only those who will risk going too far can possibly find out how far one can go." I saw the world as God's canvas and wanted its systems to be transformed or replaced by Heaven's. Work felt like play, and time was abundant. I could hear a drumbeat in my entire being, the call for UNITY. It was consistent and intense, and God's Spirit was revealing concepts and strategies at scale. I felt excited, capable, and empowered.

As with anything, sometimes things fail. We adapt, pivot, learn, grow... fail forward. Then there is loss. Loss is felt in degrees unique to its class, like replaceable or irreplaceable, and also in the recipients' level of attachment or utilization. The adages of value are applied, and investment, cost, and expense are tallied to balance the weight and justify gains. Some failures and losses, individually or in combination, are incomprehensible and insurmountable, resulting in pain, anger, shame, fear, and sadness – enter suffering.

For multiple reasons, some explainable, some not, everything I put my hand to started to burn. The harder I fought and clawed to salvage, the hotter the flames became, and the less honorable my methods and resolve grew. I needed to win; God was with me, and everything I was doing was for Him! Look to the Rolodex!! *Unity, yes, unity, that... would solve everything. Hundreds of connections, good, godly, powerful brothers and sisters, family... we can rally. With God, you cannot fail! Greater is He that is in me than he that is in the world! I can do all things through Christ that strengthens me!*

My reality was met with silence from many, prayers from few, rejection heavy, flames hotter still. This could not, would not take me down... fire burned. The failure, loss, betrayal, shame, anger, fear, and sadness was palpable – enter suffering. At the end of myself, I fell on my knees and fell into a completely new understanding of my Jesus. The level of faith and peace that was present in His arms was marvelous. The concept of doing something "for Him" was rooted in my flesh, an orphan mind. I was trying to earn something that could not be bought but is freely given to His children. As I searched His face, I found a Father who wants my partnership, not His service. He does not want me to default to doing things for Him; He invites me to do things "with Him."

Worship was my prescription, and faith was my shelter. The fire continued to burn around me, but now my heart saw *The Refiner's Fire*. I am in the fire, not on fire, and here I surrendered all of me.

Hineni is Hebrew for "here I am." Abraham, Moses, Samuel, David, and Jesus (all in surrender and resolve) answered, "Here I am, Lord, Hineni." So, me too! I would pray, "Jesus, I need more of you, Hineni, Adonai; I am suffering and need you! I am in the fire."

I met Bryan in 2022 with some other men on Zoom and felt an instant kinship. I felt like God had something for us to do together, but I knew I was in the fire. I was transparent about the current fires but a bit vague, too. I was fully aware of people's response to fire. Fire is dangerous. Over the following months, Bryan continued to reach out, sharing the adventures the Lord was taking him on, asking how I was doing, if I needed anything, and letting me know that he was praying for me. He was consistent. It was abnormal, especially with his schedule. I remember thinking, can't he see the fire?! And that, if he knew the whole picture, he would eventually do what most did and keep his distance from my suffering. Bryan didn't see it that way. He never stopped calling.

One day, not long ago, I was pleading with Jesus to end the suffering as it, to me, was lasting longer than I felt I could bear, the intense weight and heat growing hotter. I remember praying the Lord's prayer... *Our Father who art in heaven, Your Kingdom Come, Your will be done on Earth as it is in Heaven...* just then, my phone rang... it was Bryan. I do not remember much about the conversation, but what happened still amazes me. Bryan said, "You are not alone; I know exactly how you feel. I have been here before; how can I help?"

What?! Come ON! My suffering was not pushing him away; the fire was not driving him to put distance between us. Rather, THE FIRE, the suffering, was drawing him to me. The more I explained, the more resolved he became. He didn't preach at me or do risk assessments to justify non-involvement. Instead, he added grace, mercy, courage, clarity, and physical and spiritual aid. He entered my suffering with confidence, straight into the fire, like it was familiar, picked up my burden as his own, at peace in the chaos, and showed me Jesus on Earth!

If you have ever met Bryan, you will know he greets everybody with a genuine "Shalom." In John 14:27, Jesus says, *"Peace I leave you, My peace I give you; not as the world gives, do I give to you..."* As a recipient of God's peace, Bryan takes every opportunity as pure joy to bring that shalom into the lives that God puts on his path. Without reservation, Bryan does his utmost to be Jesus's hands and feet here on Earth. How wonderful! How biblically spot on. To enter the suffering of others with the fruit of the Savior Himself flowing through us. What a blessing to be a conduit for Heaven on Earth. To see people as He sees them. Praise God! The fears of this Earth will grow strangely dim in the light of His glory and grace. *Shalom.*

At present, though the fire continues, it is not touching me. My heart is full of trust and peace in The Refiner's Fire, in the confidence and faith of Jesus. I know that I will have a lot more revelation from this as time passes, more than I can see now, and for that, I continue to say, "Hineni, here I am, Lord." The horizon is full of hope, the favor of Heaven is clearly raining, chains are being broken, hearts mended and drawn closer to Jesus, and the future is bright again.

Through this process, I am full of peace that I did not have before. Jesus's peace, His shalom, shared in suffering from brother to brother and multiplied by Heaven. The more you give it, the more you receive it. I have freely received the power of His kingdom, and I am now ignited and catalyzed to release it to others freely. Not for Him but WITH Him for His people and His Glory. To be the reflection of Jesus, what a gift. Bryan was that manifestation in my life, and I praise God for him. What he shared with me caused me to lift my gaze from myself and onto Jesus, I can see clearly now. Praise God.

Lift your gaze! Enter the suffering of another and show them Jesus.

"But thou, O LORD, art a shield for me; My glory, and the lifter up of mine head."
-Psalm 3:3, KJV

Fasten me upon your heart as a seal of fire forevermore. This living, consuming flame will seal you as My prisoner of love. My passion is stronger than the chains of death and the grave, all consuming as the very flashes of fire from the burning heart of God. Place this fierce, unrelenting fire over your entire being. Rivers of pain and persecution will never extinguish this flame. Endless floods will be unable to quench this raging fire that burns within you. Everything will be consumed. It will stop at nothing as you yield everything to this furious fire until it won't even seem to you like a sacrifice anymore.
Song of Songs 8:6-7, TPT

The love of the King of the kingdom refines us, gradually transforming sacrifice into joyful surrender, as Christ is formed within.

Love is the ultimate mark of maturity, and the hallmark of maturity is self-sacrifice.[22] Sacrificial love does not love only when loved. It is modelled by the love of God and the result of God's fiery refining love. When we love others, we will sometimes experience pain as we must open our hearts, which exposes us to the inevitability of pain. However, pain is not the ultimate measure. Love is. We can continue to choose love in spite of the pain like Jesus did on the cross. If we look to Jesus on the cross, He cried out for God to forgive the very people who had Him tortured and murdered. Or Stephen, as he was being stoned in Acts 6-7, who also cried out for God to forgive his killers.

Alternately, self-focus is generally at the root of unhappiness, depression, anxiety, and general misery. Self-focus is the opposite of love, which is others focused. If you are miserable or depressed, reflect on the amount of time you spend focusing on yourself, which often looks like excessive criticism or praise. On the one hand, when we focus on God and others, God's sacrificial agape love becomes the foundation for our lives and, if we allow it, will birth greatness in us and others. On the other hand, to quote author, musician, and speaker Eric Gilmour, "Without my heart laid at your feet, it always tries to take your seat."[23]

A mother in childbirth is consumed by pain during labour. The joy and love she feels towards giving her child life enables her to push through the pain. In the same way, when we yield to what God is birthing in us through suffering and push through the pain, the newness of life and freedom and victory is ours! Like an athlete in training, "no pain, no gain." In Christ, we experience short-term pain for eternal gain. Jesus overcame the world, and we will, too, if we allow the joy of the Lord *and the presence of Jesus* to be our strength.

There is a biblical precedent to the character formed through suffering as God prepares us for what lies ahead. There is always a purpose to pain. It tells us something is out of alignment within, or something needs to change outside of us. With God, adversity is opportunity. God used suffering to prepare Joseph to steward great power and influence. God prepared Moses to lead His people to freedom through great adversity and pushback. God prepared David to be king through him fighting giants and seasons of hiding in caves. God prepared His one and only Son to be the Saviour of the world through suffering and death.

Be assured that God will never allow more suffering than we can handle *without His help*. His grace is sufficient.

Our Teacher

Though the Lord gives you the bread of adversity and the water of oppression, yet your Teacher will no longer hide Himself, but your eyes will [constantly] see your Teacher. Your ears will hear a word behind you, "This is the way, walk in it," whenever you turn to the right or to the left.
—Isaiah 30:20-21, AMP

In the words of the French mystic Jean Guyon, "It is the fire of suffering that brings forth the gold of godliness."[24] I have witnessed over and over how much more difficult it is for someone who has everything to surrender to Jesus than one who is in lack and suffering, aware of his brokenness and need of God. Consider the story of the rich young ruler in Mark 10:17-31. Though he had followed the commandments since he was a boy (an example of applying God's principles without a relationship with Him), his wealth prevented him from "needing" God. His wealth was obviously of great value to the man. Being commanded to sell everything he had to follow Jesus caused him to lower his head and literally walk away in sadness (verses 21-22). While we don't know how his story ends, we do know that this young man's "yes" to Jesus was not an immediate, abandoned surrender. Ease and comfort almost always decrease our perceived need for God. Your treasure is where your heart is.[25] Our hearts are the centre of the issues of our lives.[26] Abundant life comes about from the positioning of our hearts.

In his book *Those Who Remain*, author G. Michael Hopf summarizes the history of the world and a cycle that occurs over and over: "Good times create weak people. Weak people create bad times. Bad times create strong people. Strong people create good times."[27] It is in the hard times, in the trials and tribulations, that character is formed and tested to bring forth the kingdom of God! The rise and fall of empires throughout history is the result of the internal decay of values and character, as stated in a research paper titled "Account of Responsible Citizenship" by John Anderson: "It is never external forces that strike the fatal blow to a great civilisation, but internal decay and corruption. What causes this internal decay? The answer is unanimous: decadence, selfishness, nihilism, and hedonism."[28] The success of Rome in war made her prosperous, but this made the Romans comfortable and increasingly indifferent to living lives of virtue and uprightness.

For all that is in the world, the lust of the flesh and the lust of the eyes and the boastful pride of life, is not from the Father, but is from the world.
—1 John 2:16, NASB

Satan tempts us through the lust of our flesh (sexual lust, indulgences, etc.), the lust of the eyes (greed, envy, etc.), and the pride of life (the lie of self-sufficiency). What he offers may be pleasurable in the moment, but the more we focus on ourselves, the more miserable we will become. The key to freedom and abundant life is to focus on Jesus, die to our selfish desires, embrace the cross, and be willing to serve God regardless of the cost. When we open the door to the Spirit, the door to the flesh closes. Our internal transformation happens in the suffering or fire with Jesus. As our flesh is crucified, the things that used to attract us no longer will. They will, as the old song goes, "grow strangely dim, in the light of His glory and grace."[29]

A Pure and Spotless Bride

Sin is anything that causes separation from God or anything that is outside of God's perfect design. In addition to natural consequences, which are often delayed, one of the consequences of sin is demonization, as it opens us to agreement with the wrong kingdom. Let's embrace the power of repentance and grace! In Jesus, there is no more sin. *Sin is defeated. Sin is a dethroned monarch.*[30] Through the power of the cross, we are no longer under the power of sin and death. We are like Jesus now and learning to live from our new creation life. We are a pure and spotless bride, empowered by the Holy Spirit not to sin the more we allow ourselves to be transformed into the image of Jesus.[31] It's a process of sanctification or refinement, from glory to glory, a grace process of removing what is not of God and becoming more like God. Jesus became like us so that we could become like Him. We should all find sin unappealing and seek every day to live as the pure and spotless bride for which Jesus died.

> *For our momentary, light distress [this passing trouble] is producing for us an eternal weight of glory [a fullness] beyond all measure [surpassing all comparisons, a transcendent splendor and an endless blessedness]!*
> —*2 Corinthians 4:17, AMP*

Anything of value is costly, which is why Jesus instructed us to count the cost of following Him.[32] To count the cost means understanding and agreeing to the terms of following Him so that we will not fall away when things get difficult. Love is costly. It requires sacrifice and vulnerability. Vulnerability and intimacy are signs of courage. Both of these open us to risk, uncertainty, and the potential of pain for the sake of connection. Without real connection, what is the purpose of life?

Suffering is costly. It hurts. It is never fun. But, if done well, it produces gold as refined in the fire. It's in suffering that real transformation happens. Suffering is an accelerant. It produces eternal glory as we are moulded into the likeness of Christ. If we share in His suffering, then we share in His glory![33]

Sharing Our Comfort

When I was in the middle of the storm with the murder trial, divorce, and fighting for Bryn's healing, I wrote my first book, *More Than Gold*, with the Holy Spirit guiding me. The goal was to disciple others by sharing what I had learned, provide hope for those with life struggles by sharing my experiences, and glorify God as He carried me throughout the journey and brought me into a new place of glorious freedom. I was strengthened by sharing my story as the testimony of Jesus releases fresh faith!

Suffering, like the valley of the shadow of death, is a place to pass through, not camp out. As they say, if you're walking through hell, keep going! When we get to the green pastures, we can lie down, *but we must not lie down in the valley!*

After you have suffered for a little while, the God of all grace, who called you to His eternal glory in Christ, will Himself perfect, confirm, strengthen, and establish you.
——1 Peter 5:10, NASB

In 1 Peter 5:10, it says that after we have suffered a little while, God will restore us. When this happens, we become a gift of compassion, sacrificial love, comfort, and a testimony of hope and faith to the world.[34] As Christians, we are to share one another's burdens and regularly cast our cares upon the Lord. This is exactly what the prayer team did with me as I suffered, and now I can do it for others. Scriptures tell us we comfort others with the comfort we have first received from God, which comes through His people and our life's union with Him unto healing and restoration.[35]

When He saw the vast crowds of people, Jesus's heart was deeply moved with compassion, because they seemed weary and helpless, like wandering sheep without a shepherd.
—Matthew 9:36, TPT

God ultimately calls us to share the comfort we have received from Him with others, which is how God has used my story of suffering to bring comfort and hope to others. I am filled with gratitude as I remember all God has done for me and through me. Because of my redeemer, much of my past pain has been transformed into my purpose by His grace. Whether it is through my books or speaking, or in the day-to-day, God is using my life to be able to enter into the sufferings of others in unique ways. The Lord connects me with people in need of not only comfort but also hope. I am greatly encouraged because of what the Lord has brought me through, and I am amazed that my hope in the Lord is so strong that I can pour it out to others.[36] Regularly, God connects me with people in pain, with family problems or business trials, and uses me to speak hope and truth in love.

As God brings people in my path to encourage, strengthen, and comfort in times of hardship, I, in turn, receive encouragement, strength, and comfort. We reap what we sow! Not only that, but by doing kingdom work, I get to experience the presence of the kingdom. As an example, I recently experienced a series of losses while helping five friends who were also going through great personal hardship. Each of these five circumstances was trial by fire, God's chosen being cleansed in the furnace of affliction. God released His hope and grace through me. I had freely received the power of His kingdom, and I was freely releasing it to others. They are rapidly growing in faith and learning to live above their circumstances! It is incredible to watch God work in their lives. They are choosing to praise in hardship and cry out to God in new levels of self-abandon and dependence. In fact, to my surprise, the worse the problems, the greater the peace and hope. Why? Because my peace was not in my own strength; it was in Jesus. On my side, the last of these circumstances was a large financial loss, which came to my attention just before bed one night. In the past, I might have been up all night. But this time, I simply rolled over and slept in perfect peace. To me, this is a clear sign that the kingdom of God is taking hold of my heart, and the cares of this world are growing strangely dim. I know that only God is my provider. There was a key biblical principle at play, as my eyes were not on myself but focused on others. This opened me to receive the peace and joy of the kingdom and then release it to those around me.

All praises belong to the God and Father of our Lord Jesus Christ. For He is the Father of tender mercy and the God of endless comfort. He always comes alongside us to comfort us in every suffering so that we can come alongside those who are in any painful trial. We can bring them this same comfort that God has poured out upon us.
— 2 Corinthians 1:3-4, TPT

We are not to suffer as the world suffers.[37] Death precedes life. That's the power of the cross.[38] Suffering is an opportunity to glorify God. In it, we act as salt and light in a dark world to stand out as a beacon of hope.[39]

Don't Be Surprised!

Beloved, do not be surprised at the fiery ordeal among you, which comes upon you for your testing, as though something strange were happening to you; but to the degree that you share the sufferings of Christ, keep on rejoicing, so that at the revelation of His glory you may also rejoice and be overjoyed. If you are insulted for the name of Christ, you are blessed, because the Spirit of glory, and of God, rests upon you.
—1 Peter 4:12-14, NASB

Please don't miss this: *God's glory rests upon you.* We share in the suffering of Jesus as we share in His victory on the cross. This victory will be repeated in our tests and trials of life as we are refined and reformed. I have shared many stories of tragedies that God has used. I have also discovered that many of the refining periods of life have come through difficult or painful relational dynamics. I have felt much sadness and disappointment in betrayals, rejection, and persecution. Yet, *the Spirit of glory, and of God, rests upon me and you.* This is suffering with Christ and the key to the kingdom, His glory resting upon us, Emmanuel, God is with us. We go from glory to increasing glory as Jesus's life increases within us.

When Satan came to sift Peter as wheat (to violently shake and destroy his faith) or when Paul asked to have the thorn removed from his flesh (which was possibly meant to keep Paul from becoming arrogant after receiving incredible revelation from God but also to exercise His authority), Jesus didn't rescue them from the pain or torment. Instead, He prayed for the grace to overcome and for their faith to endure.[40] In this way, Peter was strengthened to overcome, and his story is still a blessing to this very day. Suffering with Christ builds in us grit, tenacity, resilience, and determination. It teaches us to overcome, exercise our authority, and release God's *dynamis*[41] power within us, which is made perfect in our weakness. It helps us persevere and stay strong in the faith as we walk the narrow way, the difficult way, the only way to life.

Paul sustained suffering, knowing that in the pain and loss of the things of this world, he was gaining something far more valuable, which was Christ. Paul had already counted the things of this world as "loss" or "nothing" for the sake of Christ, whether it be money, possessions, status, comfort, success, or reputation.[42] He was prepared to pay the price to grow deeper in intimacy with Christ.

Practically speaking, as Christians, we are to deny ourselves by surrendering to Jesus daily and by imitating Jesus and His submission to the Father. We do this by abiding in His Word and in Him, welcoming His presence, making His kingdom our top priority, practising agape love, putting others before ourselves, and living for the good of others by the power of the Holy Spirit. This doesn't mean life will be smooth sailing. Jesus was without sin, and He was despitefully rejected, painfully ridiculed, hatefully scorned, massively betrayed, and ultimately killed as He walked in self-denial and obedience to the Father.

"Anyone who comes to Me must be willing to share My cross and experience it as his own, or he cannot be considered to be My disciple."
—Luke 14:27, TPT

A Brief Suffering

The call of a true Christ-follower is difficult, but the rewards are unimaginable, matchless, and eternal. To be called a disciple of Jesus, we must accept the mission of Jesus and take up our cross, which is denying to ourselves and everything of the world in full surrender and making Jesus supreme in our lives. The word "disciple" means discipline, one who has been taught by the master, our perfect Father, validating us as His sons and daughters out of His great love. Our Father disciplines us for our good so that we may share in His holiness.[43]

We have this one brief opportunity while on this earth to follow in the footsteps of Jesus. It is difficult. Yet, we can still say "I love you" and give our "yes" to Jesus, even when it hurts. This is the honour of suffering. After his wife's death, Bill Johnson chose to offer the sacrifice of praise in the midst of grieving and suffering. He shared that this was the only time in all of eternity he could give God this love offering of co-suffering with His Son. We get one season (our life on earth) to offer the sacrifice of praise in and through our sufferings. I was given the same opportunity to glorify God during my daughter's funeral. Though we grieved her brief time with us on earth, we celebrated her entrance into heaven, knowing we'd be together for all of eternity. Every moment that we face hardships is a once-in-a-lifetime opportunity to glorify and worship Him. And as we demonstrate our hope in Him and live above our circumstances, we have the privilege of working out our salvation with fear and trembling.[44]

Suffering for Christ is an act of faith. It is through our sufferings that we are built up in faith and character to steward great authority. God's indescribable goodness and infinite faithfulness is our strength, our comfort, and our hope! It is not the absence of trials or tribulations that brings peace but the presence of the King and His kingdom. He empowers us to live from above here *on earth as it is in heaven*. Keep going! You will win! With Jesus, our suffering becomes transformational! We are learning to live from another world, from the kingdom of God!

After our brief journey on earth, an eternity without sorrow or tears awaits us, a place beyond our wildest dreams. As Paul reveals in 1 Corinthians 2:9, that no eye has seen, nor ear heard, nor heart imagined what God has prepared for those who love Him, highlighting the unimaginable beauty and joy of heaven.

I am convinced that any suffering we endure is less than nothing compared to the magnitude of glory that is about to be unveiled within us.
—Romans 8:18, TPT

1. Genesis 2.
2. John Lennox, "The Loud Absence: Where Is God in Suffering?," *YouTube*, accessed October 13, 2023, https://tinyurl.com/bdd26wv2.
3. John 16:33.
4. James 4:7-8.
5. Genesis 50:20.
6. Romans 8:28.
7. Daniel C. Juster, Th.D., "V. Raymond Edman, May 9, 1900- Sept. 22, 1967," *Restoration from Zion: Jerusalem, Israel*, accessed October 14, 2023, https://tinyurl.com/8aj5cb2p.
8. Hebrews 12:2.
9. Bible Ask Team, "How does suffering help the believers?," *BibleAsk*, accessed October 13, 2023, https://tinyurl.com/yjybzrf5.
10. 2 Timothy 3:12.
11. Hebrews 12:11.
12. Bryan Elliott, *More than Gold*, (Toronto: M46 Publishing, 2022), 268.
13. Rosaria Champagne Butterfield, "Bless Those Who Hate You," *The Aquila Report*, accessed October 13, 2023, https://theaquilareport.com/bless-those-who-hate-you/.
14. Ephesians 4:23-24.
15. Jeanne Guyon, *Intimacy in Christ, Her Letters Now in Modern English* (Jacksonville: Seedsowers, 1989).
16. 2 Corinthians 11:16-33.
17. Judas hanged himself after betraying Jesus (Matthew 27:5), and most believe John died of natural causes.
18. 2 Corinthians 11:24-28.
19. Revelation 4:11, Isaiah 53.
20. C.S. Lewis, "Reflections: God's Megaphone," *C.S. Lewis Institute*, accessed October 13, 2023, https://tinyurl.com/5bf6ek2a.
21. Bill Johnson, "Bold Faith Stands on the Shoulders of Quiet Trust," *Facebook*, accessed October 13, 2023, https://tinyurl.com/59j9hkm5.
22. 1 Corinthians 13:4-8.
23. Eric Gilmour, [@sonshipintl].
24. Jeanne Marie Bouvier de la Motte Guyon, "Jeanne Marie Bouvier de la Motte Guyon Quotes," *AZ Quotes*, accessed October 13, 2023, https://www.azquotes.com/quote/1345841.
25. Matthew 6:21.
26. Proverbs 4:23.
27. G. Michael Hopf, "G. Michael Hopf, Quotes, Quotable Quotes," *GoodReads*, accessed October 13, 2023, https://tinyurl.com/2anpv6k6.
28. John Anderson, "Account of Responsible Citizenship," *Arc.Research*, accessed October 16, 2023, https://www.arc-research.org/research-papers/responsible-citizenship.
29. Helen Howarth Lemmel, "Turn Your Eyes Upon Jesus," *Hymnary.org*, accessed October 13, 2023, https://tinyurl.com/49rsdzp3.
30. Romans 6-8.
31. Revelation 19:7-8.
32. Luke 14:28.
33. Romans 8:17.
34. For interest, the word "compassion" comes from the Latin root words *com*, meaning "with," and *pati*, meaning "to suffer," which come together to form "to suffer with."
35. 2 Corinthians 1:4.
36. Romans 5:3-4.
37. 1 Peter 4:12-19.
38. Luke 9:23.
39. Matthew 5:13-16.
40. Luke 22:30-32, 2 Corinthians 12:7-10.
41. Pronounced *doo'-nam-is*, meaning "strength, power, ability."
42. Philippians 3:7-8.
43. Hebrews 12:10.
44. Philippians 2:12-13.

THE KINGDOM PRINCIPLE OF TRANSFORMATIONAL SUFFERING

The kingdom of God unveils the transformative power of enduring trials with faith and trust, recognizing that God's redemptive purposes are at work even in the midst of pain. By embracing hardship, resilience and character are forged. More importantly, we can experience a deeper connection with God's love and comfort so that we can love and comfort others who are suffering.

Father, we ask for the grace to suffer well, knowing that life is not fair but that You are perfectly just. We ask for the grace to suffer unto life, knowing the cross is the pathway to Your kingdom.

QUESTIONS FOR REFLECTION

What has the Holy Spirit revealed to you through *The Kingdom Principle of Transformational Suffering*? How can you apply this to your life?

_____

_____

_____

Reflect on where God has met you in places of suffering. In what ways has it changed you or the ways you relate to others in their pain?

_____

_____

_____

Are you a living sacrifice? How? (I will say, even in writing this section, I was brought to a deeper level of surrender, offering myself more wholeheartedly to Jesus.)

_____

_____

_____

Notes

SUFFERING FOR
OUR GOOD

And have you forgotten his encouraging words spoken to
you as his children? He said, "My child, don't underestimate
the value of the discipline and training of the Lord God,
or get depressed when he has to correct you. For the Lord's
training of your life is the evidence of his faithful love. And when
he draws you to himself, it proves you are his delightful child."
–Hebrews 12:5-6, TPT

Now all discipline seems to be painful at the time, yet later it will
produce a transformation of character, bringing a harvest of righteousness and
peace to those who yield to it.
–Hebrews 12:11, TPT

In fact, you were called to live this way, because Christ also
suffered in your place, leaving you His example for you to follow.
–1 Peter 2:21, TPT

For God has graciously given you the privilege not only to
believe in Christ, but also to suffer for him. For you have
been called by him to endure the conflict in the same way
I have endured it—for you know I'm not giving up.
–Philippians 1:29-30, TPT

Part 3: Kingdom Solutions

The scriptures are full of solutions, as they are a roadmap for mankind to flourish. When we go against God's design, failure, chaos, and suffering will ensue. There are unimaginable blessings for those living in the kingdom as citizens. However, not being a citizen does not mean that you will not benefit from abiding by its laws. Biblical principles work for anyone who applies them. Even the non-believer can experience the kingdom coming near, a level of prosperity, and the fruit of living in the principles of God by honouring His commands regarding sex, marriage, loving and serving others, forgiving others, money, honouring our parents, and the sanctity of life, among others.[1] These can serve as a roadmap to flourishing on earth, no matter what you think about Christianity. Judeo-Christian values work as God graciously and faithfully abides by His own principles! The kingdom of God is the will of God done *on earth as it is in heaven*.

His Government

Most people understand the necessity of the government to maintain a civil society, establish order, and administer justice. Man-made forms of governance have clear results reflected throughout history. These attempts look nothing remotely close to heaven on earth. Democracies, monarchies, republics, and autocracies... From the far left (communism) to the far right (fascism) to governments that espouse a more "centre" perspective, there is no perfect man-made government. Every single one will fail to bring true peace and justice. This is why we need to personally submit to a heavenly kingdom government. The kingdom of heaven is the supreme government. Therefore, the kingdom of God on earth is governed by the principles and rules in the scriptures. God's perfect ways will never fail to bring perfect peace and enact God's unparalleled justice and mercy.

Heaven's kingdom realm is about a person, Jesus, who lives within us by faith and not just by adherence to principles or laws. The kingdom of God is the manifest presence of God on earth. As sons and daughters, following kingdom principles brings heavenly order to the earth and releases the power of God. When we understand how heaven functions and act accordingly, we open the doors of heaven in our relationships, families, businesses, finances, communities, and beyond.

> *"Nor will they say, 'Look, here it is!' or, 'There it is!' For behold, the kingdom of God is in your midst."*
> —*Luke 17:21, NASB*

Jesus was clear that God's kingdom does not come by simply obeying principles or waiting for signs. The kingdom realm is not discovered in one place or another but in a person, Jesus Christ; His kingdom is within and appears when Jesus lives in us by faith.

Our problems today need heaven's solutions that come through us by the power of the Holy Spirit. As kingdom citizens, we have access to solutions to the world's problems if we are humble and receive God's teachings and corrections. Every problem and crisis is an opportunity for the kingdom of light to invade darkness. One day, we will stand before Jesus and give an account of our lives. Wouldn't you like to say you were able to shine light into the darkness because you took hold of your kingdom's access to divine wisdom?

You cannot separate the kingdom of God and the wisdom of God. Jesus said the principal thing was to first seek His kingdom, and Solomon said the principal thing was to get wisdom. By their very nature, the kingdom and wisdom are inextricably linked.[2] Jesus is the King of the kingdom, and Jesus is the wisdom of God![3]

> *Jesus was once asked by the Jewish religious leaders, "When will God's kingdom come?" Jesus responded,* **"God's kingdom does not come simply by obeying principles or waiting for signs. The kingdom is not discovered in one place or another, for God's kingdom realm is already expanding within some of you."**
> *—Luke 17:20-21, TPT*

The Beginning of Wisdom

> *And to mankind He said, "Behold, the fear of the Lord, that is wisdom; And to turn away from evil is understanding."*
> *—Job 28:28, NASB*

> *The starting point for acquiring wisdom is to be consumed with awe as you worship Yahweh. To receive the revelation of the Holy One, you must come to the one who has living-understanding.*
> *Proverbs 9:10, TPT*

This is the fear of the Lord, which is the beginning of wisdom. The fear of the Lord is to live in reverence of God and His Word, loving what God loves and hating what God hates. The fear of the Lord is recognizing God as our almighty sovereign Creator of the universe.

It is the wisdom of God that allows us to co-rule with Christ and reign in life. To receive the revelation of the Holy One, you must come to the One who has living-understanding. Beginning in 2016, my hunger for God and His ways ignited, and I truly, for the first time in my life, began to seek truth. I studied the biblical worldview and how it corresponds to reality. I studied the science of God's creation. I spent more time with the Lord and in His Word. Over time, I was filled more and more with awe and wonder at our great God and the marvellous truth and the authority of the scriptures. I began to honour the Word of God and His wisdom, which caused me to think differently with new levels of understanding. This led to the writing of many books and my involvement in many organizations. As I go throughout my day, scriptures continually come to mind, which brings clarity and understanding. Living with understanding from God allows us to be heavenly-minded.

The wisdom of God is how His kingdom operates. We seek His kingdom first by seeking after and honouring wisdom. I practically do this by praying, honouring, and asking for wisdom. I also regularly read the wisdom books of the Bible (Proverbs, Job, James, and Ecclesiastes) to honour the Word of God and His presence. We attract what we honour, so when we honour wisdom, we attract it.

The Book of Proverbs, or in Hebrew, *māšāl* ("sentences of ethical wisdom"), is absolutely packed with practical kingdom principles.[4] The word māšal in the verb form can mean "to rule, have dominion, reign."[5] The Book of Ecclesiastes reminds us how meaningless the things of this world are and encourages us to focus on values that endure eternally. The Book of James offers basic advice for living in and above trials and tribulation.

But the wisdom from above is always pure, filled with peace, considerate and teachable. It is filled with love and never displays prejudice or hypocrisy in any form.
—James 3:17, TPT

The Book of Proverbs often speaks of the fools and the wicked in contrast to the wise and the righteous.

My wise correction is more valuable than silver or gold. The finest gold is nothing compared to the revelation-knowledge I can impart. Wisdom is so priceless that it exceeds the value of any jewel. Nothing you could wish for can equal her.
—Proverbs 8:10-11, TPT

I once heard someone explain that it is the fool (the one who is unteachable and rejects correction) who changes the truth to suit his opinions, but it is the wise (the teachable and open to correction) who allow themselves to be changed by the truth. When we live in the truth, we ensure the best possible outcome.

In the kingdom, we are blessed to bless others. We give to receive. Wisdom is no different. Solomon asked for wisdom so that he could lead God's people well. Because He asked for wisdom for others, great wisdom was given so that all of Israel greatly prospered and lived in peace throughout his rule. It's worth noting that there are many people who like to *hear* wisdom but don't actually *listen* to wisdom. I'm reminded of the people I know who read all the best books and go to great counsellors and seek prayer and healing, but don't actively change their lives. In order to honour wisdom, you have to actively seek to do what wisdom says to do. God wants us to be active listeners and "doers" of the Word.

The cut-off stump of Jesse will sprout, and a fruitful Branch will grow from his roots: the Spirit of Yahweh will rest upon him, the Spirit of Extraordinary Wisdom, the Spirit of Perfect Understanding, the Spirit of Wise Strategy, the Spirit of Mighty Power, the Spirit of Revelation, and the Spirit of the Fear of Yahweh.
—Isaiah 11:1-2, TPT

The Passion Translation's footnote for Isaiah 11:2 comments that the Spirit of Wisdom "...gives equipping ability for music, art, business, writing, creativity, and wisdom for judicial decisions. Paul prayed for the churches to receive this 'Spirit of wisdom' (Eph. 1:17-19)."[6] Wisdom provides us with a divine perspective to know the right thing to do and have the courage to do it. It empowers us to make the right decisions in life. It helps us to see as God sees, which is to have the mind of Christ. Wisdom knows heaven's ways and can bring them to life so we can experience life as originally intended *on earth as it is in heaven*. Wisdom is for ruling and reigning in life, kingdom style!

It is my hope that you will grasp the basic principles of the kingdom that will assist you in daily co-ruling with Christ as you journey through your time on earth. By absorbing and applying kingdom wisdom, you will step into the honour of redeeming the earth for the glory of God, the sake of the gospel, and the salvation of the nations. It's my prayer that we will all chase after wisdom and use it the way God intended from before the dawn of time.

1. See the Ten Commandments in Exodus 20:2-17 for more examples.
2. Matthew 6:33, Proverbs 4:7.
3. 1 Corinthians 1:24.
4. "H4912: Masal," *Blue Letter Bible*, accessed October 14, 2023, https://www.blueletterbible.org/lexicon/h4912/niv/wlc/0-1/.
5. Ibid.
6. Isaiah 11:2, TPT Footnote V2," *LifeBible*, accessed October 14, 2023, https://lifebible.com/bible.

EXPERIENCING THE DEPTHS OF GOD

We see God more as we are than as who He is. God cannot be fully known as He is beyond all comprehension. Here is a simple exercise to get an incredibly small taste of who God is. Close your eyes and imagine you are on the edge of an enormous cliff, a massive waterfall, the Grand Canyon, or whatever location you find most awe-inspiring.

As you stand, feel the wind swirling and take in the broad landscape visible from this height. Move your feet so they are teetering on the edge of the cliff. Look straight down, way down. Imagine your view of infinite depth as if on the edge of the universe and feel your body tighten, your senses coming alive as you tremble, and your stomach churn as you sway on the edge, facing your mortality, weakness, and your smallness.

Now imagine coming face-to-face with the one true living God, the triune uncreated One, the Creator of the universe, of greater depth than any cliff. Imagine an overpowering sense of our nothingness. (Even the beloved John fell like a deadman when He beheld Jesus in His glorified state!) What do you feel? How does this change your view of God?

If you want to continue the journey in reverential awe and wonder, take your imagination to the throne of God with Revelation 4:3-11 and Revelation 5:11-13, and imagine yourself there with 10,000 times 10,000 angels (110 million total), the four living creatures, etc.

Chapter 15: The Kingdom Principle of Co-Ruling

Yours, Lord, is the greatness, the power, the glory, the victory, and the majesty, indeed everything that is in the heavens and on earth; Yours is the dominion, Lord, and You exalt Yourself as head over all.
— 1 Chronicles 29:11, NASB

The earth is the Lord's, and all it contains,
The world, and those who live in it.
— Psalm 24:1, NASB

Kings give high positions in their government to members of their families. As sons and daughters of the King of Kings of the kingdom of God, we have legal rights, privileges, and responsibilities as members of His government. It's our job to partner with Jesus to bring heavenly order to the earth. This reflects God's will, intent, values, and nature. God created us to take dominion over the earth (never over people, but rather in service to people) with His delegated authority to govern and rule to make the earth like heaven. This is our inheritance that was lost in the fall but is now restored for all those adopted into the kingdom. As we mature, we gain access to everything because we are heirs.[1] We are simply stewards of all that we have been entrusted with. This process of growth, testing, and maturity progresses into sonship, which is the entrance into heirship and co-ownership.

The heavens belong to our God; they are his alone, but he has given us the earth and put us in charge.
—Psalm 115:16, TPT

As kingdom ambassadors, our purpose is our dominion mandate over the seen and unseen realms on earth and all of creation. All of creation is groaning for us, God's sons and daughters, to mature and set everything back into divine kingdom order, releasing it from death and decay and into abundant life.

So wake up, you living gateways! Lift up your heads, you doorways of eternity! Welcome the King of Glory, for he is about to come through you. You ask, "Who is this King of Glory?" Yahweh, armed and ready for battle, Yahweh, invincible in every way!
—Psalm 24:7-8, TPT

The footnote to this verse notes that the living gates and doors are symbols for God's people. So, "When God opens the doorway of eternity within us, no one is able to shut them. To 'lift up' our heads is a figure of speech for a bold confidence that brings rejoicing and hope."[2]

Remember, the earth is already God's. There is no "territory" to conquer, as in traditional kingdom invasions. In a kingdom, the king owns everything. In God's kingdom, God owns everything, including us! We are living gates. We are a living house of God. We get to create a dwelling place for the Lord to overflow and His kingdom to invade. As living gates, we must be aware of who rules our hearts. Do we bow to love or to fear? To God or to the power of money?

Are we rebellious or surrendered? King Jesus must first reign in our hearts before His kingdom can reign in our lives and on earth. As the kingdom expands in our hearts, there is always an outward manifestation.

Salt and Light Citizens and Ambassadors

As we humble ourselves, hunger after Him, live in repentance and worship, seeking first His kingdom and His righteousness, we create a dwelling place for the King of Glory to come in power. In our dependence, humility, and weakness, His power can flow out of our lives *today*. This is the hope and victory of the cross on display!

> *And My people who are called by My name humble themselves, and pray and seek My face, and turn from their wicked ways, then I will hear from heaven, and I will forgive their sin and will heal their land.*
> —2 Chronicles 7:14, NASB

God is sovereign and, in His sovereignty, decided to make His home in us and give us stewardship and dominion on earth. He is still the King, the King of Glory, the Creator, and the owner of all of creation.

We are called to be responsible, to partner with God and others, and to be the solution to the problems on earth. As kingdom ambassadors take their places in the kingdom and government of God, family, church, business, government, education, arts and entertainment, and media will be transformed. A kingdom citizen is salt and light and leaven, influencing and impacting the area in which he or she is planted.

The kingdom starts and expands first in our hearts before it manifests on earth. As salt and light, our values and systems will look and taste very different from the world's demonic systems. Everything we touch will radiate the light and presence of God because of the Holy Spirit's power within and because of our obedience to submit all things to Him. This is what draws outsiders into the kingdom. Remember, transformation will always start at home in the family because God's kingdom is a family. Isaiah 9:7 reminds us that His government and peace will increase with no end. With His Spirit working in and through us with His grace, wisdom, and faith, we get to bring forth this increase of His authority, character, and presence on earth. With this in mind, we have a responsibility for what is wrong in the world, as we are called to be the answer to a broken world in order to restore it to its original intent (our Isaiah 61:4 mandate). Nothing is too far gone for the Lord to redeem, and it's not someone else's job to "fix." God calls each of us to participate in the reconciliation of our world, starting in the places He has put us (our family, workplaces, church, communities, neighbourhoods, etc.).

By God's design, we are priests and kings on earth. A part of this role as priests is prayer and intercession. As priests, we minister to people on behalf of the Lord as the hands and feet of Jesus. Both are critical in accomplishing the will of God on earth.

How often does God look for someone to be His hands and feet to care for a lost or broken person, and no one responds? Yet, so many complain about the number of homeless men, women, and children living on the streets and in their cars. They ask God, "How could You let this happen?" when we could be a part of the solution. This is why we are here! To be the solution! How many married couples does God ask to adopt children? Yet, so many babies are aborted or end up in the foster care system.

Our lack of obedience and action is displayed on earth in brokenness. God calls us to pray and then act in obedience in partnership with Him. He wants to partner with us! We need to take this mandate seriously. The healing of the world depends on us working with Him, specifically through prayer, intercession, and Spirit-led action.

> Without God, we cannot, without us God will not!
> — Saint Augustine[3]

Prayer and action are essential as they are required for bringing heaven to earth! Prayer moves things in the spiritual realm, while action is the expression of faith, which reflects the practical application in tangible ways. As a very simple example, if we pray for someone who is lonely, there is a good chance God will use us to be part of the answer to that prayer, as the hands and feet of Jesus, spending quality time with that person or connecting them with others relationally. In terms of action, Romans 12:21 tells us to overcome evil with good. The kingdom is expanded, and the nations are discipled with every act of kindness. My mother often quotes John Wesley as her life mission, who beautifully and simply articulates our kingdom mandate.

> Do all the good you can,
> By all the means you can,
> In all the ways you can,
> In all the places you can,
> At all the times you can,
> To all the people you can,
> As long as ever you can.[4]

God is sovereign over the entire universe and governs over all the systems He put in place. However, a key part of His plan is to work in and through people in prayer and action so that He can intervene on earth with the resources and power of heaven. God is looking for people whose hearts are for Him and who agree with Him in prayer so that He can bring heaven to earth. God is sovereign, but He does not control everything because He is not responsible for evil, and He does not infringe upon free will. In His sovereignty (the supreme ruler, the divine orchestrator, and the ultimate authority), He makes all things work together for our good and unto the fulfillment of His sovereign plans.

> The greatest tragedy of life is not unanswered prayer, but unoffered prayer.
> —F.B. Meyer[5]

God is looking for people who will obey Him. He is looking for people who will be the hands and feet of Jesus to love others. He is looking for people who speak words of truth and life. He is looking for people who will partner with Him to bring solutions powered by heaven to establish His kingdom now.

When the kingdom of God comes, Satan's kingdom ends. Manifestations of the invisible kingdom of heaven will result in the physical realm *on earth as it is in heaven*:

- In His kingdom, there is no sickness, so people are healed.
- In His kingdom, there is no death, so the dead are raised.
- In His kingdom, we live above our temporary circumstances, so there is perpetual joy and peace.
- In His kingdom, there are no demons, so demons flee.
- In His kingdom, there is Jesus, our All in All.

> *Now the Lord is the Spirit, and where the Spirit of the Lord is, there is freedom.*
> —*2 Corinthians 3:17, NASB*

Establishing Dominion

Jesus was a disciple-maker. Specifically, He made disciples (sons and daughters) who went on to make disciples who made disciples, and so on and so forth. In fact, if you know Jesus today, it's because you were discipled by someone who (if you go back far enough) was discipled by someone who was ultimately discipled by Jesus! Making disciple-makers, mature sons and daughters who become fathers and mothers and are active kingdom ambassadors possessing kingdom authority is the mandate for every Christian.[6]

Again, God designed His power and authority to flow *through people*.

When we humble ourselves, pray, seek Him first, and repent, we are using kingdom keys to see our prayers answered and our land healed.

Jesus was given ALL authority by the Father, which gives us legal rights to govern in His kingdom's realm *on earth as it is in heaven*. We have our dominion authority restored through Christ. If it's on earth, we have authority over it. Authority legitimizes power to enforce change. But, in order to exert our authority, we must also identify and nullify the enemy's legal authority, which is the result of human partnership and man's sin. In other words, a history of sin, generational sin, curses, bloodshed, idolatry, worldly systems, etc., all give the demonic realm permission to rule. These are the areas where we can appropriate the victory of Jesus and "take back the land." In other words, all has been redeemed and now must be reclaimed. Land (nations, states, provinces, cities, etc.) is spiritual and has deposits of spiritual treasures from God, including specific redemptive gifts.[7]

An undeserved curse will be powerless to harm you. It may flutter over you like a bird, but it will find no place to land.
—*Proverbs 26:2, TPT*

Just as light displaces darkness, life swallows death, and love conquers fear, the blessings of God destroy the curse. As a word of warning, where we have compromise or sin operating in our lives, we *do not* have authority. When we agree with the lies of the enemy, we knowingly or unknowingly give legal power to Satan. Brian Orme often says something to the effect that demons are so weak they cannot even open doors themselves. Doors have to be opened for them. Let's not be the ones who open those doors to Satan. Instead, let's identify vulnerable areas in our lives and close any currently open doors that give the enemy access.

Where Are You Vulnerable?

Areas that are vulnerable to the enemy include unresolved pain, bitterness, continued habits of sin, pride, living in deception, and unforgiveness. Generational curses and iniquity may also be an open door. Where we have unaddressed wounds, there is demonic influence. This is why it is important to live a lifestyle of repentance, deeply inventorying and then addressing generational sin, uncovering ungodly beliefs, and regularly taking care of our hearts by facing traumas or life's hurts with inner healing and deliverance. Jesus is the answer to everything!

For more on this subject, I recommend connecting with ministries like Restoring the Foundations, which walks people through generational cleansing, ungodly beliefs, soul ties, inner healing, deliverance, etc.[8] HeartSync is another wonderful inner healing ministry. Both have given me tools that have helped me move into great ongoing freedom and wholeness.[9] Because God made us complex beings, there are layers to inner healing. This is why I continue to go through the HeartSync process from time to time when the Lord reveals areas that require greater healing. These ministries also teach us to encounter God in new ways.

As we walk in increasing freedom, our authority increases in our lives, families, and then into our greater spheres of influence. Imagine the kingdom expanding as you move in unity and victory over your sphere. Now imagine what could happen as other believers do the same in their spheres of influence, taking more and more ground and overlapping to expand the kingdom in our communities, cities, nations, and beyond. As love is the ultimate power in the universe, our ultimate authority is when we have the love of God moving through us. This places us in a state of obedience. Love is the fruit of abiding. Love is the person of Jesus!

Then he said to me, "Do not be afraid, Daniel, for from the first day that you set your heart on understanding this and on humbling yourself before your God, your words were heard, and I have come in response to your words."
—Daniel 10:12, NASB

In Daniel 10, an angel visits Daniel and says his prayers were heard. Daniel fasted and interceded for a breakthrough for 21 days. This empowered the kingdom of light to prevail as his prayers were enforced and brought victory from the spiritual realm into the natural realm. We get to do the same in our families, businesses, communities, and for any assignment the Lord places in our hearts. If we humble ourselves, pray, and set our hearts to understand, our prayers will be heard.

Jesus won the victory. He destroyed the enemy's legal right on earth. It is up to us to enforce victory throughout the earth by taking the battle by force in the authority of Jesus through prayer and unity in alignment with heaven. We are to function as a gate from heaven to earth so that the King of Glory may come through, allowing heaven to invade whatever sphere God has placed us in. This is our assignment on earth as co-rulers and ambassadors of the kingdom.

1. Galatians 4:7.
2. "Psalm 24:7, TPT Footnote V7," *LifeBible*, accessed October 17, 2023, https://lifebible.com/bible.
3. Saint Augustine, "Saint Augustine Quotes," *AZ Quotes*, accessed October 14, 2023, https://www.azquotes.com/quote/662102.
4. Sue Wright, "Sunday's Message: John Wesley and 3 Simple Rules," *Reisterstown United Methodist Church*, accessed October 14, 2023, https://tinyurl.com/yc3ku27a.
5. F. B. Meyer, "Top 60 F. B. Meyer Quotes (2023 Update)," *QuoteFancy*, accessed October 14, 2023, https://quotefancy.com/f-b-meyer-quotes.
6. Matthew 28:19.
7. For more information on land, see https://theslg.com/content/who-are-we.
8. Check out www.restoringthefoundations.org for more information about what they do and how to get an inner healing session with them.
9. Check out www.heartsyncministries.org for more information about what they do and how to get an inner healing session with them.

THE KINGDOM PRINCIPLE
OF CO-RULING

In the kingdom, co-ruling is a divine partnership between believers and God, where humanity exercises authority on earth in alignment with God's will. This reflects the beautiful, collaborative nature of the Father's rule. We are carriers of His presence on earth for God to reign through us and expand His kingdom.

Father, we ask for the grace to rule and reign in life.

QUESTIONS FOR REFLECTION

What has the Holy Spirit revealed to you through *The Kingdom Principle of Co-ruling*? How can you apply this to your life?

_____

_____

_____

What places or spheres of influence does God want to partner with you to bring His kingdom?

_____

_____

_____

In what ways, both through gifting and experiences, has God equipped you for these spheres?

_____

_____

_____

Notes

Chapter 16: The Kingdom Principle of Ekklesia

And the apostles went out announcing the good news everywhere, as the Lord Himself consistently worked with them, validating the message they preached with miracle-signs that accompanied them!
- Mark 16:20, TPT

Victory Is Ours

Ekklesia means "called-out ones" and is the key to the expansion of God's government on earth. The word ekklesia is a governmental term (not spiritual in nature) that comes from the Greek term for a called-out assembly or congregation "for the purpose of deliberating."[1] The ancient Greeks had an ekklesia, which referred to an assembly of citizens who would gather and make decisions about civic matters. Rome also adopted the ekklesia with legislative function, passing laws and making decisions, conducting public business, and matters of importance to the city.

Throughout the New Testament, the word is used to describe the church. It is God's legislative assembly on earth. Jesus co-opted this kingdom system of expansion and governing (both inside and outside of the Jewish religious system of His day) to expand His kingdom across the earth.

God's ekklesia are His called-out ones. They are called out to go into society with the kingdom's governmental authority. They are called out to operate 24/7 to administer the affairs of the kingdom according to the culture, values, principles, plans, and will of the King in every sphere of society. Every believer is meant to operate apostolically or sent out as a disciple-maker and to make earth look like heaven in their area of influence, regardless of their giftings or function, knowing there is no divide between the sacred and secular as it is all sacred to God. We are called to first follow and become discipled before we are sent. (This is different from the office of an apostle, which is a specific appointment by God. To operate apostolically, we must mature as disciples of Jesus, in humility, as sons and daughters who then become fathers and mothers in the kingdom, with hearts of servanthood and lives marked by love and honour.)

I like how *Transform Our World* explains it:

> An Ekklesia, as the most embryonic expression of The Church, is the gathering of at least two believers in the midst of the manifest presence of God, functioning with His authority to bind and release His will, beginning in their sphere of influence and spreading outward until The Great Commission is fulfilled.[2]

The kingdom moves us to war in the spirit realm from the place of guaranteed victory! We are not fighting for victory; we are enforcing a victory that has already been obtained. Let me say that again so that this really sinks in: *We are enforcing a victory that has already been obtained!* Jesus spoke the following words to His 12 disciples from Caesarea-Philippi, a place containing many monuments to false gods. He stood in front of a cave called *hades* ("death"), a place of human and animal sacrifice to the gods believed to be a link to the underworld.

> ***"I give you the name Peter, a stone. And this rock will be the bedrock foundation on which I will build my church—my legislative assembly, and the power of death will not be able to overpower it! I will give you the keys of heaven's kingdom realm to forbid on earth that which is forbidden in heaven, and to release on earth that which is released in heaven."***
> *—Matthew 16:18-19, TPT*

It is fascinating that God chose us (not the other way around), knowing we are a broken and imperfect people, to build His church.[3] For example, Peter, a common fisherman, was a man who fell asleep during Jesus's greatest time of need in Gethsemane.[4] He denied Jesus three times.[5] Peter sank as he attempted to walk on the water.[6] He was rebuked by Jesus as a stumbling block to His coming death with the cutting words, "Get behind me Satan."[7] Despite these flaws, Peter experienced an incredible transformation by the power of God to gradually become one of His 12 apostles and one of the church's founding fathers.

Ekklesia is rooted in relationships, as the kingdom is relational. Ekklesia starts in the heart, then the family, and expands into other spheres. Overcoming in life starts first with the things closest to us (our house must first be in order) and moves outward. It is always founded in relationships. We are designed to need one another. We are living gates of God, and as we function with other living gates as the ekklesia, it is God who will move victoriously on earth, crush Satan under "our" feet, establish His kingdom through the people of God, and implement God's solutions on earth.[8]

> …Mission was not made for the church; the church was made for mission—God's mission.
> —Cliff Jordan[9]

Interestingly, a business, community, or nation can function as an ekklesia. The church was never intended to be contained in a building. Buildings are a creation of man and a location to "see" the body of Christ. We are still called to gather, but the ekklesia is meant to be *in the world*, operating in every sphere of society. Kenn Gill likes to say that success is measured in sending capacity, never in seating capacity. Wherever we (the ekklesia) go, we cannot tolerate evil. The bedrock foundation of the ekklesia is our faith in Jesus, and the keys we are given are His governmental authority and ruling power. We get to take authority over the atmosphere as light displaces darkness, as the head and not the tail. Every believer is in the ministry wherever God has placed them!

But what if God says, "I am not raising ministries; I'm raising sons and daughters, heirs to the kingdom, joint heirs with Christ." Then, the ministry is not the goal; it's the tool.[10]

> *"I assure you and most solemnly say to you, whatever you bind [forbid, declare to be improper and unlawful] on earth shall have [already] been bound in heaven, and whatever you loose [permit, declare lawful] on earth shall have [already] been loosed in heaven."*
> *–Matthew 18:18, NASB*

When the Lord taught us to pray, He said to pray *as it is in heaven*. Consider the word "already" in the verse above; we are *already* binding and loosing (opening and closing). We are forbidding and allowing what happens on earth to match what has already been done in heaven and establishing God's will *on earth as it is in heaven*. Jesus modelled perfect obedience, the key to walking in the authority and power of heaven, by only doing what He saw the Father doing *on earth as it is in heaven*. As living gates on earth, we get our instructions from heaven and implement them on earth. God will answer our prayers that are in line with His will when we ask in the name of Jesus. *The Passion Translation* notes about Jesus: "When He would close those doors, no amount of human striving could open them."[11] We have the keys of David to open the doors that no man can shut to revelation, treasures, favour, and opportunity and to close the doors that human striving can't force open.

> *"Again, I give you an eternal truth: If two of you agree to ask God for something in a symphony of prayer, my heavenly Father will do it for you. For wherever two or three come together in honour of my name, I am right there with them!"*
> *–Matthew 18:19, TPT*

Whenever two or more gather in Jesus's name, there is an ekklesia, and He is there with them. Jesus sent His 12 and His 72 disciples out two by two for good reason. We honour God by seeing what God wants to do through us. Heaven is our blueprint. By speaking the Word of God in unity, we open the kingdom in the lives of others and the earthly realm. This is where we need to cultivate an ultra-sensitivity to the leading of the Holy Spirit. It is our prayers in faith that bring the kingdom of God to earth, which are then followed by our actions modelled after Jesus. Everything that is seen in the natural realm was first in the spiritual realm, so let's storm the heavens and the earth!

> *This is why the Scriptures say: Things never discovered or heard of before, things beyond our ability to imagine— these are the many things God has in store for all His lovers. But God now unveils these profound realities to us by the Spirit. Yes, He has revealed to us His inmost heart and deepest mysteries through the Holy Spirit, who constantly explores all things.*
> *— 1 Corinthians 2:9-10, TPT*

We must understand God's laws and principles before we can enforce and apply them on earth. The keys we are given are the eternal and unchanging laws and principles of God's. With the keys, we can operate *on earth as it is in heaven*. We have the keys to heavenly solutions and kingdom standards in our lives and relationships, but we can only use them if we know what they are and how to use them.

My people are destroyed for lack of knowledge. Since you have rejected knowledge...
—*Hosea 4:6a, NASB*

The church is always about people, living stones, uniquely designed and positioned by God for Jesus to build His church. We have the apostles and prophets as the foundation and Jesus as the chief cornerstone. In other words, the church is made of people, not bricks and mortar. Jesus is the church, which is His body, and Jesus is the head, coming together as one person. The gathering of the saints is important. We must fellowship to encourage, train, and equip, but the church was never meant to be defined by and contained within four walls. What good is salt if it is left in the salt shaker?

Living Gates

We live as portals or gateways between two realms. Living simultaneously on earth *and* in heaven takes practice to function effectively. Living naturally supernaturally is the way of the kingdom. This leads to kingdom expansion through mature sons and daughters who are heirs of the kingdom. This is how we change the world by raising and sending sons and daughters (we are all sons, just as men are part of the bride of Christ)! The ekklesia is to govern through prayer and declarations. We are to take the kingdom where darkness is entrenched and then manifest or implement these victories on earth in tangible ways. The spiritual must be followed by action in the natural.

Simply stated, see a need, meet a need, and become the solution. We need to be able to clearly and vulnerably communicate our needs and also listen to the needs of others to set each other up for success, in the spirit realm first and then in the natural realm. We are what we create or what we allow to persist, internally and externally.

The intercessory prayer team at Flō has had such an incredible impact on our company culture. The following pages contain the core guidelines we developed as a team in regards to truly becoming an ekklesia in action.

EKKLESIA IN ACTION

The practical aspects of how we operate and function as an ekklesia at Flō

by Bryan Elliott and the Flō Prayer Team

1. **Gathering in Jesus's Name:** Connect regularly in small groups with specific goals like fellowship, prayer, or practical strategy sessions. Actively contribute to discussions, ensuring everyone brings their unique strengths to the table.

2. **Honouring Wisdom:** Seek realistic solutions for everyday challenges with a humble approach. Recognize the value of wise counsel and apply divine intelligence in decision-making at home and in business.

3. **Principle of Honour:** Intentionally appreciate people in your family, company, and community. Use words of encouragement, share your time, and actively listen. Extend honour to values like justice, humility, and generosity.

4. **Unity in the Holy Spirit:** Work through differences respectfully, seeking wisdom and yielding to God's guidance. Find unity and clarity in decision-making by aligning actions with God's purposes.

5. **Kingdom Legislation Through Prayer:** Recognize opportunities to pray and declare positive change in various situations. Shape your words based on your relationship with God and seek consensus with others.

6. **Love and Service:** Support each other practically through prayer, encouragement, and assistance. View your community as a unified body, offering correction and assistance in times of need.

7. **Celebration:** Foster a joyful atmosphere by celebrating achievements, big or small. Include music, gatherings, and expressions of honour. Embrace joy as a hallmark of your community.

8. **Proclaiming the Gospel:** Share the message of Jesus through both words and actions in your daily life. Demonstrate God's mercy and justice by living in alignment with His principles, inviting others into the same.

9. **Faithfulness and Increase:** Begin with small acts of obedience, whether giving, serving, or caring for others. Watch for growth and increased responsibilities as you faithfully steward resources and contribute to the community's well-being.

PRAYER EVANGELISM [1]

Ed Silvoso outlines four simple steps of Prayer Evangelism in the Transform Our World core values, which can be used personally or in any sphere of society:

1. Bless first.

2. Fellowship and do life together, understand the needs of others.

3. Pray for these felt needs and possibly become an answer to prayer.

4. After seeing answers to prayer, declare the kingdom of God has come near and share the gospel of the kingdom of God.

BLESS

Speaking peace to people and to the systems that are around us.

I cannot change what I do not embrace.

FELLOWSHIP

Listening to find out where the pain and brokenness is.

I cannot fix what I don't know is broken.

MINISTER

Talking to God about someone else's problem.

I connect man's need with God's resources.

DECLARE

Letting it be known that the kingdom of God is near.

I confirm that the power and presence of God is "in the neighborhood."

[1] "Our Core Values," Transform Our World, accessed October 14, 2023
https://www.transformourworld.org/our-core-values/.

There was a time when Flō experienced great spiritual warfare that impacted communication and harmony. It caused everyone much confusion. Intercession often begins with removing the enemy's legal rights, including ungodly beliefs, unforgiveness, sin, etc., in order to overcome evil and maintain an open heaven. With that in mind, the Flō intercessory team used our kingdom authority from Jesus under His divine guidance to command spirits of confusion and disruption to leave.

The Lord then revealed that points of dishonour (such as words spoken in the present and the past or even what we carried in our hearts) were the seeds sown that were causing division. We each confessed and repented, then released honour to the teams and to one another. Through the power of Christ, we restored the atmosphere, which enabled us to move forward without interference. Displacement of powers and principalities happens as the kingdom comes! When evil or demonic roots are exposed and dealt with, the process breaks future repeated cycles and heals past wounds. The kingdom of God revives and reforms. It sanctifies and heals the earthly and mortal into the heavenly and eternal. Therefore, kingdom citizens will build kingdom businesses and become redemptive entrepreneurs, as we are purposing to do daily with Flō.

The ekklesia is to build the kingdom of God with kingdom foundations and not on the existing Babylonian structures, although there will be Daniels and Josephs operating within these systems. These two structures will run in parallel and co-exist, like the wheat and the weeds, until the return of Jesus. However, as life-giving kingdom entities emerge and promote human flourishing, the world will be drawn in to taste and see the goodness of God. I have seen videos describing the Jewish circular economy, which is an excellent economic model encompassing relationships, family, values, accountability, tithing, generosity, and value exchange.

As God leads and by His grace, the body is empowered to start kingdom schools, kingdom banks, kingdom supply chains, etc., unto complete kingdom economics, which are decentralized to empower, create interconnected relational networks, build equity, and create wealth for families and communities to flourish and to further the kingdom. The goal is not to centralize wealth, oppress, rule over, or enslave people, as the current world systems do. The larger the entities, whether governments or businesses, the more centralized the power becomes, and the greater the control that results.

The kingdom of God is relational, not transactional, as it is based on the desire to serve and bless others. As we live together in the realities of the kingdom, living supernaturally by faith, His values, kingdom culture, and fresh vision expand from the bottom up to transform people, families, communities, cities, and nations. We give to receive so that we can give more, working for the benefit of others. The world will never be transformed by top-down elites lording over people but by bottom-up kingdom citizens taking up their responsibility to contribute and serve. It is responsibility and growth in the capacity of self-government that place us in a position to contribute to the greater good, provide meaning, and produce resiliency in the face of trials and challenges.

Everyone has a role in making the world a better place. John Anderson, the former Deputy Prime Minister of Australia, wrote in "An Account of Responsible Citizenship" about the necessity of regaining a society where citizens are responsible.[12] He explains:

> In a way, we could say that it is the death of responsible citizenship that precedes the death of a civilisation. Responsible citizenship is when our energies are dedicated primarily to the virtue of living up to the duties that, when met, facilitate a healthy society. These duties include starting and nurturing families, looking after our parents as they age, success in the economy by working to make the most of our talents and gifts, and taking an active interest in our local communities and the welfare of our nations as a whole. Irresponsible citizenship, on the other hand, is being more inwardly focused; being more concerned with what others can do for me.[13]

This is why His kingdom calls us to take up our cross (persevere in the face of suffering unto transformation for the greater good), deny ourselves (sacrificial love in action), and follow Jesus! The kingdom is a win-win approach. It looks at the best interests of everyone involved. We take up our cross by putting others ahead of ourselves. It is only the power of God that transforms. As we build in the kingdom by creating life-giving organizations and cultures for people to flourish, non-believers will be drawn into the life, light, care, and safety of the kingdom.

Personal revival or salvation must be followed by reformation and sanctification as maturity and transformation are achieved more and more. Only a transformed heart can transform. A transformed heart begins and continues to live in repentance, a sustained change in our thinking. Repentance ushers in the presence of God.

On a side note, as we, the body of Christ, first move in repentance, repentance will spread across the world. Revival in our spheres of influence must also be accompanied by the manifestation or the outworking of new creation life on earth.[14] From my perspective, if revival does not result in transformation, then true revival has not occurred as the kingdom of God *is* revival and reformation! Through our transformation, we get to display God's kingdom to the world.

WHERE IS YOUR EKKLESIA?

If you are wondering where your ekklesia is, take some time to journal through the following questions. Make sure to stop and listen to what the Lord is revealing to you.

◊ How is your heart doing? Revival starts with you and the Holy Spirit working in you.

◊ How are your marriage and family? Ekklesia starts at home.

◊ Who are the key people in your life made for ekklesia?

◊ Describe your current communities or spheres of influence. Who is in those spaces?

◊ What are the felt needs in your communities or spheres of influence? Ask the Holy Spirit to show you.

◊ What is heaven's vision for these needs? Ask the Holy Spirit to reveal heaven's solution to the problem.

◊ What needs to be forbidden on earth?

◊ What needs to be released on earth?

◊ What are the next steps with the Lord and others to make earth look like heaven in these areas?

Ekklesia is God's instrument for global transformation, operating 24/7 to engage and govern the world.[1]

---

[1] Ed Silvoso.

Transform by Love

We cannot transform what we do not love. On the ground, this looks like God's people coming together in community, doing what God has called them to do as the hands, feet, and body of Jesus to meet the felt needs of the world. We can bring the presence of God everywhere by the presence of the ekklesia.

For example, a woman named Deniz from the Middle East moved her bakery next to my office. As we got to know each other, she began to ask many questions about Christianity and Jesus. After six months, she came to the point of deep heart surrender, accepted Jesus as Lord, and, as a result, her entire life began to change rapidly. Deniz knows her business is her ministry and is her opportunity to love and bless the local community. In fact, many ask her why she treats them differently, as they have never experienced such warmth and care, which often includes a hug.

Deniz loves the Lord and people so much that her bakery has become a hub for the community and a place to experience the kingdom, hear the gospel, receive prayer, be discipled, share testimonies, and get saved. This is a kingdom ekklesia in action! Deniz is a light in the world and a joy to be around. As I look out the window of my office, I often see people's faces light up and smile as they turn to go into her shop.

These days, we have an open invitation to everyone in our building at 8:30 a.m. each morning for prayer, which Deniz now leads. She also hosts a dinner called "The Table," where she invites people to share testimonies and glorify Jesus while feasting together, which we also host at my office. In less than one year, she is already becoming a mentor to those she leads to Christ and a mother to the lost and broken who are drawn to her. The most common words out of her mouth are, "I want others to know how beautiful Jesus is."

I love watching the leaven of the kingdom work its way through community. The ekklesia of Flō influencing Deniz's bakery, and now, Deniz's ekklesia at the bakery is influencing others — this is the kingdom at work!

Bringing Heaven to Earth in Your Sphere of Influence

It is no surprise that God's government on earth requires people as He chooses to work through mankind.

> *"For wherever two or three come together in honour of my name, I am right there with them!"*
> —*Matthew 18:20, TPT*

Did you skim over the above scripture? Please read it again. Jesus PROMISES us His presence! His manifest presence. His kingdom is at hand when we gather in His name! The key to Jesus being present with us is for us to gather in unity. *The kingdom of God is the presence of the King!* If we want

God's presence, we must be in relationship with one another, demonstrating forgiveness, mercy, love, and honouring one another and Jesus. *This goes far beyond attending a church service.*

…"Not by might nor by power, but by My Spirit," says the Lord of armies.
— Zechariah 4:6, NASB

We can trust the Holy Spirit to be the leader in all of this. It's about doing life together with other believers in discipleship, prayer, breaking bread, understanding life opportunities and struggles, and carrying each other's burdens, all in a loving community. In the kingdom, it only takes two to form an ekklesia. In the kingdom, big things often come in small packages!

We have an enormous, mind-boggling promise: The Creator of the universe, the King of Kings, our Lord and Saviour Jesus Christ, will be in our midst. The manifest presence of Jesus is with us as we gather in oneness and honour Him! This is the power source and authority of ekklesia. To quote Ed Silvoso again, "Ekklesia was a building-less mobile people movement designed to operate 24/7 in the marketplace for the purpose of having an impact on everybody and everything."[15]

The presence of the King is the presence of His kingdom. When we are alone, we have the Holy Spirit within, but when we add even one believer in unity (in close, intimate, authentic, trusting relationship), the manifest presence of Jesus is promised. The prayers of saints in line with the will of God and submitted to the Lordship of Jesus are powerful.

This is why the enemy wants to keep believers from praying together and tries to destroy families, the fabric of society, and the model of the kingdom.

If the enemy can keep us from praying and can keep families at odds with one another… we will miss out on the blessings and breakthroughs promised to us. Let's not ever forget that as ambassadors of Jesus, we have been given authority in our spheres of influence or assigned territories. We have the keys to open heaven in our families. We have the keys to open heaven in our finances, businesses, communities, cities, and nations as we come together as His body.

But are you willing to acknowledge, you foolish person, that faith without works is useless?
— James 2:20, NASB

As faith begets faith, living out our faith continually strengthens our faith, builds the faith of others, and pleases God.[16] We are to bring everything that man has created on earth into divine alignment with heaven, back to original intent, by becoming a part of God's solution on earth by diligently exercising our faith, knowing everything finds completion in Christ.

1. "Ekklesia," *Bible Study Tools*, accessed October 14, 2023,
https://www.biblestudytools.com/lexicons/greek/nas/ekklesia.html.
2. "Ekklesia Everywhere," *Transform Our World*, accessed October 14, 2023, https://tinyurl.com/sbk5bvex.
3. John 15:16.
4. Matthew 26:40.
5. Luke 22:54-62.
6. Matthew 14:30.
7. Matthew 16:23.
8. Romans 16:20.
9. Cliff Jordan, "Mission: The Activity of the Church," *International Mission Board*, accessed October 14, 2023,
https://www.imb.org/2019/01/03/mission-activity-church/.
10. Source unknown.
11. "Isaiah 22:22, "TPT Footnote V22," *LifeBible*, accessed October 14, 2023, https://lifebible.com/bible.
12. John Anderson, "An Account of Responsible Citizenship," *ArcResearch*, accessed October 14, 2023,
https://www.arc-research.org/research-papers/responsible-citizenship.
13. Ibid.
14. Revival means awakening or to live again, most often ushered in through repentance.
15. Ed Silvoso, *Ekklesia*, 17.
16. Hebrews 11:6.

THE KINGDOM PRINCIPLE
OF EKKLESIA

In the kingdom, each member plays a vital role in fostering an environment of mutual support, accountability, and shared responsibility in bringing heaven's solutions to earth, expanding God's kingdom, thereby manifesting God's rule and reign in every sphere of society, ultimately bringing about renewal and transformation.

Father, we ask for the grace to be the ekklesia on earth!

QUESTIONS FOR REFLECTION

What has the Holy Spirit revealed to you through *The Kingdom Principle of Ekklesia*? How can you apply this to your life?

How might God want you to be a part of His solution to the world's problems?

Who is the Holy Spirit prompting you to partner with in prayer and action to expand the kingdom?

Notes

Chapter 17: The Kingdom Principles of Faith and Words

Death and life are in the power of the tongue. And those who love it will eat its fruit.
— Proverbs 18:21, NASB

In the beginning was the Word, and the Word was with God, and the Word was God. He was in the beginning with God.
John 1:1-2, NASB

The Word of God

Logos and *rhema* are two Greek words used throughout the New Testament to describe the Word of God. In simple terms, logos implies God "has spoken" (His Word), and rhema is when God "is speaking." John 1:1-2 references logos or the "written" Word of God, Scripture, which is constant, unchanging, and available for all. The logos Word of God has existed since the very beginning, and Jesus, God's Son, is the logos Word in the flesh. The written Word became the living Word!

Rhema, on the other hand, means "utterance" and refers to the spoken Word of God. Rhema is what happens when God speaks directly to us; it's when the Word becomes alive and active to us by faith. For example, when Jesus told Peter to walk on the water, it was rhema (spoken) for Peter and logos (written) for us today. Logos and rhema will always reflect each other, that is, the heart of God and His commands for us yesterday, today, and forever.

The rhema Word of God carries logos (written Word) power in it. It begins the birthing process of what is not yet seen and brings it into the seen realm. God's rhema Word spoke all of creation into existence. As I journey with the Lord, I experience the rhema Word more and more.

God's Word is the primary way He speaks to us. It is by faith that we are able to receive His Word into our hearts. When we read the Word, we first open our hearts to receive God's revelation, which stirs our faith. To open our hearts is to yield afresh to the Lord, to be fully present and aware of the Holy Spirit within us. Opening our hearts means that we expect to hear His voice so that we can receive His revelation. Through Jesus, we get to continue to be His voice on earth when we speak His words. In obedience, submission, and humility, we increasingly steward the power of God and release the authority of the King on earth through our prayers and declarations!

Growing in sonship, yielded and dependent on God our Father, is the pathway to our destiny and is the key to the expansion of the kingdom!

Holiness is our eternal position with God by faith through grace alone but we still have work to do in the natural as we mature. As we work out our salvation with fear and trembling, relying not on our own ability, grace provides our divine enablement, not only to avoid sin, but also for our motives and behaviors to become pure and holy.

Now faith is the certainty of things hoped for, a proof of things not seen.
—*Hebrews 11:1, NASB*

The world says, "I'll believe it when I see it." Faith says, "I'll see it when I believe it," because faith brings the unseen into the seen. The kingdom of God is entered into by faith and is experienced by faith. Belief is an intellectual agreement, whereas faith is a heartfelt reliance that activates belief into action in anticipation of its fulfillment based on the Word of God. It is faith that proceeds the fulfillment of His promise and believes that God's Word is the final word. All heavenly faith is a gift from God, and the fruit of our faith is good works and a life that honours God. Faith expresses itself in love and love always has an expression on the earth. Faith is to be accompanied by action as faith will not do the work for us. We are called into a divine partnership with God, like Noah who built the arc by faith. Faith did not build the arc, Noah did. As James 2:14 says, faith without works is dead. We are the gateways on the earth, to manifest from the spiritual to the natural realms, *on earth as it is in heaven.*

Faith is of the Spirit and is the currency of heaven. Faith is our "title deed," and we are the "owners" of what is hoped for. In our weakness, it is faith that relies on God. The fruit of faith is an unwavering trust in the goodness and faithfulness of God. The greater our dependence on God, the greater our faith. Our courage is powered by faith. Without faith, it is impossible to please God. Faith always points to God, His character, and His promises because He is unchangeable. We cannot base our faith on what we see or on results or outcomes based on our own understanding. The 12 disciples saw all the miracles, signs, and wonders of Jesus with their own eyes over a period of three years, yet they began to doubt less than *three days* after Jesus was crucified. Seeing does not require faith, as faith is required for what is still unseen. All faith is from God, and our new life is empowered by the faith of Jesus!

My old identity has been co-crucified with Christ and no longer lives. And now the essence of this new life is no longer mine, for the Anointed One lives his life through me—we live in union as one! My new life is empowered by the faith of the Son of God who loves me so much that He gave Himself for me, dispensing His life into mine!
—*Galatians 2:20, TPT*

As an engineer, logic and reason have been my foundations for a love of learning and knowledge. Knowledge without love produces pride, and pride blinds. Even the Word of God can be reduced to head knowledge.

So faith comes from hearing [what is told], and what is heard comes by the [preaching of the] message concerning Christ.
—*Romans 10:17, AMP*

Faith comes from hearing. Often, the first way we "hear" a word from God through our emotions, creativity, innovation, imagination, etc. In other words, sometimes a word from God is most easily heard, not through human reasoning or logic. As I grew in my relationship with God, I learned that the more I gave thanks and praise and engaged my emotions and intellect in my relationship with God, the more my faith grew. An intimate relationship is one that uses the whole brain, heart, mind, and soul.[1]

Faith is about hearing God's voice, being a friend of God, receiving the revelation of God's Word, seeing God's perspective, and receiving His solutions. As believers, we are instructed by Scripture to live by faith! This is how the kingdom of God works.

The faith which you have, have as your own conviction before God. Happy is the one who does not condemn himself in what he approves. But the one who doubts is condemned if he eats, because his eating is not from faith; and whatever is not from faith is sin.
—Romans 14:22-23, NASB

Whatever is not from faith is sin. I have been rocked by this truth, as it demonstrates our absolute need for a saviour. Generally, we tend to consider ourselves good people… but this definitely shows us where the bar is with God. *Anything* outside of faith is sin. That which causes our conscience to produce guilt is sin because we are to do only what pleases and edifies God.

Thankfully, His blood covers our sins (past, present, and future). We are continually cleansed by the blood.[2] We are all forgiven, including for sins committed from a lack of faith, and saved by grace. There's nothing we can do to earn His love!

Power in Our Words

The principle of sowing and reaping applies to our words. Take a few minutes to reflect on your words. Are they birthing life or death? Knowing that our words come from the overflow of our hearts, what do your words reveal about your heart? What do your words reveal about your faith? Are your words sowing from the flesh or from the Spirit?

The kingdom of God is advanced as we move by faith outside of our comfort zone. Specifically, faith looks like:

For in Christ Jesus neither circumcision nor uncircumcision means anything, but faith working through love.
—Galatians 5:6, NASB

This tells us that the only thing that counts is faith expressing itself through love, which is living faith. This pleases God! Jesus demonstrated the principle of faith in action, which often looks like obedience in the face of the impossible or illogical. As transitioning agents between the spiritual and physical realms, we partner with the heavenly realm through prayer and move into the physical realm. Remember, it was after Jesus gave thanks that the bread and fish were multiplied

273

before the disciples distributed the meal! When Jesus prayed for the ten lepers in Luke 17:11-19, He told them to go and get examined by the priests, and they were healed as they went. They went in faith as they left Jesus's presence unhealed. Jesus didn't lay hands on them or even pray. He just told them to go to the priest as if they were cleansed. Jesus didn't use a formula. He simply did what He saw the Father doing and lived by faith. The miraculous occurred as those receiving moved in faith. Our faith will be tested, but God is with us. As we go in faith, He makes things happen. Miracles are released as we participate in obedience to Him.

So will My word be which goes out of My mouth; It will not return to Me empty, Without accomplishing what I desire, And without succeeding in the purpose for which I sent it.
—Isaiah 55:11, NASB

Remember, answered prayer requires a believing heart. It is important that we are honest in our faith position so that our words and declarations match our faith. This congruence in words and declarations moves the heart of God because our words and declarations are real and authentic. However weak our faith may seem, God will use it. Again, we are to simply steward the measure of faith we have to receive more. I have learned to be vulnerable and honest even in my unbelief, like the man in Mark 9:24 who said to Jesus, "I do believe; help my unbelief!" (NASB). Then Jesus healed His son.

However, the power of our words goes far beyond what we may consider prayer. Remember, God spoke the universe into existence! Every word we speak is important. Our words can activate the angelic or the demonic. In fact, an angel speaking to Daniel explained that his presence with Daniel was on account of his words.[3] What we say matters because our words will either release the kingdom of light or darkness. When we speak words of accusation, condemnation, judgment, murmuring, or complaining, we quench the Holy Spirit. Satan, the accuser, stands in the courts of heaven using our words against us and others as we come into agreement with him.[4] Thankfully, Jesus stands in our defence, and true repentance brings life and transformation.[5] Alternately, when we speak words of spirit and life in line with the will of God, heaven is activated, and the kingdom invades earth. His plan, before the foundations of the earth, was to make us kings and priests on earth to reign in life. Because He delegated authority to us, there is power in our words to change our lives and spheres of influence.

You will also decide and decree a thing, and it will be established for you;
And the light [of God's favor] will shine upon your ways.
—Job 22:28, AMP

"But if you live in life-union with Me and if My words live powerfully within you—
then you can ask whatever you desire and it will be done."
—John 15:7, TPT

The word "ask" means to insist, demand, or command. It is His joy to fulfill our desires. He prepares us to steward our answered prayers by faithfully managing the blessing, expressing thankfulness, and sharing our testimony for God to be glorified. When we share our testimony, we open the realm of faith for others so that God can do it in their life as well. His Word will never return void and will accomplish all that needs to be done in the spirit realm, no matter what we see in the natural.[6]

> *"Not one promise from God is empty of power. Nothing is impossible with God!"*
> *Luke 1:37, TPT*

Our words directly impact our lives (and the lives of others). We can change our world by changing our words, and we change our words by changing our hearts and filling our minds with truth. Whatever we speak is received by our subconscious mind (the part of our mind that operates outside of conscious awareness), which immediately shifts our focus and begins to form a contract for the subconscious to carry out. For example, if we wake up and say, "Today is going to be a great day," our subconscious mind looks for reasons to make this statement true. Therefore, I often start my day saying things like, "All is well and all shall be well because the kingdom of God is at hand—this is a great day!" as a declaration of my day in the natural and spiritual realms. Remember, to prophesy is to simply speak a message from God in faith in advance of its fulfillment!

Warfare and the Shield of Faith

Ephesians 6:10-18 describes the armour of God, which includes the shoes (gospel of peace), belt (of truth), and breastplate (of righteousness), which should be firmly fixed to our body. It teaches us to take up the helmet (of salvation), shield (of faith), and sword (of the Spirit). In times of warfare, the shield of faith is active in applying truth. Faith points immediately to God and relies on the power of God, the character of God, and the promises of God. This is why we must fill ourselves regularly with the Word of God. We resist the devil with the spoken Word of God that comes from our mouth, which releases the power of God. As Welsh minister and medical doctor, Martyn Lloyd-Jones explains, the sword of the Spirit must be taken up and used to quench the fiery darts of the enemy:

> The shift is because the first three pieces of armor are fixed firmly to the body, but the shield must be taken up. People do not fight some general evil, but a particular spiritual person and others he commands. What are the "fiery darts?" Commonly, they are doubting thoughts, blasphemous words, and phrases that fill the mind and come to mentally discourage, depress, and defeat. Other darts inflame desires and passions, destroying peace and contentment. Some are fiery trials of persecution, antagonistic people, or adverse circumstances. The "shield of faith" is the ability to quickly apply belief in answer to everything the devil does or attempts to do. Faith is not merely an intellectual belief or theory, but is always practical to apply truth. Faith never points to itself but to its object.

The object of genuine faith is God, His character, and His promises. When attacks come, faith is actively dependent upon God and His grace in Christ.[7]

Our words will empower the kingdom of light or the kingdom of darkness to move on earth. We know that life swallows death. God's kingdom of life and vitality displaces the kingdom of death and decay. Sometimes, we are better off silent than speaking, like Zechariah before John the Baptist was born, as we reap the consequences of our words.[8] It is vital that we live in awareness of the words we speak. Our hearts represent our internal worlds, which is why we are to guard our hearts. We are, literally, what we think.[9] Remember, from the overflow of our hearts come our words and actions.[10]

*   *   *

Father, we ask for the grace for faith and to speak life!

*   *   *

Out of Nothing

God created man with the ability to innovate or co-create with Him. We can never take the Creator's place, as He is the source of everything. *Ex nihilo* is a Latin phrase meaning "out of nothing." Only God can create something out of nothing. Satan, a created being, cannot create and must work through humans with physical bodies. He does this, beginning with our minds and words. Because our words carry so much power, it is imperative that our minds are transformed into Christ's image, so our words are aligned with His. A member of our prayer team wisely said, "If you watch the way you think, you don't have to watch what you say." The kingdom of darkness expands on earth, in and then through people. People compromised to the kingdom of darkness become agencies of destruction. Satan can get objects, substances, systems, etc., to represent him in killing, stealing, and destroying. However, he is not omnipresent and is limited in everything he does.

> **"But what comes out of your mouth reveals the core of your heart…"**
> —*Matthew 15:18a, TPT*

Recently, two of Flō's senior leaders and I were vulnerable with each other in a conversation, openly sharing about current challenges with our daughters, who were each facing significant challenges and attacks. In unity as fathers, we actively took up our shields of faith, locked our shields together over our daughters, and then began to speak life and declare our trust in the promises of God. It was a truly intimate and beautiful time of prayer and unity, followed by His shalom. It was a holy moment.

1. Whole-hearted living is the goal of inner healing.
2. *The Passion Translation's* footnote for 1 John 1:7 states, "But if we keep living in the pure light that surrounds him, we share unbroken fellowship with one another, and the blood of Jesus, his Son, continually cleanses us from all sin."
3. Daniel 10:12.
4. Revelation 12:10, John 8:44.
5. Psalm 18:2, 2 Corinthians 7:10.
6. Hebrews 11:3.
7. Dr. Martyn Lloyd-Jones, "The Shield of Faith, A Sermon on Ephesians 6:16," *MLJ Trust*, accessed October 14, 2023, https://tinyurl.com/nhdhsdkb.
8. Luke 1.
9. Proverbs 23:7.
10. Luke 6:45.

THE POWER OF
WORDS IN SCRIPTURE

"But you who are known as the Pharisees are rotten to the core like venomous snakes. How can your words be good if you are rotten within? For what has been stored up in your hearts will be heard in the overflow of your words!"
–Matthew 12:34, TPT

Guard your words and you'll guard your life, but if you don't control your tongue, it will ruin everything.
–Proverbs 13:3, TPT

When you speak healing words, you offer others fruit from the tree of life. But unhealthy, negative words do nothing but crush their hopes.
–Proverbs 15:4, TPT

Winsome words spoken at just the right time are as appealing as apples gilded in gold surrounded with silver.
–Proverbs 25:11, TPT

Guard your speech. Forsake obscenities and worthless insults; these are nonsensical words that bring disgrace and are unnecessary. Instead, let worship fill your heart and spill out in your words.
–Ephesians 5:4, TPT

Your words are so powerful that they will kill or give life, and the talkative person will reap the consequences.
–Proverbs 18:21, TPT

THE KINGDOM PRINCIPLES
OF FAITH AND WORDS

Within the kingdom, the dynamic relationship between faith and words is a foundational principle, emphasizing the importance of declaring God's promises and actively participating in the creative process of bringing heavenly realities to earth. Through faith, believers access the supernatural, and their words become powerful instruments that align with God's promises, creating a tangible impact in the natural realm. Faith is to be accompanied by action in divine partnership with God.

Father, speak to us! Use us as living gateways to declare Your words of life and truth so that Your will may be done!

QUESTIONS FOR REFLECTION

What has the Holy Spirit revealed to you through *The Kingdom Principles of Faith and Words?* How can you apply this to your life?

Reflect on key words God has used to breathe life into you. These may be scriptures, prophetic words, impactful words from leaders or other key people in your life, or those whispered to you by the Lord Himself. List them here.

What are you doing or can you do to steward those words well?

Notes

Chapter 18: The Kingdom Principle of Unity

"And a fragmented household will not be able to stand, for it is divided."
Mark 3:25, TPT

With tender humility and quiet patience, always demonstrate gentleness and generous love towards one another, especially towards those who may try your patience. Be faithful to guard the sweet harmony of the Holy Spirit among you in the bonds of peace, being one body and one spirit, as you were all called into the same glorious hope of divine destiny. For the Lord God is one, and so are we, for we share in one faith, one baptism, and one Father. And He is the perfect Father who leads us all, works through us all, and lives in us all!
Ephesians 4:2-6, TPT

The Godhead, the Trinity, the three in one is our model for unity as sons and daughters. Father is God. Jesus is God. The Holy Spirit is God. God is three distinct persons, yet one being. They work together in perfect love, cooperation, and oneness while being three distinct persons, totally void of competition, envy, or comparison. It is sonship that positions our hearts within the body and Godhead in unity. This is absolutely wild. Stop and take this in: The very glory the Father gave to Jesus, Jesus has given to us! We are now one with Him in His glory! This is the heavenly reality we are awakening to day by day as we go from glory to glory by the grace of God!

"For the very glory you have given to Me I have given them so that they will be joined together as one and experience the same unity that we enjoy."
—John 17:22, TPT

THE TRIUNE GOD

Knowing that we are all imperfect and works in progress, we can ask the Holy Spirit to help us see ourselves and others as Jesus does. This involves consciously separating behaviour and identity. Our identity is never changing as sons and daughters and new creations. However, our behaviours are in the process of refinement as we mature. Spiritually, our oneness is the ultimate source of our unity, which is to be made visible in the physical realm, following Jesus's new command.

The body of Christ is to display the wisdom of God in heavenly realms and live with the mind of Christ.[1] This can only happen collectively, in unity, sharing in God's perspective, understanding and bringing God's plans to the earth, and restoring creation for the glory of God. This terrifies the enemy more than anything. As we come close to Jesus (the key to unity), we come close to others, as unity is of the Spirit. Unity is required for the formation of a true community that follows in the ways of God and is powered by the Holy Spirit. Orphans are self-focused and self-reliant, while sons and daughters embrace our God-designed need for one another. By God's design, our destinies unfold within an interconnected community of believers.

The Community of Unity

As we recognize the fact that we need one another and look to serve others, we begin to live in interdependent and interconnected relationships. This is how community is formed, the bonds of unity are established, and the commanded blessing of God is released. This is an unstoppable broad blessing that terrifies the enemy, which is the reason he attacks unity and relationships so fervently. Especially in times of hardship, like the early church or the persecuted church, by God's design, attacks of the enemy only strengthened their bonds and deepened their need for one another.

At Flō, we have prayer teams who function in unity, though they function differently outside of the trials and challenges of the day-to-day marketplace operations. When our operational teams struggle with doubt, unbelief, or mounting pressures, we have others who are positioned to come alongside us to encourage and strengthen, holding the line of faith for the company. Most of this occurs with the believers at the company; however, non-believers also ask for prayer and are with Flō because of what we stand for and who we are as a whole. We also pray and strengthen each other in our day-to-day lives. There is such life and togetherness in the community of unity!

There's a beautiful illustration of the power of unity found in Belgian workhorses. As individuals, these horses can pull up to 4,000 pounds. But, if you yoke two Belgian workhorses together, they can pull an average of 16,000 pounds. That's not double the weight. It's *four times* the weight![2] Teamwork, whether between horses or people, equals multiplication.

Practically, unity is anchored in relationship, and any healthy relationship requires intimacy. Intimacy is anchored in trust, and trust is established in vulnerability. We first establish this with God and then with people. God is our source of belonging, identity, security, and safety. Vulnerability is anchored in humility and safety. We feel safe when we belong, and when we are safe, we can freely express our needs. We belong when we feel fully known, loved, and accepted, which is only perfectly established by God. These are the foundations for quality connections, and connection is the antidote to loneliness. I have gone through seasons of loneliness and wanted to understand the potential causes. I discovered that loneliness is a symptom of a gap between the connections we need and what we have. As the kingdom is about relationships, we can feel lonely if we have gaps in any area, including God, family, friendship, and social networks. We need them all. A large part of how we experience God is through people. When we receive this belonging, we can show up and be vulnerable with nothing to prove or earn. If we don't receive this from God, the process of vulnerability will be more difficult.

Said another way, the kingdom moves in the power of unity, founded in relationships. Relationships move at the speed of trust. Trust moves at the speed of vulnerability. Vulnerability moves at the speed of humility and honesty. The kingdom moves at the speed of relationships. By recognizing that everyone is made in the image of God and our own unique design and placement, we are able to recognize our need for one another as one interdependent body created by God and for God.

Deeply embedded in our God-given DNA is our need for family and connection. A famous Harvard Study on adult development revealed, "...the role of genetics and long-lived ancestors proved less important to longevity than the level of satisfaction with relationships in midlife, now recognized as a good predictor of healthy aging."[3] It is the quality, not the number of relationships, that matters. True connection not only makes us happier but also healthier.

Rooted and Empowered

Koinonia is a Greek word that means "fellowship, sharing in common, [and] communion."[4] The word describes an interactive relationship between God and the body of believers. Through koinonia, God offers us friendship and family rooted in Him.

Through our unity, which serves as visible proof of our invisible God, the world will know that the Father sent Jesus! Unity is an important key for the world to know Jesus.

Holy Spirit-powered unity is the key to manifesting the presence of Jesus as we gather in His name. As kingdom citizens, we get to live differently than the world, as salt and light, to love one another so the world will know we are true followers of Jesus. It is in unity that we honour others and God. In fact, as we live in unity, the Lord promises to bless us.[5] God loves unity enough that He attaches a powerful promise!

*　　*　　*

Father, we ask for the grace to live in unity and experience the life of the Trinity!

*　　*　　*

When we seek His righteousness, which is "right standing" and "right relationship" with God, we receive governmental authority through Jesus. Through a lifestyle of repentance and relationship, we experience the fruit of righteousness, peace, and joy. We honour God by honouring others and living in "right relationship" with God and man, and relationships are the foundation of unity.

In the words of Paul in his letter to the Romans:

> *So then, make it your top priority to live a life of peace with harmony in your relationships, eagerly seeking to strengthen and encourage one another.*
> *—Romans 14:19, TPT*

In the footnote to this scripture in *The Passion Translation*, it notes that righteousness, in both the modern and Hebraic context, is *kindness in our relationships*. In other words, Paul is speaking of putting others first and expressing the goodness of having right relationships with others, as well as right living.

Aligning With the Kingdom Way

We are all needed and unique by design, which removes competition. I often feel judgment come into my heart when I see believers, especially leaders, not representing Jesus well (to say it gently). When I feel condemnation coming into my heart towards another believer, the thoughts and words that follow are definitely not filled with life. My only response should be to repent and agree with God in prayer as we battle not against flesh and blood, but against powers and principalities. Yes, believers need accountability, but we must first break each other out of our spiritual prisons.

The kingdom of God is all about sound relationships! God designed us to live in community as the early church demonstrated, coming together in communion (common union in Jesus and, therefore, one another) as one body, one family of God, one church, one kingdom, in heaven and on earth—the kingdom way!

Jesus is the source of unity, and unity increases as we draw close to Him. Regularly taking communion together is an incredible way to honour and receive life from our common union with Christ. The footnote from John 6:54 in *The Passion Translation* beautifully summarizes communion:

> To eat His flesh is to take into our life by faith all that Jesus did for us by giving His body for us. To drink His blood is to take by faith all that the blood of Jesus has purchased for us. This "eating" and "drinking" is receiving the life, power and virtue of all that Jesus is to replace all that we were in Adam. Jesus' blood and body is the Tree of Life which is offered to everyone who follows Him.[6]

It is important to understand that we are the body, and Jesus is the head, and together, we make one person! As the body, we are equal in value but different in function and are in need of one another by design. We are the bride of Christ, coming together as one with the mind of Christ and known by our love. This is how His unstoppable kingdom comes and expands!

1. Ephesians 3:10.
2. "Motivation the power of unity, working together Belgian horse." YouTube.com. https://www.youtube.com/watch?v=knyXeSksH4Q. Accessed January 7, 2024.
3. Liz Mineo, "Good Genes are Nice, but Joy is Better," *The Harvard Gazette*, accessed October 14, 2023, https://tinyurl.com/3exnr3b7.
4. "What is Koinonia?," *Got Questions*, accessed October 14, 2023, https://www.gotquestions.org/koinonia.html.
5. Psalm 133.
6. "John 6:54, TPT Footnote V54," *LifeBible*, accessed October 14, 2023, https://lifebible.com/bible.

THE KINGDOM PRINCIPLE
OF UNITY

The kingdom of God is a harmonious realm where diverse individuals, bound by love and a shared purpose, reflect the image of God's triune, unified nature.

Father, we ask for the grace to unify as Your body for the sake of Your kingdom!

QUESTIONS FOR REFLECTION

What has the Holy Spirit revealed to you through *The Kingdom Principle of Unity*? How can you apply this to your life?

_____

_____

_____

_____

How does the truth of "Christian unity" impact how you see and speak about other believers and the church?

_____

_____

_____

_____

Have you agreed with the enemy when it comes to how you view or treat other believers? In what ways does agreeing with the enemy about the church hurt us and others?

_____

_____

_____

_____

QUESTIONS FOR REFLECTION *(continued)*

Can you recall a time when you witnessed the positive impact of Christian unity in operation? What was the result?

_____

_____

_____

_____

Notes

_____

_____

_____

_____

_____

_____

_____

_____

_____

_____

_____

_____

_____

_____

_____

_____

Chapter 19: The Kingdom Principles of Tithing, Generosity, and Faithfulness

"Bring the whole tithe into the storehouse, so that there may be food in My house, and put Me to the test now in this," says the Lord of armies, "if I do not open for you the windows of heaven and pour out for you a blessing [until] it overflows. Then I will rebuke the devourer for you, so that it will not destroy the fruit of your ground; nor will the vine in the field prove fruitless to you," says the Lord of armies. "All the nations will call you blessed, for you will be a delightful land," says the Lord of armies.
Malachi 3:10-12, NASB

Tithing: A Heart-check and Kingdom Investment

Firstfruits, the first and best, is a powerful principle of giving an offering at the beginning of the harvest, and the tithe is the firstfruits of our regular income. God established the tithe in Leviticus 27:30-33. In this verse, God commands the Israelites to give the first 10 percent of any income or increase back to Him.

We honour God by giving the tithe to Him first, before anything else. The tithe acknowledges that all we have belongs to the Lord. The tithe is our opportunity to give back to God in faith what is already His. As a tithe is sown in faith, God says in Malachi 3:10-12 to test Him to watch how He unfolds supernatural increase and rebukes the devourer! When we tithe, we can actively declare and call on God's promise to rebuke the devourer (or anything that would attack our God-given prosperity). I encourage you to take God up on His promise and test Him!

Abram (before his name was changed to Abraham) presented the first tithe to God in the Old Testament:

And He blessed him and said, "Blessed be Abram of God Most High, Possessor of heaven and earth; And blessed be God Most High, Who has handed over your enemies to you." And he gave him a tenth of everything.
Genesis 14:19-20, NASB

God does not *need* our tithe, but the kingdom on earth does need practical resources. Heaven contains infinite abundance. He does not need our money. Rather, the tithe is a tool to expose the condition of our hearts. Money reveals what we believe in and whom we trust. In giving, we acknowledge that all we have is from God. It demonstrates we believe He is our provider. The tithe is a principle in the kingdom. The tithe was made for us and our hearts today; it was not just an Old Covenant requirement. Many Christians say the tithe is an Old Covenant requirement of the law and we are currently under the New Covenant of grace, but the entire Bible is a treasure chest of ancient wisdom and goodness to be lived out.

"Woe to you, scribes and Pharisees, hypocrites! For you tithe mint and dill and cumin, and have neglected the weightier provisions of the Law: justice and mercy

and faithfulness; but these are the things you should have done without neglecting the others."
—*Matthew 23:23, NASB*

We know from the gospels that Jesus did not abolish the tithe. Jesus confirms in Matthew 23:23 that they should be tithing, along with following His other instructions. He also commanded us to be willing to give *everything* for the sake of the kingdom.[1] This is for our good! It trains us to be generous, and it is a privilege to give towards the promotion of the Gospel and the building up of the church. Generosity always yields abundant life.[2] Tithing is an act of faith and obedience that demonstrates our surrendered lives to God in a tangible way. It really is faith in action.

Tithing reminds us with every increase that all we have is from Him.

All we need, God will provide. He is the owner, and we are His stewards. Interestingly, as we are faithful with earthly riches, God will entrust us with true riches that can never be stolen. This includes the grace to walk out all He has planned for our lives. Many, like me, remember being a child in church. As the offering plate was passed around, our parents would put some money in our hands to put into the plate. The same is true today with our Heavenly Father. Ultimately, He provides our tithes, gifts, and offerings. Everything we have is from Him. The tithe is the Lord's.

Like any biblical principle, you are free not to follow them. However, it is wise to follow all of God's principles and the many dimensions of giving, including firstfruits, tithe, alms, legacy, and offerings. If you are not tithing or feel you don't have enough to start, consider building up to the tithe, starting with one percent the first month, two percent the second month, and so forth. This will create discipline and instill the habit of tithing.

Divine Stewards: Co-heirs and Servants in God's Economy

"How could you worship two gods at the same time? You will have to hate one and love the other, or be devoted to one and despise the other. You can't worship the true God while enslaved to the god of money!"
—*Matthew 6:24, TPT*

We demonstrate stewardship and servanthood as we mature. Then, we can fully understand co-ownership and the power and privilege of our identity as sons and daughters and co-heirs with Jesus.

Baal, an ancient idol worshipped for fertility, means "master" or "owner."[3] When we become the owner of money (i.e., put our faith in money over God), it owns us. When we own our possessions, they will ultimately own us. This is why we are to claim nothing as our own. Consider the power our money and belongings have over us when not stewarded well. If you purchase a large house beyond your means, you will be controlled by a big mortgage, expensive electric bills, and land and property that needs constant tending. As a result, your time will be consumed with thoughts of how you will manage the expenses looming over you, not to mention the hours of work to tend or pay for this massive responsibility.

On a more emotional level, money can often represent our value or worth in the world. We think the more we have to show for ourselves, the higher standing we have in the world. More money equals more power and influence, which is exactly what the kingdom of darkness (and the world) wants us to seek out first. In the kingdom, affluence is for godly influence and impact. We are blessed to be a blessing.

Rethinking Tithing for Kingdom Impact

Tithing also serves very practical purposes. On this side of the cross, tithing to the Lord go towards where you are fed and blessed spiritually and receive the Word of God. Typically, this is your local church. By giving our tithe to God through the church, we provide for the tangible needs of those in vocational ministry. This allows pastors, leaders, and other church workers to continue serving the church, acting as managers to bless the community's relational, spiritual, and emotional needs. As the church is a place of outreach, our giving to the church also supports those in need locally, sends missionaries abroad, feeds the poor, and enables other acts of kindness in our communities. I believe we are moving from the age of the traditional church to the age of the kingdom! I believe we are moving from passive to active engagement, from sitting within the four walls of a church and being fed to the ekklesia operating 24/7 across every sphere of society, tearing down the walls between the sacred and secular. Christ created everything, visible and invisible. All things were created by Him and for Him. Christ is supreme in everything! This means there is no such thing as a sacred/secular divide. All things belong to Christ! God is tearing down the religious walls so people can enjoy where He has planted them, as God is bringing His kingdom everywhere! This type of church, or a church moving in this direction, is where I choose to sow my tithe.

> Wealth is a gift from God, but it needs to be brought under the power and authority of our Lord, which is the purpose of the tithe. As stewards, if we can't be faithful with the 10 percent, which is the Lord's, why would we think we would be faithful with the remaining 90 percent? Redeemed wealth is key to God's plans to establish His kingdom on earth.
> — Ed Silvoso[1]

For the love of money is a root of all sorts of evil, and some by longing for it have wandered away from the faith and pierced themselves with many griefs.
— 1 Timothy 6:10, NASB

Giving is surrendering control of our finances and trusting God as our provider, guarding our hearts from the love of money (money as an idol). Money is not good or bad in and of itself. But it must be submitted to God on all levels. Money can be a great blessing to many! When we give control of our finances to the Lord, they can be used mightily! A big house (or a home of any size, for that matter) can be a place to host church gatherings, bless those who need a safe place to stay, and create opportunities for ministry of all kinds. Wealth can also be stewarded to provide for the needs of others, the church, or ministries (and ministers) needing funding. As we use our money to tithe, give generously, and care for the poor, widows, and orphans in advancing the kingdom, we are actually worshiping God with the money we are stewarding!

In the past, I debated how much I would give, where I would give, how much the tithe should be, etc. I was inconsistent in keeping the tithe and played mental games to justify my decisions. I got mixed up with firstfruits, tithes (the first 10 percent of income), and offerings (anything beyond the tithe). I now know how straightforward it is. Simply put, I give 10 percent to the church without argument. Anything I give to the church or those in need over and above that amount is a gift and an offering.

In fact, if we follow Jesus's model of giving in the New Testament, we would give away *everything*… not just 10 percent. Through giving, Jesus demonstrated the importance of our heart position and willingness to purchase the pearl of great price.

Jesus said to him, **"If you want to be complete, go and sell your possessions and give to the poor, and you will have treasure in heaven; and come, follow Me."**
—*Matthew 19:21, NASB*

He then turns to His disciples and says in verse 24 that it is difficult to enter the kingdom when you are rich.

We can pass through with heavenly riches but must shed earthly entanglements. We are required to go low and recognize our spiritual poverty to enter the kingdom. The more we realize our poverty and total need for God for everything, the more we realize the kingdom. Following God requires full submission of your life and everything in it, including money.

The position of stewardship promotes generosity as we become set free to obey more and more! The tithe is a statement of stewardship, sanctifies our money, and frees us from the influence of both. This is true financial freedom, as opposed to the world's system, which is characterized by, first, *mammon*, second, greed, and third, riches. Mammon is a term used in Scripture meaning "riches" or "wealth" and is considered unrighteous.[5] It refers to a demonic principality that deceives people into idolatry by encouraging us to believe that the source of power is money rather than God.

Each of the disciples was called to leave everything behind to follow Jesus. They left their jobs, families, time, control of their lives, and especially… their pride. As a reward, Jesus declared:

"And everyone who has left houses or brothers or sisters or father or mother or children or farms on account of My name, will receive many times as much, and will inherit eternal life. But many who are first will be last; and the last, first."
—*Matthew 19:29-30, NASB*

290

*   *   *

Father, we ask for the grace to honour the tithe and to live for You.

*   *   *

The Joy of Giving: Living Generously in God's Kingdom

Remind the wealthy to be rich in remarkable works of extravagant generosity, willing to share with others. These spiritual investments will provide a beautiful foundation for their lives and secure for them a great future, as they lay their hands upon the meaning of true life.
1 Timothy 6:18-19, TPT

Generosity has always been a core value of mine, which I attribute to the model set by my parents. Ever since I was little, I witnessed my parents caring for the poor, needy, broken, and struggling families. My father has since passed away, but my mother still loves to open her house to refugees, missionaries, and people from out of town needing a place to stay as she serves and exercises her gift of hospitality.

In everything I showed you that by working hard in this way you must help the weak and remember the words of the Lord Jesus, that He Himself said, **"It is more blessed to give than to receive."**
—Acts 20:35, NASB

We have all experienced the power and joy in the words of Jesus: *It is more blessed to give than receive.* As we give what He has blessed us with (time, words of life, encouragement, money, acts of kindness, prayer, etc.), the joy we experience is the kingdom of God in action! Generosity is not about money but a heart position to faithfully share our blessings and gifts with others, including intellectual, emotional, and spiritual gifts. Someone can give all the money in the world and be mean, rude, and unloving. God cares more about our hearts than about our bank accounts. He cares more about you being generous with love and kindness. There are times when a warm smile directed towards a stranger or taking the time to help someone talk through an issue can transform someone's day. I've witnessed great generosity in areas of extreme poverty. God has blessed me financially, so this has become an expression of generosity in my life, but it is not the only or most important expression. The point is that whatever God has blessed you with is meant to be used to bless others.

Sometimes, being generous means shifting my priorities when someone is in need and giving them the gift of listening and being truly present. This is boots-on-the-ground activation of the kingdom of God. The kingdom responds to a heart of generosity and giving without expecting a return. When we know we are to be faithful stewards and live according to the ways of the kingdom, we can freely give what we have freely received. We have wealth to be generous to others and advance the kingdom. Giving from a cheerful heart results in God pouring out more provision in and through you, whether that's money, time, love, support, friendship, serving, healing, etc. When we give in faith, we can expect to receive true riches and abundant life. When we understand that everything we have that is good is from God, we are only giving back from that which He has already blessed us with. Everything is by the grace of God. However, we must be discerning in our giving as to what is seed and what is fruit. We are to give away our fruit *and not our seed* which is meant to be multiplied. One apple seed can produce an apple tree from which there will be a great harvest for generosity with much new seed to sow for new trees to grow.

> *Those who live to bless others will have blessings heaped upon them, and the one who pours out his life to pour out blessings will be saturated with favor.*
> *—Proverbs 11:25, TPT*

From Barns to Blessing: The True Treasure

As we give, we transfer our earthly riches to a far superior account, an eternal treasury with rewards that remain! We are called to be distribution centers, not storage houses. Those who selfishly store up riches for themselves, trusting in their assets instead of God, are like the man Jesus describes in the parable of the wealthy fool in Luke 12:16-21:

> *And He told them a parable, saying,* **"The land of a rich man was very productive. And he began thinking to himself, saying, 'What shall I do, since I have no place to store my crops?' And he said, 'This is what I will do: I will tear down my barns and build larger ones, and I will store all my grain and my goods there. And I will say to myself, "You have many goods stored up for many years to come; relax, eat, drink, and enjoy yourself!"' But God said to him, 'You fool! This very night your soul is demanded of you; and as for all that you have prepared, who will own it now?' Such is the one who stores up treasure for himself, and is not rich in relation to God."**

The Cycle of Kingdom Abundance

Any form of blessing coming in and through us is one we can turn around and give to others. The love we have is from God. The life we have is from God. The family we have is from God. Our unique gifts and strengths are from God. The list is infinite. It is in giving that we receive. When we need a breakthrough, contend for the breakthrough of others. When we need strengthening, look to encourage and strengthen others. When we need healing, contend for the healing of others, and so on. Even our lifestyle of obedience profoundly impacts the lives of others, which in turn will yield powerful fruit in our own lives.

Consider the following scriptures:

- *Generosity brings prosperity, but withholding from charity brings poverty. Those who live to bless others will have blessings heaped upon them, and the one who pours out his life to pour out blessings will be saturated with favor. —Proverbs 11:24-5, TPT*

- *You will never go without if you give to the poor. But if you're heartless, stingy, and selfish, you invite curses upon yourself.* — *Proverbs 28:27, TPT*

- *Here's my point. A stingy sower will reap a meager harvest, but the one who sows from a generous spirit will reap an abundant harvest. Let giving flow from your heart, not from a sense of religious duty. Let it spring up freely from the joy of giving— all because God loves hilarious generosity! Yes, God is more than ready to overwhelm you with every form of grace, so that you will have more than enough of everything —every moment and in every way. He will make you overflow with abundance in every good thing you do.* — *2 Corinthians 9:6-8, TPT*

Giving is thanksgiving! We display God's generosity as we give. If the body of Christ were truly generous without holding anything back, there would be an incredible, unstoppable multiplication of blessings. The entire world would be overwhelmed by blessings in and through kingdom citizens, as the abundance of the kingdom of heaven would be on display for all the earth. No one would know what to do with so much blessing!

APPLIED WISDOM

We need wisdom to balance the multiplication of resources and financial generosity to continually increase our capacity for generosity. A great example of this sort of applied wisdom is found in the life of Arthur Guinness.

The Guinness Beer Story

In 18th century Ireland, Arthur Guinness of the famed Guinness Beer, still popular today, began brewing beer as an antidote to "The Gin Craze." Pure water was unsafe to drink at that time due to germs and contamination. Since liquor importation had been banned by Parliament in 1689, people began making their own liquor, which was much stronger and led to gross drunkenness. By producing a beverage lower in alcohol, the people were provided with a safer and healthier drinking option.

> Then, apparently, [Arthur Guinness] went to church on a Sunday [when] John Wesley was preaching. Wesley—who founded the Methodist Church—was known to commonly preach the same message: "Earn all you can. Save all you can. Give all you can. Your wealth is evidence of a calling from God, so use your abundance for the good of mankind."[1]

Guinness was so impacted by Wesley's sermon that he began giving away large sums of money to help the poor. His generosity went against the money-obsessed upper class and influenced his family to follow in his footsteps.

Please never forget that every act of kindness, every word of life, and every dollar is a seed sown. *Father, we ask for the grace to be free and wildly generous!*

[1] "Bristol Palin, "The Christian Origin of the Guinness Beer Company," Patheos, accessed October 14, 2023, https://tinyurl.com/2dy3y8te.

"And if you've not proven yourself faithful with what belongs to another, why should you be given wealth of your own?"
—Luke 16:12, TPT

The tithe is the Lord's and is a foundational qualification of our faithfulness. Two stories come to mind when I hear the word "tithe." The first is the story of the woman who gave the little she had described in Mark 12:41-44. This is what Jesus had to say about her: "Truly I tell you, this poor widow has put more into the treasury than all the others. They all gave out of their wealth; but she, out of her poverty, put in everything — all she had to live on." The second is the story of the Widow's Olive Oil in 2 Kings 4 (if you are unfamiliar with this story, now's your chance to read it for yourself). Both women demonstrate faithful stewardship.

The first step in establishing ourselves as faithful stewards is to give to the storehouse of God. If you are faithful with little, you will receive more. If you manage what you have been given well, God will increase your capacity. Alternately, what we mismanage, we lose. I have mismanaged my budget and investments and experienced loss and lack. In business, I have mismanaged people and have experienced relational loss and people leaving the company. I have mismanaged my family and have experienced many hardships as a result.

As you demonstrate good and faithful stewardship in relationships, family, finances, management, leadership, and business, you are given more responsibility. This is no different from a child growing up and maturing to take on increasing responsibility as they increase in ability and wisdom. Our faithfulness is an external demonstration of our internal character and growth. This is why we must first get our house in order before we can effectively go beyond. If our personal finances are not in order, how can we be entrusted with a great increase in our businesses?

More will be given to those who learn to multiply whatever God has given them (relationships, creativity, finances, etc.). God loves fruitfulness. Many of Jesus's parables deal with how servants steward what their master gives them. They demonstrate that God treats us equitably, not equally (although He loves us equally), as the faithful receive increase and those found unfaithful lose what little they have, as Jesus's parables on the talents attest. The poor become poorer, and the rich become richer. We are to take risks and build our skills and capabilities to create value and multiply wealth. We must first be found faithful in the natural realm to be trusted in the supernatural realm. It is often the poverty spirit that stops people from moving forward with whatever they have. As we lean into God and do the little things, we gain authority over the poverty spirit and begin to walk in our design. Ultimately, Jesus is our master and will return as the King to judge how we stewarded His resources entrusted to our care! This is our time to shine and be found faithful with little to increase in wealth, authority, and influence!

"The one who faithfully manages the little he has been given will be promoted and trusted with greater responsibilities. But those who cheat with the little they have been given will not be considered trustworthy to receive more."
—Luke 16:10, TPT

From Shepherd to King: The Faithful Journey of David

King David is a great example of a man after God's heart. He was a shepherd boy who was faithful with little, defeated the lion and the bear, then Goliath, and eventually rose to be king after many seasons of preparation and growth. "Faithful with little" starts with personal internal mastery. Personal mastery results in meekness, achieving internal order and self-control to live in submission to the will of God. Having internal order opens the doors to bringing external order into our lives. Internal transformation comes before external transformation. Jesus testifies that the meek will inherit the earth.[6] Faithfulness in every area of life is important in the formation of our character, which ultimately gives us the capacity to steward greater things.

The Courageous Path of Faithful Stewardship

Faithfulness and stewardship apply to everything, especially faith. How do we steward our current measure of faith to receive more? Are we exercising our faith regularly? Do we pray for healing or miracles when prompted by the Holy Spirit? Do we follow the promptings of the Holy Spirit, especially when it is uncomfortable, illogical, or risky? Are we allowing the fear of man to hinder our stewardship? Are we allowing ourselves to stretch and experience discomfort to receive the gift of faith to move into a greater realm of faith?

In the journey of wisely stewarding what we have been given so that God will entrust us with more, we must be careful not to chase glamour and riches. God's provision does not look like the world's. God looks at the heart, not external success, riches, or power. Hence, it is more important to remain faithful to our current assignment than to worry about what it looks like from the outside. As we prove ourselves faithful with little, God will bring the increase *at the right time* (i.e., not always in *our* timing). As we increase in our stewardship and mature as sons and daughters, God can release more of our inheritance as we become about our Father's business and represent our Father.

1. Matthew 19:21.
2. Luke 6:38.
3. The Editors of the Encyclopedia Britannica, "Baal: Ancient Deity," *Britannica*, accessed October 14, 2023, https://www.britannica.com/topic/Baal-ancient-deity.
4. Ed Silvoso.
5. See Matthew 6:24; Luke 16:9, 11, 13.
6. Matthew 5:5.

THE KINGDOM PRINCIPLES OF TITHING, GENEROSITY, AND FAITHFULNESS

In the kingdom of God, the principle of tithing is an act of worship and obedience, acknowledging God's ownership of all things and expressing gratitude for His provision.

Generosity in the kingdom is a heart posture, reflecting the goodness and grace of our heavenly Father. It involves sharing God's blessings, meeting the needs of others, and creating a culture of love, compassion, and interconnectedness in the community of believers.

Father, we ask for the grace to faithfully tithe and be generous as You are generous!

QUESTIONS FOR REFLECTION

What has the Holy Spirit revealed to you through *The Kingdom Principles of Tithing, Generosity, and Faithfulness*? How can you apply this to your life?

_____

_____

_____

Do you tithe regularly? Is tithing easy or difficult for you?

_____

_____

_____

Jesus sacrificed everything for us. What is God calling you to sacrifice for the sake of the kingdom?

_____

_____

_____

Notes

Chapter 20: The Kingdom Principle of Wealth

"So above all, constantly seek God's kingdom and his righteousness, then all these less important things will be given to you abundantly. Refuse to worry about tomorrow, but deal with each challenge that comes your way, one day at a time. Tomorrow will take care of itself."
Matthew 6:33-34, TPT

Even the strong and the wealthy grow weak and hungry, but those who passionately pursue the Lord will never lack any good thing.
Psalm 34:9-10, TPT

Eternal Abundance: The Kingdom Citizen's Wealth

For you have experienced the extravagant grace of our Lord Jesus Christ, that although he was infinitely rich, he impoverished himself for our sake, so that by his poverty, we become rich beyond measure.
—2 Corinthians 8:9, TPT

We are drenched with wealth! Jesus is the ultimate treasure of heaven! True prosperity is eternal life, spiritual well-being, exhibiting the fruit of the Spirit, relationships, wholeness, righteousness, contentment, peace, wisdom, revelation, knowledge, understanding, and reflecting the love of Jesus. Jesus did not become poor so that we could be rich and in need of nothing. The Beatitudes reflect the heart condition of those truly blessed in the kingdom: those who are poor in spirit, who mourn, who are meek and gentle, pure in heart, and love righteousness. In essence, they are those who are utterly dependent on God for EVERYTHING. This is sonship. Obviously, none of these things can be purchased for any amount of money. As kingdom citizens and ambassadors, we mature as sons and daughters to gain full access to the abundance of the kingdom. We also have the mind of Christ, which, by faith, opens us to the unlimited nature of the kingdom. The principles of tithing, generosity, and faithfulness prepare the heart, build up, and support the acceleration of kingdom wealth generation. Our role now is to first seek His kingdom and let the King provide all the lesser things for us as His ambassadors. As we mature into sons and daughters, we become heirs with full access to everything our Father has! I once heard someone say that when the presence of God is more important than entering the promised land, we are ready to enter the promised land.

This is very different from (the less helpful aspects of) the prosperity gospel, which (generally speaking) views material wealth as evidence of one's faith. I encourage you to read Revelation 3:13-22, the letter to the wealthy church of Laodicea who thought they needed nothing. The truth was, they were blind, poor, wretched, miserable, and naked! In contrast to the prosperity gospel, the goal of kingdom wealth is to apply biblical principles of wealth within the context of growing in spiritual maturity by seeking His kingdom first.

Kingdom Economics

Financial integrity is a moral principle of the kingdom of God, honouring God through our financial practices, intertwining the virtues of integrity, stewardship, and compassionate giving. Biblical principles laid the foundation for our societal norms, economic systems, and governance, which led to the incredible prosperity and social well-being enjoyed by the Western world. Regrettably, we are now reaping the consequences of veering away from these foundations. Now is the time for His kingdom to come *on earth as it is in heaven!*

Throughout our lives on earth, those in the kingdom are constantly learning His ways of wealth and stewardship. Money and wealth are different. Money is a medium of exchanging value and a store of value. Wealth refers to an abundance of resources and can be generated by creating different forms of value that range widely from assets to resources, intellectual property, quality of life, time, etc. Money is created by man, belongs to the world's systems, and in some cases has a limited supply, whereas wealth is unlimited as it is created. As you create wealth, money can be a byproduct and used to provide a quantitative value of wealth. To live out these fundamental truths, kingdom citizens must understand that money is simply a tool for trade, moving wealth, and creating wealth. For believers, the ultimate purpose of both money and wealth is for the kingdom's expansion on earth.

Financial Freedom: Serving God, Not Money

The Bible uses the term mammon to refer to a spirit that attempts to enslave by making the pursuit of riches, money, or material possessions a primary focus in life. Mammon wants us to believe that money, rather than God, is our source of power and security, making it our master. God is our source and our security. Jesus is the Lord of our lives, never money. Satan relentlessly seeks to ensnare us, whether through the shackles of poverty or the seduction of wealth. As stewards, we follow God's directives on the use of wealth and the tithe to honour God as our source, which guards our hearts from the spirit of mammon and leads to contentment.

"How could you worship two gods at the same time? You will have to hate one and love the other, or be devoted to one and despise the other. You can't worship the true God while enslaved to the god of money!"
—*Matthew 6:24, TPT*

Money, as our servant, is to serve God's kingdom. It is a form of power that enables us to exchange value for the benefit of the kingdom as we are obedient and let our light shine before men to glorify our Father. As the saying goes, money is a terrible master but a wonderful servant. Money frees us to be flexible, obey any call of God in our lives, and not be tethered to lack and limitations. We can use money to serve and love others well rather than become slaves to the love of money. When we exercise discipline over our money by budgeting, investing, or any financial planning, we are moving towards being a master of money rather than slaves to it. When we borrow for consumption and not for investment, we become slaves to the lender. The opposite of a meek (who inherits the earth) approach to finances (living below your means) is debt (which is living above our means). We are designed to be financially free! The poverty or scarcity mindset, often present within the church, fosters division and competition, as it views resources as limited and finite. However, the kingdom operates from a perspective of infinite abundance, transforming dynamics and promoting collaboration.

We can learn to love problems because understanding problems paves the way for solutions. Albert Einstein said it well, "If I had an hour to solve a problem, I'd spend 55 minutes thinking about the problem and five minutes thinking about solutions."[1] God has a solution for every problem and wants to partner with us to bring kingdom solutions.

Building Through Unity, Honour, and Partnerships

Wealth generation requires intentional communication, active cooperation, unity, honour, partnerships, and the creation of or participation in relational networks. Relationships are a form of wealth that increase in value over time. They also serve as a currency of the kingdom, uniting us in the shared pursuit of God's purposes.

The more we serve and meet the needs of others, the more we are rewarded. We are designed to serve well, take responsibility and risk, grow, adapt, and live interdependently as we learn to understand our need for one another and our unique design. As members of God's family, we get to live out God's principles and trust Him for the impossible as risk becomes an adventure of obedience, faith in action, and dependence.

"Use the wealth of this world to demonstrate your friendship with God by winning friends and blessing others. Then, when it runs out, your generosity will provide you with an eternal reward."
– Luke 16:9, TPT

Commonwealth of the Kingdom: Embracing Heaven's Abundance

Dr. Myles Munroe captures the infinite abundance of heaven in his book *Kingdom Principles*. Consider the following excerpt:

> Why is wealth so important in a kingdom? So the king can take care of his citizens. A righteous and benevolent king does not amass wealth for himself but for the welfare of his citizens. This is why it is only in a kingdom where we truly find commonwealth; that is, the wealth is common to all the people… No kingdom is greater or richer than the kingdom of heaven because it encompasses all that exists. And no king is wealthier than the King of heaven because He owns everything everywhere in both the natural and supernatural realms. Consequently, no citizens of any government are more prosperous or have greater

welfare than do citizens of the kingdom of heaven because all the infinite wealth of that kingdom is their common wealth.[2]

When we adopt the kingdom's culture of tithing, generosity, faithfulness, etc., while loving the King, we will experience life as heaven intended and release the power of God on earth. We will be truly wealthy. Wealthy people pursue purpose, not money. The scriptures support diligence, discipline, development, perseverance, service, excellence, integrity, and creativity in the generation of wealth.

The Blueprint of Wealth: Mindset, Strategy, and Kingdom Principles

Wealth is a mindset (beliefs, attitudes, and thinking patterns that shape our perspective and behaviour) filled with abundance, curiosity, creativity, and possibility. We must align our mindset with heaven as God's kingdom is one of unlimited abundance, and we have full access to His kingdom. Wealth is also practical and requires strategy, consistency, and vision. Without a plan, wealth is only an elusive wish. Strategy is more than a plan; it's an act of discernment, aligning our actions with heavenly wisdom—as in heaven.

From Toil to Dominion: Wealth Building With God

As we bring kingdom solutions to the world through starting businesses or investing wisely, our money will release us from toiling and *work for us* rather than us *working for it*. Wealth of all kinds empowers our purpose and accelerates transformation on earth. Wealthy people learn to multiply money. To multiply is to use leverage. We can leverage money, investments, knowledge, ideas, creativity, time, solutions, businesses, systems, and people to increase results exponentially. I once heard the definition of Christian charity as "productivity plus generosity." Financially speaking, we cannot be generous if we are not productive in generating wealth.

But you are to remember the Lord your God, for it is He who is giving you power to make wealth, in order to confirm His covenant which He swore to your fathers, as it is this day.
—Deuteronomy 8:18, NASB

We are designed to work with God on earth as our work is a form of worship. We worship as we obey God in our day-to-day lives. It is not perfection we should seek but excellence, growth, learning, and continuous improvement. God may shift our specific channel of provision in new seasons; we simply need to be attentive to His leading. His wealth strategies enable wealth generation, even while we sleep.[3]

Time, much like currency, is a form of wealth. Echoing Miles Monroe's wisdom, "Whatever you trade your time for, you become."[4] We are to assess how we allocate our time to enhance our quality of life. Just as we intentionally budget and prioritize our finances, so should we govern our time. We can learn to leverage time through people, structures, and systems. It's about mastering our moments, making each count towards our growth, fulfillment, and contribution to the world around us.

All true wealth and heavenly riches are the Lord's. All the gold, silver, and cattle on a thousand hills are His and must go into His kingdom treasury to expand His kingdom on earth. The earth is the Lord's, and all that is within.[5] The land is the Lord's and is part of our domain stewarding our dominion mandate. It is God who gives us the ability to create wealth and steward land or property. As we honour wisdom, we attract wisdom, and wisdom attracts wealth.

> *Wisdom extends to you long life in one hand and wealth and promotion in the other. Out of her mouth flows*
> *righteousness, and her words release both law and mercy.*
> *Proverbs 3:16, NASB*

15 KINGDOM STEPS TO WEALTH

by Bryan Elliott and Wesley Wright (CEO, Money Fitness Expert)

 Faithful Stewardship: Demonstrated through giving to the storehouse of God, managing resources well, and proving faithful in relationships, family, finances, management, leadership, and business.

- **Practical Application**: Regularly evaluate and manage your finances, ensuring that giving to God's purposes is a consistent priority. Caution, do not give out of and from a position of financial deficiency unless clearly called or invited to so, by a rhema word from God.

- **Action Steps**: Develop a budget, understand what your bottom line is, maintain and increase a positive cash flow, set financial goals, and commit to regular tithing. Seek financial advice for effective management from trusted experts.

 Increase through Faithfulness and Wisdom: Faithfulness in wise stewardship leads to increased responsibility and capacity, both in the natural and supernatural realms.

- **Practical Application**: Identify areas in your life where you can demonstrate faithfulness in wise stewardship and appropriate responsibility, both personally and professionally. Remember, everything, whether forming intention or the subsequent actions and resulting deeds, are all personal in the kingdom.

- **Action Steps**: Take on additional and appropriate responsibilities at work or in your community (n.b., is the responsibility just a good thing or is it a God thing?). Reflect on personal growth areas and commit to learning how to be reliable. Where there is room for improvement, take heed of wise counsel.

 Multiplication: God loves fruitfulness, and as faithful and wise stewards, we are called to multiply what we have been given, and more will be entrusted.

- **Practical Application**: Look for opportunities to multiply your character, skills, efforts, and resources.

- **Action Steps**: Explore ways to expand your impact in your workplace, community, or ministry. Mentor others to multiply your influence.

Risk-taking and Skill Development: Taking risks, developing skills, and creating value are essential to multiplying wealth. Faithfulness in the little things leads to authority over much and has the potential power to arrest the poverty spirit.

- **Practical Application**: Embrace calculated risks and invest in skill development. Seek advice from trusted experts and take heed to such advice.
- **Action Steps**: Identify areas where you can take strategic risks, such as starting a new project or business. Invest time and resources in improving skills relevant to your goals.

 Kingdom Wealth Definition: Kingdom wealth is redefined as eternal life, spiritual well-being, living in the fruit of the Spirit, loving and healthy relationships, righteousness, contentment, peace, wisdom, revelation, knowledge, and reflecting the love of Jesus.

- **Practical Application**: Prioritize spiritual well-being by spending quality time with God, creating, building, and sustaining godly relationships, and living righteously.
- **Action Steps**: Cultivate a daily spiritual practice, invest time in building meaningful relationships, and pursue righteousness in your decisions and actions.

 Tithing, Generosity, and Faithfulness: Kingdom citizens mature as sons and daughters and then as friends of God, to gain full access to the abundance of the kingdom through principles like wisdom, tithing, generosity, and faithfulness.

- **Practical Application**: Make wisdom, tithing, generosity, and faithfulness integral parts to your financial habits.
- **Action Steps**: Be guided by God, create a giving plan, allocate a portion of your income for charitable acts, and consistently demonstrate faithfulness in your financial stewardship.

 Financial Integrity: Financial principles are moral in the kingdom of God, and believers are called to learn and apply His ways of wealth and stewardship throughout their lives.

- **Practical Application**: Continuously educate yourself on financial principles aligned with biblical values.
- **Action Steps**: Attend financial literacy workshops, read books on biblical finance, and seek guidance from financial advisors who share your values.

Money vs. Wealth: Money is a tool for trade and wealth creation, with the ultimate purpose of expanding the kingdom on earth.

- **Practical Application**: View money as a (multi) tool for serving God and advancing His kingdom.
- **Action Steps**: Regularly evaluate your financial decisions to ensure they align with kingdom principles and values. Practice generosity as a way of using money for the benefit of others.

 God as the Source: God is the source of power, not money. (However, money on earth is a practical form of power in the world system; the more money you have, potentially the more power on earth you possess.) Believers are called to love and serve God first, and out of and from that loving relationship use money as an effective tool for the benefit of the kingdom.

- **Practical Application**: Cultivate a mindset that recognizes God as the ultimate provider.
- **Action Steps**: Spend time with God, experience Him, follow His leading and guiding hand, learn to trust Him by experiencing His goodness and love, and have faith in who He is and who He has made you to be. Develop a habit of prayerful decision-making regarding finances. Partner with God and trust His guidance when faced with financial challenges.

 Creating Wealth: God has given us unique gifts and abilities to create wealth by serving, solving problems, and adding value to others' lives.

- **Practical Application**: Identify and utilize your unique gifts and abilities to create value. Be alert and open to opportunities, and remember, opportunity is when preparation meets the occasion.
- **Action Steps**: Explore entrepreneurial ventures, invest in skills that align with your strengths, and seek opportunities to create value in your community. Look for and be aware of God's signposts.

 Leveraging Resources: Believers can leverage various resources, including money, knowledge, ideas, creativity, time, and relationships, to multiply results.

- **Practical Application**: Strategically use your resources to maximize impact, but remember, the end does not always justify the means.
- **Action Steps**: Identify areas where you can leverage your skills, time, and relationships to create more significant outcomes. Collaborate with others to achieve shared goals. In all situations, hold dear, implement, and never depart from God's fundamental principles or values (e.g., love, honesty, truthfulness, integrity, compassion, and humility, to name a few).

God's Partnership: Believers are designed to work with God on earth, and their financial plans and strategies should align with God's wealth-generation principles.

- **Practical Application**: Align your financial plans with biblical principles. Know where you are on your journey with God. Are you in a training season, or have you entered into manifesting the calling in your life? These two positions are very different; therefore, the focus and results are also different.

- **Action Steps**: Regularly assess your financial goals to ensure they align with God's purposes. Seek wisdom from mentors or financial advisors who share your faith.

 True Prosperity: True prosperity comes from seeking God's kingdom first, pursuing purpose over money, and applying biblical principles in wealth creation.

- **Practical Application**: Prioritize seeking God's kingdom first in your daily life.

- **Action Steps**: Establish a daily spiritual practice, consistently seek God's guidance in decision-making, and align your goals with His purposes.

 Character Development: Christlike character, including meekness, humility, and teachability, is crucial for inheriting the earth and leaving a lasting legacy.

- **Practical Application**: Actively cultivate Christlike character in all areas of life.

- **Action Steps**: Practice humility, meekness, and teachability in your interactions. Seek accountability from mentors or a supportive community.

 Mindset Shift: A shift in mindset, breaking old beliefs, and aligning thoughts with kingdom principles are essential steps in achieving internal and external prosperity.

- **Practical Application**: Actively work on changing old beliefs and aligning thoughts with kingdom principles.

- **Action Steps**: Engage in regular self-reflection, challenge limiting beliefs, and replace them with biblical truths. Enroll in courses or join groups that focus on mindset transformation.

Wesley Wright is the CEO of Money Fitness Expert, a company focused on empowering individuals to master money management.

To learn more, visit moneyfitnessexpert.com and @moneyfitnessexpert.

CREATING WEALTH

God has given us unique gifts and abilities that are to be cultivated for us to prosper by creating value. God also gives us the power to create wealth as we use our gifts to benefit others. We have an innate need to contribute, living with a focus beyond just ourselves, which is met as we love and serve. We serve one another directly or indirectly as we apply our gifts and abilities. Serving requires us to work together, which requires relationships. We are designed to serve and bless others. As we serve, it causes others to experience love. To know the need, we must connect and seek to understand others.

We create wealth as we create value. The better we serve and meet the felt needs of others (people, companies, communities, etc.), the more value we provide. As we create different forms of value (products, intellectual property, skills, relationships, services, etc.), we create different forms of wealth. As we specialize, our value creation becomes more specific and increasingly valuable, thereby increasing wealth. As wealth is created, there are no limitations, only possibilities and abundance. We can multiply those we serve by raising leaders to reproduce ourselves. As the ways of the kingdom progress, kingdom culture is formed, and new godly economic systems will emerge.

To all the rich of this world, I command you not to be wrapped in thoughts of pride over your prosperity, or rely on your wealth, for your riches are unreliable and nothing compared to the living God. Trust instead in the one who lavishes upon us all good things, fulfilling our every need.
— 1 Timothy 6:17, TPT

Money is important, so much so that the Bible mentions money, tithing, and possessions more than 2,000 times.[6] Contrary to historical or popular opinion, money (as with technology) is not good or evil, but it takes on good or evil depending on the person who has the money and what they choose to do with it. It is the love of (or rather, lust for) money that breeds issues and many different forms of evil, not the money itself.[7] The world bases "worth" on wealth, power, and reputation. While money allows us to feed the poor, print copies of the Bible for unreached people groups, sponsor missionary work, and care for our families (a biblical responsibility), it can also have another side. Money can easily become an idol, where we trust it to provide for our needs instead of God. Money can quickly become a distraction, obsession, and an open door to sin. Jesus makes this clear.

"The seeds that fall into the weeds represent the hearts of those who hear the word of God but their growth is quickly choked off by their own anxious cares, the riches of this world, and the fleeting pleasures of this life. This is why they never become mature and fruitful."
— Luke 8:14, TPT

I have enjoyed some of the best things the world offers, which enables me to share different perspectives. From NBA courtside season tickets, luxurious vacations, expensive nights out to getting engaged in the foothills of the Andes in a vineyard in Argentina, and married on a 900-acre estate in Tuscany, I had it all (according to the world). Before 2019, I even lived in a house valued at six million dollars. If I wanted something, within reason, I could buy it. I was under the deception of self-sufficiency, not understanding that everything is by grace.[8] I was generous with my giving, but I still had more security in money than I knew, making money a master more than a servant. I am not saying anything is wrong with any of these things in and of themselves. Rather, I'm saying that these experiences have given me perspective on what truly matters and the potential emptiness and traps of wealth, the illusion of self-sufficiency, and the dangers of self-focus and self-indulgence.

God made beautiful things for us to enjoy in moderation. They must not be our highest focus or distract us from our call to serve others, our pathway to joy and fulfillment. I can say from experience that, after a period, we become accustomed to things, even when they are luxurious. Any luxury can become a new normal, which requires another upgrade and then another to keep feeling the "wow factor," no different from drugs. Chasing fulfillment through items and experiences is chasing after the wind. The solution is gratitude (which leads to contentment and moderation), generosity (the antidote to greed), and humility (the antidote to pride). Proverbs 10:22

says, "True enrichment comes from the blessing of the Lord, with rest and contentment in knowing that it all comes from him," (TPT). This proverb emphasizes that true rest and contentment stem from recognizing that all blessings originate from God and highlights the importance of divine providence in our lives.

Aligning With Kingdom Wealth

Putting His kingdom first ensures God is our (loving) master. When God is our master, money is our servant. As we shift our hearts by the power of the Holy Spirit, our lives will gradually come into proper alignment as the things of this world fade away. As our faith deepens, the natural realm loses its impact. When the world no longer has a hold on us, then we are prepared to steward kingdom wealth. In the words of Paul, "May my only boast be found in the cross of our Lord Jesus Christ. In him I have been crucified to this natural realm; and the natural realm is dead to me and no longer dominates my life."[9] This is spiritual maturity, that is, sonship.

One who is an heir can be entrusted with material and spiritual wealth. *Things* cannot define sons and daughters of God. Like the rich young ruler whom Jesus asked to give up the "things" that defined him and the ways of the world to join the countercultural kingdom, He asks us to do the same. Your identity is the key to not allowing wealth to keep you tethered to the world. If you see yourself as a steward of what God's given you rather than as an owner, staying free from the trappings of wealth is much easier.

To become a citizen of the kingdom, the young ruler needed to understand that he was a steward of the King's wealth. He was to be a steward of resources. He had to demonstrate a heart that was willing to place God above his money. He thought he was rich, but he was poor.

> **"For where your treasure is, there your heart will be also."**
> —*Luke 12:34, NIV*

This idea is no different from the letter to the church of Laodicea in the Book of Revelation. I resonate much with this letter's recipients, who were living a compromised and prideful life.

> *Because you say, 'I am rich, and have become wealthy, and have need of nothing,' and you do not know that you are wretched and miserable and poor and blind and naked.*
> —*Revelation 3:17, NASB*

Revelation 3:17 describes my blindness prior to making Jesus Lord in 2016. Jesus advises the church in this passage and us today in verse 18 to buy gold as refined in the fire so that we can be truly rich. I have experienced the false and fleeting safety and security of money. I have lived apart from God and partially with God and have discovered the immense blessing of living my life *all in* for God. When our finances are surrendered to God, the pressure and burden of self-reliance shift to an appropriate reliance on God as our provider. The amount of anxiety and fear around finances or, conversely, the amount of peace we experience from above is a good indicator of our mindsets, especially in trying circumstances. Shalom is priceless!

I am convinced that my God will fully satisfy every need you have, for I have seen the abundant riches of glory revealed to me through Jesus Christ!
Philippians 4:19, TPT

The Narrow Path: Finding True Security in God's Kingdom

When Jesus tells the disciples it's easier for a camel to go through the eye of a needle than for a rich man to enter the kingdom of heaven, He didn't say this because He has something against wealth.[10] Rather, He said it to make us question who rules our hearts. God or money? It is harder for a rich man to see his need for God because his faith and security can easily be placed in the wrong areas. While wealth may provide temporary insulation from repercussions of actions and circumstances, true security only comes from God. Any security outside of security in God is aligned with the kingdom of darkness. It's not impossible for those with financial wealth to maintain dependence on God, but it is difficult as our perceived need for God can easily be diminished. Giving Jesus absolute lordship is a costly and narrow path few are willing to take. It takes moving from operating as an orphan in our finances to operating as a son of God! After experiencing everything the world could offer, Solomon said it was all "meaningless, meaningless, utterly meaningless."[11]

Jesus alone shows us the way to true wealth.

At the end of the day, money will magnify what is in our hearts, either good or evil. It is an expression of these two things on earth. Suppose you have any serious issues around health, marriage, or family. Will your trust be in money or a loving Heavenly Father of an unshakable, eternal kingdom of light, abundant life, perfect peace, and joy?

I advise you to buy from Me gold refined by fire so that you may become rich, and white garments so that you may clothe yourself and the shame of your nakedness will not be revealed; and eye salve to apply to your eyes so that you may see.
--Revelation 3:18, AMP

Kingdom Impact in the Marketplace: Grow Where You're Planted

There is no separation between the sacred and secular for the believer; everything is consecrated or holy to the Lord. We are to see every task as sacred. Recognizing work as a form of worship allows us to see how using our God-given gifts and talents to pursue our divine calling can transform our perspective on where He has placed us, creating and stewarding wealth. Our work reveals God and His kingdom as it reflects our beliefs and whom we serve to the world. The crucial factor is maintaining God's supremacy in our lives by seeking first His kingdom. Whether you're a minister in the church in the marketplace, it is all the same to God. Your ministry happens wherever He plants you.

I believe there is much more prophetic gifting (envisioning new ideas, innovations, etc.) at work in the marketplace than we realize. Our infinitely creative God created us in His image. We can glorify God with our work and the application of wealth as salt and light in a dark world. As we grow in affluence, we grow in influence and can provide a platform to disciple the marketplace and impact culture. The key to accomplishing all these things is having a Christlike character. A Christlike character includes meekness (power under control, humility, gentleness, and discipline).

> ***"Blessed are the gentle, for they will inherit the earth."***
> —*Matthew 5:5, NASB*

> *A good person leaves an inheritance to his grandchildren, And the wealth of a sinner is stored up for the righteous.*
> —*Proverbs 13:22, NASB*

> *Who is the person who fears the Lord? He will instruct him in the way he should choose. His soul will dwell in prosperity, And his descendants will inherit the land.*
> —*Psalm 25:12-13, NASB*

A Divine Exchange: Kingdom Priorities

The Bible teaches that the meek, those who are submitted, teachable, and humble of heart, shall inherit the earth. This refers to God's blessings that include land, as does our covenant of Abraham restored through Jesus. Leaving a secure inheritance to our children's children is the continuation of this generational blessing.

When we are truly humble and meek, *we claim nothing as our own and live in total dependence on God.*

However, the Proverbs 13:22 wealth transfer from the unrighteous to the righteous isn't merely about acquiring tangible riches; it embodies a divine exchange aligned with God's kingdom priorities. This includes seeking His kingdom first, embracing heavenly wisdom to generate wealth through systems such as businesses and work, and understanding that the true purpose of wealth is not only for personal enrichment but also for the advancement of His kingdom. It calls for spiritual maturity and stewardship aligned with kingdom values and principles. Chantal Fowler, our prayer team leader at Flō, shared her revelation on this topic:

> This wealth transfer goes beyond material assets to encompass the riches of heaven, the principles of God's economy, the empowering presence of heaven, and the government of the kingdom of God to rule and reign in righteousness. It is a system that works and fosters prosperity for all, advancing His kingdom on earth as it is in heaven.

Everything is a gift. Character results in consistent stewardship, leaving margin in our lives for what God wants us to do. This means having clear priorities (focused on God), actively avoiding distraction, living simply, and being wise stewards of our finances. Practically, this looks like not being over-extended, having savings, being ready to capitalize on opportunities, making your money work for you, etc. Character also means being patient, faithful, having self-control, and sacrificing in the short-term for long-term gain. As we remain steadfast in prayer and the ways of God, we will rule and reign on earth. We are designed for victory, and living victoriously brings joy and peace as the kingdom advances, living above our circumstances.

> *The lovers of God will have more than enough, but the wicked will always lack what they crave.*
> *— Proverbs 13:25, TPT*

> *Worship in awe and wonder, all you who've been made holy! For all who fear him will feast with plenty. Even the strong and the wealthy grow weak and hungry, but those who passionately pursue the Lord will never lack any good thing.*
> *Psalm 34:9-10, TPT*

Christlike character emerges when we actively change our mindsets to look like Jesus. There are kingdom wealth courses that begin by addressing the lies and issues of the heart around identity and mindsets and then continue to build towards creating a vision and a wealth plan.[12] It is an inside-out process, helping us develop internal prosperity before realising external prosperity.

Embracing Kingdom Wealth Principles

Breaking agreement with old, ungodly beliefs and stepping into agreement with kingdom principles of wealth is necessary for every believer. When we come into agreement with an ungodly belief, we come under its influence. It is important that this is not done simply at face value (e.g., simple affirmations). We all need a complete perspective shift. It's vital to look at what created those old beliefs, then see what the Word of God says about wealth and align our thoughts with His. When we put these new beliefs into action, it breaks the spirit of poverty. When a solid biblical foundation has been laid, it is time to gather practical tools and strategies for wealth creation and multiplication unto freedom and kingdom expansion. This is to ensure that wealth is attainable, a cycle of gain and loss does not occur, and that money does not have a hold on your heart.

Ultimately, the best way to steward God's resources well is to learn to listen to and obey His voice.

As Christians, we must take wealth creation seriously and understand the strategies of finance. The church has taught on the power of tithing and generosity but not on how to generate wealth.[13] Today's problems and frustrations are the fuel to create new solutions and wealth. We spoke previously about strongholds in the mind, which can also foster non-biblical views or ungodly beliefs about money and wealth. The kingdom works through faithfulness or management. If you want to grow financially, first look at how you manage what you have. True financial freedom begins with surrendering our finances to God, believing He is our provider, honouring His ways, and obeying His commands. Wealth in the form of financial freedom gives us the freedom to obey God and use our gifts and resources to serve and bless others, planting more and more good seeds!

Wealth is a powerful weapon in the hands of a son or daughter of God that can be used to bring a massive expansion of His kingdom.

And don't allow yourselves to be weary in planting good seeds, for the season of reaping the wonderful harvest you've planted is coming!
—Galatians 6:9, TPT

Wealth Transfer: Manifesting Kingdom Prosperity on the Earth

As we multiply what we sow, let's initiate a wealth transfer from heaven to earth as we sow good seeds according to the Spirit and reap a kingdom harvest! To deepen your journey in accumulating kingdom wealth, consider these expanded steps:

1. Generously share not just money but also your time, knowledge, and connections, reflecting God's endless generosity. (Luke 6:38)
2. Use your skills and talents to serve God's purpose, transforming every act into an offering to Him. (Matthew 25:14-30)
3. Acts of service carry eternal significance; by helping others, you mirror Jesus's compassionate ministry. (Matthew 20:26-28)
4. Spread the gospel of the kingdom and guide others in their spiritual growth, multiplying the kingdom's reach. (Matthew 28:19-20)
5. Faithfully manage all God has entrusted you with intention and wisdom, ensuring they're used in ways that honour Him. (1 Peter 4:10)
6. Apply God's wisdom in solving the world's problems, showcasing the kingdom and its principles in practical actions and inspired solutions. (James 3:17)

By living out these principles, along with others like unity, honour, prayer, faith, and forgiveness, you're not merely accumulating eternal wealth that can never be lost or stolen; you're also creating significant value, impacting the present for the kingdom of God. As we seek first His kingdom in faith and action, living by His principles, it is God alone who will provide for all our needs.

As an aside, the Bible does not talk about retirement for good reason. By God's design, our lives are meant to be continuously productive until the end. We are to continue to steward whatever resources and abilities God has given us and not to grow weary in doing good. The later years of life may look different but there is an incredible opportunity for ongoing generosity and legacy, transferring the wisdom and practical understanding gained over the course of a life well lived. Every believer is meant to live a life of service as a blessing to others. These are biblical keys to a wonderfully fulfilling life filled with purpose.

By seeing our lives and resources as channels or instruments of God's grace entrusted to us for the purpose of advancing His kingdom, we align with the biblical principle of stewardship, reflecting the economy of God's kingdom. We get to be conduits of God's kingdom, participating in God's divine plan, reflecting His nature, and bringing His provision, manifesting His kingdom from heaven to earth! We are blessed with the opportunity to honour God in our financial actions, living out the principles of integrity, stewardship, and compassionate generosity. Doing wealth God's way and with His wisdom results in both eternal wealth and temporal wealth generation, pressed down, shaken together, and running over!

Honor the LORD with your wealth And with the first fruits of all your crops (income); Then your barns will be abundantly filled And your vats will overflow with new wine.
Proverbs 3:9-10, TPT

1. Laura Haarakalju, "How Can Conversational Analytics Assist You in Solving Business Problems?," *Feelingstream*, accessed October 14, 2023, https://tinyurl.com/4kyhhhzu.
2. Myles Munrow, *Kingdom Principles: Preparing for Kingdom Experience and Expansion* (ReadHowYouWant, 2010), 93.
3. Psalm 127:2.
4. Dr. Myles Munroe, "You are a product of how you manage time and change," *TikTok*, 2024, https://www.tiktok.com/@jacquesjudejohnsonsr/video/7341229821931267370.
5. Psalm 24:1.
6. Jesse Wisenski, "Bible Verses About Money," *Tithely.com*, Accessed October 16, 2023, https://tinyurl.com/rcjv5mmz.
7. 1 Timothy 6:10.
8. 1 Corinthians 4:7.
9. Galatians 6:14, TPT
10. Matthew 19:23-24.
11. Ecclesiastes 1:1-11.
12. I recommend Jim Baker's online workshop, "Wealth with God" available at www.wealthwithgod.com.
13. I also recommend Dave Ramsey's "How to Win with Money in 7 Easy Baby Steps," at www.ramseysolutions.com.

THE KINGDOM PRINCIPLE OF WEALTH

In the kingdom, wealth is redefined as stewardship, where abundance is a means to bless others, advance justice, and participate in God's redemptive purposes on earth. Kingdom wealth emphasizes spiritual abundance over material riches, focusing on eternal life, righteousness, and serving others. Believers steward wealth as a tool for kingdom expansion. By prioritizing spiritual maturity and aligning with God's values, wealth is used to glorify God and to bless others, fulfilling the role of kingdom ambassadors.

Father, we ask for the grace to be humble, to seek first Your kingdom, to serve well, to create wealth, and to expand Your kingdom.

QUESTIONS FOR REFLECTION

What has the Holy Spirit revealed to you through *The Kingdom Principle of Wealth*? How can you apply this to your life?

_____

_____

_____

What types of wealth has the Lord given you?

_____

_____

_____

_____

Has the Holy Spirit revealed any ungodly beliefs you have about money and wealth? Explain.

_____

_____

_____

QUESTIONS FOR REFLECTION *(continued)*

I challenge you to dream with God! What gifts and abilities has God given you? How can you expand the kingdom with wealth in service to others?

_____

_____

_____

_____

Notes

_____

_____

_____

_____

_____

_____

_____

_____

_____

_____

_____

_____

_____

_____

_____

_____

Chapter 21: The Kingdom Principle of Business

Living for eternity NOW is the best life on earth!

"And he called ten of his own slaves and gave them ten minas, and said to them, 'Do <u>business</u> with this <u>money</u> until I come back.'"
—Luke 19:13, NASB

From Pioneering to Prosperity: A CEO's Journey in Kingdom Business

God loves people, and He loves partnering with us in all aspects of life, including business. The purpose of business is to be a redemptive blessing to the world, not exploitative. Business is an operational expression of love.

As the CEO of Flō Energy Solutions Inc., I am first and foremost the CSO (Chief Spiritual Officer, a key element of my CEO role), a custodian of kingdom DNA as positioned by God. As the CSO, it's my job to put and keep things in God's order as I serve those who serve the company. This book highlights God's kingdom principles, which serve as a kingdom plumbline for Flō, and this section was a collaborative effort with many of our leaders. By following God's design and applying God's truth, kingdom culture is formed within our company, which leads to human flourishing for all involved, believers and non-believers alike.

As a father figure to those in my company, I have the privilege of teaching others how to live blessed lives, care for the souls of our people, and model healthy sonship by pointing people to their Heavenly Father. You know my story by now; it certainly hasn't been easy on the personal side or the business front. My heart is to freely share what I have freely received. I want my experience of pioneering, persevering, and breaking through to prepare a way for others to accelerate and prosper in the kingdom in whatever sphere of society they operate in.

For this section, I will use the example of the business the Lord has entrusted to our team and me. However, please keep in mind that we are always learning, and I am simply sharing our process and where we are today. I suspect that in the coming years, it will look very different as the process of transformation continues incrementally, day by day. As a company, we are in the process of bringing business back to its original intent, first receiving and then releasing the kingdom through everything we do. This is according to the biblical principle that we cannot give what we have not received or experienced, described in Luke 6:38. At Flō, I can confidently say that our people are transforming, and faith is rising!

The Kingdom Company Model: A New Era for Business

Aside from our primary mission to serve and bless the food retail sector, Flō's function is to model and share what we are learning as a kingdom company. Our core belief is "A Better Way," which fuels our innovative engineering solutions and business in general. We strongly believe in having a win-win attitude rooted in an "abundance mindset." Knowing that we have access to everything in the kingdom allows us to seek mutually beneficial deals for everyone involved.

Please keep in mind that we have believers *and* non-believers at Flō who all engage in creating our value system and are proud to support the ethos of Flō. However, we hire based on a person's alignment with the needed role and according to our values, not their faith. God loves believers and non-believers equally, and so do we. Here is a small example. As a company, we sponsored a Syrian family eight years ago. They are not believers but needed a fresh opportunity to start over. We hired the father, who could barely speak English. We gave him simple tasks as he began to learn the language and culture. Today, he is flourishing at Flō and is a great contributor to our accounting team and our business. He has become a dear friend, and although he doesn't yet know Jesus, we pray together and have walked through some very difficult life challenges together. Often, when he comes into the office, he gives me a big hug and tells me how much he loves me and this company. (His wife also makes dinner for us from time to time, which is absolutely incredible!)

What's taking place at Flō is called "ekklesia." An ekklesia is the assembly of two or more people gathering as God's legislative assembly in Jesus's name to make decisions and declarations based on the Word and will of God, for it to be *on earth as it is in heaven*. Ed Silvoso's ministry, *Transform Our World*, explains ekklesia well:

> An Ekklesia, as the most embryonic expression of The Church, is the gathering of at least two believers in the midst of the manifest presence of God, functioning with His authority to bind and release His will, beginning in their sphere of influence and spreading outward until The Great Commission is fulfilled... Ekklesia [is] a building-less mobile people movement designed to operate 24/7 in the marketplace for the purpose of having an impact on everybody and everything.[1]

These principles and practices apply to kingdom leaders running organizations or teams. If you don't run a business or are not in a position of leadership at your place of work, keep in mind that it only takes two people to form an ekklesia. Not only can you apply some of these practices to your role, but you can find one or two other believers to form an ekklesia and begin to pray for your leaders and the company. The kingdom is often packaged in small things, so do not despise small beginnings. As you model the kingdom, bringing heaven to earth through a process of going deep and building solid foundations, growth will occur.

And by the blood of His cross, everything in heaven and earth is brought back to Himself— back to its original intent, restored to innocence again!
Colossians 1:20, TPT

Living Stones: Building Kingdom Businesses with God's Presence

God's kingdom resides in the hearts of people. We are living stones with Jesus as the chief cornerstone and capstone. With this in mind, a kingdom business is simply a business of people who love God and seek first His kingdom and His righteousness. The believers at Flō value His presence and act as living gates for Jesus. Our businesses are gateways for the kingdom to come into the marketplace. The expression of every kingdom business on earth will be unique, as it is God's designed expression. Each organization, whether a business, government, parachurch organization or otherwise, has a specific redemptive purpose and plays a role in discipling the nations. This means that each believer is called to play a role in advancing the kingdom wherever he or she is positioned.

What expression of love does God want to express to the world through your life and business?

Building His Kingdom: The Transformation of Business in Sonship

As we grow in sonship, the areas of Flō that are aligned with the orphan systems of the world continue to get exposed and replaced. Orphans think like slaves. They are self-focused, self-reliant, and motivated by self-promotion, fear, control, etc. These are the result of the Fall and are the fruit of the Tree of Knowledge of Good and Evil, and they are a fallen mindset.

An orphan-minded business looks like "my business," building "my kingdom," and is susceptible to fear, control, and greed, whereas a son builds "His business" and "His kingdom." Kingdom business is about partnering with God to birth the desires He has put in our hearts to fulfill our destinies. The orphan is self-led, and the son is Spirit-led. An orphan builds a company, and a son builds a family, a safe place of honour and belonging for all to grow and flourish. Orphans tend to surround themselves with people like them, whereas leaders who are sons build diversified teams.

God uses sons and daughters as heirs to build His kingdom. Just like Jesus, a son is about His Father's business. When we mature from an orphan mindset to sonship, we move from independence to dependence on God and then to interdependence with others in the family of God. Orphans' relationships are transactional and prone to focus on win-lose outcomes. On the other hand, a son or daughter is others-focused, values relationships, and looks for a win-win that blesses everyone who participates.

Kingdom Companies: Stewarding God's Business for Eternal Impact

Flō is an ekklesia, a church, a kingdom business, an embassy of heaven, a marketplace ministry, a light set on a hill, and an apostolic outpost (a place that equips and sends out people to expand the kingdom). There is no divide between the sacred and secular, as we are meant to live a unified life. This shatters the religious paradigm. As believers in His kingdom, all things are sacred. His kingdom encompasses all of creation. Your workplace and home are as important and holy to God as the church. The church is made up of people, not buildings, which makes Flō a church where

320

we minister to the needs of our people and industry. As sons and daughters, we are called to be ambassadors of the King in the marketplace.

A kingdom company is a company that values what God values—fruit, much fruit, and fruit that remains.[2] This fruit comes not through religious activities or human striving but by His Spirit. As Ed Silvoso teaches, the marketplace, as modelled by the first-century Christians, is the heart of cities and nations, has been redeemed by Jesus, and must now be reclaimed. We can work passionately, regardless of our position or calling, knowing that what we do will make an eternal difference.

We are designed to faithfully steward what the Lord entrusts to us. Because the company is the Lord's, He carries the weight, burden, and responsibility of the business. The outcomes are His, and the glory is His. We know that all success is from God, and all that we are is a gift from God. Flō and the impact we have on people is God's legacy on earth.

In 2017, I tried to "make" a Christian company by following a religious recipe to create what I thought a Christian company should look like. I gave Jesus 51 percent "ownership" to honour His lordship over my life. However, this just revealed the level of orphan thinking still present in my life at the time. And because it was a religious decision and model, even the Christians within the business didn't like it! I was working for God to earn His approval out of an orphan identity. My intentions were noble, but they lacked genuine surrender and divine revelation.

It wasn't until 2020, as I grew in my identity of sonship, that I truly caught on to the principle of stewardship. That was when I began to understand that *nothing* in this life is mine alone. As we mature, we come into our inheritance as heirs of God, making us co-owners and partakers in ALL of God's promises. To steward well, I have to know the owner! I can't steward successfully what I've been given unless I intimately know what the owner wants! This allows me to work with God from a place of pre-approval and full acceptance in relationship and submission.

Recently, I had a discussion on the kingdom with an Uber driver who was a former pastor. He said, "We can do church without God, but we can't do the kingdom without God." Of course, he was speaking of religion. So true! We are a people of God carrying God's presence for His kingdom to expand in and through us. The kingdom is the church (His body), which is the church as God intended, operating everywhere, all the time.

Embracing Vulnerability: The Power of 360 Discovery

In 2019, I had 18 people on my team rate me on a 360 evaluation. My results were intriguing, revealing many positive areas of my life alongside many weak areas needing attention as they negatively impacted the company. As the CEO and owner (steward/servant), I decided to openly share my results and comments with everyone at a town hall meeting, making myself accountable to everyone at Flō. I then looked at my greatest weaknesses and created a development plan to address the top weaknesses impacting the company, which, to name a few, included me being inconsistent, impulsive, reactive, distracted, and lacking clear strategic direction.

Impulsivity, the bias for action with a high sense of urgency, is a good trait for an entrepreneur, but this can also lead to problems if the actions are not strategic and intentional. I've read many books with lots of good ideas, but trying to implement them without a system led to inconsistency within Flō. It gave others the feeling that we were only and always pursuing the "flavour of the month." Without a clear strategy for our company and its goals, I tended to be reactive and distracted rather than responsive to the challenges and opportunities available. Shining a light into these areas created awareness; once acknowledged, half the battle was already over.

Empowering Leadership: Building Capacity Through Feedback and Development

The following year, I engaged in another 360 evaluation and shared my results. I put the 2019 and 2020 results side-by-side with the same audience to show my growth and improvement. There were marked improvements, but there was still room for growth. Once again, I made the focus of my development plan to continue growing in these key areas known to my team. By doing this, I measured myself against myself (and continue to do so), from where I was before to where I am now. By opening up and sharing my weaknesses, I removed any mask I could hide behind. Understanding my weaknesses was a gift as it helped me recognize and hone in on my strengths. People could really see who I was, for better or for worse. I experienced great freedom in not needing to be perfect or pretend I had it all together when I didn't. This opened the door for others to follow suit, as many began requesting 360 evaluations as openness begets openness.

From Weakness to Strength: Harnessing Growth Opportunities

When I started this process, I was involved "hands-on" in almost every aspect of the business. This limited the growth of the company and our team. My strengths were overplayed, which became a weakness. This was resolved by empowering leadership across the company. We hired a new president who has a much stronger skill-set in strategic execution, allowing me to leverage my strengths more fully. I went from spending over 80 percent of my time "in" the business to less than 10 percent. I let go of many daily activities to make room for more high-level strategic endeavours. Through this process, I removed myself as the bottleneck for others dependent on me and instead built and empowered the team to lead and grow in new ways. As a leader, I discovered I didn't need to have all the skills. Instead, I surrounded myself with others who had the specific skills and gifts required.

Many executives and people in general suffer from imposter syndrome, including myself for many years. When I became transparent about my strengths and weaknesses, light rushed into the darkness, bringing a new level of freedom. I no longer needed to pretend to be something I'm not. Knowing our weaknesses also makes our need for others obvious, leading to valuing others and strengthening unity.

Not long ago, our president at the time took a one-month sabbatical, and everything ran well while he was gone. His teams are now empowered to lead themselves. He created greater freedom by removing himself from the day-to-day to operate in his unique sweet spot to grow, innovate, strategize, and build greater leadership capacity at Flō. This is our goal for everyone. Although this is a piece of the puzzle, ultimately, sonship is the answer to identity, value, and purpose. He has since transitioned to a new company with which we've partnered to infuse the DNA and systems of excellence of the kingdom. We've dubbed this initiative a "kingdom incubator" and are excited to see what God will do through the process.

This process of being stretched continues within the organization, empowering people in the areas of their giftings, narrowing in specialization as they develop mastery, increase in ability, grow in self-accountability, and, as a result, are accountable to others.

> A leader is one who leads as he follows and follows as he leads and no one will know which one he is doing.
> — Oswald J. Saunders[3]

Self-Government in Leadership: Fostering Accountability and Growth

Another way to describe the process is for us to use authority to lead those under us to mature in responsibility. Delegation is about management, while leadership focuses on empowerment. This enables us to give authority by creating accountability. This is how we multiply authority so that others can do the same in building other responsible leaders. The kingdom is all about self-government, as described in Genesis 1:28. We are building leaders who can govern themselves. This process increases capacity, effectiveness, and freedom with discipline. We support growth by holding one another accountable, which accelerates the process.

"The greatest among you will be the one who always serves others."
–Matthew 23:11, TPT

Be free from pride-filled opinions, for they will only harm your cherished unity. Don't allow self-promotion to hide in your hearts, but in authentic humility put others first and view others as more important than yourselves. Abandon every display of selfishness. Possess a greater concern for what matters to others instead of your own interests.
–Philippians 2:3-4, TPT

The greatest in the kingdom shall be the servant, and as we grow in humility, we will put others first. The lines of leadership and followership beautifully blur as we honour and submit to one another, which is practically demonstrated by Jesus who served His disciples by washing their feet. In the kingdom, we gain authority when we are under authority. Our gifts are to serve and build up others, which creates successors so that what is built can endure.

FOLLOWERSHIP is a prerequisite for LEADERSHIP, as true leadership flows out of followership.

In 1988, a Harvard Business Review article on leadership titled "In Praise of Followers" masterfully defined leadership and followership.

"The Qualities of Followers: Effective followers share a number of essential qualities:

1. They manage themselves well.

2. They are committed to the organization and to a purpose, principle, or person outside themselves.

3. They build their competence and focus their efforts for maximum impact.

4. They are courageous, honest, and credible."

The best followers are independent, self-managed, self-developers, critical thinkers, consistent, and actively engaged as risk-takers and self-starters.[1]

---

[1] Robert Kelley, "In Praise of Followers," Harvard Business Review, accessed October 14, 2023, https://hbr.org/1988/11/in-praise-of-followers.

A Paradigm Shift in Leadership

Every person at Flō is a steward of their giftings and the company. The goal of the steward is to lead with honour, even when honour has not been extended to us. We honour because all people are to be honoured as they are of infinite value and made in the image of God. We must lead with honour to create a transformational culture of honour. Honour begets honour. When we honour, it stops people from becoming objectified, which is sadly commonplace in business. At Flō, we seek to see people as human beings made in the image of God and loved by God rather than just assets or tools.

The Father's family business must be faithfully stewarded by maturing sons and daughters within the culture of honour. As we grow in sonship, we can lead others differently, knowing each person is uniquely created with special giftings to bring to the world. Given the kingdom's dominion mandate, every person is created to be a leader. The greater the leader, the greater the servant. The greater the servant, the greater the humility. All this enables submission to one another in honour. To submit is to place our desires beneath the desires of another, sacrificial love in action. Remember, the kingdom's mandate is to rule over *the earth*. We are not called to rule over *people*; every man and woman is meant to live submitted to the rulership and authority of Jesus in the kingdom of God. Like Jesus, we walk in authority when we are under authority.

Lowering Expectations, Elevating Relationships: Insights from Kenn Gill

Pastor, founder of The Ripple Centre, and my good friend, Kenn Gill, recently shared the "life word" God gave him in the 1970s that changed everything. He was told, "Heighten your investment in people and lower your expectations." At first, this confused me. In the context of the marketplace, people are paid based on the expectation of high performance. Healthy relationships require open communication around our needs and expectations for both parties. This requires vulnerability. However, after reflecting on Kenn's word from God, I recognized that most judgment or disappointment I have experienced was based on an expectation I had placed on another that wasn't met. Or it was based on assumptions of them being like me or how I would do something, and they weren't. In addition, I have found that being disappointed or having unmet expectations of someone can open the door to offense, which presents a choice to take the offense or not. Honouring people allows us to separate identity and behaviour and to move in curiosity rather than judgment.

Working from the Heart: Integrating Faith and Excellence in the Workplace

In the workplace (and in life), you will often find yourself sharing common goals or outcomes with others. This is the "what" you are both working towards. While the *what* has been collaboratively established, it's important to let the other person determine "how" the outcome is achieved.

As we believe in and build up and align people around the key objectives, including caring for their hearts and well-being, positive outcomes naturally emerge. We have real faith in them because we hired them for a purpose. The culture of honour must be established first. With Kenn as a model, I have discovered the difference between holding expectations and believing in people with a 1 Corinthians 13:4-7-style love.

Love is large and incredibly patient. Love is gentle and consistently kind to all. It refuses to be jealous when blessing comes to someone else. Love does not brag about one's achievements nor inflate its own importance. Love does not traffic in shame and disrespect, nor selfishly seek its own honour. Love is not easily irritated or quick to take offense. Love joyfully celebrates honesty and finds no delight in what is wrong. Love is a safe place of shelter, for it never stops believing the best for others. Love never takes failure as defeat, for it never gives up.
—1 Corinthians 13:4-7, TPT

God cares more about our hearts and where our focus is than what we produce, although working diligently will produce great fruit—physically and spiritually. What we carry in our hearts has an expression on earth, so it is important to examine our hearts regularly.

Do you carry His heart, priorities, and perspective in your areas of influence?

What is in the way of a breakthrough?

We are designed to work with all our hearts unto the Lord as a form of worship. We honour God with the pursuit of excellence. This is a process of wholehearted engagement, bringing out the extraordinary in people and faithfulness in developing extraordinary stewardship in all that we do.

Put your heart and soul into every activity you do, as though you are doing it for the Lord Himself and not merely for others. For we know that we will receive a reward, an inheritance from the Lord, as we serve the Lord Yahweh, the Anointed One! A disciple will be repaid for what he has learned and followed, for God pays no attention to the titles or prestige of men.
—Colossians 3:23-25, TPT

Excellence is not an elusive future state but an attitude in the here and now. It applies to everything, from the smallest to the largest tasks of the day.

The secret of joy in work is contained in one word —excellence. To know how to do something well is to enjoy it.
—Pearl S. Buck[4]

TALENT AND CULTURE

The kingdom of God is made of people and relationships. It is a blessing that we get to do life together, but we must recognize our need for each other first. At Flō, we invest in people because we value people. We believe that treating people with love encourages others to bring their best selves to the workplace because it allows them to flourish.

This core belief led to creating a talent and culture strategy with the help of my good friend and kingdom strategist, Glem Dias, and his associates. To maintain consistency and build maturity, we implemented an annual activation calendar, which includes facilitated quarterly strategic reviews, quarterly coaching sessions, monthly town halls, weekly operational reviews, and continuous two-way performance feedback, with intentional quarterly employee driven coaching or check-ins to access OKRs. Employees take on the responsibility for their career and personal development.

In addition, we have a talent and culture roadmap to enable the vision and strategy of Flō. This includes leadership development, accelerated development plans with action learning projects, talent calibration, defining pivotal roles with succession planning, and an internal CEO advisory panel. Part of the strategy includes something we call "Leadership Profiles," which are descriptions of leading performance indicators that demonstrate our culture in action and the character of a leader. Leadership development is key to creating a kingdom ecosystem. The values of the kingdom are ultimately what everyone on our team wants, both believers and non-believers, as they bring life for all to flourish.

ACTIVATION CYCLE

Strategy, Operations, and Talent

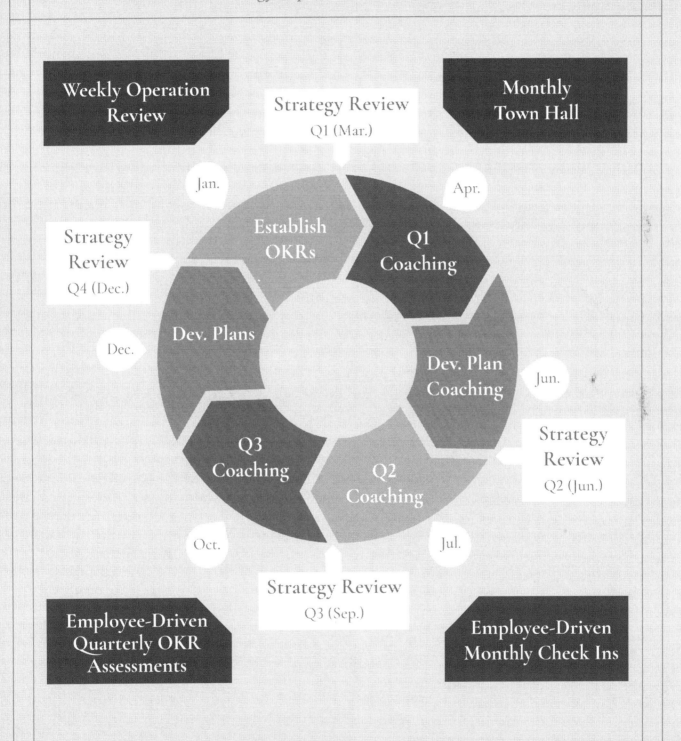

Positioned for Kingdom Impact: Expressing God's Love Through Business

When we seek first His kingdom, we align with heaven and the will of God for people. Love will say what needs to be said. Sometimes, this includes difficult conversations. Kindness will provide honest, hard feedback and hold people accountable. Loving people first is the key. Because this is our priority, Flō offers and pays for inner-heart healing for everyone on the team to assist in their journey to wholeheartedness. We are also implementing prayer support for anyone who desires prayer ministry. This enables people to serve their employer (and employers to serve their employees) wholeheartedly.[5] It can also empower them to process their pasts, disagree with lies, and believe the truth. Healed, whole hearts are free to love God wholeheartedly.[6] As people are faithful with little, more will be given, and if they mismanage what they are given, they will be given less to manage or steward.[7] As people thrive, the company thrives.

Kingdom Leadership Blueprint: What Makes People Extraordinary

As disciplers, we get to multiply by mentoring and developing people as leaders. We honour people by seeing and understanding their unique designs and gifts. We want to discover God's design (giftings and calling), which is the place where they do well, are most creative, and most satisfied. God created us to have His life flow through us by honouring His design and His ways. This moves people from "wanting to be seen" to instead look for opportunities where they will thrive. The antithesis of belonging is conformity, as it requires one to alter their identity, whereas our desire is for people to authentically embrace who and how God made them. We must position people where they will shine – the right person in the right place with role clarity. This will directly relate what they do with the outcomes of the company, so they know that what they do matters. Said another way, they understand how they directly impact the business from the chair they occupy. They don't have to try to be something they are not. This also involves providing honest and direct feedback, even when it is hard. As a leadership team, we aim to maximize our strengths and combine our giftings and talents, working in harmony around common goals.

Unlocking Potential: Equipping Individuals for Collective Impact

Flō has progressed to a new form of outcome-based goals called OKRs (objectives and key results).[8] This new collaborative goal-setting process leads to greater focus, empowerment, ownership, alignment, consistency, and agility as we progress towards our key strategic objectives as measured by our key results. We understand that to accelerate growth, we must set stretch goals and continue to identify bigger problems to develop innovative solutions to create more value, naturally leading to increased revenues and profitability. We are implementing employee-driven monthly check-ins where they lead the meetings and real-time OKR assessments of progress.

Leaders demonstrate honour by serving, equipping, and empowering others, not lording over people. As kingdom citizens who honour the ways of the kingdom, we are called to equip and grow people capable of self-government. More accurately, we provide the conditions and opportunities for growth and our people do the growing. Freedom comes with discipline, self-control, and the responsibility to do what is right through character development. Leaders are meant to help people discover where they thrive.

Unveiling Excellence: Nurturing God's Design in Individuals

Leaders understand that purpose or calling is cultivated as people are empowered to use their giftings and skills to make a meaningful difference. With this in mind, the Flō leadership team worked with Donna Tadych from Wisdom's Way to initiate a new process of utilizing assessments using DISC®, 360 Evaluations, Myers Briggs Type Indicator®, Working Genius, the 5 Love Languages®, the 5 Apology Languages™, leaderPOP™, the Team Dimensions Profile, and finally, the redemptive giftings, to begin to understand the design of God within our team. We want to harness the strengths of our whole team by loving and honouring each member individually to maximize influence and impact together as we advance His kingdom.

Practically, we have created a spreadsheet for each team member with the top two attributes of each assessment to narrow the information and make it readily actionable. In addition to helping us understand and stretch each person in their role, we also use this spreadsheet for everyday activities. For example, suppose there is an issue requiring an apology. In that case, we can glance at the sheet and know their top two apology languages to guide the discussion and ensure reconciliation is effective. If we want to know how to support or show appreciation for someone, we can see their top two love languages. If we are holding an innovation meeting, we can look at the top two working genius and team profiles to ensure we have the right people in the room to brainstorm effectively.

Discovering Redemptive Gifts: Unveiling God's Design

The Romans 12 redemptive gifts consist of seven God-given gifts to be used in our personal callings. These gifts manifest themselves in a natural tendency to be an (a) exhorter, (b) ruler/leader, (c) teacher, (d) giver, (e) servant, (f) prophet, and (g) mercy-giver. We use the book *Designed for Fulfillment* by Charles R. Wales, Jr., for our redemptive gifts assessment and utilize the checklists in the book. The results have been incredibly accurate and insightful in understanding how God designed us.

Jesus had all seven gifts in perfect measure. We have a primary gift that motivates everything we do, plus secondary gifts. Together, these gifts are our God-given design, hard-wired into our souls and given at birth. Though we can grow in our gifts as we become more like Christ, we are also called to rely on the gifts of others. Working for the kingdom is the epitome of teamwork!

For what makes a distinction between you and someone else? And what do you have that grace has not given you?
And if you received it as a gift, why do you boast as though there is something special about you?
— 1 Corinthians 4:7, TPT

At Flō, starting with the senior team, we have begun using the redemptive gifts results as the umbrella or context for which all the other test results are filtered. Essentially, our goal is to build a multidimensional identity model of each person to help us as leaders and disciplers to best steward those entrusted to us. This aids us in building people the way God made them and helps us proactively understand our differences so that we can see them as an advantage. Understanding and valuing one another encourages honour and interdependence. It allows people to be authentic. These God-given redemptive gifts are different from the nine gifts of the Holy Spirit listed in 1 Corinthians 12:7-11 and the gifts of Jesus to the church in Ephesians 4:11-12. No matter how you apply them, your redemptive gifts and abilities are simply how God made you. Those who are inexperienced in their giftings need to experience success through practice.[9] Experience is the harvest of life, and every harvest is the result of a sowing.

Strengthening Relationships for Kingdom Flourishing

People long to be known, accepted, valued, and loved. Only God meets this need perfectly, which provides our ultimate sense of belonging. However, we can continually grow in these areas so people around us feel seen, heard, and valued. These exercises and assessments not only honour the person because we care and recognize their makeup but also help remove competition and comparison. Because competition is removed, a culture of celebration is established. Fear destroys connection and love casts out fear. Loving people brings freedom, and freedom allows people to be real and connect.

In God's kingdom, trust fuels strong relationships, and the kingdom flourishes through these close ties. When we have quality connections, we can have real relationships. When we have real relationships, we can more easily be curious, listen, and seek to understand. In this place, assumptions and judgments are reduced, trust is strengthened, and people feel safe. As leaders, we start by extending trust to our people and then work to gain their trust. As we grow in character, the bonds of trust increase. When trust is present, we can all be more open and vulnerable. Vulnerability results in trust, so a reinforcing foundation is built. The greater the trust, the greater the ability to engage in healthy conflict (including speaking the truth with honest feedback), and healthy conflict results in greater commitment and trust as we are being authentic with one another. Orphans find it hard to trust. Sons and daughters trust because they know the Father unconditionally loves and accepts them! When we trust God, it enables us to yield to God and extend trust to others. God honours our choice to trust Him by showering us with His grace.

Your capacity to lead is directly proportional to your capacity to trust God.[10] When we think of how much God trusts us with His kingdom on earth, His people, His creation, the Gospel, our family, our work, and our businesses, it gives us reason to pause in gratitude. Like the biblical concept of loving God, because He loved us first, we can trust God because He entrusted us with certain responsibilities, specifically the dominion of the earth.[11] God is good and infinitely faithful!

Cultivating Growth: The Flōurish Approach to Personal Development

To help build a strong foundation for our coaching conversations and peer accountability, we created "Leadership Profiles." Because of the culture we have established, people are hungry to receive feedback as it is unto growth. We also have an annual employee engagement survey, allowing us to baseline our improvement across various categories. The results are shared each year along with our past results to see growth and progress. We also have "Grow with Flō," a regular personal development series. Our current theme is personal finance, and we have made one-on-one financial coaching available to everyone to get their financial house in order. We are also exploring strategies to accelerate the elimination of employee personal debt by partnering with those eager and willing to take responsibility in the process.

We are gradually creating a kingdom culture and community at Flō for both the believers and non-believers to taste and see that the Lord is good. We understand that labour is worship, so we work unto the Lord and practice living in constant awareness of God. We know that only love transforms by the power of the Holy Spirit, so we made agape (sacrificial love; a choice, not a feeling) our foundational value, as work is meant to produce love in serving, blessing, and advancing His kingdom. Love always releases life! All the while, we actively avoid religious language when we articulate our value system, which is our vision for who we will become through the development and transformation of our mindsets, as seen in the Leadership Profiles graphic on the following page.

LEADERSHIP PROFILES

Leadership Vision   *Expression*

AGAPE IN ACTION

A servant who establishes a foundation of trust, honour, and family

HONOUR HEARTSET
- Prioritizes and invests in meaningful connections
- Enables others to flourish in their uniqueness
- Honours others by listening, empathizing, and having compassion for their journey
- Puts the interest of others above their own
- Pursues unity through honour and shared purpose
- Demonstrates servant leadership; is humble, kind, and generous, especially when it's hard
- Sees and believes the best in others
- Looks for opportunities to bless, have fun, and celebrate

BUILDS FOR THE FUTURE

A strategic multiplier who leads through influencing, empowering, and inspiring others with a compelling vision

GROWTH MINDSET
- Leaders making leaders
- Aligns goals and tasks to steward our vision, strategy, and succession
- Provides input to the strategic direction
- Self-led with clear accountabilities and takes action on personal development
- Applies creativity to their responsibilities
- Participates in defining problems to create opportunities
- Understands strength in interdependence
- Curious to uncover tomorrow's problems to drive growth through innovation

DELIGHTS OUR CLIENTS

An empathizing "solutionary" who thinks from the outside in

CLIENT-CENTRIC MINDSET
- Honours relationships
- Is curious to understand the needs of others and seeks to define the root problem
- Prioritizes solving customer challenges in collaboration
- Seeks win-win opportunities in all interactions
- Believes there is always a better way
- Delights in excellence in delivering outstanding client experiences
- Creatively adapts
- Relentless focus on value creation within our ecosystem

LEADS WITH CHARACTER

An authentic leader, living from a heart of integrity, honour, and peace

LEVEL 5 LEADER MINDSET
- Earns respect and builds trust by maintaining a high say/do ratio
- Values transparency, vulnerability, and wholeheartedness
- Intentional with communication
- Confronts issues, holds oneself and others accountable
- Honest about challenges and opportunities
- Champions hope
- Builds strong interdependent relationships, committed to one another's success
- Grows in self-awareness of one's strengths and weaknesses

RESOLUTE

A tenacious yet humble leader with an attitude of gratitude in all things

OUTCOME DRIVEN MINDSET
- Diligent and disciplined in the day-to-day challenges
- Hungers to deliver on goals, even in adversity
- Takes ownership and trusts in the power of our team
- Sees problems as opportunities and learns from failures
- Adaptively perseveres until the desired outcome is achieved
- Is proactive to communicate and resolve challenges
- Focuses on the positive, even when it's hard
- Is comfortable being uncomfortable

PRAYING IN KINGDOM CULTURE

Until 2020, I had a team of prophetic intercessors whose sole job was to pray for Flō.[1] However, we did not practice corporate prayer. Then, in 2020, we began to incorporate prayer within Flō following a process called "Transforming Your Business," which was introduced to me when I met Chester and Betsy Kylstra, founders of Restoring the Foundations ministry. The process is designed to restore the foundations of the business so His kingdom can come to *earth as it is in heaven*. It includes removing the rights of the enemy related to the business, addressing generational issues (past and present founders and leaders), cleansing the land, identifying ungodly beliefs, and addressing hurts, areas of unforgiveness, and wounds. This paves the way for deliverance and the displacement of powers and principalities with an open heaven. We use apology language to aid in relational repair and ongoing reconciliation. Afterward, as a company, we must continue to occupy what God has given us, which involves maintaining an open heaven. (You could consider all this inner healing and spiritual cleansing for a business.) Like the Israelites, God brings us into the promised land, but there are enemies to overthrow by the power of His Spirit.[2] God has formed and prepared us to occupy the land amid future attacks and continue to expand His kingdom.

> *Because we don't focus our attention on what is seen but on what is unseen.*
> *For what is seen is temporary, but the unseen realm is eternal.*
> – 2 Corinthians 4:18, TPT

Now, we have set apart times of corporate prayer and fellowship for those who want to come. We also have key roles for prayer intercessors, whose job is to pray, discern, and prophecy as directed by the Lord. We pray for our families, marriages, customers, employees, businesses, or any other area as the Holy Spirit directs.

When we first began our prayer time was mainly focused on ourselves and Flō. However, as we have matured, our prayer assignments have greatly broadened to come alongside and strengthen many, specifically others in the marketplace. Opportunities to build up other companies and industries through encouragement and edification (but also financial and wisdom sharing) are a two-way blessing! As we pray, a healthy atmosphere is established that benefits everyone. The Lord continues to bring people in need of prayer from outside the company to receive prayer from our team, which has been a massive blessing to all involved.

We honour our apostolic and prophetic foundation with Jesus as the chief cornerstone (and master builder) to build kingdom structures. In addition, we introduce others from outside the company gifted by grace in the five-fold ministry to build up and equip the team so they can do the same for others.[3] There are many marketplace prophets who have visions and dreams and see ideas and solutions to bring into the world. We typically have worship music playing and have a "24/7 house of prayer" in the main office space that is open to the community. We are mainly a remote work environment, so the office is more of a meeting hub for some.

A few employees from various departments meet every morning online for prayer. On Wednesdays, we invite employees and the prayer teams to pray together. The cross-pollination of this greatly diverse group results in accelerated growth for all. This process has grown to include ongoing inner-heart healing made available to employees and facilitated restoration conversations[4] as required with the goal of heart-to-heart connection. Everything is a process that can sometimes be messy and requires hard work. However, we have discovered blessings in the process, as heart issues must be revealed so they can be healed.

> *The only clean stable is an empty stable. So if you want the work of an ox and to enjoy an abundant harvest, you'll have a mess or two to clean up!*
> – Proverbs 14:4, TPT

Remember, there is no exact recipe for what a kingdom company should look like. God will have a unique expression of His kingdom coming in and through your job, business, or whatever sphere of influence the Lord has called you to. As disciples, we learn and then apply kingdom principles over and over and grow in understanding and purpose in our callings.

---

[1] These were paid intercessors because we honour their calling and time with no sacred/secular divide.
[2] Joshua 21:44.
[3] This includes the grace gifts of apostles, prophets, pastors, teachers, and evangelists as listed in Ephesians 4:11.
[4] Facilitated by Wisdom's Way.

> I believe that one of the next great moves of God is going to be through the believers in the workplace.
> —Billy Graham[12]

Every company has a redemptive purpose and the opportunity to be a spiritual entity and influence the world. Flō is blessed to be a blessing in the marketplace and connect with people the traditional church typically has a more challenging time connecting with. We get to glorify God wherever we are planted. In 1 Peter 4:10, we are exhorted to use our gifts to serve one another. As we function and serve with our gifts, talents, and acquired skills, we are engaging in ministry with the marketplace as our mission field.

It is tempting to look at size, money, and significance as key indicators of success. However, as a kingdom company, we are unlearning the ways of the world and embracing the ways of the kingdom. The kingdom starts small and increases gradually as deep foundations are the key to long-term strength and growth. For a couple of years, it looked like very little was happening, but the roots were developing before the new growth could be seen above the surface. We were going deep with the Lord, building the foundations, before going high. Unless the Lord builds the house, we labor in vain.

Part of my passion is to live out and demonstrate the heart of God in kingdom business to the world so that others can see what is possible. God makes the rules, and only He decides what success looks like. When we are obedient to the call of God and stay in our lanes, individually and corporately, the need to compare or compete (which comes from a place of scarcity) is replaced with freedom and gratitude because we are living and working from a place of abundance. There is great distinction here, as we are in the world but not of the world.[13]

A New Success: Joy in the Lord

We recently welcomed Chad as the new president of Flo. He is a godly man deeply rooted in the principles of the kingdom. As we crafted his 90-day plan and discussed our markers of success, a prompting came to me from the Holy Spirit: joy. Understanding that joy is an essential indicator of God's presence and His kingdom, I shared this insight with the team and everyone enthusiastically embraced it.

That evening, during our time of prayer in the office prayer room, our worship leader began prophesying over Chad, and another voice echoed with the joyful declaration of "Glad Chad!" repeated joyfully. Laughter and joy filled the room, serving as a beautiful confirmation from heaven that joy is a measure of success in the kingdom.

Balancing Empowerment and Accountability: A Kingdom Company's Approach

Accountability and results (the fruits of our labour) are, however, still important. There is a natural tension between empowerment and accountability. Being responsible to one another, discipline, and natural consequences are necessary to set people up for success, to mature, and to flourish by God's design. The goal of what needs to be done can be agreed upon with delegated authority and creative autonomy regarding how it is accomplished. We set targets and goals built within the context of strategy, but we must always seek His kingdom first. Remember, it's impossible to have both God and money rule over your life according to Matthew 6:24-26. You must choose whom you serve. We have chosen to make money our servant and God our master.

The path to success with God is simply being obedient and faithful with whatever God entrusts to us (including our callings) and leaving the outcomes to Him. In this process, God will entrust true riches, the riches of heaven, leading to abundant life and fruitfulness. We provide faithfulness, and God provides fruitfulness.

Multiplying Blessings: The Fruit of Kingdom-centered Investments

With generosity as a key kingdom principle, much of our profits have been seeded into wonderful ministries and organizations, which have yielded much fruit for the kingdom! In fact, new organizations have been birthed through Flō. We are seeing a broad impact far beyond our industry. We now operate directly and indirectly in all seven spheres of society (family, religion, business, education, government, media, and arts/entertainment) to bring redemptive solutions to the world's problems. A redemptive solution is a transformational approach that addresses the root cause rather than symptoms, resulting in restoration, healing, and reconciliation. Flō has become a channel for the kingdom to flow from M46 Ministries (family, media in the form of TV, podcast, social media, books, etc.) to Bee Me Kidz (which works directly with families, schools, and the Canadian government). We seek to wisely steward profits as we sow through generous giving, reinvestment, and investment, and to employees through profit-sharing.

From Renters to Owners: The Journey of Stewardship in God's Kingdom

In addition to our profit-sharing program that targets a percentage of our profits to our employees, we are investigating employee-shareholder programs. I am the stockholder (the owner who issues the shares), and the employees are the shareholders with individual units of ownership. As stewards, the purpose is to mature in faithfulness and position. This parallels the kingdom journey, from orphans to sons and daughters, from renters to owners, from slaves to stewards to co-heirs with

Christ, and from citizens to ambassadors, being about our Father's business. From working for a blessing to receiving an inheritance. Another way to say it is that God is the owner and gives us the right of possession or delegated authority. God rules, but He chose to reign on earth through His people. Kingdom expansion happens through sons and daughters who can gain entrance as heirs of God and co-heirs with Christ and reproduce themselves in others.[14]

As we journey with Christ, we mature into the fullness as sons and daughters of the King of the kingdom of God. We cannot reproduce what we are not, and we cannot lead people where we have not gone. As such, spiritual fathering can only go as far as you have become a son to the Father. One of the greatest kingdom investments is a father's investment in sons and daughters, as this is how the kingdom of God is expanded: through heirs. Sons become fathers who produce sons, which is an investment that will keep on paying long after you leave the earth. This is kingdom business and the culture of the kingdom *on earth as it is in heaven*. Hierarchy exists in kingdom organizational design as a structure to provide clarity and order unto fruitfulness. Remember, just like Jesus, the greatest position in the kingdom is to be a faithful servant to all, as the least will be the greatest.[15]

> Leadership is the capacity to influence others through inspiration motivated by a passion, generated by a vision, produced by a conviction, ignited by a purpose.
> —Myles Munroe[16]

Manifesting the Kingdom: Glorifying God through Personal and Corporate Transformation

I have discovered that my personal journey of growth, maturity, sonship, and healing impacts not only my family, but also Flō. God is using me in ways I never could have dreamed. The more I am being transformed, the more it instigates transformation in others. My heart is to be a faithful servant in my life and with Flō to be yielded, open, and prepared for God to use the company to advance His kingdom. At the end of the day, all that matters is that I do my part to show the marketplace and the world a better way, which is God's way.

> *And so that we would know that we are his true children, God released the Spirit of Sonship into our hearts—moving us to cry out intimately, "My Father! My true Father!" Now we're no longer living like slaves under the law, but we enjoy being God's very own sons and daughters! And because we're his, we can access everything our Father has—for we are heirs because of what God has done!*
> *—Galatians 4:6-7, TPT*

My heart is for my life and Flō to glorify God. Peace and prosperity are manifestations of the kingdom of God on earth. As such, the following verse has been an anchor for me for years. I want my life and business to be like this description of Jerusalem, and I long for the world to be in awe of the goodness of God and His kingdom on earth:

338

Jerusalem will be to Me a name of joy, praise and glory before all the nations of the earth which will hear of all the good that I do for it, and they shall fear and tremble because of all the good and all the peace (prosperity, security, stability) that I provide for it.
—Jeremiah 33:9, AMP

God is also bringing new people to Flo for kingdom purpose, which we could not be more grateful and excited.

As I mentioned, we recently hired Chad as our president. We had been in conversation with Chad for some time, unsure of what role he might take as there were no apparent openings. When we invited him to our prayer meeting for the second time, just before he arrived, I distinctly heard God's voice saying, "Welcome to Flo." At the meeting's start, I acknowledged this as an unusual way to begin but shared what I heard, saying, "Chad, welcome to Flo!" Surprisingly, Chantal from our prayer team affirmed she had received the same message. This is a testament to how God orchestrates events in the kingdom.

HOW TO BUILD A KINGDOM ECOSYSTEM

There is much to ponder as we transition from thinking of the world to thinking of the kingdom of God as we cast our nets to the other side of the boat. Let's consider the following questions as we explore new ways of thinking in the marketplace to build a kingdom ecosystem.

- Are we seeing people as Jesus sees them, or are we seeing them through the eyes of harsh, flawed human judgment?

- What if we truly believed everyone is of infinite value? How would this change the way we operate in the marketplace?

- What if we were to help people discover their purpose (or kingdom assignment) through discovering and helping them grow in their gifts and talents?

- What if everyone used effectiveness evaluations rather than performance evaluations? Effectiveness evaluations are kingdom reviews that provide opportunities for growth rather than the fear of punishment.

- What if issues and problems with people were first met with prayer and intercession? Assuming the right person is in the proper role, what if the consequence of ineffectiveness was targeted investment in training and growth?

- What if reassignment into their area of giftedness was an option?

- What if people could live fearlessly within the safety of His family business?

- What if people were all valued enough so that decisions were made through consensus (general or directional agreement, all fully committed to the decision), and consensus was reached through stewarded dialogue by calling on the wisdom of the team?

- What if sonship or character formation were the highest qualifications of leadership?

- What if we were to embrace God as our source and provider, no longer bound by fear, scarcity, or competition, but on adding value by freely giving and blessing others, and knowing it is God who will bring the increase or harvest as we seek first His kingdom?

- What if the Beatitudes attributes were looked upon as strengths?

- What if the company was known for its love?

- What if businesses were relationally "aligned" with an apostle for counsel, covering, insight, wisdom, and prayer, exemplifying an integrated relational model rather than a hierarchical one?[1]

- What if the leader with the grace gift of an apostle (the office) or those operating in the apostolic (sent ones, builders of the kingdom) were meant to be largely unseen, relational first, lift others up, create the culture and atmosphere for people to flourish, create alignment, ensure a plumb-line of the faith, serve and empower others, and build a solid foundation for the success of others for an ongoing legacy? We must never forget that only Jesus belongs on the throne. Jesus made Himself of no reputation (no desire for fame or recognition) and humbled Himself as a servant. We can't look up to any human leader in a way that displaces Jesus from His rightful place as Lord. In the kingdom, there is no "celebrity." We must be cautious when fame and fortune distract from the Gospel, for God pays no attention to the titles or prestige of man.

- What does a heavenly corporate structure look like in the marketplace with the right balance of structure, hierarchy, and authority when modeling heaven?

These questions (and others like them) will definitely stir up a clash of kingdoms!

 Change your mindset: Live and lead in a kingdom way.

 Adopt a new lifestyle: Remove strongholds and display kingdom principles.

 Experience the power of the Holy Spirit: Be open to more of the Holy Spirit's influence.

 Advance the kingdom of God: The kingdom advances in the expression of love, kindness, justice, and righteousness.

[1] This is directed towards Christian leaders and is a much larger topic to be discussed.

Bringing Heaven to Earth: Manifesting the Kingdom in the Marketplace

Like Jesus, we are about our Father's business! We know that we are all called to succeed in family and business as we place things in their proper order: (1) God, (2) family, (3) business, and (4) everything else. We get to be Jesus in the marketplace to build His kingdom together, knowing Jesus is the master builder. People are God's top priority. We are meant to blur the boundaries between heaven and earth in the marketplace by receiving His unshakable kingdom and then releasing heaven on earth. What we have been given, various types of gifts, resources, and favour, is for others. This sacrificial or selfless lifestyle advances His kingdom and creates human flourishing. We are meant to bring the power of the Gospel into the marketplace with the salvation, freedom, healing, restoration, and transformation described in Isaiah 61. This is the power of the gospel of the kingdom of God.

> Live in the kingdom of God in such a way that provokes questions for which the Gospel is the answer.[17]

Changed people change things. Transformed people transform things. The kingdom works everywhere and changes everything!

*Many of the assessments described in this chapter are available at M46ministries.com on the "Extras" page.

1. "Ekklesia Everywhere," *Transform Our World*, accessed October 14, 2023, https://tinyurl.com/sbk5bvex.
2. John 15:16.
3. Oswald J. Saunders, *Spiritual Leadership* (Chicago: Moody Publishers).
4. Pearl S. Buck, *Forbes Quotes*, https://www.forbes.com/quotes/7381/, accessed April 4, 2024.
5. Ephesians 6:7-8 also tells us that God rewards us when we work as though we are serving Christ, whether employee or employer.
6. Mark 12:30.
7. Luke 16:10.
8. John Doerr, *Measure What Matters: How Google, Bono, and the Gates Foundation Rock the World with OKRs*.
9. Henry Ford, "Henry Ford Quotations," *The Henry Ford*, accessed October 14, 2023, www.thehenryford.org.
10. Kris Vallotton, "Your Capacity to Lead is Directly Related to Your Capacity to Trust God," *Facebook*, accessed October 14, 2023, https://tinyurl.com/muj82ndh.
11. 1 John 4:19.
12. Os Hillman, "Is This Billy Graham Prophecy About the Next Great Move of God Coming to Pass?," *Charisma News*, accessed October 14, 2023, https://tinyurl.com/3trwwcbt.
13. John 17:16.
14. See the Beatitudes in Matthew 5:3-12 for the description of the heart of a mature son.
15. Matthew 19:30.
16. Myles Munroe, "Flight Leadership," *A Comprehensive Definition of Leadership*, accessed Februrary 23, 2024, https://www.facebook.com/reel/6893206384121046.
17. Chris Seay, "The Gospel, Church, and Culture According to Lesslie Newbigin," *Ecclesia*, accessed October 14, 2023, https://tinyurl.com/yc7p9z9p.

THE KINGDOM PRINCIPLE
OF BUSINESS

Business is an opportunity to glorify God, create value, foster innovation, and contribute to the common good, aligning with principles of honesty, fairness, and ethical conduct. In the kingdom of God, work is worship and business is a platform to expand His kingdom by expressing love, integrity, and service to others, reflecting the character of God in every transaction and interaction.

Father, we ask for the grace to steward our marketplace callings and glorify You in all we do!

QUESTIONS FOR REFLECTION

What has the Holy Spirit revealed to you through *The Kingdom Principle of Business*? How can you apply this to your life?

How does having access to a limitless kingdom impact how you approach the marketplace?

Reflect on the "How to Build a Kingdom Ecosystem" questions in this chapter. Which question(s) stands out most and why?

QUESTIONS FOR REFLECTION *(continued)*

If you are an employee (versus employer), how can you integrate this kingdom key into your work?

_____

_____

_____

_____

What sphere of influence(s) has God placed you in? How can you implement this kingdom key into your life?

_____

_____

_____

_____

Notes

_____

_____

_____

_____

_____

_____

_____

_____

_____

_____

Chapter 22: The Kingdom Principle of Leadership

"The leaders who are served are the most important in your eyes, but in the kingdom, it is the servants who lead. Am I not here with you as one who serves? Because you have stood with me through all my trials and ordeals, I am promising you the kingdom that the Father has promised me."
—Luke 22:27-29, TPT

Although the Kingdom Principle of Business chapter already highlights many aspects of kingdom leadership, I wanted to introduce leadership from a distinct angle.

Answering the Call to Kingdom Leadership

At Flō, we are on a path to grow in kingdom leadership. Jesus exemplifies kingdom leadership. We cannot lead unless we have first learned to follow, which develops humility and character. We are in the process of finding a balance between structure, hierarchy, roles of authority, and "round table" operations as the maturity process unfolds, built upon the foundation of love and honour. Implementing objectives and key results (OKRs) are very helpful in this area.[1]

Leadership is essential in every aspect of our lives, extending beyond the marketplace into our families and societal roles God has placed us in. Within His kingdom, we are designed to lead and reign in life as modeled by Jesus. This call to expand His kingdom necessitates a leadership approach that transforms our immediate surroundings and has a broader impact on society.

Level 5 Aspirations: Something Unexpected

In one of the most profound books ever written on business, *Good to Great*, author Jim Collins defines a leadership development journey as culminating in "Level 5 Leadership." Characteristics of Level 5 Leadership include:

1. A personal sense of humility
2. A deep personal understanding of one's strengths and weaknesses
3. A laser-like focus on the organization's purpose
4. A passionate commitment to continuous learning
5. A relentless determination to do what is right, not what is easy[2]

This culmination, as defined by Collins, represents the absolute best of global leadership, complete with executive skill sets and character development often based on biblical values and principles. However, many world-class companies struggle with greed, fear, and control, which are embedded in their mindsets and systems.

In 2018, friend and award-winning Leadership and Talent strategist Glem Dias and I started envisioning the transformation of Flō into a kingdom-class company (going beyond what is considered "world-class"). We initiated this journey by examining the best practices in the corporate world. Then we began implementing strategic tools, systems, and resources focusing on developing leaders founded in biblical values and principles with a passion for excellence. Though we continue to grow and mature towards greater levels of leadership, we believe it is possible to transcend even these rarely achieved, world-class leadership limits when empowered by the Holy Spirit.

> **"For the natural realm only gives birth to things that are natural, but the spiritual realm gives birth to supernatural life!"**
> —John 3:6, TPT

Surprisingly, amidst our journey, something else began to unfold that was not built by mere human endeavour, something far beyond structures, systems, tools, and principles. God was doing a new thing powered by His Spirit. Fueled by surrender, hunger, and prayer, God was taking us on a journey of spiritual maturity. We were enlightened to our union with Jesus, with new levels of intimacy and deepening revelations of the kingdom of God. As a result, we continue to experience a spiritual awakening. *As in Heaven* is a spiritual fruit of this journey.

A Spiritual Journey to Kingdom 5 Leadership (K5)

> *For the Lord God is one, and so are we, for we share in one faith, one baptism, and one Father. And he is the perfect Father who leads us all, works through us all, and lives in us all!*
> —Ephesians 4:5-6, TPT

Initially, we perceived a shift from world-class to kingdom-class leadership, aiming to identify three distinct levels of growth beyond the levels of world-class Level 5 Leadership. We began using the term Kingdom 5 (K5) to highlight the shift from Level 5. Now, it's evident to me that kingdom-class leadership is an entirely new dimension of leadership that is cultivated alongside world-class leadership development, frameworks, and excellence systems.

> *I was flooded with such incredible grace, like a river overflowing its banks, until I was full of faith and love for Jesus, the Anointed One!*
> —1 Timothy 1:14, TPT

K5: The Leadership of Jesus

Kingdom-class leadership transcends prescriptive methods, emerging from a state of being. "Being" is led by the Spirit and founded in identity, where our actions and decisions flow naturally from our character and relationship with God rather than from external guidelines or strategies. Prayer teams (including executives), not just executive teams, spearheaded this transformation, guiding us towards a unity that embodies God's love and wisdom, essential for world transformation.

This is all new, and we are still learning; however, we've outlined these areas or aspects of heavenly leadership, recognizing that growth can occur in each area throughout our journey. As spiritual growth in the kingdom is more about "being" rather than "achieving," we will refer to these as areas or aspects of leadership rather than levels. Each area of growth champions or facilitates various aspects of the Ephesians 4:11-13 grace gifts of the five-fold ministry (pastor, teacher, apostle, prophet, and evangelist, with evangelism being a common expression among them all). This journey includes three forms of leadership: redemptive leadership, transformational leadership, and Kingdom 5 or K5 Leadership, which encompasses all the areas.

What's required to embark on the path to kingdom-class leadership?

Remarkably, it begins with a simple and heartfelt "yes" to God!

Our "yes" is rooted in the Lordship of Jesus! We are called to be conduits of heaven, making the invisible kingdom visible. In the process, we've shifted from focusing on "performance indicators" to emphasizing "leadership expression" in our kingdom-class leadership approach. This change underlines a transition from merely *what we do* to *who we are*, shaped by our connection with Jesus. Practically, this means being Spirit-led with our actions naturally flowing from our core identity, values, and beliefs.

K5 Leadership is the culmination of all other forms of kingdom leadership, marked by significant growth in the revelation of sonship. These leaders embody spiritually mature fathers and mothers in the marketplace. They have embraced an inside-out process, demonstrated strong character, and exemplified the principles, values, and ethics of the kingdom of God, which they impart to those they serve and disciple.

Every K5 Leader embraces the call of a CSO (Chief Spiritual Officer) to uphold the kingdom's DNA in the areas they lead. I have described how God has practically positioned me in this role; however, this aspect of K5 Leadership will be an authentic expression of each leader depending on their unique positioning, design, redemptive giftings, calling, purpose, etc.

A K5 Leader operates with a profound understanding and alignment with the kingdom's principles and integrates them into their daily life. They embrace the process of inner-heart healing unto wholeheartedness and place enormous value on relationships and authentic connections. A K5 Leader lives by bold faith, expecting to go beyond what is reasonably possible because of their belief in God, who makes all things possible. Like Jesus, they function from a position of alignment with God's will, timing, and placement within these areas:

- Their unique giftings (unique abilities and design to fulfill their calling)
- Their calling (God-given assignment or vocation)
- Their purpose (the reason for existence, giving life meaning)
- Maturity in their redemptive gifting (tied to purpose) — dependent on and empowered by the Holy Spirit

K5 | THE LEADERSHIP OF JESUS
The Spiritual Journey of Kingdom-class Leadership

Leadership Strength | *Expressions of Leadership*

REDEMPTIVE LEADER

Champions hope-filled possibilities and change, nurtures renewal, reconciliation, unity, and wholeness for broken people, relationships, situations, and organizations, embodying the redemptive power of the gospel of the kingdom. They embody and promise a restoration mindset unto wholeheartedness and unity. Embraces and champions the roles of pastor and teacher.

- Trust-building
- Compassion and mercy
- Peacemaker
- Healing and restoration
- Active listening
- Conflict resolution
- Internal transformation
- Wholehearted loving

TRANSFORMATIONAL LEADER

Catalyzes growth and innovation, shaping and empowering future leaders to create godly transformation in individuals, organizations, and communities, aligned with God's will and the transformative power of the gospel of the kingdom. They live out and inspire a high-impact stewardship mindset. They are carriers of shalom that brings chaos into order. Embraces and champions the roles of the prophetic and apostolic.

- Influences visionary change
- Servanthood
- Inspires stewardship and continuous growth
- Fosters self-governance
- Holy Spirit-inspired innovation
- Outward transformation as the fruit of internal transformation

KINGDOM 5 (K5) LEADER

Leads from their life union with Jesus and as a son or daughter, spiritual fathers and mothers, embodying their heirship in God's kingdom. This Spirit-led servant embraces kingdom principles and operates in divine love, heavenly wisdom, and authority, on earth as it is in heaven, demonstrating the gospel of the kingdom through the invincible power of God's love. They demonstrate an agape heartset. They live from sabbath rest where doing flows from being. Rules and reigns as son or daughter, a king and priest.

- Childlike trust and confidence in God
- Radiating joy in constant celebration
- Heavenly minded seeing God in everything
- Catalytic in lives and destinies
- Divine partnership and alignment with heaven
- Exercise kingdom authority as kingdom ambassadors
- Kingdom generosity
- Followership, servanthood, and sacrifice
- Bold faith expressing itself through love – practically followed by signs, wonders, and miracles
- Kingdom influence and expansion

And consider the example that Jesus, the Anointed One, has set before us. Let his mindset become your motivation. He existed in the form of God, yet he gave no thought to seizing equality with God as his supreme prize. Instead he emptied himself of his outward glory by reducing himself to the form of a lowly servant. He became human! He humbled himself and became vulnerable, choosing to be revealed as a man and was obedient. He was a perfect example, even in his death—a criminal's death by crucifixion! Because of that obedience, God exalted him and multiplied his greatness! He has now been given the greatest of all names!

—*Philippians 2:5-9 TPT*

In the gospel of the kingdom of God, following Jesus calls us to surrender all that we were never meant to be, enabling us to dedicate our lives in service to others. Leadership is love and Jesus shows us that love expresses itself in selfless service and self-giving. True leadership is not about dominance or power. It's about humility, compassion, and the willingness to lay down one's life for others. It is in serving others with love and selflessness that true leadership is demonstrated, revealing the very nature of God Himself.

In Scripture, self-emptying, self-giving love is the essence of God's nature, a tangible display of His divinity. Jesus lived out this truth by doing only what He saw the Father doing, emptying Himself to serve humanity and reveal the love of God. Therefore, to be like Yahweh, our Heavenly Father, is to be a servant, serving with joy. Denying oneself allows us to fulfill our purpose and become who we are meant to be. The highest calling is shown by Jesus washing feet. Following Jesus means embracing this downward path of humility and selflessness. To be like God is to be a servant with Jesus as the perfect representation of the invisible God. Surrendering our lives leads to true fulfillment.

Embracing the path of self-emptying, self-giving love exemplified by Jesus is the essence of divine living on earth as it is in heaven. As we follow His example of servanthood and sacrificial love, we discover our true purpose and identity. Denying ourselves and surrendering to His ways leads to the highest fulfillment and the truest expression of our humanity, mingled with divinity in Christ. As the way up is down, it is in losing ourselves that we truly find ourselves and experience the abundant life God intended for us. Therefore, let us embrace the way of Jesus, for in Him, we find the ultimate expression of God's love and the path to our highest calling. In His kingdom, true power, leadership, and greatness are redefined through acts of love and selflessness.[1]

---

[1] Matthew 10:39; 16:24-25; 20:28, Mark 10:45, John 5:19, 13:4-17; 15:13, Romans 8, Philippians 2:5-8, Colossians 1:15.

Divine alignment enables K5 Leaders to lead with clarity, wisdom, and effectiveness, partnering and co-creating with God and others to advance the kingdom for the glory of God. A K5 Leader honours God, is selfless, motivated by love, and operates in the authority and anointing of God. In our Heavenly Father's family business, leadership is rooted in servitude from the bottom up, not power from the top down. The K5 Leader seeks alignment with heavenly principles to achieve heaven-to-earth outcomes, embodying the servant leadership model Jesus demonstrated. From this place, the K5 Leader demonstrates and reveals the heart of our Heavenly Father to the world.

A K5 Leader lives in constant awareness of their union with Jesus. From this place of oneness, their actions naturally lead to fruitfulness, recognizing that all fruitfulness comes from God, and apart from Him, they can do nothing. For a K5 Leader, work is worship and comes from a place of rest as they are Spirit-led, operating out of the overflow of the Holy Spirit. They understand that everything is made by God and for God, and that everything finds completion in Him. A K5 Leader embraces the abundance of the kingdom, free from the scarcity or poverty mindset (fear leading to greed, resulting in hoarding and competition), and becomes an open conduit of heaven's resources.

Living in meekness (living below their means, strength under control) and simplicity (detached from materialism and the distractions of this world), K5 Leaders are freed from the worldly shackles of business, power, status, possessions, time, and money, operating in true freedom and in service to others. This stage of leadership marks the end of toil and the beginning of true dominion, as they rule and reign in life in alignment with God's will from a place of rest, manifesting hope, peace, and joy in the Holy Spirit. Jesus describes it beautifully in John 12:25-26, TPT:

> *"The person who loves his life and pampers himself will miss true life! But the one who detaches his life from this world and abandons himself to me, will find true life and enjoy it forever! If you want to be my disciple, <u>follow me</u> and you will go where I am going. And if you truly <u>follow me</u> as my disciple, the Father will shower his favor upon your life."*

The original call of the King of the kingdom was, **"Come, follow me."**[3] A K5 Leader and all kingdom leaders first follow Jesus, understanding that leadership flows from followership and submission. This means that the essence of K5 Leadership is rooted in the deep, personal discipleship and imitation of Christ's example, embodying His teachings and actions in every aspect of leadership because they know that in Him, they breathe and live and have their being.

Cruciform Leadership: Embracing the Pathway to the Kingdom

> *"And since we are his true children, we qualify to share all his treasures, for indeed, we are heirs of God himself. And since we are joined to Christ, we also*

inherit all that he is and all that he has. We will experience being co-glorified with him provided that we accept his sufferings as our own."
—*Romans 8:17, TPT*

Untethered from worldly concerns and trappings, K5 Leaders become heavenly leaders, journeying through the cross and embracing a crucified lifestyle of self-sacrifice and humility as the pathway to the kingdom. Marked by sacrifice, followership, servanthood, generosity, and prayer, they receive from God and overflow with blessings to others. A K5 Leader does not shy away from problems or people in need but brings the kingdom's power through signs, wonders, and miracles while also being the hands and feet of Jesus in tangible ways. Empowered by the Holy Spirit, the K5 Leader manifests the peace, provision, and joy of heaven to every person and sphere they encounter.

By embodying the values of the kingdom, K5 Leaders create environments of flourishing and empowerment where individuals and communities thrive spiritually, emotionally, and economically. Their visionary leadership inspires innovation, collaboration, and sustainable growth, fostering a culture of excellence and purpose-driven impact. Jesus emptied Himself of power and embraced servitude. The K5 Leader will look more and more like Jesus, living above circumstances, embodying humility, and serving others with a heart full of grace and love, regardless of life's trials. The K5 Leader is anchored in the sovereignty of God, His goodness, and the fear of the Lord. As Jesus's life is dispensed into this leader, their life is dispensed into the world.

Rising Together: Envisioning K5 Leadership in the Body of Christ

My old identity has been co-crucified with Christ and no longer lives. And now the essence of this new life is no longer mine, for the Anointed One lives his life through me—we live in union as one! My new life is empowered by the faith of the Son of God who loves me so much that he gave himself for me, dispensing his life into mine!
—*Galatians 2:20, TPT*

Ultimately, K5 Leadership glorifies God by advancing His kingdom agenda on earth, ushering in a new era of hope, restoration, and fulfillment of God's redemptive purposes. A K5 Leader is a sold-out son or daughter in the kingdom. It is not only for the so-called "elite" few. Each and every one of us can mature into a K5 leader wherever God has positioned us.

Why is K5 available to every believer? It's because, through our new life in Jesus, every believer is in life union with Jesus, sharing in a life of oneness.

K5 Leadership is for the entire body of Christ in every sphere of society, with each member of His body uniquely coming together to reflect the fullness of Christ on the earth, ruling and reigning in life as kings and priests. **Jesus is the ultimate K5 Leader, making K5 the leadership of Jesus.** He is our King, brother, and friend. As He is, so are we on the earth, and we will do even greater things because of the Holy Spirit within us. We are all called to kingdom-class leadership!

He raised us up with Christ the exalted One, and we ascended with him into the glorious perfection and authority of the heavenly realm, for we are now co-seated as one with Christ!
— *Ephesians 2:6, TPT*

Never doubt God's mighty power to work in you and accomplish all this. He will achieve infinitely more than your greatest request, your most unbelievable dream, and exceed your wildest imagination! He will outdo them all, for his miraculous power constantly energizes you.
Ephesians 3:20, TPT

Hunger In the Marketplace

In March 2024, Glem Dias and I used Flō's journey as a case study to present "Building a Kingdom Company" at a kingdom business conference named "EPIC — At Work," a board I had recently joined. After we presented the journey of Flō and a very brief vision for K5 Leadership, a businessman named Kevin jumped up and said, "I want this. I need this. I commit to becoming a K5 Leader! Glem, would you pray for God to release this anointing?" Someone then asked, "Who else would like to commit to K5?" and most of the room stood up to receive prayer and impartation. It was a powerful move of the Holy Spirit to launch the conference! It was even clearer at that moment: people are hungry for the kingdom.

Here is Kevin's statement given to us the following day:

> Within five minutes into "Building a Kingdom Company," I was convicted that I was allowing the logistics of an expanding company to distract me from spending face time with the King of the kingdom. Instead of operating in peace, I found myself consumed by stress. Rather than attending to the needs of people's souls, I was barking orders at them. By the end of the session, I made a solemn commitment before God. I resolved to entrust our companies to trustworthy leaders whom God had already provided, so that I could implement His blueprint and become a true K5 Leader. My priority became hungering for God above all else and measuring our companies' success by the spiritual transformation of our people. I pledged to step up as one of the kings under the King of the kingdom, leading with spiritual confidence and authority to extend God's kingdom on earth as it is in heaven.
> Kevin White

Shortly after the conference, an employee from Kevin's company contacted me to discuss his personal development. During our conversation, he excitedly highlighted the significant transformation in Kevin's leadership, reflecting his deep commitment to growth and change.

The Kingdom Principles of Leadership

As Satan is totally defeated, requiring him to work through lies and deception, our agreement is necessary to open the door which empowers a disempowered foe. A mind full of truth, the mind of Christ, allows us to see Satan rightly, see God rightly, and see ourselves rightly, as those who are made from heaven, infinitely valuable, loved, and victorious. Living in the truth, our very lives become a living expression, a manifestation of worship, and the domain of the King! The kingdom of God is sovereign!

Within each of us resides the fullness of King Jesus, unlocking the realm of endless possibilities where it is not *we* who live but Christ living through our surrendered lives as we relinquish control. We embody His presence on earth for God to reign through us and expand His kingdom.

Jesus demonstrated this realm of love through His ministry. This ministry was marked by signs, wonders, and miracles, fueled by the fullness of the seven spirits of God, the redemptive gifts, and the solution to every need, demonstrating the transformative power of the five-fold ministry and the unlimited power, authority, and provision of heaven released on earth.[4] As His joyful kingdom comes and His sovereign plan unfolds, powers and principalities of darkness are displaced.

It is unfathomable that God would allow Himself to endure crucifixion, the most monstrous and humiliating torture known, reserved for the lowest. Yet, the cross exemplifies that even in the most seemingly powerless and gruesome circumstances, the greatest demonstration of power can be unleashed. As the Beatitudes teach, the first shall be the last and the last shall be first, revealing divine wisdom in the midst of apparent weakness. Blessed are those who are pure as they shall see God and see Him in others. Knowing His power is made perfect in our weakness, how does this change your perception on kingdom leadership?

Just as Kevin and those at the conference stood to answer their call to becoming K5 Leaders, we invite you to join us on the same journey! By embracing this journey of spiritual growth, you not only enhance your own leadership capabilities but also contribute to a broader mission of societal revival and reformation *on earth as it is in heaven.*

Your crucifixion with Christ has severed the tie to this life, and now your true life is hidden away in God in Christ. And as Christ himself is seen for who he really is, who you really are will also be revealed, for you are now one with him in his glory! … He is the divine portrait, the true likeness of the invisible God, and the firstborn heir of all creation. For in him was created the universe of things, both in the heavenly realm and on the earth, all that is seen and all that is unseen.
—*Colossians 3:3-4 and 15-17, TPT*

1. John Doerr, *Measure What Matters: How Google, Bono, and the Gates Foundation Rock the World with OKRs,* (Portfolio: 2018).
2. Christine Kininmonth, "Good to Great: The Key Traits of Jim Collins Level 5 Leadership," *Growth Faculty Learn,* accessed October 14, 2023, https://www.thegrowthfaculty.com/blog/levelfiveleadership.
3. Matthew 4:19, NIV.
4. Revelation 1:4, 3:1, 4:5, 5:6.

THE KINGDOM PRINCIPLE OF LEADERSHIP

The kingdom of God is the foundation of K5 Leaders, emphasizing a Spirit-led life of encountering God that transcends all leadership models. Love, the pinnacle of spiritual maturity, is the bedrock of K5 Leaders, servant leaders who blend spiritual growth and stewardship. Through their leadership and heavenly positioning in Christ, they release the transformative power of the gospel of the kingdom of God, aligning the church and broader society with the principles and power of heaven. The K5 Leader brings about renewal and reformation *on earth as it is in heaven.*

Father, will You empower us through the Holy Spirit to become kingdom leaders who lead with love and in service to others as we steward all You have entrusted to us?

QUESTIONS FOR REFLECTION

What has the Holy Spirit revealed to you through *The Kingdom Principle of Leadership*? How can you apply this to your life?

_____

_____

_____

Where are you called to lead?

_____

_____

_____

Are you able to envision yourself as a K5 Leader? Why or why not?

_____

_____

_____

QUESTIONS FOR REFLECTION *(continued)*

How does inner-heart healing and faith contribute to K5 Leadership?

_____

_____

_____

_____

In what ways do K5 Leaders honour God and operate in love?

_____

_____

_____

_____

How does maintaining awareness of union with Jesus impact K5 Leadership?

_____

_____

_____

_____

What is the overall impact and significance of K5 Leadership?

_____

_____

_____

_____

Understanding that Yahweh, our Heavenly Father, embodies servanthood as part of His divine nature, how does this reshape your understanding of our role and responsibilities as His followers?

_____

_____

The Unstoppable, Ever-expanding Fruitfulness of the Kingdom of God

"You did not choose Me but I chose you, and appointed you that you would go and bear fruit, and that your fruit would remain, so that whatever you ask of the Father in My name He may give to you."
—John 15:16, NASB

We are like common clay jars that carry this glorious treasure within, so that this immeasurable power will be seen as God's, not ours.
2 Corinthians 4:7, TPT

The Snowball Effect: Multiplying God's Kingdom in Ordinary Lives

God chose ordinary, imperfect, and broken people made of the dust of the earth to be His dwelling place. We are a chosen people who carry the glorious treasure of the glory of Jesus Christ within so that the power of God can be displayed through us. It is God who is unstoppable! It is God who is the source of all transformation and fruitfulness!

The Lord has established His throne in heaven and His kingdom rules over all.
—Psalm 103:19

We all know how a small and seemingly insignificant snowball starts slowly and gradually picks up speed, building energy and mass as it rolls down a hill, growing larger, heavier, and faster. The higher the mountain, the greater the potential of the snowball. The same is true of the kingdom of God, which is God's perfect design bringing divine order *on earth as it is in heaven.* The higher and harder the climb, the more powered by God for supernatural expansion and multiplication we become in order to bear much fruit that remains. This is the lifestyle of the kingdom in action! Our surrendered lives and our "yes" spur others on to do the same! As we speak and others hear and experience the gospel of the kingdom of God, they will receive Jesus and learn to live as Jesus did with the mission to expand His kingdom on earth.

I planted the church, and Apollos came and cared for it, but it was God who caused it to grow. This means the one who plants is not anybody special, nor the one who waters, for God is the one who brings the supernatural growth.
— 1 Corinthians 3:6-7, TPT

We all play a unique part in God's kingdom, but only God brings supernatural growth! This removes competition or comparison, as we all have a unique part to play as God ordains. We just need to be faithful, with the grace and gifts God has given us… and God gets the glory! Everything is by grace. As we sow in the kingdom, we reap a harvest that will produce many new seeds for the next harvest. We grow the kingdom as disciple-makers, making disciple-makers. Doing so impacts today and the generations to come! This is supernatural multiplication as kingdom seeds go into good soil.

"But what was sown on good, rich soil represents the one who hears and fully embraces the message of the kingdom. Their lives bear good fruit—some yield a harvest of thirty, sixty, even one hundred times as much as was sown."
—*Matthew 13:23, TPT*

"Give, and it will be given to you. They will pour into your lap a good measure—pressed down, shaken together, and running over. For by your standard of measure it will be measured to you in return."
—*Luke 6:38, NASB*

Living as Conduits: Unlocking Kingdom Multiplication in Our Lives

As we faithfully steward God's resources, we prepare for an increase. As we give, we are given more and more to give once again. There is sowing and reaping, and there is also God's wonderful favour. With God's favour we get what we don't deserve and reap where we haven't sown! We have the privilege of receiving from our Heavenly Father! The kingdom principles allow for God's supernatural multiplication in the world. God's principles create biblical thought patterns, which become the pillars of our lives, allowing us to live out the truth of God's design. As we bless, we are blessed. We cannot give what we have not received first from God. What we freely receive from God, we can freely give. As we forgive, we are forgiven. As we sow mercy, we reap mercy. As we minister to others, we are ministered to. This releases us and creates a multiplication in the kingdom in others, which goes on and on. We are an ever-expanding conduit of kingdom goodness and blessing! This is how we increase—simply pour out to be filled!

As conduits of the kingdom, we know it is no longer us who live but Christ who lives in us. Our self-focused life is over; *Christ lives in us, and He alone is our hope of glory.* This means our lives reveal the testimony of Jesus, removing the enemy's claim on our past, present, and future.

God is excited about the future—Satan is not! Satan is already defeated and knows how the story ends, as the Bible clearly articulates his position and fate. We simply need to break free from deception, close the doors to Satan, and appropriate the victory of Jesus in every area of our lives. Remember, deception influences us, even when we don't realize it. When you recognize the lie you've been living (a wrong way of thinking), you must repent and receive God's truth in its place. This allows us to live in wild freedom, blasting forward into the kingdom of God. We are the ones who get to display God's kingdom to the world. When Satan looks at us, he will only see Jesus.

As we engage with the process of the cross, suffering is inevitable until its transformative work is complete, taking us to a new level of surrender, intimacy and freedom. This journey, marked by both challenge and change, allows us to see not just the power but also the beauty of the cross. It serves to remove everything we were never meant to be, freeing us to become who God intended us to be. This understanding of the cross highlights its crucial role in our spiritual transformation and the profound growth it fosters in living sacrificially.

The more we allow Jesus to live through us by dying to ourselves, the less in common we have with the enemy. Hence, we will have more authority. This is the pinnacle of life in the kingdom of God. It is where we truly overcome and see victory![1]

Then I heard a triumphant voice in heaven proclaiming: "Now salvation and power are set in place, and the kingdom reign of our God and the ruling authority of his Anointed One are established. For the accuser of our brothers and sisters, who relentlessly accused them day and night before our God, has now been defeated—cast out once and for all!
Revelation 12:10, TPT

Transforming Hearts: The Power of the Kingdom for Real Change

The kingdom of God is both revival and reformation as His kingdom brings power for real change and to fix what is broken. A heart that truly returns and continues to turn to God results in an inward transformation, demonstrated in outward action, led by the Spirit and inspired by love. It's all about living out our faith by loving others in real, practical ways.

As we share our testimonies of Jesus, the grace we have received is multiplied again and again around the world to others! Love displaces hate. Generosity displaces greed. Humility displaces pride. Seeking His kingdom first displaces idols. Serving displaces selfishness. Light displaces darkness. Truth displaces lies. The kingdom displaces powers and principalities. Life swallows death. All this is "because through Christ Jesus the law of the Spirit who gives life has set you free from the law of sin and death."[2] The kingdom of God is a realm where grace and truth come together in boundless mercy and unwavering righteousness for all to flourish authentically.

Cultivating a Culture of Honour: The Ripple Effect of Kingdom Values

As we honour, we are honoured, and honour begets honour. As we are open and vulnerable, openness begets openness. As we trust, trust begets trust. As we love, love begets love. As we bless, blessing begets blessing. As we sow in the kingdom, we reap, pressed down, shaken together, and run over—divine multiplication! Indeed, sometimes people do not respond kindly, but we must keep following Christ's example. Like leaven or a tiny mustard seed, seemingly small acts of faith or kindness have a significant impact, gradually influencing and changing the spiritual and moral climate through the influence of God's kingdom's reign. This is the kingdom in action! As we consistently apply the values and principles of the kingdom, they become embedded, and restoration happens and expands as the life of the kingdom takes hold. We recognize that we first receive from God, as apart from God, we have nothing. We recognize the gift of our salvation, our total dependence on Jesus, and know that everything we have is a gift from God. As we are one with Jesus, we are never apart! Whatever we receive, we give, and it is multiplied. Generosity begets generosity in ourselves and in the receivers. We can turn a giver into a greater giver by giving to them!

> *The generous man [is a source of blessing and] shall be prosperous and enriched,*
> *And he who waters will himself be watered [reaping the generosity he has sown].*
> —*Proverbs 11:25, AMP*

Bringing Heaven to Earth: Living with a Kingdom Mindset

The kingdom of God is God's original intent for the world, seeing the unseen realm manifest in the seen realm. As we begin to see our circumstances with a kingdom mindset or kingdom consciousness, we can rule and reign in life with Jesus and live *on earth as it is in heaven*. Our new creation life allows us to bring the unseen heavenly realities into physical reality. What we receive in the spirit realm, we can translate into the natural realm. In other words, we are not waiting to escape and die to go to heaven; we are bringing heaven to earth here and now!

The Ekklesia: Plundering the Enemy's Strongholds

The ekklesia, God's people operating 24/7 in every sphere of influence, is to plunder the enemy and overtake the gates of hell. When God allows an attack (as Satan needs permission, typically based on a door we opened), it is an invitation to grow. The attack exposes an area we are to overcome, grow, rule, and reign. We must go through things to get to our destinations. When the enemy is caught, he must pay seven times in return.[3] His kingdom of darkness is quickly diminishing as we hold him accountable. This is a powerful Old Testament truth, but there is so much more. We now have full access to everything the Father has. We can receive the rewards and blessings of God. We will harvest what we plant, plus so much more!

Reaping an Abundant Harvest: Accessing God's Rewards and Blessings

We frequently concentrate and prioritize addressing generational iniquities and curses, yet they can readily be resolved. When, in fact, there are incredible generational blessings and spiritual treasures stored up in our generational lines all the way back to the promises of God for Abraham and his descendants, to Adam, the original son of God. There are incredible blessings and spiritual treasures stored up in the land as well. We get to ask God to release them to us and to our generations in God's perfect timing and for His grace to steward these blessings. We have all the incredible blessings from our new covenant through faith in Jesus. These blessings are intended for His life to flow abundantly through us. His presence brings the blessings of the kingdom realm!

As we continue to move forward, the kingdom of God displaces the kingdom of darkness! Light always displaces darkness! We know that EVERYTHING finds completion in Jesus Christ!

Materializing Solutions: Ambassadors of Heaven in Action

And because of God's unfailing purpose, this detailed plan will reign supreme through every period of time until the fulfillment of all the ages finally reaches its climax — when God makes all things new in all of heaven and earth through Jesus Christ.
Ephesians 1:10, TPT

In the episode "Death, Dominion and Decay" from Brian Orme's *Seated Above* podcast, he captures the enormity and gravity of our heavenly assignments.[1] He said one of our purposes in the body of Christ is to liberate physical creation from bondage to decay. From God's realm of delight, we are to reform the systems of physical creation, having dominion over creation or, in other words, cosmic governance. Ambassadors of heaven direct their authority (the right to rule or govern) in the direction of problems and then demand results.

We have been deputized to materialize in another world with infinite solutions. This is the kingdom of heaven. We are the solution to death and decay in the cosmos. We are to extend the resurrection life of God into creation as Jesus broke the power of death. We have been given the dominion to reign over death and time as the solution to the cosmos.

Bottom-up Transformation: Empowering Kingdom Disciple-makers

I am on the board of Transform Our World Canada, an organization on a mission to see God's presence and power meet felt needs and address systemic challenges in our nation. We aim to equip and help people connect in divine relationships, cross-pollinate, and extend His kingdom in their spheres of influence. We see this as starting at home. Societal transformation begins with family, as it is a bottom-up culture and values-based movement.

Our goal is to empower and equip kingdom disciple-makers who build the kingdom in whatever sphere God has called them to. This is not done by an elite few but by ordinary people who have a vision for transformation and discipleship and, therefore, journey with others as they transform their spheres and then release their disciples to do even greater works. This will lead to a movement that not only multiplies in number but transforms everything it touches.

The King's Triumph: From Captivity to Freedom

Then Jesus made a public spectacle of all the powers and principalities of darkness, stripping away from them every weapon and all their spiritual authority and power to accuse us. And by the power of the cross, Jesus led them around as prisoners in a procession of triumph. He was not their prisoner; they were His!
— Colossians 2:15, TPT

I pray that you will continually experience the immeasurable greatness of God's power made available to you through faith. Then your lives will be an advertisement of this immense power as it works through you! This is the

362

mighty power that was released when God raised Christ from the dead and exalted him to the place of highest honour and supreme authority in the heavenly realm!
—Ephesians 1:19-20, TPT

Releasing the Power of the Kingdom: Fulfilling the Great Commission

The power of God is very different from the power of this world, as His kingdom is not of this world. Our pursuit is not for power or anointing but of God Himself, with a deep desire to live in purity and surrender. Jesus shows us that real power is love! God's kingdom co-exists with evil on earth, as He honours free will and choice. God's kingdom is available to all. God's kingdom does not use power to conquer people or territories but to bring freedom and life to its people. God's kingdom is not geographical or nationalistic, as it transcends nations, denominations, social classes, and people groups. It exists within its citizens. His kingdom is not visible with outward signs of power but invisible and expands in surrendered and contrite hearts. His kingdom does not use force or coercion to expand like earthly kingdoms, which rise and fall. His kingdom expands slowly and humbly, eternally secure, unshakable, and forever increasing. His kingdom is already and not yet; it is now and in the future.

Kingdom Ambassadors: Channels of Divine Power and Love

His kingdom is one of love, hope, forgiveness, and grace, and stands for righteousness and justice. His kingdom is marked by self-denial and self-sacrifice, which leads to great joy and peace, not selfishness and worldly indulgences. His kingdom starts with the small and seemingly insignificant and expands by His Spirit, not by earthly power or might.

Jesus charges His disciples in Matthew 28:16-20 to go out into all the world and make disciples of all nations. This is known as the "Great Commission" and calls us to bring heaven's realities to earth. Created from heaven, the earth and its people are meant to reflect its divine origin. Through Jesus, we are kingdom ambassadors. As living gateways and a colony of heaven on earth, Jesus dispenses His life into ours, aligning and transforming our world to be *as it is in heaven*. Unlike worldly kingdoms that grip tightly to power for themselves, we are instructed to freely release the power of the kingdom we have received to others because it is for others.

"Freely you have received the power of the kingdom, so freely release it to others."
—Matthew 10:8, TPT

God's kingdom power and use of power by His citizens (ambassadors) are very different. Grace is the limitless power of God, and those in the kingdom host the presence of God. We have been given authority and the right to rule and reign as His grace works through us. When we receive the revelation of what God has already done by the blood of Jesus and enforce it, His *dynamis* power is released by faith, as faith is our victorious power that overcomes the world.[5] Kingdom citizens have access to God's *dunamis* power expressed through His anointing, as Jesus Himself works through people. In this, the Holy Spirit comes upon them in power by faith.

Cultivating the manifest presence of God brings heaven to earth to…

- Preach the Gospel
- Know and love God
- Love others
- Bless
- Endure
- Act and exert influence
- Release peace
- Live in the kingdom above our circumstances
- Experience transformation through repentance
- Walk in the grace of God
- Walk in humility, gentleness, and meekness
- Do the impossible
- Bear much fruit
- Walk in forgiveness
- Overcome sin
- Set people free
- Deliver and restore
- Rule and reign
- Overcome with explosive power
- Govern *on earth as it is in heaven*
- Shift atmospheres
- Create wealth
- Build the kingdom
- Speak life
- Miracles in hearts, lives, health, relationships, families, etc.
- Fulfill the Great Commission
- Be transformed
- Glorify God
- Fulfill our calling and destiny

For the kingdom realm of God comes with power, not simply impressive words.
—1 Corinthians 4:20, TPT

From the moment John stepped onto the scene until now, the realm of heaven's kingdom is bursting forth, and passionate people have taken hold of its power.
—Matthew 11:12, TPT

"Whoever continually humbles himself to become like this little child is the greatest one in heaven's kingdom realm."
—Matthew 18:4, TPT

Embracing God's Power: The Path of Humility, Unity, and Surrender

It is God's power that fulfills His kingdom principles. The power of God reveals the nature and character of God on earth, specifically through HUMILITY. As we live more fully from our new creation life, we let God's glory saturate us. His power is our strength, and His authority is our authority in accordance with His will and purposes. There is power in proximity to the presence of God, and this power is increased as we come together in agreement as His ekklesia. The power of His presence makes our lives an advertisement for His glory. Salvation is just the door to the kingdom. This is why the Beatitudes describe the condition of the mature heart of a son or daughter (meekness, humility, brokenness, yieldedness, and a hunger for righteousness) to receive and move in the power of the kingdom as His power is made perfect in our weakness.

You see, every child of God overcomes the world, for our faith is the victorious power that triumphs over the world. So who are the world conquerors, defeating its power? Those who believe that Jesus is the Son of God.
—1 John 5:4-5, TPT

Unleashing the Power of the Kingdom: Overcoming Satan's Schemes

We have a guaranteed and unstoppable formula to overcome Satan. It is by releasing the power of God! The kingdom provides all the solutions we need to solve our problems on earth. When we apply kingdom principles, life and victory always follow. Jesus already won the victory by His blood. As we overcome, we grow in authority over what we have overcome. This helps us to embrace our challenges, knowing God is sovereign. The kingdom empowers every person to live in the freedom of our new creation lives. As called-out ones, we are to build His kingdom within the family of God and out into all the world. As we live out the values of the kingdom, the aroma of Jesus and the nature of the kingdom are on display, which COMPELS people to want to know the King. People are longing to know this is real! Many will be drawn into the kingdom. We are to simply invite people to "come as they are," lost and broken, to encounter Jesus, regardless of their sin or current lifestyle. Remember, sinners were drawn to Jesus as they were drawn to His life. As their hearts turn to Jesus, they will become transformed trophies of His grace and love.

"The law of Moses and the revelation of the prophets have prepared you for the arrival of the kingdom announced by John. Since that time, the wonderful news of God's kingdom is being preached, and people's hearts burn with extreme passion to receive it."
—Luke 16:16, TPT

*Looking around, she replied, "I see no one, Lord." Jesus said, **"Then I certainly don't condemn you either. Go, and from now on, be free from a life of sin."***
—John 8:11, TPT

Living in Grace Consciousness: Embracing Our Union with Jesus

When people experience His kingdom, presence, goodness, and power, they will want to share it with the world. The law condemns and punishes, but Jesus fulfilled the law. Grace does not condemn or punish. Jesus did not condemn the woman caught in adultery in John 8:11. Rather, He forgave her and said, "Go, and from now on, be free from a life of sin." The law would have stoned her to death, but Jesus came with grace. The law kills because no one can keep it, and it condemns to eternal death, but the spirit gives life because it brings grace by faith. Grace is God's goodness. It's love in action that frees and transforms from the inside out. Because of God's grace, mercy triumphs over judgment. We don't need to be holy and pure to approach God; we just need a heart that wants more of Him; He draws us closer. His holiness invites us to transform into His likeness, and in this divine encounter, by His great grace, God makes us holy and pure. Sin consciousness results in the illusion of separateness, whereas grace consciousness draws us in. Living in awareness of our life union with Jesus, knowing there is no condemnation for those in Christ Jesus, we are free!

Citizens of the Kingdom: Embracing Our Identity as Gateways of Glory

The kingdom of God is our new reality as kingdom citizens. We are gateways or doors for the King of Glory to come through. And ultimately, we are members of God's family. This book and my life are testaments to this truth! By removing ourselves from the throne of our own lives and submitting all things to Christ, God can do incredible, beyond-your-imagination, miraculous things, bringing heaven to earth.

You are the Lord who reigns over your never-ending kingdom through all the ages of time and eternity! You are faithful to fulfill every promise you've made. You manifest yourself as kindness in all you do.
— Psalm 145:13, TPT

Living Sacrifices: Embracing Our Role in God's Inheritance

As we offer ourselves as living sacrifices who are fully His, we are offering ourselves as the inheritance of God to be progressively conformed into the image of Jesus. When we focus on God getting His inheritance, our inheritance will come supernaturally. These are the hallmarks of sonship and the family of God seeking His kingdom first.

The inheritance of Jesus gives us a stake in the kingdom of God! We share in Jesus's sufferings and His victories over sin and death. We are heirs of the kingdom of God, adopted into His family, and are responsible to live out the values, principles, and mission of His kingdom on earth.

Our inheritance is an abundant life in an eternal kingdom, now, *as in heaven*, and future glory. This is mind-boggling. As Jesus is in heaven and on His throne, so are we on earth NOW as partakers of His divine nature, as we are co-heirs with Jesus. By faith, we also move in the realm of signs, wonders, and miracles to fulfill the will of Jesus.

Seeking His kingdom is impossible without first receiving "the ultimate key" to the kingdom—Jesus! As we discover our kingdom purpose, we can move into our God-given purpose wherever He has planted us. We do so by learning the principles of the kingdom and partnering with God and His body to bring kingdom solutions to the earth, which leads the way to producing eternal kingdom fruit. Let's embrace kingdom realities and live out the kingdom *on earth as it is in heaven*!

Expanding Channels: Partnering with God to Release Heaven's Blessings

These are all keys to the kingdom that create harmony between heaven and earth. What you have done to bless, love, and serve others, God will do for you. As we practice partnering with God, we become a larger and larger channel of the kingdom of heaven to be released into the world. In this process, we also accumulate heavenly treasures that can never be stolen! The enemy cannot stop, counteract, or nullify a kingdom principle because these principles are the way God created the earth to operate. The ONLY way we can lose is if we QUIT! We are accumulating eternal treasures, kingdom wealth that endures forever!

1. Liz Wright, "Encountering God, A Higher Altitude," God.tv, accessed February 25, 2024, https://www.god.tv/video/w1_eglw24_8-mov/zype.
2. Romans 8:2.
3. Proverbs 6:31.
4. Brian Orme, "Seated Above: Death, Dominion and Decay," *Listen Notes*, accessed October 14, 2023, https://tinyurl.com/2j662nhr.
5. "G1411: Dynamis," *Blue Letter Bible*, accessed October 14, 2023, https://www.blueletterbible.org/lexicon/g1411/niv/mgnt/0-1/.

ACTION STEPS FOR ADVANCING THE KINGDOM UNTIL KING JESUS RETURNS

1. Choose to make decisions based on love, not fear. This ensures we are aligned with the Holy Spirit when making choices about the future. Anxiety is a terrible leader, but perfect love casts out fear. When you feel anxious or afraid, take the time to step back into God's peace and then choose to walk forward with Him.

2. Actively seek inner and outer peace. When you sin, confess, repent, and receive God's forgiveness as soon as possible! As much as you can, make peace with others. Do not stir up ungodly strife or participate in petty disagreements. (This doesn't mean you will not have to confront evil when necessary. Sometimes, we must "fight for peace," as God's peace cannot rest where evil, abuse, or sin is permitted.)

3. Choose to show humility and honour others, even when it is difficult. All men are made in God's image, even if they are not walking according to His ways or have outrightly rejected Him. Sarcasm, bitterness, cynicism, meanness, cruelty, making fun of others, etc., have no place in the kingdom.

4. Intentionally sow seeds of faith. To reap a good harvest, we must sow good seeds physically, emotionally, and spiritually. This includes what we carry in our hearts. Let God pour into us so that we can pour out to others.

5. Choose to forgive others quickly and show mercy. Do you want the same treatment from God and others? It starts with you.

6. Embrace a lifestyle of Sabbath rest. Approaching work from a place of rest demonstrates our dependence on God rather than drawing from a place of self-reliance (which is a form of idolatry and symptomatic of the orphan spirit). In the same vein, choosing to honour the Sabbath is a physical act of trusting God to provide for us when we honour His commands.

7. Choose to suffer well, unto life (not death). We can choose to be a people who know how to suffer. When you lose your life, you will find it. Allow God into your suffering like a refiner's fire, giving the sacrifice of praise in the process. Give Him permission to use your suffering to make you more like Jesus. Suffering has the power to make you a victor and literally mold you into Christ's image. However, if we do not allow God to use our suffering, we give the enemy an open door to plant seeds of depression, self-pity, shame, and victimization in our lives. Once these seeds are planted, they can be difficult to uproot.

⟨8⟩ Use our God-given authority as co-rulers with Christ over sin, disease, and lack. God rules, but He chose to reign on earth through His people. That includes casting out demons, healing the sick, and seeing other incredible miracles that will lead many into the kingdom. We are not to tolerate evil. We are to tell the enemy what he cannot do by declaring things like: *Sickness and disease cannot come into my house; cancer cannot come into my house; death cannot come to my house; I will not be stolen from; I say no to chaos in my home or business; I determine the atmosphere and declare the atmosphere of righteousness; peace and joy are in my home and business; I am not subject to worldwide depression or recession, etc.*

⟨9⟩ Stay engaged in a Christ-centred community. Isolation leaves us vulnerable to attacks of the enemy. We need to surround ourselves with trustworthy believers who help us stay on the straight and narrow, correct us when we mess up, encourage us to go "higher up," and help us discern God's voice.

⟨10⟩ Remember to speak words of life. Our words have real power in the natural and in the spirit. Don't fool yourself into thinking your words don't matter. If you want God's blessing, speak it out over your life and the lives of those around you. There is no room for death-words in the kingdom.

⟨11⟩ Remember that we begin as stewards of everything He places in our hands. As mature sons and daughters, we are co-heirs with Christ. Live life without the secular/sacred divide. Do everything unto God's glory. A disciplined life of tithing and radical generosity paves the way for generating kingdom wealth. We give so we can give even more!

⟨12⟩ Be firmly rooted in the Word of God. Let's read the Bible daily. Ideally, be in the Word for a significant portion of time. I challenge you to gradually build up your daily reading of the Word, which is an act of worship. Remember, work is also worship as done unto the Lord. Just one month of worship as a lifestyle will drastically change your life.

⟨13⟩ Give thanks without ceasing, no matter your circumstance. This is the key to joy, healed brains, and transformed emotions. In other words, a kingdom mindset (the mind of Christ) begins and ends with praise and thanksgiving.

⟨14⟩ Make a point to remember everything God has done in our lives and share these testimonies often, especially with our children.

⟨15⟩ Be the ekklesia on earth with the promise of the manifest presence of Jesus! We are the family of God who has the privilege of discipling the nation and legislating as the government of God on earth.

Epilogue

"So above all, constantly seek God's kingdom and His righteousness, then all these less important things will be given to you abundantly."
Matthew 6:33, TPT

Seeds of Redemption: Turning Tragedy into Testimony

Like the lifecycle of a seed, death precedes life. At some point, the old ceases to exist. Jesus was a single seed before His death. Jesus's death resulted in the greatest victory of all time for those who repent, believe, and receive His new creation life. His life and Spirit have been multiplied into His entire body of believers through the Holy Spirit. Resurrection life has saved us from sin and death. This is our inheritance of eternal life in Christ. By God's grace, my daughter Abbe's death was not in vain.

Life from Death: The Seed and His Resurrection Power

In the midst of extreme tragedy and brokenness, the thought of Bryn and me coming together to start a ministry was impossible, but by the grace of God, it was possible. God opened door after door, and soon, we were provided with many opportunities to share our stories, which the Holy Spirit was using to breathe hope into hopeless situations. I have discovered that God is the source of all hope. He is our redeemer and the guarantee of our eternal destiny. Our hope is not based on blind optimism, but on the futuristic certainty of the promises of God.

As mentioned previously, on May 23, 2022, four years to the day of Abbe's murder, Bryn and I launched M46 Ministries (founded upon Malachi 4:6 and Isaiah 61) with the release of Bryn's book, *Dying to Live*. Bryn's book testifies to the promise of God in John 12:24 of Abbe's death, producing many seeds, her glorious new creation life, and Bryn's process of being conformed to the image of Jesus. I released my first book, *More Than Gold*, on March 17, 2023, which would have been Abbe's 26th birthday. Though Abbe's life will be missed for a short while on this side of eternity, God is using her tragic loss to bring new life to the Elliott family and so many more.

Abbe is safely home with her Father in heaven. My Heavenly Father gave me a gift of the revelation of Abbe in heaven after she passed, which has shaped my life in the revelation of the goodness of God and hunger for the heavenly realities of His kingdom. Her life continues to bear much fruit through the ongoing testimony of our family. Nothing wasted. Nothing ultimately lost because He is a redeemer. This is His kingdom. What the enemy intended for evil, God is now using for good through us.[1]

Today, we are on a mission to share the gospel of the kingdom and draw fathers and children to the heart of the Father through books, blogs, podcasts, speaking engagements, and various social media platforms. Our lives are ongoing testimonies of God working all things together for the good of those who love Him.[2]

Majestic Creator, Majestic Creation: Reflecting on God's Handiwork

Yahweh claims the world as His. Everything and everyone belong to Him!
—Psalm 24:1, TPT

Creation reveals the Creator and the Creator is manifested within creation; the universe and all it encompasses reflect the attributes and divinity of God. As all people are made in the image of God, everything beautiful and lovely, from the artwork of an artist and the verses of a poet to a musical composition, a scientist making a discovery, a doctor treating a patient, a pastor teaching the word of God, a janitor cleaning a school, an architecturally significant building, a herbalist caring for an ailment, a chef's culinary masterpieces, a businessman creating a new product or service, a child's coloring, a nurse caring for the hurting, a missionary living in the slums with the poor, the innovative technologies of an engineer, the tender care of a mother for her children, and a father teaching his son to play baseball, mirrors the beauty of God. Each beautiful thing unveils a unique aspect of the King of the universe. Consider Jesus, a carpenter whose work with His hands was done unto the Lord. Everything is holy and sacred to God, as the gifts and talents He has given us serve to glorify and reveal Him. Let's never forget that everything good is a gift from God, and He is revealed in what is good.

However, we can too easily become familiar with our surroundings and with our God! The goodness of God declares His glory! Consider these astounding facts about just how awesome our God really is…

The Infinite Majesty: Exploring God's Immeasurable Greatness in the Cosmos

In the beginning, God created the heavens and the earth. Our universe is over 90 billion light-years long. The speed of light is 186,282 miles per second, equivalent to traveling 7.5 times around the earth every second. It takes light just over eight minutes to travel 93 million miles from the sun to the earth, whereas it would take a jet over 21 years to make that same trip. To travel across the universe, you would need to travel at light speed for over 90 billion years, yet God measures the universe *by the span of His hand!*

The heavens cannot contain God. He cannot be contained in the largest space imaginable, yet *we are a house of God!* The heavens are the work of His fingers, making the creation of solar systems and galaxies comparable to the work of a potter.

Behold, like the clay in the potter's hand, so are you in My hand, house of Israel.
—Jeremiah 18:6b

369

Our earth seems big, but did you know:

- More than one million earths would fit into our sun;
- More than five billion of our suns would fit into some of the largest stars in our universe. Quasars are celestial objects found in some galaxies, powered by black holes. They are billions of times brighter than our sun, which is 400,000 times brighter than a standard incandescent floodlight; this offers incredible insight into the infinite brightness or glory of our Creator.
- Our solar system revolves around the sun, a tiny star, and is one of 100-300+ billion stars in our Milky Way Galaxy;
- In total, there are 100-300+ billion galaxies in our universe, meaning there are 1 to 6 x 10(22), which is 1 to 6 septillion stars suspended in the sky.[3]
- It takes the earth between 225-250 million years to complete one full orbit around the center of our Milky Way galaxy, known as one galactic year.

Counting the Grains of Sand: Reflecting on God's Infinite Love

For context, if you hold a dime in your fingers and stretch out your arm towards the sky, that one dime blocks more than 15 million stars from your view.

How precious also are Your thoughts for me, God! How vast is the sum of them! Were I to count them, they would outnumber the sand. When I awake, I am still with You.
Psalm 139:17-18, NASB

The Bible says God's thoughts for us are more than the grains of sand on earth. There are roughly 60,000 grains of sand in just one five-gallon bucket. Think of how many grains of sand there are on a small beach, not to mention the seemingly countless grains of sand across all the shores and deserts of the earth! Yet, there are more stars in the universe than grains of sand on the seashore. So, every time you look to the night sky and see the infinite array of stars twinkling, these number the wonderful thoughts of God towards you.

Beyond Measure: Contemplating God's Infinite Wisdom in the Cosmos

It is remarkable to think of all this movement and rotation, yet we enjoy an incredibly stable and consistent existence of life here on earth and across the entire universe. Much more remarkable than any of the above figures is the fine-tuning of the universe or the unfathomable precision of physical constants and conditions required for our universe and life to exist.

In the book *Jesus Among Secular Gods*, Vince Vitale so poignantly states:

> Right now, I am standing on a rock that is rotating at one thousand miles an hour and flying around the sun at sixty-seven thousand miles an hour, as part of a galaxy that is

hurling itself over a million miles an hour through a universe with laws so orderly that human life exists.[4]

There is an array of constants, such as the gravitational constant or the ratio of electromagnetic force to gravity (which are 1:10(37) and 1:10(40) respectively). To try and grasp these incredible numbers, picture a ruler extending across our entire solar system, measuring a vast expanse of 27,000 light-years. Now, consider that adjusting this ruler by a mere one inch represents a precision ratio of 1 in 10 to the power of 40.[5] While this fact is mind-boggling, it's worth noting that other constants exist with even greater levels of precision.

Marvels of Creation: Exploring the Miracles Within the Human Body

Then there are the orderly laws of the universe, such as the laws of thermodynamics, physics, gravity, biogenesis, etc. Within the human body alone, there are so many miracles to consider, including the design of the human eye, which contains ~1,000,000 optic nerves per eye connecting to the brain. Each eye contains ~130 million light-sensitive rods and cones that meticulously convert light to chemical impulses. Yet, it is with awe-inspiring precision that we possess the innate software to decipher and extract the extraordinary gift of vision.

We are truly living miracles of creation. Our bodies have an astounding network of more than 40 billion blood vessels. If you connected all the blood vessels (arteries, capillaries, and veins) in one human body into one continuous line, it would extend ~60,000 miles or 2.5 laps around the earth.

One square inch of human skin has "65 hairs - 9,500,000 cells - 95 to 100 sebaceous (oil) glands - 19 yards (17 meters) of blood vessels - 650 sweat glands - 78 yards (70 meters) of nerves - 78 sensory apparatuses for heat - 19,500 sensory cells at the ends of nerve fibers - 1,300 nerve endings to record pain - 160 to 165 pressure apparatuses for the perception of tactile stimuli - 13 sensory apparatuses for cold."[6]

The human body is made up of 37.2 *trillion* cells.[7]

The human mind has 60,000 thoughts a day, which are enabled by more than 100 *billion* neurons.[8]

The human nose's 1,000 olfactory receptors recognize 50,000 smells.[9]

One human has roughly 30 trillion red blood cells that make up 1.6 gallons of blood, which flow through 42 billion blood vessels.[10] If all the blood vessels (arteries, capillaries, and veins) in one human body were connected into one continuous line, it would reach 100,000 km or 60,000 miles or 2.5 times around the earth.

Our hearts beat roughly 155,000 times a day (that's over 2,000 gallons of blood).[11]

Our skin secretes up to 10 liters of sweat a day to regulate our temperature.[12]

After three months, an unborn child has fingerprints, their own unique barcode differentiating them from every other human ever born.[13]

We have a DNA code of instructions consisting of more than three billion characters; this instruction set is within each of the 40+ trillion cells in our body, all working together as one unit using chemical and electrical signals for mass collaboration. Our DNA is supercoiled within our cells; however, if you stretched out the DNA in one cell, it would reach approximately two meters long. If you were to stretch out all of the DNA in your cells, it would be about twice the diameter of the solar system or to the moon and back 178,000 times — well over 10 billion miles.[14]

The Astonishing Human: Delving into the Depths of Our Divine Design

Perhaps the greatest miracle of all is that one cell consists of approximately 100 trillion atoms and does not originate from DNA. Rather, the cell was created separately and must work with other cells to build the body plan, not to mention the wild complexity of cell division (we begin by the division of one cell with the exact genetic instruction to create an entire person) and intercellular communication, the miraculous functioning of our immune system, the intricacy of the wiring of our brains and the billions of electrical signals simultaneously pulsing through our bodies. The existence of our minds (which are separate from the brain), plus our wills and emotions, reveals that we are a truly masterful creation. Add these physiological miracles to the mystery of being created in the image of God as a triune multidimensional being (body, soul, and spirit) living in union with Jesus, and the wonder only increases! We are fearfully and wonderfully made!

Marvels of Creation: Exploring the Beauty and Wonder of God's Handiwork

Every living thing and all of creation declares His glory and goodness. All of creation reveals His nature as God wants to show people who He is!

I am in awe of so many of His wonders, like:

- A smiling baby who showcases the goodness, warmth, and joy of our Creator;
- The miracle of eyesight with the depth of vision and colours to enjoy the beauty of His creation;
- Our ability to smell flowers and fragrances or our favourite baked goods and fresh mountain air that makes life so enjoyable;
- The unique and wonderful sounds of all the various birds with their colourful designs that make every day more special;
- Breathtaking sunrises and sunsets, like a giant painting that showcases God's beauty across the sky;
- Awe-inspiring cloud formations and storm patterns that remind us of the power of our Creator;
- The magnificence of mountains that reflect the magnificence of God;

- The expanse of the oceans, full of mystery and adventure just like the heavens;
- The unique and spectacular world that exists beneath the waters (most of which still awaits discovery);
- The vast array of flowers and trees, each one a gift of beauty;
- The countless creatures, big and small, on the land and in the waters, which all play a specific part in the world;
- The comfort of family and friends, a true reflection of the love of our heavenly Father;
- The ability to create art and discover God in the sciences within an orderly universe, which testifies to the divine spark of creativity within each of us;
- The intricacy of each snowflake, a one-of-a-kind creation, demonstrating God's attention to every detail of creation;
- Masterfully constructed and interdependent ecosystems that attest to the wisdom of God;
- The incredible workings of God that enable life to even exist on this tiny little planet called earth;
- The unfathomable precision of the universe which generates awe and wonder;
- The joy of a pet greeting you at the front door, another generous gift from our joyful Heavenly Father;
- The infinite possibilities held within each and every day, an opportunity to make the world a better place wherever God has placed you.

All of this is possible *because God is good!* All of this declares His goodness and glory! It is impossible to exaggerate His goodness! Can you even imagine what a new heaven and a new earth, our eternal home, will be like? His glory and His limitless attributes will be on full display! All of His marvellous creation is created by love and for love. His goodness is inexpressible. His greatness is incomprehensible. His power is without comparison. His presence is inescapable. His love is indescribable. Jesus's victory is absolute.

Kingdom Dawning: Unveiling the Glory of God in Dark Times

Arise, shine; for your light has come, And the glory of the Lord has risen upon you. For behold, darkness will cover the earth And deep darkness the peoples; But the Lord will rise upon you And His glory will appear upon you. Nations will come to your light, And kings to the brightness of your rising.
—Isaiah 60:1-3, NASB

Hundreds of years before Jesus, Isaiah prophesied that the kingdom would come in times of incredible darkness, so take great hope! Our light shines the brightest in the most difficult season, which will cause the nations to be drawn to our brightness for the glory of God. Jesus came at a very dark time in human history to declare His kingdom has come!

Remember, the kingdom is the wheat that continues to grow among the weeds. Times of intense darkness serve to awaken His ekklesia to arise as God's legislative assembly on earth. Jesus said to invade the darkness and that the gates of *hades* would not prevail![15] Even when the church as we know it may decrease, we can always be sure the kingdom within His body is expanding as it has since Jesus's grand announcement 2,000 years ago— the kingdom of God is at hand! It is no longer dark where your light shines.

Like Randy Alcorn said (and we previously quoted), "For Christians, this present life is the closest they will come to Hell. For unbelievers, it is the closest they will come to Heaven."[16] So, on the cusp of the great harvest of souls, let's bring heaven to earth and share the gospel of the kingdom with the world! As Isaiah prophesied, "Nations will come to your light," so let your light shine brightly![17]

> ***"Let it shine brightly before others, so that your commendable works will shine as light upon them, and then they will give their praise to your Father in heaven."***
> *—Matthew 5:16, TPT*

> ***"And this Light never fails to shine through darkness— Light that darkness could not overcome!"***
> *—John 1:5, TPT*

The Eternal Kingdom: Abundant Life under the Reign of King Jesus

At some point, Jesus will return to rule and reign as our King on earth. But today, we can enjoy life in His spiritual kingdom, *on earth as it is in heaven*. He was, He is, and He will be a King of unprecedented, unmatched, and unlimited power and authority. Jesus, our King, has unlimited resources. His kingdom is unshakable and eternal. It is always increasing and without end.

King Jesus unconditionally and perfectly loves His subjects. He is a King who is humble and meek. His kingdom is built on honour. It is a kingdom of family and a kingdom of heavenly relationships in unity and oneness. This is a kingdom where everyone flourishes, lives abundantly, and is governed and defined by love. In this kingdom of perfect righteousness and justice, perfect peace, joy, fun, and celebration all exist all the time.

We do not have to imagine a kingdom of hope, destiny, and legacy. We get to live in one, *now* and into eternity, as citizens of heaven. The kingdom is a place bursting with fruitfulness, life, and light. Our King is responsible for providing for us and protecting us. He is glorified by our fruitfulness. Those in the kingdom share an inheritance with the King as adopted sons and daughters of God. And as we wait for our King's physical return, we are privileged to serve as His ambassadors and stewards.

> *For the earth will be filled With the knowledge of the glory of the Lord, As the waters cover the sea.*
> *— Habakkuk 2:14, NASB*

Anticipating the Kingdom: Living in Hope and Expectation

"The Spirit of the Lord is upon me, and He has anointed me to be hope for the poor, healing for the brokenhearted, and new eyes for the blind, and to preach to prisoners, 'You are set free!' I have come to share the message of Jubilee, for the time of God's great acceptance has begun."
—Luke 4:18-19, TPT

As kingdom heirs, it is His sons and daughters who will bring the kingdom, which results in breakthrough, healing, deliverance, freedom, provision, life, and reformation on earth. One of the greatest kingdom investments is a father's investment in sons and daughters who become fathers and mothers, as this is how the kingdom of God is expanded through a family of heirs. As we saw with Jesus, He produced sons who became fathers who produced sons, and now there are sons and daughters throughout the world.

Embracing the Kingdom Mandate: Sons and Daughters of the King

The time is now to enter the battle and run forward in the spirit of victory! Now is the time to take our place in the kingdom and press through the darkness and confusion in the world to bring people life and freedom. Our breakthroughs and victories become His testimony for His glory. We are in a time of testing and learning, which will impact our eternity and our final rewards. We are preparing for what is to come. Jesus has restored our partnership with the Father to take dominion and steward the earth.

We have a role to play as His dominion agents on earth and beyond! We are representing Jesus on earth so that His kingdom can come *on earth as it is in heaven*. Another world, the kingdom of heaven, is infiltrating the earth through us *now* as we fulfill God's divine plan and design for all of humanity.

The Ultimate Triumph: Reigning with King Jesus in the Eternal Kingdom

Then the seventh angel sounded his trumpet, and a loud voice broke forth in heaven, saying: "The kingdom of the world has become the kingdom of our God and of His Anointed One! He will reign supreme for an eternity of eternities!"
—Revelation 11:15, TPT

The seventh trumpet will sound at the return of Jesus when He arrives as the conquering King. This day will be great or terrible, depending on which side you are on. Ultimately, the armies of heaven will prevail and bring God's kingdom of peace to the earth. King Jesus will rule from the capital city of Jerusalem, the kingdom of God will reign over all the earth, and the kingdoms of this world will be no more. The wicked will be removed, and the meek shall inherit the earth.

Then in a vision I saw a new heaven and a new earth. The first heaven and earth had passed away, and the sea no longer existed. I saw the Holy City, the New Jerusalem, descending out of the heavenly realm from the presence of God, like a pleasing bride that had been prepared for her husband, adorned for her wedding.
—Revelation 21:1-2, TPT

Final Thoughts: Embracing the Kingdom Reality

"So don't ever be afraid, dearest friends! Your loving Father joyously gives you his kingdom with all its promises!"
Luke 12:32, TPT

I have been corrected, convicted, challenged, awakened, and transformed while writing this book. The process with the Lord was so profound and intimate that I grieved when this book was finished as it was a labour of love. My hope is that, as you read, the Holy Spirit does the same for you. Through this journey, I've come to realize that everything is by God's grace, and the Gospel stands as the greatest expression of love. From this place of love, Jesus's new command to love others as we love ourselves becomes the focal point and expression of our faith.

Embracing Our Identity: Chosen, Loved, and Destined for Holiness

The kingdom of God is not a distant utopia but a transformative reality meant to be lived out NOW! Before the creation of the world, we were chosen to be holy and blameless in His sight. In love, He predestined us for adoption to sonship through Jesus! Our eternal position is one of holiness, which God is currently working out in our lives while we are on earth. Sonship is the path to destiny. Before we were knit together in our mother's womb, God knew us, had a plan for our lives, and has good works prepared for us. At His appointed time, we were born from the heavenly realm into the earthly realm on a divine assignment to establish His kingdom on earth. Please slow down and take a moment to absorb these incredible truths: God loves the way He made you. You are a magnificent one-of-a-kind masterpiece, fully known, deeply cherished, immensely valued, and uniquely essential on this earth by God's loving design.

Everyone can benefit from kingdom principles, but as believers, when we live by these principles (like love, honour, generosity, and forgiveness), He empowers us to do more than we could ever imagine. Whatever is born of God overcomes the world. This empowerment brings blessings, strengthens our bond with Him, and shines brightly to others, showing them God's kingdom in action and all for His glory.

Gateways of Glory: Bringing Heaven to Earth

As God is love and delights in showing mercy, He made THE way that by faith through grace alone, we have been born again into His eternal, unshakable kingdom. The kingdom of God on earth is established through the finished work of Christ and expanded through God's family as co-heirs with Christ. We are no longer of this world but now belong to a holy nation, a nation from above, one kingdom nation. We have been gifted with words from heaven, the Word of God, empowering us to live by heaven's principles *on earth as it is in heaven.*

We are seated with Christ in heavenly places, meaning our spirits are already in heaven, and, as living gates, we get to bring heaven to earth as the King of Glory comes through us. Where the King of Glory is, so is His kingdom! By the power of the Holy Spirit, we are transformed by the renewing of our mind as we live a lifestyle of repentance, changing the way we think to become heavenly-minded, experiencing a totally new kingdom reality. Remember, the kingdom of God is at hand! The kingdom of God is an others-focused kingdom based on serving, blessing, and faithfulness, with its principles meant to be lived out. Our lives become the evidence of transformed hearts that glorify God in our families, work, communities, and those who cross our path in need.

Fear of the Lord: Awe, Wisdom, and Perspective

Living in the fear of the Lord means having awe, reverence, and adoration for God and His Word. It involves loving what God loves and hating what God hates. This fear is the starting point of wisdom, acknowledging God as the almighty sovereign Creator of the universe. When we see God with awe and wonder, we gain heaven's perspective. This fear also helps us see ourselves rightly, fostering humility, childlikeness, and complete dependence on God.

Blessed and Joyful: Embracing the Beatitudes

The Beatitudes reveal the heart of God's mature children, lives marked by blessedness and joy, characterized by humility, gentleness, patience, and awareness of one's need for God, and a repentant heart. Living by the Beatitudes is the path to true blessing, joy, and fulfillment, reflecting the maturity of those who fully embrace their identity as heirs in God's kingdom. The expansion of His kingdom is propelled by mature sons and daughters who embody these virtues and reproduce them in others, empowered by the Holy Spirit. As followers of Jesus, we are promised persecution. When we are persecuted for the sake of righteousness, we will be blessed and receive eternal rewards.

The Beatitudes convey a simple truth: finding the true treasure of heaven allows us to rejoice even in life's toughest moments. The enduring presence of God's Spirit and the reality of His eternal kingdom outweigh any temporary challenges.

Kingdom Transformation: Dying to Self and Living in Christ

Consider suffering the "grace path" to the heart position of the Beatitudes and holiness. Jesus opens the door to the kingdom and we enter into His kingdom through the cross. This is a process of dying to self so that it is no longer we who live but Christ who lives in and thorough us. If we suffer well, it has the power to turn our world upside down, allowing the kingdom to explode in and through us. It is grace that changes us, and all change involves suffering. We are to live for God and not for ourselves. In this process, we become a light to the world as we take up our cross and follow Jesus. Let your light shine. We are like mirrors, brightly reflecting the glory of Lord Jesus! It is no longer dark where His light shines.

We can all draw close to him with the veil removed from our faces. And with no veil we all become like mirrors who brightly reflect the glory of the Lord Jesus. We are being transfigured into his very image as we move from one brighter level of glory to another. And this glorious transfiguration comes from the Lord, who is the Spirit.
— 2 Corinthians 3:18, TPT

Remember: Jesus opens the door to the kingdom, and we enter through the cross. Sacrifice requires suffering in the beginning, which lessens as love is formed within. As we live sacrificially, receiving from God and pouring out our lives to others, the kingdom expands.

As ambassadors of His kingdom and followers of Jesus, we are called to deny ourselves and take up our cross. There is suffering in the process of dying. In the fire or hardships, impurities rise to the surface and are exposed. As we own what is revealed and repent to align our thinking with heaven, they are removed, and we are transformed. The fire precedes promotion as God prepares us for increase. This is the process of character formation to be able to steward the anointing of God. The more dead we are to the world and worldly concerns, the lesser the suffering becomes as the reality of heaven becomes more vivid.

When Jesus is our Lord, Satan's attacks are used to propel us towards our destinies. All things work together for our good, with the highest aim being to mold us into His image, often involving suffering, not necessarily for our comfort or desires. If we don't address our challenges now, including caring for our heart, we will deal with them later.

Surrendered Hearts: Embracing the Way of the Cross as the Pathway to the Impossible

Our lives are to mirror His crucifixion, a life of self-sacrifice, humility, and letting go of our desires. It is from this surrendered heart position that His resurrection power flows. By His grace, as we yield to God, we can willingly pay the price to overcome, not holding onto our lives, even unto death. As Jesus said in John 15:13, "**Greater love has no one than this: to lay down one's life for one's friends.**" In the same spirit, we demonstrate our love for God by surrendering our lives to His will, embodying this profound love through our actions. This is agape, the sacrificial love Jesus demonstrated as our model. Submission is holy and beautiful. It is to place our desires beneath the desires of Jesus and HIS commands, making Him Lord. Paradoxically, giving our lives away leads to abundant life and freedom as we become dispensers of the life of Jesus. Regardless of earthly challenges, we can rest assured, knowing that our future is glorious, as the kingdom of God is glorious!

God has not called us to do what seems possible, reasonable or normally attainable; He has called us to do the impossible. He wants us to stretch beyond our ability, our faith and

our capacity to reason. He wants us to do more than we could ever imagine or dream. If you are reading this and think that your call is attainable, it's time for an upgrade. We are not supposed to be doing what is possible. We're supposed to be doing what is impossible and outrageous. To accomplish our calling, we must put our hand in the hand of God, learning to be completely dependent on the Holy Spirit for everything.
—Graham Cooke[18]

The Book of Life: Fulfilling Your Divine Assignment

As believers, we're assured of our heavenly destination. However, our lives will be judged not only for our actions but also for fulfilling our God-given purpose and stewarding His call on our lives, including our motives and deeds. Each of us has a book of life written by God with good works prepared for us. Will we live according to our desires or align with God's plan? Will we be faithful to steward what He has given us, no matter how large or how small it may appear? Did we learn to love? Simple faithfulness to our call is all that's required, whether you are called to be a mom, a pastor, a fireman, a chef, a community leader, a world leader, or a CEO. Our God-designed path brings the greatest fulfillment and eternal impact as intended by Him. This is success, plain and simple! (This also eliminates any and all competition and comparison between members of the body because everyone is needed and secure in living out their God-ordained role on earth.) The kingdom of God is an others-focused kingdom based on serving, blessing, and faithfulness, with its principles meant to be lived out. Lives become the evidence of a transformed heart that glorify God in their families, work, communities, and those in need who cross their path.

One Chance, Eternal Consequences: Seizing the Moment for Heavenly Rewards

Ultimately, we'll all stand before Jesus on the judgment seat. This single chance on earth determines our eternal rewards or not. It's the only opportunity to earn rewards for eternity. This determines how we'll spend eternity. Imagine if how we lived just one hour would determine how we would spend our entire life on earth. There is no question we would be totally present and live fully for God and His kingdom! In view of eternity, the returns are infinitely greater. Let's be heavenly-minded and live with an eternal perspective—striving for life AS IN HEAVEN, divinely empowered by grace! An eternal heavenly perspective helps us get through anything in life because we see the horizon of hope, knowing God is always with us.

Acknowledging that everything originates from and belongs to God, we become stewards—entrusted with our lives and resources to join His body to make *earth as it is in heaven*. We must never forget that God owes us nothing; we are grateful recipients of His continual goodness, mercy, and grace.

Let's aim for heaven, practice the kingdom lifestyle with Jesus as our friend and King, and demonstrate the kingdom everywhere and always! The principles of the kingdom work for everyone as they are the way God created the universe to work, but only the power of the Holy Spirit will change the world as the kingdom of God is the presence of the King! As we honour and live out His principles, His power is released. The transformation and the resulting actions of each person create a ripple effect that contributes to the community's collective growth and further expands the kingdom.

Proclaiming the Kingdom Gospel: Bringing Healing and Restoration to the Nations

As we proclaim the kingdom gospel that the good news is here and now we take action, and by faith, witness displays of power that reveal the kingdom and honour the King. This gospel of wholeness is destined for every corner of the globe to bring healing and restoration to people, families, and nations. As members of God's family, we get to live out God's principles and trust Him for the impossible as risk becomes an adventure of obedience, faith, and dependence. Not by power, nor by might, but by His Spirit! Enjoy the journey and embrace this grand adventure!

Jesus is the ultimate K5 Leader making K5, the leadership of Jesus, as demonstrated by the King of the kingdom. As the body of Christ, let's embrace the journey to maturity and the call to K5 Spirit-led grace-empowered leadership to advance His kingdom! This is what He died to give us as co-heirs with Christ. This is the gospel of the kingdom of our God and of our Lord Jesus Christ!

> My identity is royalty. My assignment is servanthood. My life source is intimacy with God. Before God, I'm intimate. Before people, I'm a servant. Before the powers of hell, I'm a ruler, with no tolerance for their influence.
>
> Bill Johnson[19]

In this new move of God, marked by Spirit-led believers and God's continual empowerment, we are experiencing a profound shift a sentiment shared by our prayer teams and believers globally. When the enemy looks at us, he sees Jesus! This is the Gospel. We are united with Christ and seated with Him in heavenly places. Our lives are hidden in Christ, in God! This is life in God's kingdom! It's a life of ruling and reigning in His grace, bringing heaven's reality to earth. This is for everyone—NOW!

Finishing Strong: The Eternal Impact of a Life Devoted to God

At age 46, I finally gave God my full "yes" and continue to do so each day. Now, at 53, I feel like my life and adventure in His kingdom are just getting started. No matter your age, I pray that you feel the same. I pray for the grace for all of us to continually seek first His Kingdom and His righteousness, to seek His presence, to live by His kingdom principles, and to make Jesus the king in every area of our lives, family, community, and beyond! We have work to do in the kingdom and all of eternity to see it through! In His kingdom, it's not how we begin our journey; it's how we ultimately finish that truly matters. Let's ask daily for a fresh baptism of the Holy Spirit, to baptize us in His love, His fire, and in the Spirit of the fear of the Lord to be all that He created us to be so that, by His great grace, we can complete the good works He prepared for us in advance! We get to participate in God's sovereign plan! His kingdom reigns supreme!

> *His destiny-plan for the earth stands sure. His forever-plan remains in place and will never fail.*
> *—Psalm 33:10, TPT*

The kingdom of heaven is within… let it flow out into the world!

Yours is the kingdom! Yours is the power! Yours is the glory! Forever and ever. Amen!

God is good! Shalom!

Bryan Elliott

1. Genesis 50:10.
2. Romans 8:28.
3. A septillion is a one followed by 22 zeros.
4. Vince Vitale. *Jesus Among Secular Gods*. (Faithwords: 2017), 66.
5. Visually that looks like: 10,000,000,000,000,000,000,000,000,000,000,000,000.
6. "What's Contained In One Square Inch of Skin," www.stephanietourles.com, accessed January 10, 2024, https://www.stephanietourles.com/post/whats-contained-in-one-square-inch-of-skin.
7. "Your body is a miracle," Fitstream.com, accessed January 10, 2024, https://www.fitstream.com/articles/your-body-is-a-miracle-a6393.
8. "Your body is a miracle," Fitstream.com.
9. Ibid.
10. Ibid.
11. Ibid.
12. Ibid.
13. "10 miraculous things about your body," Allprodad.com, accessed January 10, 2024, https://www.allprodad.com/10-miraculous-things-about-your-body/.
14. Amounts are approximate as some figures vary slightly depending on sources.
15. Matthew 16:18.
16. Randy Alcorn, *Heaven*, Goodreads.com, accessed April 9, 2024, https://www.goodreads.com/work/quotes/86257-heaven.
17. Isaiah 60:3, NASB.
18. Graham Cooke, public message, date unknown.
19. Bill Johnson, "Bill Johnson Quotes," QuoteFancy, accessed October 13, 2023, https://rb.gy/2y7s7.

In Memory of Abbe

Life Verses

My life anchors! My life verses!

So we are convinced that every detail of our lives is continually woven together for good, for we are his lovers who have been called to fulfill His designed purpose.
—Romans 8:28, TPT

Here's the one thing I crave from Yahweh, the one thing I seek above all else: I want to live with Him every moment in His house, beholding the marvelous beauty of Yahweh, filled with awe, delighting in His glory and grace. I want to contemplate in His temple.
—Psalm 27:4, TPT

My declaration!

May He subdue and take dominion from sea to sea; may He rule from the river to the rim.
—Psalm 72:8, TPT

"Pray like this: 'Our Beloved Father, dwelling in the heavenly realms, may the glory of your name be the center on which our lives turn. Manifest your kingdom realm, and cause your every purpose to be fulfilled on earth, just as it is in heaven. We acknowledge you as our Provider of all we need each day. Forgive us the wrongs we have done as we ourselves release forgiveness to those who have wronged us. Rescue us every time we face tribulation and set us free from evil. For you are the King who rules with power and glory forever. Amen.'"
—Matthew 6:9-13

About the Author

Bryan is an entrepreneur, engineer, author, speaker, and philanthropist. He is the co-founder and CEO of Flō Energy Solutions, and holds multiple technology patents. Bryan is also the co-founder and chairman of Bee Me Kidz, co-founder and president of M46 Ministries, board member of Transform Our World Canada, board member of EPIC at Work, and serves in various advisory roles.

He is the author of *More Than Gold* and *As in Heaven*, with more projects underway. His adventurous side is highlighted by cycling across Canada, bungee jumping 364 feet off Victoria Falls Bridge in Africa, and skydiving, reflecting his dynamic life approach.

"LIVING FOR ETERNITY NOW IS THE BEST LIFE ON EARTH!" —Bryan Elliott

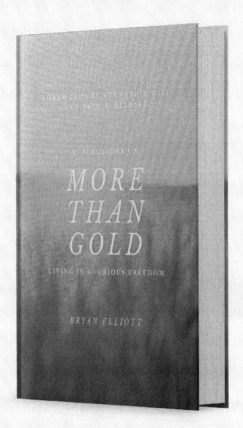

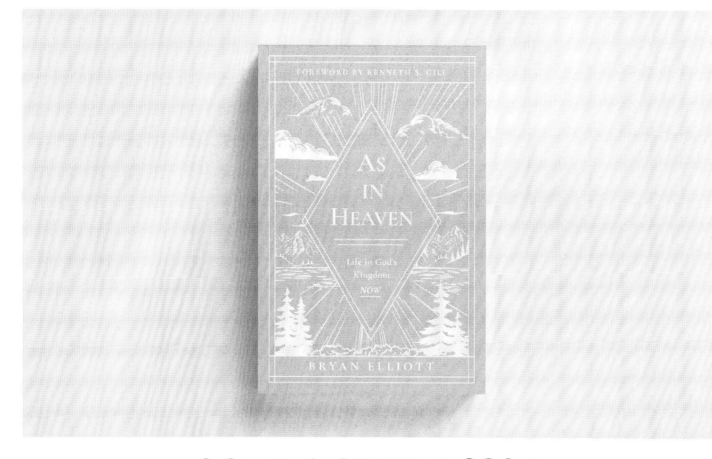

LISTEN AS YOU READ ALONG

SEASON 2 COMING SOON!

AVAILABLE NOW ON YOUR FAVORITE STREAMING PLATFORM

The Father Pursuit, featuring Bryan and Bryn Elliott along with Matt Davis, takes a real look at what it means to be an intentional father who pursues his children, learning and growing from his mistakes to become the loving father our Father wants us to be.

EPISODES:

1 • A Story of a Father, a Daughter, and God
2 • Starting with the Gospel
3 • The (Often) Missing Link in the Church
4 • Out of Religion and into Relationship
5 • Living as Sons and Daughters
6 • An Invitation to Prayer & Worship
7 • Listening for His Voice
8 • When Forgiveness Feels Impossible
9 • The Faith to Rest
10 • Growing Good Fruit
11 • Why Suffering
12 • The Blessing of Suffering
13 • Hope, Holding on, and Heaven's Perspective

M46MINISTRIES.COM

DYING TO LIVE

Experiencing God's Redemptive Power in the Midst of Tragedy

Bryn S. Elliott

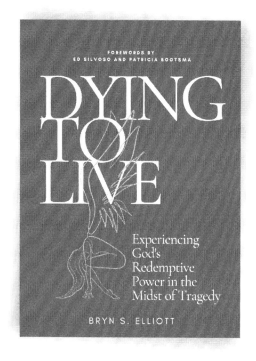

Dying to Live is the captivating true story of Bryn Elliott, whose life was marked by trauma, abuse, addiction, rape, rebellion, and the tragic murder of her older sister, Abbe. Once hopeless, alone, and wishing for death, Bryn candidly shares her journey of overcoming the enemy to experience a life transformed by the Savior.

Today, Bryn's testimony declares God's love to a generation marked by depression, addiction, and a total loss of identity. Her story shines light on the darkness and gives hope to the weary. For those who have struggled with addiction, abuse, and severe personal loss, Bryn's experience gives purpose to their pain.

This two-part book invites readers into the most vulnerable parts of a daughter's journey to freedom, and then offers practical insight, wisdom, tools, and encouragement toward an intimate relationship with Jesus. A surrendered life might not always be easy, but it will always be worth it.

"THIS BOOK IS A PROFOUND, EVEN SACRED MASTERPIECE. IT HAS LEFT ME BREATHLESS WITH WONDER AND AWE IN CELEBRATION OF THE GOODNESS OF GOD'S OUTRAGEOUS LOVE."
-MICHELE OKIMURA EXECUTIVE DIRECTOR, EXPLICIT MOVEMENT

www.M46Ministries.com

Made in the USA
Columbia, SC
01 February 2025

52711077R00236